# THE HISTORY

OF THE

# WORKING AND BURGHER CLASSES.

# HISTORY

OF THE

# WORKING

AND

# BURGHER CLASSES.


BY

M. ADOLPHE GRANIER DE CASSAGNAC,

PARIS, FRANCE, A.D. 1838.

TRANSLATED BY

BEN. E. GREEN,

OF DALTON, WHITFIELD CO., GEORGIA.

PHILADELPHIA:

CLAXTON, REMSEN & HAFFELFINGER,

819 AND 821 MARKET STREET.

1871.

STEREOTYPED BY J. FAGAN & SON, PHILADELPHIA.

# Translator's Dedication.

TO THE

WORKING AND BURGHER CLASSES OF AMERICA,

UNDER WHICH DESIGNATION I INCLUDE, NOT ONLY "LABORERS, MECHANICS, HUSBANDMEN, AND MERCHANTS IN GENERAL," BUT ALSO LAWYERS, PHYSICIANS, MINISTERS OF THE GOSPEL, AND ALL OTHERS OF THE LEARNED PROFESSIONS, — ALL, WHO LIVE, AND SEEK TO GROW RICH, BY THE FRUITS OF THEIR OWN LABOR AND INDUSTRY, WHETHER OF THE HEAD, OR OF THE HAND; AND NOT BY THE "SUBTLE AND ARTFUL FISCAL CONTRIVANCES" OF MODERN CLASS LEGISLATION, NOR BY PUBLIC OFFICE AND PUBLIC PLUNDER, — THIS WORK IS RESPECTFULLY

Dedicated

BY THE TRANSLATOR.

# CONTENTS.

## CHAPTER IV.

### ORGANIZATION OF SLAVERY BY POSITIVE LAWS.



## CHAPTER V.

### EMANCIPATION OF SLAVES AND FORMATION OF BURGHERS.



## CHAPTER VI.

### GENERAL IDEA OF THE COMMUNE — TWO KINDS.

## CHAPTER VII.

### THE FRENCH COMMUNE.



## CHAPTER VIII.

### SYMPTOMS OF THE ANCIENT COMMUNE — HIRELINGS AND BEGGARS.



## CHAPTER IX.

### SYMPTOMS OF THE ANCIENT COMMUNE — ARCHITECTURE.

## CHAPTER X.

### SYMPTOMS OF THE ANCIENT COMMUNE — JURISPRUDENCE.



## CHAPTER XI.

### THE PEASANTS.



## CHAPTER XII.

### ANCIENT TRADES' UNIONS — FORMATION.

## CHAPTER XVII.

### THE COURTESANS.



## CHAPTER XVIII.

### BANDITS.



## CHAPTER XIX.

### MODERN TRADES' UNIONS.

## CHAPTER XX.

# TRANSLATOR'S PREFACE.

FOR several years prior to the Civil War in America, the late STEPHEN COLWELL, of Philadelphia, withdrawing from active business, had shut himself up in his library, devoting himself principally to the study of Political Economy, on which subject his work on "The Ways and Means of Payment" is, perhaps, one of the ablest ever given to the public. Absorbed in this study from his own personal standpoint, that of a retired merchant and manufacturer, he gave little attention to matters of general politics occurring around him.

The news of the "Great Rebellion" reached him in the privacy of his library, and he again emerged into active life. Believing, like many other able and good men at the North, that the war was a "slaveholders' rebellion," and that everything should be sacrificed to the preservation of the Union, he took an active part in sustaining the Government. By degrees he became, under the excitements of the war, a thorough-going Abolitionist. He took great interest, and was one of the most active agents and liberal contributors, in sending teachers South to instruct the negroes.

When the war was over, he went to Paris, and again shut himself up in the libraries of that city. There he found De Cassagnac's "History of the Laboring and Burgher Classes." Struck with the great erudition of the work, and its peculiar views, he went to a book-dealer, and gave orders for the purchase of every copy that could be found for sale in Paris. It was out of print, and he could only secure three copies.

I met him in Philadelphia in 1868. In a brief interview, in which I gave him my views of the causes and results of the war, he paid me the compliment of saying that I had studied and understood the subject better than any one whom he had met; that he had brought this book from Paris to have it translated and published in the United States; that he was too old to do it himself, and had been looking for some one qualified for the task. He urged me to do it, and gave me the book.

Perhaps it is due to myself, and to my old preceptors of Georgetown College and the University of Virginia, to whose thorough training I am indebted for whatever merit there may be in the translation, that I should disarm the critics in advance, by an apology for any errors. Most of this work has been done hurriedly, under the pressure of much business and many cares, of my own and of others, at my home in Georgia, without access to dictionaries or books of reference, to compensate for twenty years' disuse of the Latin and Greek, and fifteen years' disuse of the French language; and I have sought always to give the author's exact meaning, sometimes perhaps sacrificing classic English to the exigencies of a close translation from the French.

This History was published in Paris in 1838, and is now for the first time offered to the American public. Heretofore it has been accessible to a very few only of the very few American readers of this class of French works. But through these few, some of the author's ideas, very soon after their publication in Paris, began to permeate into the American mind, and in course of time they became part of the political creed of a great party in the United States, resulting in the greatest and bloodiest civil war of recorded time.

De Cassagnac starts out with the declaration that his book is one of history, and not of politics. Evidently he was a student; poring over musty tomes; delighting in books, old and new; absorbed in the solution of the facts and philosophy of history. Certainly, so far as depends on ancient and modern law, history, and literature, he has in his seven years of preparatory study treated his subject exhaustively, and, as an historian, faithfully. But he probably little dreamed that in less than a quarter of a century, and on another continent, his ideas would take a new form of expression in the dogma that "free labor is cheaper than slave labor," and drench that continent in blood.

De Cassagnac dedicates his work to M. Guizot. Guizot was not a mere closet student. He was a statesman, intent on giving to the facts of history a gloss to suit the political purposes of the royal master, whose throne he sought to establish. He was the trusted minister of King Louis Philippe, whose every thought was directed to the perpetuation of his dynasty, and the repression of the "fierce democracie" of France. A translation of Guizot's Lectures on the History of Civilization was published in this country in 1838, about the time that De Cassagnac's book appeared in Paris. Those lectures were prepared for a special purpose: to strengthen the throne of Louis Philippe, by presenting to France *centralization and monarchy*, as represented by the Orleans dynasty, in their most attractive lights and colors. Guizot taxed his great abilities to the utmost to prove that "*whenever the reflection or the imagination of men has especially turned toward the contemplation or study of legitimate sovereignty, and of its essential qualities, it has inclined toward monarchy*," and that "*republicanism, under the most favorable circumstances, does not contain the principles of progress, duration, and extension.*"

Perhaps for the reason that the Americans are a more book-reading people than the French, it is probable that M. Guizot had more readers — and it is not going too far to say, more converts — in the United States than in France; and what was written with special reference to a political effect in France, exerted a potent influence in bringing about the civil war in America. M. Guizot has lived to see a great party in the United States, under the name of that republicanism which he sought to disparage in France, preparing the way for that *centralization*, which, to use his language, "naturally and as if by instinct," inclines the minds of men to monarchy. Lest any of my readers should be startled at this assertion, and a prejudice be thereby aroused to hinder a dispassionate reception of what more I have to say, I ask, have they ever heard Mr. Sumner's lecture on "Are we a Nation?" and read M. Guizot's Lecture XI., on the "Centralization of Nations and Governments?"

Lest any of my readers may have fought under Grant or Sherman, and should throw down this book in disgust at the bare intimation that they carried fire and sword and famine into the South, in the interests of centralization and monarchy, let me here quote briefly from M. Guizot's eleventh lecture:

"Europe, however, was then (at the close of the fourteenth century) very far from understanding her own state, such as I have now endeavored to explain it to you. She did not know distinctly what she required, or what she was in search of, yet set about endeavoring to supply her wants as if she knew perfectly what they were. When the fourteenth century had expired, after the failure of every attempt at political organization, Europe entered, naturally and as if by instinct, into the path of centralization. It is the characteristic of the fifteenth century that it constantly tended to this result; that it endeavored to create general interests and general ideas; to raise the minds of men to more enlarged views; and to create, in short, what had not, till then, existed on a great scale — *nations* and governments.

"The actual accomplishment of this change belongs to the sixteenth and seventeenth centuries, though it was in the fifteenth that it was prepared. It is this preparation, this silent and hidden process of centralization, both in the social relations and in the opinions of men — a process accomplished, without premeditation or design, by the natural course of events — that we have now to make the subject of our inquiry.

"It is thus that man advances in the execution of a plan which he has not conceived, and of which he is not even aware. He is the free, intelligent artificer of a work, which is not his own. He does not perceive or comprehend it till it manifests itself by external appearances and real results; and even then he comprehends it very imperfectly. It is through his means, however, and by the development of his intelligence and freedom, that it is accomplished. Conceive a great machine, the design of which is centred in a single mind, though its various parts are intrusted to different workmen, separated from and strangers to each other. No one of them understands the work as a whole, nor the general results, which he concurs in producing; but every one executes, with intelligence and freedom, by rational and voluntary acts, the particular task assigned to him. It is thus that by the hand of man the designs of Providence are wrought out in the government of the world. It is thus that the two great facts, which are apparent in the history of civilization, come to co-exist; on the one hand, those portions of it, which may be considered as fated, or which happen without the control of human knowledge or will; on the other hand, the part played in it by the freedom and intelligence of man, and what he contributes to it by means of his own judgment and will."

When the true history of yet recent events shall have been written, many, who have been accustomed to believe that President Lincoln was the author and father of emancipation, will be surprised to learn that to the very last he was averse to it, and anxious to prevent the adoption of the Thirteenth Amendment to the Constitution, which was carried, not only without the concurrence of, but in direct opposition to, his judgment and will. When he visited Richmond, immediately after the evacuation in 1865, a message from my father, General Duff Green, asking an interview, reached him after he had re-embarked and the command had already been given to go ahead on the return to Washington. He immediately stopped the steamer, and waited for my father to come aboard. When they met, Mr. Lincoln said, "My dear old friend, how are you, and what can I do for you?" My father replied: "Mr. President, I went to see you at Springfield in December, 1860, at the instance of Mr. Buchanan, and with the concurrence of Mr. (Jefferson) Davis, to ask what you were willing to do to avert the war. (*a*) I come now on my own account, to ask on what terms you are willing to grant us peace." To this Mr. Lincoln said: "If the South want peace, all they have to do is to lay down their arms and acknowledge the authority of the Government of the United States. I cannot recall my Emancipation Proclamations, but I am perfectly willing that the Supreme Court shall decide them to have been unconstitutional, null, and void. If the South do not wish to give up their slaves, let them call their Legislatures together, and vote down the Thirteenth Amendment." The result of this interview between my father and Mr. Lincoln, followed up by another, in which Judge Campbell participated, was that General Weitzel was authorized to call the Virginia Legislature together, for the twofold purpose—first, of repealing the Act of Secession and recognizing the authority of the General Government; and, secondly, of voting down the Thirteenth Amendment. On Mr. Lincoln's return to Washington, a pressure was brought to bear on him, that forced him very reluctantly to cancel the authority given to General Weitzel to convene the Legislature. It is well known to many that Mr. Lincoln was with great difficulty induced to sign the Emancipation Proclamations. Perhaps no disputed fact in history is susceptible of clearer proof. But few know the historical fact that he was avowedly willing, and secretly desired, that the Thirteenth Amendment should be defeated.

(*a*) See account of General Duff Green's visit to Mr. Lincoln, in the New York Herald, of 8th January, 1861.

Much has been already, and ably, written on the causes that led to the late civil war. The ablest, who have written on the subject, are probably the Hon. Alexander H. Stephens, and Judge Nicholas, of Kentucky, whose views were condensed in a correspondence between them, published in the National Intelligencer, in the summer of 1868. Mr. Stephens said:

"Slavery so called, or that legal subordination of the black race to the white, which existed in all but one of the States when the Union was formed, and in fifteen of them when the war began, was unquestionably the occasion of the war, the main exciting proximate cause on both sides. But it was not the real cause, the *causa causans*, of it.

"The war grew out of different and directly opposite views as to the nature of the Government of the United States, and where, under our system, ultimate sovereign power, or paramount authority, properly resides."

"The truth is well established that the seceding States did not desire war. Very few of the public men in these States even expected war."

The gist of Judge Nicholas's rejoinder was that the question of the right of secession was the real cause of the war; that even a distinct recognition of rights in the Constitution could never be used for any available purpose; because, if at any time attempted to be exercised by a weaker portion of the country, the only result would be giving the Government the trouble of declaring war against and conquering it; that, as a remedy, the right of secession proved unavailable, and had to be abandoned; and that, therefore, expediency and policy required that the South should, by a total abnegation, deny that there was ever any legitimacy in their assertion of that right.

Mr. Stephens is, and Judge Nicholas was, a man of great force and ability. The former writes always in the spirit of a great constitutional lawyer and statesman. The argument of the latter on this occasion amounts simply to an assertion of the utter worthlessness of all constitutional guarantees; that might makes right; and that the weaker party, to avoid worse punishment, should always submit to whatever conditions the stronger thought proper to impose. On this occasión he sank far below himself; for on others he was unquestionably able. But with all deference to such authority, it must be said that neither have gone far enough back to discover the real causes of the war. Both agree that secession was adopted as a peaceful remedy — as a bloodless solution of pre-existing questions, involving the alternatives of civil war on the one hand, or submission to, what the weaker party believed to be, intolerable wrong on the other. How then can that be said to have been the real cause of the war, which was only resorted to as a peaceful remedy to prevent war?

We do not understand Mr. Stephens to mean that so many valuable lives were sacrificed, such heavy burdens imposed on both sections, merely to decide an abstract question of constitutional law; but only that the war would not have taken place when it did, if the North, under the lead of Massachusetts, had acquiesced *then* in the doctrine of State rights, including the right of secession, which Massachusetts asserted in the war of 1812, and on the acquisition of Louisiana.

The real causes of the war existed long before the right of secession was thought of in the South; long before it was asserted by Massachusetts; long before the Constitution or the Union was formed; long before New England began to grow rich by the importation and sale of negro slaves; and they still exist in full force, now that slavery has been abolished and the right of secession suppressed. They were —

1st. The irrepressible conflict between monarchy and democracy.

2d. The irrepressible desire of capital to cheapen labor.

From the beginning, the New England mind inclined to

monarchy, with established orders of nobility. Shortly before the adoption of the Constitution, John Adams, their greatest and favorite leader, with as much ability, with more zeal, and with less disguise than M. Guizot, published a defence of the New England ideas of government, from which the following are extracts:

"The people in all nations are naturally divided into two sorts, the gentlemen and the simple men, a word which is here chosen to signify the common people. By the common people we mean laborers, mechanics, husbandmen, and merchants in general, who pursue their occupations and industry without any knowledge in liberal arts and sciences, or in anything but their own trades and pursuits." (See John Adams's Defence of the Constitution, vol. iii., p. 458.)

"The distinctions of poor and rich are as necessary in states of considerable extent (such as the United States) as labor and good government: the poor are destined to labor, and the rich, by the advantages of education, independence, and leisure, are qualified for superior stations." (Ibid., p. 360.)

"*A nobility must and will exist.* . . . Descent from certain parents and inheritance of certain houses, lands, and other visible objects (titles) will eternally have such an influence over the affections and imaginations of the people, as no arts and institutions will control. *Time will come, if it is not now,* that these circumstances will have more influence over great numbers of minds than any considerations of virtue and talents." (Vol. iii., p. 377.)

"The whole history of Rome shows that corruption began with the people sooner than the Senate." (Vol. iii., p. 327.)

"Powerful and crafty underminers have nowhere such rare sport as in a simple democracy, or single popular assembly. Nowhere, not in the completest despotism, does human nature show itself so completely depraved, so nearly approaching an equal mixture of brutality and devilishism, as in the last stages of such a democracy, and in the beginning of despotism, which always succeeds it." (Ibid., vol. ii., p. 329.)

"It is the true policy of the common people to place the whole executive power in the hands of one man." (Vol. iii., p. 460.)

"By kings and kingly power is meant the executive power in a single person." (Vol. iii., p. 461.)

"There is not in the whole Roman history so happy a period as this under their kings; . . . in short, Rome was never so well governed or so happy." (Vol. iii., p. 305.)

"I only contend that the English Constitution is, in theory, the most stupendous fabric of human invention. . . . In future ages, if the present States become a great nation, their own feelings and good sense will dictate to them what to do; they may make *transitions* to a nearer resemblance of the British Constitution." (Vol. i., pp. 70, 71.)

"It (the aristocracy) is a body of men which contains the greatest collection of virtue and character in a free government; is the brightest ornament and glory of the nation, and may always be made the greatest blessing of society, if it be judiciously managed in the Constitution." (Vol. iii., p. 116.)

"Mankind have universally discovered that chance was preferable to a corrupt choice, and have trusted Providence rather than themselves. First magistrates and senators had better be made hereditary at once, than that the people should be universally debauched and bribed." (Vol. iii., p. 283.)

Such were the ideas to which the reflection and imagination of the leading men of New England inclined them at the time of the adoption of that democratic form of government, the denunciation of which as "a league with death and covenant with hell," has been in vogue in New England down to the time when that *transition* period, anticipated by their great leader, commenced by amending the Constitution.

That these ideas have not lost ground in New England, but have been spreading to the Middle and Western States, appears by the following extract from the Monthly Gossip of Lippincott's Magazine for February, 1868:

"The *Revue de Quinzaine*, of October last, has a paper on Harvard University and Yale College, which shows a considerable knowledge of the subject. The writer says, that while the system and the division of studies are, in the main, the same as those of the English universities, yet important improvements have been introduced from time to time; and he truly remarks that, while Harvard has a certain aristocratic tone, in Yale the forms and the prevailing ideas are democratic. (*a*)

"The proposition recently made in Congress to tax the use of armorial bearings on carriages and household furniture is an eminently proper one, though it may perhaps cause some amusement at our expense in monarchical countries. If enacted into a law, the impost ought to yield a handsome return from New England, if one may judge from the fact that the *Heraldic Journal*, published by Wiggin & Lunt, Boston, has completed its third volume. A similar periodical in England, the *Herald and Genealogist*, edited by John Gough Nicholls, has also just completed its third volume, in the course of which there are five articles on 'Anglo-American genealogy and coat-armor.' The *New England Historical and Genealogical Register* has just issued its twenty-first volume, having started in 1847; and it is a curious fact that the New England Historic-Genealogical Society is the first one, particularly devoted to the pedigrees of families, ever formed. The interest which Americans take in this subject is also evinced by the increasing number of family histories which are issuing from the press. Heretofore these works were

(*a*) The truth of this statement, as to Harvard, is unquestionable; but if it be true that any democratic ideas prevail at Yale, the explanation of that phenomenon is to be found in the fact that, until recently, Yale has been mainly supported by students from the South and West, while Harvard was altogether sustained by New England.

mainly confined to New England and New York, which were settled before Pennsylvania and the Western States; but they are now appearing in other parts of the Union. Histories of the Sharpless, Darlington, Levering, Du Bois, Cope, Montgomery, Shippen, Wolfe, Coleman, and Hill families have been printed in this State, and those of the Buchanan and Sill families in Ohio. We hear that the pedigree of the Wentworth family is about to be published in Chicago; and that Mr. D. Williams Patterson, of Pittston, Pennsylvania, has in preparation the genealogy of the Grant family, which will include the pedigree of General Ulysses S. Grant. It appears that his ancestor was Matthew Grant, whose name first occurs on the town records of Dorchester, Massachusetts, April 3, 1633. Noah, the grandfather of the General, born in Connecticut, June 20, 1748, and the sixth generation in descent from the Dorchester emigrant, came from Coventry, Connecticut, to Pennsylvania, after the Revolutionary War, and settled here. The Rev. Mr. Headley's statement, that the ancestor of Grant settled in Pennsylvania on his arrival in this country, is therefore erroneous. Although very frequently indeed these pedigrees are fit subjects of ridicule, some link in a chain being assumed without proof, or some sign of vanity being exhibited by the degenerate offspring of worthy sires; yet at the bottom of all this there is, on the whole, a healthy family-pride, which benefits society, and to which no one, who comes of virtuous and honorable parentage, is insensible."

Speaking of an *elective* chief-magistrate, Mr. Adams said, "This hazardous experiment the Americans have tried, and if elections are soberly made, it may answer very well; but if parties, factions, drunkenness, bribes, *armies*, and delirium come in, as they have always done, sooner or later, to embroil and decide everything, the people must again have recourse to conventions, and find a remedy for this 'hazardous experiment.' Neither philosophy nor policy has yet discovered any other cure than by prolonging the duration of the first magistrate and senators. The evil may be lessened and postponed by elections for longer periods of years, until they become for life; and if this is not found an adequate remedy, there will remain no other but to make them hereditary." (Vol. iii., p. 296.)

Observe that Mr. Adams also said, "*The time will come, if it is not now;*" and among the signs of the time he enumerated "bribes, armies, and delirium." In this connection, the organization of the "Grand Army of the Republic," and the establishment of the *Imperialist* newspaper in New York, just after the war, to test whether the time had come for the realization of these views, by making General Grant emperor, are signs of the time not to be overlooked. The "Grand Army of the Republic," with all its commanderies and commanders, has so far only served to strengthen the Democratic vote, by a reaction from the delirium of the war; and the *Imperialist* newspaper expired with the death of General Rawlings, Grant's Secretary of War. (*a*) This, however, does not prove that the monarchical and aristocratic spirit of New England is dead, but only that the time has not yet come.

But there were in New England then, as now, some

(*a*) Of all the converts to the logic of Adams and Guizot, General Rawlings was perhaps the most sincere, the purest, the least influenced by selfish considerations. He had come to believe that Rome was never so well governed or so happy as under her kings, and that the good government and happiness of this vast country required that it should be centralized into a *nation* and governed by an emperor. There is reason to believe that his death was hastened by chagrin at finding out that General Grant, whom he had selected as the instrument for that *transition*, was not the right man. Bribes and armies are potent for the subversion of democratic government and the establishment of empires; but the former must be given, not received, by the aspirant for imperial sway. Plutarch relates of Sylla that, while prætor, he happened to be provoked at (Sextus Julius) Cæsar, and said to him, angrily, "I will use *my* authority against you." Cæsar answered, laughing, "You do well to call it *yours*, for you *bought* it." Whether true or false, it soon came to be believed of General Grant that he was more ready to *sell* than to *buy* his authority.

earnest and able advocates of free government, as, for instance, Samuel Adams. The sentiment against monarchy was so strong in other portions of the Union, and especially in the slaveholding States of the South, that after the adoption of the Constitution, the monarchical party deemed it prudent to assume the name of Federalists, as being less unpopular than one more indicative of their peculiar ideas and theories of government. In the Boston Monthly Anthology, for March, 1807, the curious reader will find some verses (*a*) denunciatory of the Republican party, in which this policy of assuming a name for political purposes is thus referred to:

> "And if we cannot alter things,
> By G—, we 'll change their *names*, sir!
> . . . . . . . .
> True, Tom and Joel now no more
> Can overturn a nation:
> And work by butchery and blood,
> A great regeneration,—
> Yet, still we can turn inside out
> Old nature's constitution,
> And bring a Babel back of *names*,—
> Huzza! for REVOLUTION."

The advocates of the Constitution as adopted were, and called themselves, Republicans; but their opponents in New England called them Democrats in derision. In course of time they accepted this name, as indicative of their theory that legitimate sovereignty resides in the whole body of the people, and not in a king and nobility; and, as soon as they dropped the name of Republicans for that of Democrats, their opponents, the monarchists, took it up, and assumed it as their own party appellation.

During the session of Congress of 1807–8, Mr. John Q.

(*a*) The authorship of these verses was attributed, and no doubt correctly, to John Quincy Adams. By Tom and Joel, Tom Paine and Joel Barlow, anti-monarchists, were referred to.

Adams surprised his former political opponents as well as his own party friends, by what Governor Giles, of Virginia, in an address to the public, dated February 28, 1828, calls "a complete political somerset from the Federal (or monarchical) to the Republican (or democratic) party." In explanation of his course, Mr. Adams told Governor Giles and Mr. Jefferson that the object of the Federal (or monarchical) party in New England "had been for several years the dissolution of the Union and the establishment of a separate confederacy; that he knew this from unequivocal evidence, although not provable in a court of justice; and that, in case of a civil war, the aid of Great Britain to effect that purpose would be as surely resorted to as it would be indispensably necessary to the design." (*a*)

The following is an extract from a letter from Mr. Jefferson to Governor Giles, dated Monticello, December 26, 1825:

"You ask my opinion of the propriety of giving publicity to what is stated in your letter, as having passed between John Q. Adams and yourself. Of this no one can judge but yourself. It is one of those questions which belong to the forum of feeling. This alone can decide on the degree of confidence implied in the disclosure: whether, under no circumstances, it was to be communicable to others. It does not seem to be of that character, or at all to meet that aspect. They are historical facts, which belong to the present as well as future time. I doubt whether a single fact, known to the world, will carry as clear a conviction to it, of the correctness of our knowledge of the treasonable views of the Federal party of that day, as that disclosed by this most nefarious and daring attempt to dissever the Union, of which the Hartford Convention was a subsequent chapter; and both of these having failed, *consolidation* becomes the first book of their history. But this opens with a vast accession of strength,

(*a*) See Mr. Adams's own statement in National Intelligencer, October 21, 1828.

from their younger recruits, who, having nothing in them of the feelings or principles of '76, now look to a single and splendid government of an aristocracy, founded on banking institutions and moneyed incorporations, under the guise and cloak of their favored branches of manufactures, commerce, and navigation, riding and ruling over the plundered ploughman and beggared yeomanry. This will be to them a next best blessing to the monarchy of their first aim, and perhaps the surest stepping-stone to it."

When it was made known that Mr. John Quincy Adams, in explaining to Governor Giles and Mr. Jefferson his reasons for joining the Republican or Democratic party, had charged these treasonable views upon the Federal party of New England, some of his late political associates, who claimed to be patriots, while conscientiously believing the monarchical form of government the best, retorted on him, by charging that he was still a monarchist at heart, and that his conversion to democracy was only pretended. They asserted that "in 1807, at the table of an illustrious citizen now no more, he (Mr. Adams) *lamented* the fearful progress of the Democratic party and of its principles, and declared that '*he had long meditated the subject, and had become convinced that the only method, by which the Democratic party could be destroyed, was by joining with it, and urging it on with the utmost energy to the completion of its views: whereby the result would prove so ridiculous, and so ruinous to the country, that the people would be led to despise the principles and to condemn the effects of Democratic policy; and* THEN,' *said he*, 'WE MAY HAVE A FORM OF GOVERNMENT BETTER SUITED TO THE GENIUS AND DISPOSITION OF OUR COUNTRY THAN OUR PRESENT CONSTITUTION." (*a*)

This charge made against Mr. John Quincy Adams by his then late associates was denied; and the attempt was made to prove it by the affidavits of Messrs. Townsend and Derby, of the monarchical party, both men of high standing in Mas-

(*a*) See Boston Statesman, November, 1824.

sachusetts. The case made by these affidavits against Mr. Adams was strong, but not conclusive, although they afterward acquired much additional force from Mr. Adams's subsequent reaffiliation with the party whom his father, John Adams, in one of his letters to Cunningham, styles the "*Absolute Oligarchy*," and by the bitterness of his hatred of Democracy, and of its stronghold, the Southern slaveholding States.

But whether the charge was true or false — whether this idea originated with John Quincy Adams, or with the monarchical party, who brought the charge of having originated it against him, certain it is that they have since then pushed it vigorously and successfully. For what can be more or better calculated to "lead the people to despise the principles and to condemn the effects of Democratic policy," than to see a parcel of ignorant negroes, recently slaves, with no knowledge of history or jurisprudence, controlling the destinies of States like Virginia and South Carolina, in the place of such men as George Washington, Thomas Jefferson, Madison, Sumter, Marion, and Calhoun?

New England was not only monarchical. She was also a negro-slave trader; and it was not until it was discovered that the effect of negro slavery was to strengthen the democratic principle of equality among the whites, that negro slavery became odious to New England. In course of time, it was seen that the ownership of negro slaves carried with it the necessity of making color and good conduct (not wealth and poverty) the only basis for distinction. In the presence of their black slaves and of the poor white men, whom they employed as overseers, and whose authority it was necessary to maintain, the slave-owners found themselves compelled to treat the poor white man as an equal, because he was white, and the negro slave as an inferior, because he was black. In no other way could they teach the negroes lessons of obedience to their poor white overseers, or keep up the personal pride, self-respect, and character of the overseers, which was indispensable, that they might more easily control the slaves. When, at a later period, the Southern slaveholders learned that Old England was seeking to abolish slavery in the United States, as a means of securing for her own East-India possessions a monopoly of the production of cotton and sugar, and that the monarchists and aristocrats of New England had united with Old England against them, they found it more than ever necessary to strengthen themselves by inculcating upon their children and neighbors that color and good conduct were the only proper foundation for *castes*.

It was this *necessity* of the slave-owners—the necessity of employing poor white men as overseers, and of treating them with respect in the presence of the negro slaves, so as to secure respect and obedience to them from the slaves—which, perhaps more than all else, led to the marked contrast between the social relations and distinctions in the non-slaveholding and in the slaveholding States. In the former, if a laboring man had occasion to call at the house of a rich man, he was kept standing at the front door, or at best in the passage-way, until his business was accomplished. In the latter, he was invited to be seated in the parlor; was offered a glass of wine, or whisky and water; was asked to dinner, if that hour was nigh; his family and business affairs, the weather, the crops and politics were discussed, as between equals and friends. M. Guizot, in his History of Civilization, comments on, and attaches great importance to, an analogous effect of the Crusades on the social relations of Europe. He says:

"During the Crusades, small proprietors found it necessary to place themselves in the train of some rich and powerful chief, from whom they received assistance and support. They lived with him, shared his fortune, and passed through the same adventures that he did. When the Crusaders returned home, *this social spirit, this habit of living in intercourse with superiors*, continued to subsist, and had its influence on the manners of the age. . . .

"Such, in my opinion, are the real effects of the Crusades: on the one hand, the extension of ideas and the emancipation of thought; on the other, a general enlargement of the social sphere, and an opening of a wider field for every sort of activity; they produced, at the same time, more individual freedom and more political unity."

Such was the effect of negro slavery in the South on the social relations of the rich and poor whites.

I remember, when a boy, hearing the striking contrast between the social relations of the rich and poor whites at the South and at the North, commented upon by my father. It was before the days of railroads, when travelling was by stage coach, and before the Abolition agitation had begun to attract attention. He had always lived in the South, and was accustomed to the social equality among the whites there prevailing. In a tour through the Northern States, he rode generally with the stage-driver, to see the country. At the first meal-stand in Pennsylvania, he was struck with the fact, that the *white* stage-driver was not permitted to take his seat at the same table with the passengers; and, as he progressed northward, he found the rule universal that, in the non-slaveholding States, the driver was required to eat at a separate and inferior table. He was long enough in the Northern and Eastern States to become somewhat familiarized with this distinction there made between the rich passengers and the poor drivers; and as he passed through Maryland on his return, he did not notice whether the driver was permitted to eat at the passengers' table or not. From Washington City he started on a similar tour through the Southern States. The first day out in Virginia, he reached the meal-stand with a traveller's appetite, and, seeing dinner ready, he was about to take his seat; but was stopped and told by the waiter that the passengers must wait until the driver — a white man — who was washing his hands, was ready to take his seat with them. This little circumstance caused him to be more observant of the absence of the New-England social distinction between the poor and the rich, and of this social equality among the whites, which he found everywhere a prominent characteristic of the slaveholding States.

From having heard my father speak of this, now nearly thirty years ago, and often since, my own attention was called to it, and in a very extensive observation in all the slaveholding States, I have found it universal, and more strongly developed as the Abolition agitation progressed. Shortly before the war, I was visiting one of the largest slaveholders, (*a*) a truly representative man of his class, who had a poor white neighbor employed digging a well. When the first bell rang for the ladies to dress for dinner, this well-digger came out of his hole in the ground, washed and dressed himself, took his seat at the table with the family and guests, and seemed as much at his ease as if he had been governor of the State.

This privilege of color could be forfeited by bad conduct, and by bad conduct only; and when so lost, the negro slaves despised the losers, and spoke of them contemptuously as "mean white trash;" sometimes as "poor white trash;" not because they were *poor*, but because, being white, they had forfeited by misconduct the respect due to them by virtue of their white skins.

This tendency of negro slavery, as it existed in the South, to break down "the distinctions of rich and poor" whites, which the monarchical-aristocratic party of New England held to be "as necessary in states of considerable extent (such as the United States) as labor and good government," gave a great impulse to the agitation against negro slavery, which had been originally set on foot by paid agents of Old England, with a view of securing a monopoly of the pro-

(*a*) The planter here alluded to was the late Colonel Andrew P. Calhoun, eldest son of John C. Calhoun; and the well-digger's name was, I think, Boggs, of Pickens District, South Carolina.

duction of cotton and sugar for the British East-India possessions.

But there was another remarkable tendency of negro slavery, which made it still more odious to those who desired a transition to a nearer resemblance of the "British Constitution," and therefore "lamented the fearful progress of the Democratic party and of its principles." This was its political effect on the character of the poor whites, or "common people," of the South. Their social elevation, the more respectful treatment secured to them by the *necessity* of the slave-owners, as above explained, increased their self-respect, and caused them to value more highly their political franchises, which, at the same time, made them the superiors of the negroes, and the political, as well as social, equals of their rich white neighbors. For this reason bribery at elections was a thing almost unknown at the South. Even the most abject of those, whom the very negro slaves despised as "poor white trash," recoiled from that lower depth of degradation — selling his vote. This was strikingly illustrated by the testimony elicited by the Covode Investigating Committee, 1st Session, 36th Congress, vol. v., p. 490. It there appears that bribery at elections had grown to be a customary thing with all parties in the free States. The witness, a Northern man, being asked, "Have all your contributions been in Northern States?" replied, "Yes, sir; I do not remember spending a dollar politically in Southern States. I have tendered contributions there, but they allowed they did not use money as we use it in the Northern States."

In course of time, another remarkable result of negro slavery was developed and came to be understood by the master minds of W. H. Seward, Salmon P. Chase, and a few others, although the great majority of the free and intelligent artificers of the work, which they designed, did not perceive or comprehend it, while executing the particular tasks assigned to them, and even now comprehend it very incompletely. Mr. Seward misled the productive classes of the free States by the specious dogma of "an irrepressible conflict between free labor and slave labor," when in fact there was no such conflict; the interests of all labor, whether free or slave, being identical, viz., to keep up wages and keep down the cost of living. The real conflict was — not between free and slave labor — but it was between the capital that hired free labor, and the capital that owned slave labor. The interests of the former required a system of legislation that would put down wages and put up the cost of living. The interests of the latter required a diametrically opposite system. Wages went into, and the cost of living came out of, the pockets of the capital that owned slave labor. Wages came out of, and the cost of living went into, the pockets of the capital, that hired free labor. Mr. Seward and Mr. Chase were not long in discovering that herein consisted the philosophy of Mr. Jefferson's celebrated aphorism, "The Democracy of the North are the natural allies of the Republicans of the South." They were not slow to see that, while the interests and inclination of the capital that hired free labor called for a system of taxation imposing heavy burdens on the laboring classes, the interests and inclination of the capital that owned slave labor required a system of light taxes, high wages, fair prices for the products of labor, and cheap living. While many of their less discerning "workmen" were surprised to see the Southern slaveholders voting and exerting their influence to shape the legislation of the country to this end, and were astonished that those whom they were taught to consider as the "slave aristocracy," should thus act *against* the interests of those whom they were taught to consider the *true* aristocracy, and *for* the interests of the "common people," (the laboring and productive classes of the North,) Mr. Seward's astute mind solved the mystery. He saw that one peculiar result of negro slavery was to identify the interests of the Southern slaveholders and of the northern working-men; that it gave to Northern labor in its conflict with Northern capital — to the "laborers, mechanics, husbandmen, and merchants in general" of the North in their conflict with the aristocracy — a potent ally in the slaveholders of the South; that it joined them together, as the priest joins man and wife, and that to abolish slavery would be to *divorce* Southern capital from Northern labor.

[Since the foregoing was written, Mr. Attorney-General Akerman has been to Washington City, and was initiated into the counsels of those, in whose minds the designs of the Government machine are centred. Returning to Georgia, he made a speech in Representatives' Hall, Atlanta, 1st September, 1870, by which it clearly appears that, among other things learned by him in the Cabinet councils, was this fact: that one of the main objects and results of the war was to *divorce* Southern capital from Northern labor. His speech, whether prepared by him or for him, evinces much adroitness in view of the objects to be accomplished by it. They were, first, to call the attention of Southern capital to the fact, that it is no longer interested in opposing high taxes, low wages and prodigal Government expenditures; that it has no longer any interests in common with the laboring classes, the "common people," of the North; secondly, to prepare the way for an election bill, by which the ignorant negroes of Georgia, voting early and often, on several different days and in several different counties, could be used to neutralize the votes of intelligent white Democratic workmen in Ohio or Pennsylvania. He said:

"My friends, I am touching now a serious topic. . . . In the United States, looking at the white population alone, the cry of a conflict between capital and labor has generally been the cry of the demagogue, for the reason that capital has seldom been organized against labor, and labor has seldom, except in the small way of trades' unions, been organized against capital. . . .

"*How is the problem affected by the elevation of colored men to freedom? Labor and capital were in the same hands here in the South. They have now become* DIVORCED *by emancipation.*"]

In a speech, at Boston, shortly before the inauguration of President Lincoln, Mr. Seward avowed that, in his theories of government, he was a disciple of John Adams. The quotations we have given from Mr. Adams's book show what those theories were. Mr. Seward, then, believed that "a nobility must and will exist;" that "the aristocracy is the brightest ornament and glory of the nation;" that "first-magistrates and senators had better be made hereditary at once, than that the people should be universally debauched and bribed;" that "the distinctions of poor and rich are as necessary in states of considerable extent (such as the United States) as labor and good government;" and that these States, having become a great nation, should "make transitions to a nearer resemblance of the British Constitution." (*a*) But a thorough, statesman-like, philosophic investigation of the social and political effects of negro slavery in the South also disclosed to him the fact, that its tendencies were all anti-monarchical and anti-aristocratic; that the slaveholder was surrounded by necessities, which, in his social treatment of his poor white neighbor, forced him to become what John Adams would call a "vulgar democrat," (*b*) and in his political action forced him to vote with the "common people," and against the monarchical aristocracy of the North, for light taxes, high wages, and cheap living; and, seeing this, he declared that "these States must become all free;" that negro slavery must be abolished, and capital *divorced* from labor.

M. Guizot says:

"The struggle of classes constitutes the very fact of

(*a*) Query: Russian?

(*b*) See John Adams's Letters to Cunningham.

modern history, of which it is full. Modern Europe, indeed, is born of this struggle between the different classes of society." (*a*)

The same is true of the United States. We see this struggle of classes in Mr. Adams's book; we see it in the dogma of the political party that elected Mr. Lincoln and made war on the South to abolish slavery, that "free labor might be made cheaper than slave labor;" we see it in Chief-Justice Chase's son-in-law's declaration at the Memphis Commercial Convention that labor must be cheapened; (*b*) we see it in the substitution of negro for white printers in the Government printing-office at Washington City; we see it in the attempt to *cheapen* the labor of shoemakers in Massachusetts and negroes in the South by the substitution and competition of the "heathen Chinese;" we see it in the trades' unions of the North, and in the National Labor Union of the United States.

It has long been held by a certain class of statesmen that the United States could never take that rank among nations, to which their vast territory and great resources entitle them, without manufactures; and that they cannot compete with Europe in manufactures without reducing the wages of labor in the United States to the standard of wages in Europe. Among the living advocates of cheap labor, we again find Mr. Seward and Chief-Justice Chase the ablest. The only difference between them, in this respect, is that Mr. Seward, residing in the East, was a high-tariff man, seeking to cheapen labor, by taxing labor for the benefit of the capital that employed labor, as well as by abolishing slavery; while Mr. Chase, though born and educated in New England, moved in early life to the West, where the protection theories were

(*a*) See Guizot's History of Civilization, D. Appleton & Co., New York, 1837, p. 184.

(*b*) See Senator Sprague's speech at the Memphis Convention.

unpopular, and therefore relied mainly on abolition to cheapen labor.

In searching for the origin of the dogma that "free labor may be made cheaper than slave labor," I find it in M. de Cassagnac's book. He proves, demonstratively, that all voluntary emancipations on a large scale have been made for the benefit of the master, to get rid of the care and expense of supporting the slaves; and that the invariable result of all emancipations has been to produce four classes, viz., hirelings, beggars, prostitutes, and thieves. The corollary is that pauperism increases competition in the struggle for the means of existence, and increased competition tends to a further reduction of wages, below the cost of feeding and clothing a slave, and taking care of him in infancy, sickness, and old age.

About the same time, viz., in 1837, Mr. Calhoun, in his speech on the reception of Abolition petitions, threw out, with less elaboration, similar ideas: that the tendency of negro slavery in the South was to strengthen the principle of republican equality among the whites, and that no laboring class in any part of the world were so well treated and cared for, or received so large a share of the products of their labor, as the negro slaves of the South. He said:

"I appeal to facts. Never before has the black race of Central Africa, from the dawn of history to the present day, attained a position so civilized and so improved, not only physically, but morally and intellectually. It came among us in a low, degraded, and savage condition; and, in the course of a few generations, it has grown up under the fostering care of our institutions, as reviled as they have been, to its present comparative civilized condition. This, with the rapid increase of numbers, is conclusive proof of the general happiness of the race, in spite of all the exaggerated tales to the contrary.

"In the mean time, the white or European race has not

degenerated. It has kept pace with its brethren in other sections of the Union, where slavery does not exist. It is odious to make comparisons; but I appeal to all sides whether the South is not equal in virtue, intelligence, patriotism, courage, disinterestedness, and all the high qualities, which adorn our nature. I ask whether we have not contributed our full share of talents and political wisdom in forming and sustaining this political fabric? and *whether we have not constantly inclined most strongly to the side of liberty, and been the first to see, and first to resist the encroachments of power.* In one thing only are we inferior — the arts of gain: we acknowledge that we are less wealthy than the Northern section of this Union; but I trace this mainly to the fiscal action of this Government, which has extracted much from and spent little among us. Had it been the reverse — if the exaction had been from the other section, and the expenditure with us — this point of superiority would not be against us now, as it was not at the formation of this Government.

"But I take higher ground. I hold that, in the present state of civilization, where two races of different origin, and distinguished by color and other physical differences, as well as intellectual, are brought together, the relation now existing in the slave-holding States between the two is, instead of an evil, a good — a positive good. I feel myself called upon to speak freely upon the subject, where the honor and interests of those I represent are involved. I hold, then, that there never has yet existed a wealthy and civilized society in which one portion of the community did not, in point of fact, live on the labor of the other. Broad and general as is this assertion, it is fully borne out by history. This is not the proper occasion; but if it were, it would not be difficult to trace the various devices, by which the wealth of all civilized communities has been so unequally divided, and to show by what means so small a share has been allotted to those, by whose labor it was produced, and so large a share given to the non-producing class. The devices are almost innumerable, from the brute force and gross superstition of ancient times to the subtle and artful fiscal contrivances of modern. I might well challenge a comparison between them and the more direct, simple, and patriarchal mode, by which the labor of the African race is among us commanded by the European. I may say, with truth, that in few countries so much is left to the share of the laborer, and so little exacted from him, or where there is more kind attention to him in sickness or infirmities of age. Compare his condition with the tenants of the poorhouses in the most civilized portions of Europe. Look at the sick, and the old and infirm slave, on the one hand, in the midst of his family and friends, under the kind superintending care of his master and mistress, and compare it with the forlorn and wretched condition of the pauper in the poorhouse. But I will not dwell on this aspect of the question. I turn to the political; and here I fearlessly assert, that the existing relation between the two races in the South, against which those blind fanatics are waging war, forms the most solid and durable foundation on which to rear free and stable political institutions. It is useless to disguise the fact. There is and always has been, in an advanced stage of wealth and civilization, a conflict between labor and capital. The condition of society in the South exempts us from the disorders and dangers resulting from this conflict; and this explains why it is that the political condition of the slaveholding States has been so much more stable and quiet than the North. The advantages of the former in this respect will become more and more manifest, if left undisturbed by interference from without, as the country advances in wealth and numbers. We have, in fact, but just entered that condition of society where the strength and durability of our political institutions are to be tested; and I venture nothing in predicting that the experience of the next generation will fully test how vastly more favorable our condition of society is to that of other sections for free and stable institutions, provided we are not disturbed by the interference of others, or shall have sufficient intelligence and spirit to resist promptly and successfully such interferences. It rests with ourselves to meet and repel them.

"Be assured that emancipation itself would not satisfy these fanatics; that gained, the next step would be to raise the negroes to a social and political equality with the whites; and that being effected, we would soon find the present condition of the two races reversed. They and their Northern allies would be the masters, and we the slaves; the condition of the white race in the British West Indies, as bad as it is, would be happiness to ours. There the mother country is interested in sustaining the supremacy of the European race. It is true that the authority of the former master is destroyed, but the African will there be a slave, not to individuals, but to the community; forced to labor, not by the authority of the overseer, but by the bayonet of the soldiery and the rod of the civil magistrate."

Mr. Calhoun was an ardent, a passionate devotee of the Union under the Constitution; and it is questionable whether Governor Joseph E. Brown, of Georgia, could have succeeded in hurrying the Southern States into secession in 1861, if Mr. Calhoun had then been living. Entering public life in 1811, he was one of the ablest and most zealous supporters of the war of 1812 with Great Britain, in defence of the rights and interests of the seamen of New England; and his earnest nature was soon shocked by discovering that the object of the so-called Federal party in New England "had been, for several years, the dissolution of the Union and the establishment of a separate confederacy," by the co-operation of Great Britain.(*a*) The study of his life, therefore, was to find in the Constitution some balance-wheel, or regulator, which would

(*a*) See statement of John Quincy Adams in the National Intelligencer, October 21, 1828.

guard against the danger of secession on the one hand, or centralization and despotism on the other. Hence his modification of Mr. Jefferson's doctrine of *nullification*, as an antidote to the New England doctrine of the right of secession,(*a*)

(*a*) The doctrine of *nullification*, as laid down in the Virginia and Kentucky Resolutions, and as maintained by Jefferson, Madison, and others, made *each* State, *for itself and separately*, the judge of any alleged infraction of the Constitution, and of the "*mode and measure of redress.*"

Mr. Calhoun's modification of that doctrine proposed to make "*all the States in convention assembled*" the judge; and meanwhile, until such a convention of *all* the States could be called together for the decision of the question, to give to each State the right to nullify, or *suspend* the execution of an obnoxious and unconstitutional law *temporarily* within her borders. By this State right of temporary suspension, analogous to the Presidential veto, Calhoun sought to protect the weaker States from hasty and unjust legislation; while he relied on the calm deliberations of a convention of *all* the States to effectually suppress the spirit of secession.

Mr. Thomas Ritchie, of the Richmond Enquirer, Mr. Francis P. Blair, of the Washington Globe, the National Intelligencer, and others, admitting the right of secession, opposed Mr. Calhoun's modification of the doctrine of the Kentucky and Virginia Resolutions, on the ground that its effect would be to place a State *in* the Union and *out of* the Union at the same time. See Calhoun's address to the people of South Carolina. (Jenkins's Life of Calhoun, pp. 172–173.) He said:

"How the States are to exercise this high power of interposition, which constitutes so essential a portion of their reserved rights that it *cannot be delegated without an entire surrender of their sovereignty*, and converting our system from a *federal* into a *consolidated* government, is a question that the States only are competent to determine. The arguments, which prove that they possess the power, equally prove that they are, in the language of Jefferson, '*the rightful judges of the mode and measure of redress.*' But the spirit of forbearance, as well as the nature of the right itself, forbids a recourse to it, except in cases of dangerous infractions of the Constitution; and then only in the last resort, when all reasonable hope of relief from the ordinary action of the Government has failed; when, if the right to interpose did not exist, the alternative would be submission and oppression on one side, or resistance by force on the other. That our system should afford, in such extreme cases, an intermediate point between these dire alternatives, by which the Government may be brought to a pause, and thereby an interval obtained to compromise differences, or, if impracticable, be compelled to submit the question to a constitutional adjustment, through an appeal to the States themselves, is an evidence of its high wisdom; an element, not, as is supposed by some, of weakness, but of strength: not of anarchy or revolution, but

and to the New England spirit of centralization and monarchy. His last words in the Senate of the United States, when the hand of death was upon him; — when the ambition of this world was over; — were a plea for the Union under the Constitution. His speech of 1837, from which we have just quoted, was an earnest and able appeal to the justice, good sense, and self-interests of the laboring and productive classes of the North, for the Union under the Constitution, against the Abolitionists, then few in number and generally regarded

of peace and safety. *Its general recognition would, in a great measure, if not altogether, supersede the necessity of its exercise, by impressing on the movements of the Government that moderation and justice so essential to harmony and peace, in a country of such vast extent and diversity of interests as ours;* and would, if controversy should come, turn the resentment of the aggrieved from the system to those who had abused its powers, (a point all-important,) and cause them to seek redress, *not in revolution or overthrow, but in reformation.* It is, in fact, properly understood, *a substitute, where the alternative would be force, tending to prevent, and, if that fails, to correct peaceably the aberrations, to which all systems are liable, and which, if permitted to accumulate, without correction, must finally end in a general catastrophe.*"

See also Calhoun's letter to Governor Hamilton, of 28th August, 1832, in which he said:

"If the views presented be correct, it follows that on the interposition of a State in favor of the reserved rights, it would be the duty of the General Government to abandon the contested power, or to apply to the States themselves, the source of all political authority, for the power, in one of the two modes prescribed by the Constitution. If the case be a simple one, embracing a single power, and that in its nature easily adjusted, the more ready and appropriate mode would be an amendment in the ordinary form, on a proposition of two-thirds of both houses of Congress, to be ratified by three-fourths of the States: but, on the contrary, should the derangement of the system be great, embracing many points difficult to adjust, the States ought to be convened in a general convention, the most august of all assemblies, representing the united sovereignty of the confederated States, and having power and authority to correct every error, and to repair every dilapidation or injury, whether caused by time or accident, or the conflicting movements of the bodies, which compose the system.

"With institutions every way so fortunate, possessed of means so well calculated to prevent disorders, and so admirable to correct them, when they cannot be prevented, he, who would prescribe for our political disease, *disunion* on the one side, or *coercion* of *a. State* in the assertion of its rights on the other, *would deserve* and *will receive the execrations of this and all future generations.*"

with contempt, as being either paid agents of Great Britain or crazy fanatics.

But here we have an illustration of the truth of M. Guizot's remark that some portions of history are without the control of human judgment and will. Mr. Calhoun intended to arrest the Abolition agitation by appealing to the justice and reason of that portion, who were actuated by an honest zealotry, hoping thereby to withdraw them from the support of the *paid* emissaries of the British East-India cotton and sugar monopoly. His speech, however, had a directly contrary effect. By it he drew attention to the republicanizing, levelling, democratizing influences of negro slavery, in its social and political effects upon the whites. By it he called attention to the peculiar influence of negro slavery in its bearing on the irrepressible conflict between capital and labor. By it, and by the cotemporary publication of M. de Cassagnac's book, Mr. Seward and Mr. Chase were brought to understand *why* the influence of the South was always exerted, in the legislation of the General Government, to keep up wages, and keep down the cost of living—in favor of light taxes, high wages, cheap living, and an economical administration of the Government. From Mr. Calhoun's speech and De Cassagnac's book the advocates of low wages learned that Abolition would produce pauperism; that pauperism would increase competition in the struggle for bread; that increased competition would reduce wages, with cheaper food and coarser clothing and fewer of the necessaries of life to the laborers. The result was, not to detach the zealots from the British agents, but to bring the monarchists, the aristocrats, the capitalists, and the advocates of low wages into an alliance with the British agents and the zealots; fusing them all, together with some other elements, into the great party, that elected Mr. Lincoln, made war upon and subjugated the South, and abolished slavery, that "free labor might be made cheaper than slave labor;" which simply means a reduction of the wages of free labor below the cost of feeding and clothing a negro and taking care of him in sickness and the infirmities of age.

We have referred to other elements in the fusion, that produced the party that elected Mr. Lincoln. The two *major* causes that led to that fusion and the consequent war, were unquestionably the conflict between despotic and free government; between the spirit of aristocracy and the spirit of democracy: and between capital and labor; the desire to make transitions to a monarchical and aristocratic government, and the desire to reduce wages. But there were other *minor* causes that deserve a passing notice.

And, first in importance, should be mentioned foreign intrigue to foster division between the North and the South, as shown in President Madison's message to Congress, with the accompanying correspondence of John Henry, the British emissary at Boston, to which the reader is referred.

In a letter from Boston, 20th March, 1809, to Sir James Craig, Governor-General of British America, John Henry said:

"It should, therefore, be the peculiar care of Great Britain to *foster division between the North and the South;* and by succeeding in this, she may carry into effect her own projects in Europe, with a total disregard of the resentments of the democrats on this continent."

Unfortunately too many of the politicians of the United States have aided to make this British policy effective, "thus advancing (to use Mr. Guizot's language) in the execution of a plan, which they had not conceived, and of which they were not even aware."

One great statesman, unquestionably the ablest of his party now living, Mr. Seward, conceived the idea of governing this country by sectional animosities, as a permanent system. In a speech to the Maryland Legislature at Annapolis, shortly after the war, he suggested that, the sectional conflict between the North and South having been terminated, the time had arrived for a reorganization of parties, on the basis of a combination of the Eastern and Southern Atlantic States *against* the West.

Another of the minor causes of the war was the personal pique of disappointed aspirants for public office or patronage. Among these the most notable were John Quincy Adams, Martin Van Buren, and Francis P. Blair.

Mr. Adams left the Federal party and joined the Democratic party, assigning, as his reason for so doing, that the former were traitors and disunionists; but when the Democratic party rejected him as a candidate for the Presidency, he renewed his affiliation with his old party, and thereby gave color to the charge, made by some of the old Federalists, that his conversion to Democracy was pretended. The bitterness of his subsequent hostility to the Democracy and to the South, their stronghold, leaves no room to doubt that his views were colored by the jaundice of disappointed ambition.

Mr. Van Buren, having been deserted by the Southern Democracy in his second race for the Presidency, took his revenge by the Free-soil Buffalo platform, and thereby gave an impulse to the fusion, which finally resulted in the election of Mr. Lincoln and the war.

Francis P. Blair had grown rich at Washington, as the editor of the Democratic newspaper, and by the public printing. Mr. Thomas Ritchie had grown old as a Democratic editor at Richmond, and was still poor. On the election of Mr. Polk, the Virginia delegation in Congress, wishing to provide for Mr. Ritchie, urged that Mr. Blair had enjoyed the public patronage long enough, and ought to make room for Mr. Ritchie. Mr. Polk admitted the force of the demand, and required Mr. Blair to sell out the Globe to Mr. Ritchie and General Armstrong of Nashville, who changed its name to the Union. Mr. Blair yielded to superior force; but held the South responsible for it. He took his revenge by joining in the fusion that elected Mr. Lincoln and brought on the war;

aided greatly to break down the Democratic party; and only forgave and returned to his first love, when his revenge was full by the surrender to superior force at Appomattox Court House.(*a*)

Another of the minor causes that led to the war was the Pacific Railroad. That portion of the Democracy, who supported Breckinridge, were opposed to giving to a few individuals the enormous grants sought to be obtained from Congress in aid of that road, and had defeated the bill known as the Curtis Bill. Mr. Douglas himself, probably — certainly, Governor Herschel V. Johnson — and very many of those, who voted for them, were not aware of the plan, the execution of which was to be advanced by their nomination; but it was brought about by a *ring* of those, who expected to be the beneficiaries of some such Pacific Railroad Bill as that of Mr. Curtis; — to defeat Breckinridge, who would oppose it, and elect either Douglas or Lincoln, both of whom were pledged to its support. But, as it is my purpose to give a full history of the Pacific Railroad in another publication, I refer now to Duff Green's Facts and Suggestions, chap. xxvi., p. 215, for further information on this point.

In this connection, however, there was another remote, but very potent, cause of the war, that ought not to be passed unmentioned: the cession by the State of Virginia to the United States of her great territory northwest of the Ohio River. Mr. Calhoun doubtless had it in mind, when claiming for the South, among the other high qualities that adorn our nature, disinterestedness. Mr. Webster, in his speech in the Senate, March 7, 1850, said of it:

"And a most magnificent act it was. I never reflect upon it without a disposition to do honor and justice; — and justice would be the highest honor; — to Virginia, for the cession of her Northwestern territory. I will say, sir, it is one of her fairest claims to the respect and gratitude of the United States, and

(*a*) See note (*a*) to page xliii.

that, perhaps, it is only second to that other claim that attaches to her; that, from her counsels, and from the intelligence and patriotism of her leading statesmen, proceeded the first idea put into practice of the formation of a general Constitution for the United States. . . . I have said that I honor Virginia for her cession of this territory. There have been received into the Treasury of the United States eighty millions of dollars, the proceeds of the sales of the public lands ceded by her. If the residue should be sold at the same rate, the whole aggregate will exceed two hundred millions of dollars."

In the light of more recent events, the historian may lose sight of the disinterestedness and magnificence, in the prodigality, of the gift; for those, to whom she gave it, turned upon and rent her in twain. Nay, more; while they heaped honors on those, whose boast was that they desolated the fair fields of Virginia, until a crow flying over them had to "carry his rations with him," they sought to realize Mr. Calhoun's prophecy by putting the negro slaves, as political masters, over the sons of those, whose intelligence and patriotism called forth these expressions of respect and gratitude from Mr. Webster.

I remember to have seen, shortly after the war, the idea advanced in a New York paper (I think the Journal of Commerce) that the South must thank her own statesmen and leaders for her defeat; because it was wholly due to that sentiment of love for the Union, which Southern statesmen had striven so hard to arouse, and which Northern leaders had striven with as much earnestness to suppress.

The proofs of this truth are multitudinous, but space admits only the following extracts from the resolutions adopted at a convention of the (so-called) Republican party of Massachusetts, at Worcester, not long previous to the war:

"Resolved, That the necessity for disunion is written in the whole existing character and conditions of the two sections of the country—in their social organization, education, habits, and laws — in the dangers of our white citizens in Kansas, and of our colored ones in Boston — in the wounds of Charles Sumner and the laurels of his assailant — and no Government on earth was ever strong enough to hold together such opposing forces.

"Resolved, That this movement does not seek merely disunion, but the more perfect union of the free States by the *expulsion* of the slave States from the Confederation, in which they have ever been an element of discord, danger, and disgrace.

"Resolved, That henceforward, instead of regarding it as an objection to any system of policy, that it will lead to the separation of the States, we will proclaim that to be the highest of all recommendations and the grateful proof of statesmanship; and will support, politically or otherwise, such men and measures as appear to tend most to this result.

"Resolved, That the sooner the separation takes place the more peaceful it will be; but that peace or war is a secondary consideration in view of our present perils. Slavery must be conquered, 'peaceably if we can, forcibly if we must.'" (*a*)

(*a*) For twenty years, from the time that Mr. Polk required him to give place to Messrs. Ritchie and Armstrong, in 1845, until Columbia was burned and Richmond evacuated, in 1865, Mr. Francis P. Blair more or less openly co-operated politically with the men, who passed these resolutions. In a letter addressed, in 1855, to Daniel R. Goodloe and Lewis Clephane, Corresponding Committee of the Republican Association of Washington City, he assigned the reasons of his hostility to the Democratic party and to the South, as follows:

"The cause, which your organization is intended to promote, may well draw to its support men of all parties. Differences on questions of policy, on constitutional construction, of modes of administration, may well be merged to unite men, who *believe* that nothing but concert of action on the part of those, who would arrest the spread of slavery, can resist the power of the combination now embodied to make it embrace the continent from ocean to ocean."

It is impossible for any one, who knows Mr. Blair, to believe that he *believed* what he here assigns as the reason of his combination with the men, who passed these resolutions. He was too well informed, knew too much of geography, understood too well the climatic influences, which necessarily confined negro slavery to the Southern States, where alone it could be made profitable, to believe any such thing. But as the close of a lady's letter is said to open the window of her heart, so the close of Mr. Blair's letter opens the window of his. He said:

"Incumbents and expectants of office and dignities claim a sort of patent-right

Here we have disunion avowed in Massachusetts, for the purpose of getting rid of the social and political influences of negro slavery. I have already shown that its social influence was to make the well-behaved poor white man the equal of his rich neighbor, and its political influence was exerted to secure light taxes, fair wages, and cheap living. Some of the party, like Mr. Greeley, were willing to "let the Union slide," if thereby they could be left free in the North and East to enjoy the distinctions between poor and rich, reduce wages, and tax labor and its products for the benefit of an aristocracy. But when the Union sentiment, created by Southern statesmen, showed itself, then the men, who passed these resolutions, were the loudest in crying "rebel," and in denouncing those, who took them at their word and proposed to separate peaceably. Then the monarchists, aristocrats, and advocates of low wages, previously avowed disunionists, endeavored to make, and did make, the "simple-hearted citizens," who loved the Union, believe that the South had begun the war. This was not true: for the first act of war was the military movement of Captain, now General, Robert Anderson, in taking possession of Fort Sumter; unless, perhaps, it would be more correct to say, that the first act of war was done by the men, who passed at Worcester the resolutions above quoted, when they sent John Brown and his band to Harper's Ferry, to incite a servile insurrection in Virginia.

The dominant party of Massachusetts demanded disunion, "peacefully if they could, forcibly if they must." The South, in answer to this demand, offered to withdraw peace-

in the machine of Government, to create a Democracy adapted to their purposes. Their innovations in the machinery are contrivances to renew their privileges for new terms."

Mr. Blair had long been the incumbent of the very lucrative office of public printer, and was forced to give way for Mr. Ritchie and General Armstrong, at the instance of the Virginia delegation. His long "incumbency" made him feel that he had "a sort of patent-right" in the profits of that office, and that his removal was an "innovation" in the machinery contrived by the Democratic party and the South.

fully; tendered the olive-branch; sent commissioners to Washington to arrange the terms of peaceful separation. Secession was resorted to as a peaceful measure, to satisfy the dominant party at the North, who had demanded the "*expulsion*" of the South from the confederation. Some, as I have said, cared only to get rid of negro slavery; so that the North, relieved from its democratic tendencies, might more readily make transitions to a monarchical and aristocratic form of government, with high taxes, low wages, and large Government expenditures. Another class saw, in the larger expenditures of a war, the chance of making fortunes by contracting for army supplies; and their purpose to provoke a war was disclosed by the remark about "blood-letting," made by Senator Chandler, whose display of gorgeous liveries and other insignia of pretensions to nobility, on his tour through Europe since the war, in some measure compensated newspaper men for the dearth of excitements when the war was over. But there was another class of men at the North, those, whom M. Guizot calls the "simple-hearted citizens," whom Southern statesmen had taught to love the Union, and who, full of courage and virtue, though little mindful of political affairs till something startling happens to arrest their attention, rose up to declare that the Union should be preserved. The South was willing — anxious — to remain in, and even after secession to return to, the Union, if permitted to do so with their rights inviolate under the Constitution. In December, 1860, President Buchanan despatched to Mr. Lincoln a gentleman, (*a*) a connection by marriage of the latter, to invite him to come to Washington at once; with assurances that he would be received as a guest at the White House, with all the honors due to him as President elect; and that

(*a*) This was my father, General Duff Green. Mr. Buchanan selected him to be the bearer of his invitation to Mr. Lincoln, supposing that through the marriage connection he would have more influence with Mr. Lincoln than almost any other messenger, who could have been selected. Ninian Edwards, of Springfield, Illinois, was my mother's nephew, and he and Mr. Lincoln had married sisters.

by uniting their influence, they could yet satisfy the South that they could remain in, or return to the union, with safety to their rights, and honor to their character; that thus the farther progress of secession could be arrested, and the States, that had already acted, be brought back. Mr. Lincoln declined to accept Mr. Buchanan's invitation without the approval of Mr. Ben Wade, of Ohio, and some others, who would not consent to it; and the result was that the blood-letting and contracting portion of the aristocratic party carried their point, and succeeded in provoking the war.

A great effort was subsequently made to produce the impression at the North that the war was "the slaveholders' rebellion." Nothing could be farther from the truth. The slaveholders, with rare exceptions, were averse to war, and opposed to secession, lest it might lead to war. Only a few, very few, slaveholders, (who were misled into believing the Worcester declaration that the sooner the separation took place, the more peaceful it would be,) favored the movement. Let the candid reader bear in mind that property-holders are proverbially timid and averse to all political movements calculated to endanger property; and that the slaveholders had multiplied reasons for caution, in the peculiar nature of their property, which had legs and a will of its own to take itself off.

It is generally, but erroneously, believed at the North that Yancey, Rhett, Toombs, Benjamin, and some others, were the chief agents in bringing about secession. Their influence, however, was small, compared to that of Governor Joseph E. Brown, of Georgia; and for the reason that their arguments;—(such, for instance, as the offer to "drink all the blood that was spilled," attributed, truly or falsely, to Mr. Toombs;)—were intended to prove that secession would be peaceable, and were addressed to the slaveholders, who were in a minority of one to fifteen; while Governor Brown addressed himself to the non-slaveholders, who were a vast majority, as the census of

1860 will show. (*a*) Governor Brown was born in South Carolina, a self-made man, sprung from the non-slaveholding class of poor whites; and his influence with that class, who were proud of his talents and success, was not much less in South Carolina than in Georgia.

While Governor of Georgia before the war, he issued several papers addressed to the non-slaveholders, advocating secession with great adroitness and ability. His argument was in substance as follows:

That the (so-called) Republican party was coming into power, pledged and determined to abolish slavery, and to make the negro the equal of the poor white man.

That, inasmuch as slaves were property, and private property could not be taken without just compensation, the first result would be to tax the non-slaveholding mechanics, small farmers, croppers, and others of their class, to pay for the slaves.

That another result would be to reduce wages by the competition of the freed negro, who would make up by petty larceny for lower wages; that this would fall upon the laboring whites; because the slave-owners also owned the lands and the bank and railroad stocks, and could still provide for their

(*a*) The vast preponderance of the non-slaveholders appears by the following tabular statement, taken from the census of 1860. (See volume of Population, pp. 592 and 593, and volume of Agriculture, pp. 223 to 245.)

| | Slaveholders. | White population. | Ratio of slaveholders to white population. |
|---|---|---|---|
| Alabama | 33,730 | 526,271 | 1 in 15 |
| Arkansas | 11,481 | 324,143 | 1 " 28 |
| Florida | 5,152 | 77,747 | 1 " 15 |
| Georgia | 41,084 | 591,550 | 1 " 14 |
| Louisiana | 22,033 | 357,456 | 1 " 16 |
| Mississippi | 30,943 | 353,899 | 1 " 11 |
| North Carolina | 34,658 | 629,942 | 1 " 18 |
| South Carolina | 26,701 | 291,300 | 1 " 11 |
| Tennessee | 36,844 | 826,722 | 1 " 22 |
| Texas | 21,878 | 420,891 | 1 " 20 |
| Virginia | 52,128 | 1,047,249 | 1 " 19 |

children without labor; while the non-slaveholders would be further impoverished by taxation to pay for the slaves; and that it would be they — the non-slaveholders and their children — who alone would have to compete with the negroes for employment.

That another result would be to degrade their social position; because the freed negroes would not attempt to intrude into the well-furnished drawing-rooms of their late masters, but would force their way to the humble firesides of the poor mechanic and laborer, and insult them by demanding their daughters in marriage. (*a*)

By such arguments as these Governor Brown "fired the hearts" of the vast non-slaveholding majority, and by their votes swept the reluctant slaveholders into secession. When at a later period it was proposed by General Lee and others to put negroes into the army, it was the non-slaveholders, who most bitterly opposed it; because they shrank from a contact, which they feared would bring them down to a level with the negroes.

The war was not a slaveholders' rebellion. Notwithstanding the declaration passed by Congress, at the instance of the late President Johnson, that the only object of the war was to preserve the Union — though very few on either side conceived, or were even aware of, the plan, the execution of which they were advancing — it was fought on the one side — by those, who controlled the Government, and in whose minds the design of the vast machine was centred,— in the interest of monarchism and of the capital, that employs free labor; to destroy negro slavery; because its tendencies were anti-mon-

(*a*) It is due to Governor Brown to add that, as Chief Justice of the Supreme Court of Georgia, since the war, he has sought to shield the poor whites of that State from one degradation, by the fear of which he sought to "fire their hearts," when advocating secession, by deciding that the intermarriage of whites and negroes is prohibited. (See his opinion in the case of Charlotte Scott, plaintiff, *vs.* The State of Georgia, which those, who have not access to the Georgia Reports, will find in McPherson's Handbook of Politics for 1870, p. 474.)

archical, and its influence exerted in legislation to maintain the price of labor and cheapen the cost of living. On the other side, it was fought by the Southern non-slaveholders to avert pauperization by taxation, reduction of wages, and social debasement.

The great majority of the brave men, who did the hard fighting of the war, fought and bled and died, to keep the Southern States in the Union; yet their "judgment and will" were subordinated to the control of the men, who, in the Worcester resolutions, declared their purpose to be "the expulsion of the Southern States from the confederation."

Many conscientious men thought they were fighting to secure justice and liberty for the negroes; yet their "judgment and will" were subordinated to the control of men, who seized the first moment of power to oppress the negroes, by an unjust and unconstitutional tax upon the product of negro labor, cotton, while seeking to use the negroes as voting-machines, to oppress free white labor at the North by similar unjust and pauperizing taxation.

Mr. Attorney-General Akerman, in his speech in Representatives' Hall, Atlanta, Georgia, 1st September, 1870, sought to impress upon Southern capital the fact, that emancipation was a decree of *divorce* of its interests from those of labor.

He, or whoever prepared his speech for him, was aware, however, that this was a "serious topic." He therefore endeavored in that speech to ride on both sides of the "serious topic," by adding that, "looking at the white population alone, the cry of a conflict between labor and capital has generally been the cry of the demagogue, for the reason that capital has seldom been organized against labor; and labor has seldom, except in the small way of trades' unions, been organized against capital."

But what are the historical facts?

The following is an extract from a late report of the Massachusetts Bureau of Labor Statistics:

"BOSTON AND THE WORKING-WOMEN — A PITIABLE PICTURE.

Extract from the last Report of the Massachusetts Bureau of Labor Statistics.

"In Boston, a large proportion are workers in shops. We will take one trade, that of tailoresses and cloakmakers: they go to their work at seven, almost always without any warm breakfast; they work till ten, and then perhaps have a few minutes' rest, when the little teapot is set on the range and a lunch of dry food eaten; but in most of the establishments the girls do not stop work till twelve, when, in all, they are allowed from thirty to sixty minutes for dinner. Work ends at five P. M., and many of the girls take work home with them, work not ceasing till midnight. Room-rent costs not less than two dollars to three dollars each, with often two or more double beds in a room. In good shops and with brisk work they can earn a dollar a day. Some machine girls receive more, but the work is very wearing, and induces spinal disease. One of our largest as well as kindest custom-work merchant tailors testified to a committee of inquiry, that few 'machine girls' could work over two years before becoming so broken down that they were ever after unfit for labor. In slopwork shops, girls can seldom earn more than their room-rent except by overwork. In slack times their suffering is extreme, girls having been known to work weeks with only water and bread or crackers for food, and fortunate if able to procure an ounce of tea. In dull times many have lived for weeks on five cents' worth each of stale bread per week while seeking work. The lodging-house keepers charge working-women higher rates than men, and many refuse to have them in their houses at any price. Hence they are often obliged to live and sleep in localities, where they would be ashamed to let any one know they ever went. Yet few ever break down morally or become untidy in dress. Those women, who take work home from the slopshops, provident, aid, and other charitable societies, receive as follows: Shirts, 4 cents to 7 cents; fine-bosomed shirts, 10 cents to 25 cents; satin vests, 20 cents; pants, 15 cents, 20 cents, and 37 cents; coats, 50 cents; French calico suits, lined sacks, faced skirt, 20 cents; long white night-dresses, 50 cents. Of the 30,000 women in and about Boston, who live by sewing, very few earn over $12 a week; the average wages do not exceed $2.75. Many poor women take this slop and charity work in quantities, and give it to others to do, still further lessening the receipts of the actual workers, who are usually women with small families dependent upon their labor for support. Paper-box makers average about $3 per week.

"Factory life is much harder on women than it was twenty-five years ago. Instead of tending two looms, as then, she is required to tend six; while a week's work now will not procure as much comfort as when she only tended one loom. Very few working-women of any class ever have a good bed, with sufficient bed-covering. Their wages will not allow them to purchase warm flannel undergarments or serviceable shoes, water-proofs, etc. Few are ever exempt from diseases caused by scanty clothing, insufficient and innutritious food, and long-continued labor in deleterious conditions. The constant pressure of anxiety breaks down many girls physically, and too often morally, before they reach the prime of life. All avenues of employment are overcrowded."

The New York Times, under Mr. Raymond's management, was, and still is, one of the ablest exponents of the doctrine that "free labor is cheaper than slave labor." On the 14th July, 1868, it said editorially:

"The New Orleans Commercial Bulletin says that the Southern planters, 'profiting by free labor, have now discovered that more money can be made out of a freedman's labor than from that of a slave.' We are glad to hear it. In the old days of slavery, we always told the Southern people that this was the case."

On the 21st July, 1869, the New York Times spoke editorially of the great Asiatic slave-trader of the nineteenth century, Koopmanschap, as follows

"It was only a few weeks ago that the name of Koopmanschap was unknown to fame. Suddenly it has emerged from the obscurity, with which the appellations of ordinary mortals are surrounded, and *occupies a lofty niche within the nation's fame.* Everybody is asking 'Who is Koopmanschap?' Fortunately he has arrived in the city just in time to answer for himself this question, as propounded to him by our reporter yesterday."

Now why does this advocate of cheap labor and dear living give such *a lofty niche in the nation's fame* to this trader in human bones and flesh and muscle? Is there, can there be, any other reason than because this new organization of the labor system of the United States proposes to furnish capital with cheaper labor, giving to capital all the advantages of the slave system, and at the same time relieving capital from the expense and burden of taking care of labor in sickness and the infirmities of age? Oh, admirable, money-making philanthropy!

But let the New York Times speak for itself. It says: "It is the importation of these coolies in the past, and the proposed transportation immediately of hundreds of thousands more, to supply the demand for labor everywhere, and in every industrial department, and especially to cultivate the neglected plantations of the South, that have *made the name of Koopmanschap famous* in the land.

". . . The woollen factory of Lazar frères, in San Francisco, employs 300 Chinamen, who make splendid hands, although they were entirely ignorant of the business when first employed by that firm. This was two years ago, when the Irish hands refused to work more than eight hours a day. The firm immediately discharged them, and employed the coolies, paying the latter for ten hours' labor a day only $1 per diem on an average, while to the Irish laborers they had paid on an average \$3 per diem, or from \$60 to \$100 per month. . . .

"Mr. Koopmanschap says that he does not bring over Chinese women. They are sure to follow wherever the men go. The Chinamen will import them for themselves."

The Cincinnati Commercial is another noted advocate of these politico-economical ideas. It also sings pæans to Koopmanschap, and revels in the thought of a coming millennium of cheap labor. It says:

"Weavers of cotton and silk can be had in China for two or three dollars a month, and skilled artisans receive from five to eight dollars for that period of time. . . .

"Women are found in abundance in China to do the labor of households for their mere bread and clothing. Laborers can be got in the tea districts of China for six or seven cents a day. . . .

"The American laborer consumes enough meat, tea, and coffee, two or three times a day, to keep a Chinaman for a week. The price of meat, as is well known, is about four or five times that of bread. . . .

"The subsistence of the great mass of the Chinese is extremely simple. The great staple, of which it consists, is rice, and this, mixed with a little bread, a few vegetables, a little fruit, and a little meat, (more frequently fish,) constitutes the whole diet of millions. Indeed, the small consumption of animal food in China is one of the wonders of the country to a stranger. The flesh of beef or mutton is scarcely ever tasted except by the rich, and no Chinese ever use either milk, butter, or cheese."

Such is the Barmecide feast to which the so-called Republicanism of 1871 invites the laboring and productive classes of America.

On the other hand, the question of cheap labor and cheap production, which are the great problems of the age, has been so well treated by Ex-Governor Horatio Seymour, in a recent address to a mass meeting of working-men in Utica, New York, that I here insert it entire.

### SPEECH OF EX-GOVERNOR SEYMOUR.

At a mass meeting of working-men in Utica, New York, Ex-Governor Seymour spoke as follows:

"At the last six annual elections in this State the Republican leaders have asked that they should be kept in power, because they claimed they had saved the country, and we are left to the conclusion that they saved it for their own special benefit. We do not see the grounds for this claim, so far as the war is concerned, as we sent our full share of men to the field. The city of New York, the stronghold of the Democracy, did more than its share in filling the ranks of our armies. If we look at the action of the party in power, the question comes up, what kind of salvation have they given us.? Our whole people are grievously burdened by taxation. Military power still tramples upon the judiciary in many parts of the South, and even threatens the sanctity of the ballot-box at the North. Great armies are kept up upon the pretext that they are needed to save the negroes at the South, and to kill the Indians at the West. The country is harassed by Indian and African problems. It is now also perplexed with the Asiatic question. It comes up like a black cloud upon our Western borders, taking unusual forms and proportions. To all, who have studied it, it causes great anxiety. Its shadows fall upon us, and we cannot get rid of its dangers by shutting our eyes to its evil forebodings. It enters into this election, for we are about to choose our lawmakers, who must deal with it. Some months ago I wrote a short letter in answer to an invitation from a body of working-men to speak to them upon this subject. I took ground not only against the way, in which the Chinamen come to our country, but to their coming here at all. That letter was sharply censured, but it was not written without thought or study. As the subject is fairly up in this canvass, I will speak of it to-night. Heretofore, except at the time when the people of New York and New England were bringing negroes from Africa to sell to the people of the South, immigration has always brought us people kindred to ourselves in manners, customs, and religion. Even their languages had much in common. The literature of Europe, translated into different tongues, was more or less known to them all. They had the same habits of thought, and were used to the same form of civilization. Their coming gave no shock to our institutions, laws, or habits. They rapidly became part of ourselves, and added to the general wealth and prosperity. Europe was not so overcrowded with people that they were sent to us in great numbers, or more rapidly than they could be assimilated. We therefore welcomed them to our shores. The Chinese immigration is a different thing. It comes from a land crowded with people beyond what our civilization could tolerate. They outnumber us ten to one. It brings to us a people who are in conflict with all our methods of thought, with all our ideas of morals, and with all our conceptions of government. While we find much to commend in their industry, there is more to condemn in their cunning, their cruelty, and in that stolidity of character, which makes them unimpressible by any influences we can bring to bear upon them. They will always be an undigested, hurtful thing in our political system. The idea prevails that they are a docile, harmless race; and so they are while they remain a few individuals scattered through the community. But study their characters at home, and you will find thieving, corruption, and falsehood in the interior of the state, piracy upon its coasts, and robbery upon its inland borders.

"They are hated by all other Asiatics. While some urge that we should welcome them here, they are debating the question if they shall go on with the massacre of Americans and Europeans, which they began with the awful slaughter of the men and women, who are engaged among them, as missionaries, in works of charity and religion. Unfortunately for our country, our difficulties in dealing with this question are increased by the late amendments to the National Constitution, which have stripped the States of rights needed for their good government. Otherwise this question could have been left to the Pacific States, who would have dealt with it in the light of their own experience. But the Fifteenth Amendment binds California and Oregon hand and foot, and lays them prostrate before the Chinaman, who strides over them, and we are forced to confront him here. It is urged by some that Chinese immigration will lower the wages of our labor, cheapen production, and add to the national wealth. This is not true. Cheap labor does not add to a nation's wealth, neither does it cheapen production, as I will show. Look over the map of the world, and you will find universal poverty where labor is most poorly paid. In Africa, you can buy a man's labor for life for a string of beads, but they are too poor to get the string of beads. In Asia, the laborer gets a little better pay; but how little is its wealth, and how small is its commerce, compared with its countless millions of people! Men, who wear scanty cotton clothing, cannot uphold arts or industry. They cannot give life and prosperity to the workshop, to the counting-house, or to fleets of vessels upon the ocean. If you compare Asia and Africa with Europe, you will find that, while the laborers of England, of Germany, of France, and other countries are much better paid, the national wealth is greater, and that they are sending their products to the very regions where the pay of labor is at the lowest ebb. The labor of Europe, whose wages are so much higher than those of the other continents I have named, can still produce all the products of art for a much less price, and can and does sell them to those countries, where labor starves for want of pay. But we must turn to our own country to learn how true it is that labor must be well paid to give wealth and prosperity to a land. If the laborers and mechanics of the United States were put upon the same pay given to the Chinamen, we should have universal bankruptcy throughout the bounds of our country. Three-quarters of the stores of this city would be closed. Why is it that a town with 10,000 people here does more business than a city of 100,000 in Asia? It is due to the fact that our mechanics are able to build houses; to furnish them with the comforts of life; to clothe themselves and their families, not only in a way which protects their persons, but also gratifies their tastes; which enables them to support the arts and industry in all its forms. Why are the people of these United States able to pay a percentage of taxation, which would crush any other nation? It is simply because the wages of labor here enable men to consume all those varied articles, which pay a duty to Government. Go where you will, the world over, and you will find the greatest general wealth, the greatest prosperity, and the greatest happiness, where you find the greatest wages for labor. Men confound cheap labor with cheap production. These are not only different, but at times they are opposite things. Sometimes cheap labor is an element in cheap production, but that is not the rule. We see the fact to be that, where labor is the highest, production is the cheapest, and sends its works of art and of skill all over the world. The reason of this is, cheap production is the result of intellect as well as labor; of mind as well as of toil. It is wrought out by those, who are in that condition of comfort and respectability, that their minds are educated and alert. Starving labor never yet invented machinery to till the ground and gather in its crops; it never yet worked out those wonders in mechanics, which have borne our country on to its greatness. Men can cheapen their productions and add to their earnings when they can call to their aid science and learning, but these two cannot live where labor is pinched down to the point of starvation. If man invents a machine, which enables him to make more, he can yet sell for less and grow rich. But force him to sell for less by the competition of the Chinaman, which does not increase his power of production, and he starves. And when the laborer sinks, the whole structure of society, of which he is the basis, sinks with him. This may be laid down as a law — that cheap production and general prosperity are the results of high civilization and general intelligence; that these can only exist among a people, where the great mass of the working men are well paid and placed in the condition of respectability, where their minds are fed as well as their bodies. But it is said there is no danger that the Chinamen will come to this country in such numbers as will harm our working-men. Is this true? We find that the character and condition of the Chinese is such that they can be sent for as readily as so many boxes of tea. We learn every day of orders that are sent out for thousands of them for special purposes. Orders are now under way for bands of them to make boots and shoes. It does not take a large number, thrown into this branch of business, to overstock the demand for this labor, and to unsettle the wages of those, who are skilled in this business. Already the artisans engaged in this trade are uneasy. They do not know how soon that skill, which they have gained in it, may be made valueless to support their families in the condition they have heretofore lived. The men who make clothes or hats, or other classes of our mechanics, may be treated in the same way. Those, who work in our factories, are liable to be driven out by orders, which are even now on their way to Asia. Navigation on the Pacific, as its name implies, has always been less costly and dangerous than that of the stormy Atlantic. There are now about one hundred and fifty thousand Chinamen in our country. An equal number, brought here by selfish and designing men, may be so placed as to force down the wages of working-men. The mere fact, that this can be done, destroys the independence and clouds the hopes of the body of our mechanics. There is a growing belief in men's minds that the mission of Mr. Burlingame was contrived by a class of manufacturers to effect this very object, at the moment they were appealing to Congress for special legislation in their own behalf. Short-sightedness is always incident to selfishness and greed. Let these men bear in mind that, when they have broken down the body of the laborers of this country, they will have destroyed their ability to be the consumers of manufactured products. The evils of underpaid labor will not fall upon the working-men alone. All classes must suffer when they are made poor. The owners of real estate, the merchant, the manufacturer, will find that the laws of trade and the rules of value are universal and unvarying. They will operate in Europe or America, as they do in Asia or Africa. True statesmanship and generous wisdom ever look to building up the interests of labor. Where the homes of toil are happy, and where prosperity waits upon the hand of industry, there is national greatness, wealth, and glory. But we are asked, What can we do to avert these evils? How can we hinder the landing upon our shores of swarms of Asiatics, without overturning the established maxim as to immigration? We need no change of our policy in this respect. We put the Asiatic and the European upon the same footing. Our laws have never allowed any nation to send here a hurtful or a dangerous class of men. When in some instances they have shipped paupers to our shores, we have sent them back. We forbid the violators of laws, men who endanger the public health or order, to land here. The statutes of the different States and of the nation are full of such regulations. We welcome the great body of European immigrants, because it is for our advantage to have them here. The Chinaman has no better rights than the German, the Irishman, the Englishman, or the Frenchman. If his coming here is hurtful to the good order of society, to the great interests of industry, we have a right to keep him away. If there is danger that they will pour into the Pacific States in such numbers as to shape their customs and habits by Asiatic rules, then they endanger our Union, for the end of this must be their utter severance from the rest of our country. The Mormons are not so much in conflict with our ideas of morals and civilization as are the Chinese. Yet no one would tolerate the idea that the Mormons should gain control of the Pacific coast. This Government is even now adopting sharp measures to hold them in check, at their colony in the midst of the great deserts of the West. A simple law, such as has been adopted with regard to foreign immigration, will settle this whole question. Let Congress declare that no more than ten Chinamen shall be landed from one vessel, and they will close to a safe degree those floodgates, which are now wide open, and through which we are threatened with an invasion from Asia as hurtful as that, which once desolated Europe under Genghis Khan. I have spoken thus plainly upon this subject, because I believe it more deeply concerns the welfare of the American people than any topic involved in this election. I have no censures for those who may differ from the views I hold. I have no prejudices, which will hinder me from changing those views, if I find that I am wrong. What I have said is the result of much thought and careful study. I wish that those, who are charged with the conduct of national affairs, or that their supporters, who are active in this canvass, had in a plain and open way stated their views with regard to this great Asiatic problem. I think that, by so doing, they would stand in a better light before the country and the world, than by efforts to keep alive sectional hate and partisan malice."

To the editorial comments of the New York Times on the fact noticed by the New Orleans Commercial Bulletin, it is only necessary to add one single example, out of millions, to illustrate that the effect of emancipation has already been to reduce wages, and to diminish the share of the products of labor, allotted to those, by whose labor they were produced. A negro woman, who was an excellent cook, was, by the casualties of the war, separated from her owners in 1864. In January, 1870, she was most happy to get back to them. She told them she had been doing her best to support herself, but had not been able to get more than her food and forty dollars a year, out of which she had to clothe herself, and pay for medicine and medical attendance. Before the war she could be hired readily for $125 to $150 per annum, with food, clothing, medicines, and medical attendance in addition.

Yet the Republican cry is still for cheaper labor! and Senator Sprague attended the Memphis Commercial Convention for the sole purpose of impressing on the mind of Southern capital that, having been *divorced* by emancipation from labor, it should now unite with Northern capital in measures to cheapen labor. (*a*)

In this *divorce* case, labor is the feebler party;—the poor deserted wife, left without alimony, and with a brood of hungry children crying for bread, and dependent on her for support!

Emancipation has taken from her that "natural ally," which a community of interests secured to her in the old days of negro slavery, as expressed in Mr. Jefferson's aphorism, above quoted. Wages no longer, at the South, go into, but they come out of, the pockets of capital. The cost of living, at the South, no longer comes out of, but goes into, the pockets of capital.

And now we have the authoritative declaration of the Attorney-General, the first law-officer of the Government, that Mrs. White Labor and Mrs. Black Labor are two lonely grass widows.

(*a*) See Senator Sprague's speech at the Memphis Commercial Convention.

The question arises, Where can they, in their lonesome grass-widowhood, turn for aid and comfort, food, and shelter?

Shall they "go to Chicago"? Alas, they are already *divorced by emancipation!* They would be glad to make an honest living, as hirelings, if they could get wages to keep soul and body together. But they shrink from living by beggary, prostitution, or theft. Then there is no use in their "*going to Chicago.*"

Shall they appeal to what is called *Republicanism* in 1871? Alas! with the old rakes of that set, who misled, deceived, and betrayed them, the heyday of the blood is over; their hearts are withered and callous! Besides, they brought about the *divorce*, of malice prepense, with set purpose to ruin these two poor women; that they might thereby be forced into one of De Cassagnac's four classes of the proletariat, viz., hirelings at cheap wages, or else beggars, prostitutes, or thieves!

Shall they appeal to the younger bloods of the set—any of the "smaller fry," who call themselves Republicans? Alas! they never had either hearts or brains; or, if they had, there was not phosphorus enough in their composition to light up the one, or warm the other! Besides, they belong, body and soul, to capital, and believe that, in the progress of civilization, the great need of the hour is *cheap labor!*

Can they find relief in what the Attorney-General calls "the small way of trades' unions"? Alas, alas, alas! our author shows that all history proves that to be a poor and vain reliance! Egotism, selfishness, appear there, as elsewhere. I attended the National Labor Convention in Baltimore in 1866, as a spectator, from curiosity, to see what it was composed of, and what were its objects. I was at the National Labor Convention in Chicago in 1867, as a delegate from the Pattern-makers' Union of Baltimore. I had not much to say at either Convention, but was a close observer at both. Of all the men, whom I saw at Baltimore or Chicago, only two impressed on me the idea that their purpose was to relieve the distress of the two poor *divorced* widows, Mrs. White Labor and Mrs. Black Labor. All the rest impressed me with the idea that their "judgment and will" were under the control of the few, in whose minds the designs of the machine were centred; or that egotism, selfishness, was their only motive; that their purpose was "to grind their own axes," and to get some control over the two poor lonesome grass widows, on which they could trade, for their own profit, with the advocates of cheap labor.

Can wan, pallid Mrs. White Labor find an asylum in the cabin of her dusky rival, Mrs. Black Labor, now the favored mistress of that wild *enfant perdu*, Imperialism, who is travelling, *incog.*, through the United States, under the assumed name of Republicanism?

Pshaw! Let Pharisees, who trade upon, and grow rich by, negrophilism, falsely prate about the equality or superiority of the negro over the white race, in all intellectual, moral, physical, social, and political aptitudes. Let charlatans in statesmanship vainly delude themselves with the belief, that, by such legislation as the Akerman Election Bill of Georgia, they can vote negroes, without challenge, as often as their party necessities require. Let would-be emperors fondly imagine that, because the "*colored troops fought nobly*," the colored vote can be used to make them small Neros or Caligulas. All this is vanity and vexation of spirit. It is historically certain — at least I firmly believe — that thirty millions of the Caucasian race will not long consent to leave their destinies under the control of four millions of ignorant negroes, misled by bad white men, of very little more intellect than the negro, and with hearts blacker than the negro's skin.

Oh, that these poor divorced women could turn to some one of the noble and gallant men, whom they called "rebels," when in fact they were risking life and fortune, and lost everything but honor, for their sakes and in their cause! I could speak to them of men, whose names are synonyms for all that is great in intellect, noble in conduct, pure in morals, knightly in courtesy. I could point to one in Georgia, a native Georgian; brave as Marshal Ney, eagle-eyed and skilful as the first Napoleon, devout and sincere as Havelock or Robert E. Lee, the great Christian soldier, Major-General John B. Gordon, who was on the battle-field and in the Episcopal Church, what Stonewall Jackson was on the battle-field and in the Presbyterian Church. Near to him, in South Carolina, I could point to General William S. Walker, a Pennsylvanian by birth, but, like Gordon, "sans peur et sans reproche;" one who never deceived man or misled woman. I might name others. But, alas! all these men were Southern rebels. They fought bravely and conscientiously in a cause they believed to be right; yet, they were conquered — subjugated. Now they are prostrate. The dusky mistress of Imperialism has her pearl-embroidered slipper (*a*) on their necks.

Is there, then, no hope for the widows — is there no help for the widows' sons and daughters?

Yes. In the Democracy of the Great West, there yet remain traces of the pure republicanism of Jefferson and Madison, of Calhoun and Webster. There labor can find statesmen, who have never bowed the knee to Baal or to Mammon, nor accepted the idea that, in the progress of civilization, the great objects of social and political science are to cheapen labor, and to regulate the diet of American working men and women by the smallest quantities of rice and fish, on which an Asiatic can exist.

The first great need of labor is an honest and economical administration of Government. Prodigal expenditures require oppressive taxation, which, however disguised by the subtle and artful contrivances of modern legislation, labor and the products of labor in the end have to pay. (*b*)

(*a*) See chap. xvii.

(*b*) See chap. xiv., on the Fall of the Ancient Trades' Unions.

But what, more than all else, oppresses labor, and all, who employ labor in the pursuits of productive industry, is the subtle and artful fiscal contrivance, by which the control of the money of the country is centred in a few hands, enabling them by combination and concert of action to raise or lower the prices of the products of labor at pleasure, by making money scarce when they wish to buy, and abundant when they wish to sell. "Never," said Mr. Calhoun in the Senate, October 3, 1837—"Never was an engine invented better calculated to place the destiny of the many in the hands of the few, or less favorable to that equality and independence, which lie at the bottom of our free institutions."

I wish here to repeat, what I have said in my dedication, that under the designation of "The Laboring and Burgher Classes of America," I include all of the learned professions—all, who labor with the brain or with the hand—all, who wish to live and grow rich by the fruits of their own honest industry—all, who do not seek to live by plundering the Federal or State treasuries, nor by Congressional or State class legislation.

What they all require is an abundant and cheap measure of prices, of uniform and stable value.

But a further discussion of this subject would make this preface too long, and I propose to treat of it in another book.

If I have succeeded in dispelling some few of the many errors, under which the Northern and Western mind have been befogged, in reference to the causes and results of the late Civil War in America, my present purpose will have been accomplished.

BEN. E. GREEN.

HOPEWELL, near Dalton,
Whitfield County, Georgia,
*February*, 1871.

# INTRODUCTION

TO

# UNIVERSAL HISTORY.

---

## PART FIRST.

---

Note.—Part Second, by the same author and translator, will contain the History of the Noble Classes.

# Author's Dedication.

## TO M. GUIZOT.

I DEDICATE THIS BOOK TO YOU, AS THE PRINCE OF THE HISTORIANS OF OUR AGE. YOU WILL RECOGNIZE IN IT THE TRACE OF YOUR PRINCIPLES AND THE FRUIT OF YOUR COUNSELS, IF I HAVE BEEN ABLE TO COMPREHEND THE FORMER AND PROFIT BY THE LATTER. BE PLEASED TO BELIEVE THAT I WOULD HAVE DESIRED TO ADDRESS IT TO YOU, AS THE MAN, WHOM I MOST RESPECT, IF I HAD NOT OFFERED IT TO YOU, AS THE HISTORIAN, WHOM I MOST ADMIRE.

A. GRANIER DE CASSAGNAC.

# AUTHOR'S PREFACE.

THIS is not a political work. It is a book of history. I do not propose, nor attack, nor defend, any social theory. I relate and discuss facts.

I hasten to express myself thus; because, in spite of the great liberty of thought that this age enjoys, we live in a time when political parties, like the ancient doctors of the Sorbonne, assume an absolute jurisdiction over every idea, whatever it may be, in literature or in art. They pretend that every poet who sings, every dramatist who writes, every painter who designs, every sculptor who chisels, every wise man who calculates or analyzes, should direct their verses, their scenic combinations, their paintings, their statues, their theorems, to certain results of constitutional progress and representative amelioration, as the theologians of former days required poets and philosophers, jurisconsults and astronomers, Vanini and Ramus, Servetus and Galileo, to conform to the letter of the decretals and the canons.

Small as I am among the young laborers, who work on the ethics of this age, I, for my part, protest against the tyranny of parties. Poets, artists, and learned men, when God gave them the knowledge of the elevated things of this world, became invested with a supremacy too noble and too kingly, to descend, without abasement, to become the servants of political cabals, or to be required, in searching for the object and conditions of their works, to satisfy any other exigencies than those of poetry, science, and art.

I know that for some years there has been a desire to accustom the public to other principles. I know that the desire has been to have it believed that what constituted great writers and great artists was to give their time, their heads, and their hands, to the study and satisfaction of what is called the *wants of the age;* but I know also that those, who put forward these ideas and use this jargon, never did, and beyond doubt never could, write a book, or execute a work of art, and that they have their reasons for wishing to steal by fraud into the family of the learned, and to taste the joy of triumph, without having passed through the anguish of the strife.

I have already said, my ideas are different; and I have put them at the beginning of this book; that those, who may be tempted to open it, may not be surprised by finding it a stranger to all the pretensions, to all the cliques, to all the grudges of the moment.

Nevertheless, little as I revere the parties, who oppress France; little as I respect their bright lights; little confidence as I have in their duration, I would not have it thought that I am indifferent to the destiny of my country, and that I consider the different theories now contesting for mastery as equally unworthy the attention of a man of study. During the seven years, which I have devoted to collecting the materials for this book, I have been witness to many outrages and many crimes; and at each hurrah, that the dishevelled rioters gave in the streets; at each grimacing bravado, that assassination threw up from the planks of the scaffold, I have found it necessary to plunge deeper into the solitude of old books, to find in this necropolis of the illustrious dead of Greece and Italy silence enough to guard me from the noise, that distracts, and calmness enough to guard me from the emotion, that excites.

No, indeed; I have not abstained from politics, because I disdained it, but because I feared it.

For more than fifty years, the greater part of the men, who have written, or who now write, on politics, seem to me to have misunderstood its nature and its temper. It has always seemed to me that every science had its proper place and its special necessities. For example, geometry lives by the logical deduction of abstract ideas, and chemistry by the exact analysis of material objects. By analogy, I have been pressed to believe, and I believe firmly, that politics, to become a science, must take history for its base; and that, its object being to rule and govern men, who are neither blind matter nor abstractions, and who consequently are beyond the customary methods of the exact sciences, it becomes necessary to observe in history the laws peculiar to man and to peoples, to lay aside generalities, theorems, syllogisms, all the apparatus of ideologists and dreamers, and search in the jurists, the philosophers, the poets, among all those, who have written concerning man and nations, about his heart and mind, his feelings and his ideas, the secret tendency of individuals, of families, and of society.

Outside of this path, politics appear to me barren and worthless. For thirty centuries it was obstinately tried to study chemistry by reasoning; and they did not succeed in the decomposition of a pebble-stone. Since forty years it has been studied by observation, and already the half of the secrets of nature have been discovered. Now, politics are, in the order of moral things, what chemistry is in the order of material things, a science of observation and analysis; only much more difficult; because man, whom it has to observe and know, is much more complex than matter. Let us not, then, be surprised at the vanity of our long domestic strifes. Politics are like a gun: when we pull the trigger, it only emits what has been put into it. For forty years we have loaded it with crude phrases, and it throws out crude phrases. Load it with well-observed facts, and it will give you solid institutions.

The science of politics, then, needs to be preceded by another science, which is history. Without this guide, it is not a science, but poor nonsense, unworthy the leisure hours of a man of sense. Now, if I have abstained from politics, it is because, in my opinion, history has not yet been written, and I had no wish to set on the pillory a book of generalities, the use of which is sterile, and the abuse fatal.

Now, as I think history has never yet been written, I will explain what I mean, for the benefit of those good and patient readers, who never get angry with their books; who find how never to open one without learning something, and who can believe, that when the pending works of the day are brought to an end, we should leave the old chronicles to rest in peace, and declare to the present, that it should, hereafter, hold itself to be sufficiently instructed in all the secrets of past times.

Certainly, if any age has reason to be dissatisfied with its historic labors, ours has not. Men of the greatest learning, others of the greatest merit, have, for twenty years, treated many difficulties of ancient and modern history. Each one of them has cleared away some part of the immense mass of the rubbish of past ages, and has reconstructed in some one of its essential parts the monument of their lives, which the people of former days have erected: a monument, which is called politics, when it is standing; and history, when it has been overthrown.

Thus I delight to recognize, first of all, that few epochs have done in history more or better than ours. And first, in this matter, we should mention M. Guizot. His monographs on different questions of Roman history and of the middle ages, have marked the path we must all follow, if we wish to give to history the elements of strict demonstration and a positive basis. Moreover, by his lessons and his general ideas on modern civilization, M. Guizot has produced in France, a true, pure, and correct historic sentiment, which will be the cause, and the precursor of rapid progress and lasting conquests. It is not impossible, that his later works, which in the mind of the author were only a sketch, may perhaps some day be surpassed by a finer and more delicate analysis of facts, and a more elevated and complete synthesis of ideas. For, as Buffon justly observes, it is the fate of inventors to be despoiled by those, who come after them; but it is none the less certain, even on this hypothesis, that whatever may be done hereafter in history, correct and great, M. Guizot will have rendered it possible.

Thus the *Spirit of the Laws* is now a book half dethroned — no one, however, will wish to take away from Montesquieu the glory of having produced in his time, as M. Guizot has in ours, a certain sentiment of elevated, calm, and profound criticism. This sentiment may be said to be the soul of good books — a soul, which lives always, even when the books are no more. After this, who will so far forget his condition as to *promise* himself all the future? When one really labors at intellectual work, which the human mind pursues incessantly, it matters little when he is buried. God always finds him.

After, and alongside of, M. Guizot, other men, younger and of less elevated ideas, have, nevertheless, undertaken and accomplished works, which all, more or less, enter into this new historic spirit, of which we speak; works, which are more seed than fruit, but of which any epoch might be proud, and of which ours boasts, with good reason.

M. Augustin Thierry, in whom, perhaps, we do not find that great elèvation of view necessary to measure the vast historic horizon, nor that complete and abundant learning required for the explanation of far separated epochs, is, nevertheless, a wonderful workman, in restoring, by his very confused episodes, the personal and dramatic aspect of the middle ages. His ideas, generally, only touch, or penetrate very little below, the surface of things; but the patient carving of his embellishments is always that of a work at once vast and severe, capricious and exact.

M. Michelet is a very noble and great historian. His ideas always step along with head erect and high, and the poet might have said of him, that he sought the royal road to heaven, *viamque affectat Olympo.* Nevertheless it is in my opinion questionable whether the time has yet come to undertake what he has undertaken. In my eyes, M. Michelet is a sculptor, who has mistaken the hour and has arrived at the foot of the monument before the masons had left it. Certainly it is a very legitimate curiosity, worthy of the brightest minds, to wish to learn the most elevated, the most ideal, the most accurate signification of the history of nations. But is it not necessary to wait for that, until all the preparatory work shall have been, if not finished, at least commenced? In every edifice, must not the foundations first be laid? M. Michelet may then be said to have occupied himself prematurely with the abstract and supreme meaning of history. The last word in the life of nations is composed of many letters. How many of them have yet been written legibly?

Along with these didactic historians, who directly, and we may say professionally, teach and study history, we must name a writer, who has illuminated one whole immense and obscure side of the middle ages — that of arts, of public manners, and of the feudal family. This was M. Victor Hugo. Those, who may be astonished to hear us speak of M. Victor Hugo as one of the most eminent historians of the age, have not observed that great poets seize upon certain aspects of the life of peoples more readily than the learned and the chronologists. Besides, it is not to be doubted that there is more of Greek history in Homer than in Pausanias, and more of Latin history in Virgil than in Sallust.

I have said and freely repeat, then, that our epoch is rich in remarkable historians, and especially opulent in historic intelligence and aptitude. But what great and definitive results has it obtained? We scarcely dare to count them. The historians have not understood each other, either in their plan of work, or in their critical ideas. Hence the works of one have not added to the works of another; their efforts have not aided each other, are not complete, do not make parts of a whole; in the collection of their works there is neither logical sequence nor design. With profound learning, great intelligence, and indefatigable research, history has not been written and settled, except in some very limited matters, like the map of those unknown countries, on which only a few harbors and rivers are marked with certainty.

General history, significant history, conclusive history, has not yet been written, as we have said. More than that, it is not yet possible. The traditions of the ancient and modern world are in fact like that geographical chart just mentioned. We have only the position of a very few points exactly and geometrically indicated. The position of all the others is vague, uncertain, speculative, very questionable and very much disputed, without counting the numerous and immense blanks, which serve to indicate deserts and unexplored regions.

These gaps, still left in general history, terrify by their numbers and extent, and we dare not ask when at last we can know the exact and real configuration of humanity.

For example, who has thought of writing the history of the family; that is to say, the history of all the variations, which the relations of husband and wife, father and son, father and daughter, master and servant, mother and children, have passed through, since the commencement of nations, and among all people, both as to moral authority and in respect to property?

Who has thought of writing the history of law; that is to say, to determine, by the laws, every kind of association, that men have been led to form with each other, and to discover the general tendency of human associability in the special character of all its local and temporary conjunctions?

Who has written the history of language and literature; the history of religion; the history of administrative institutions; the history of judicial institutions; the history of the military art; the history of commerce; the history of agriculture; the history of architecture; the history of heraldry; the history of furniture, dress, and domestic life?

Here we have so many series of facts, running through and through the history of all peoples, and of which it is impossible for any one to say anything precise and clear, without danger of fatal or ridiculous errors. All that the writers of general history can do is to make more or less mistakes on all these unknown matters, and to fall back upon dates, battles, lists of emperors, the passages of rivers, and the captures of cities. But, in good conscience, is this the history of the peoples? No.

What is to be done, then, in this situation of studies? In my opinion, the position is difficult, but simple. Each one must take his particular task, and accept the consequences of the want of accord and consecutiveness, which has heretofore prevailed in the works of historians. It becomes necessary to renounce general history, which is impossible, and grapple resolutely with monographs, dissertations, and special treatises. We must become learned; (I return to the comparison, because it is clear and exact,) we must write history as they make geographical charts, measuring with precision each portion of land, and not passing to the second, until the first has been indicated with all possible exactness. When we shall have thus solved, one after another, all the special difficulties of tradition, we need not trouble ourselves to know who will write general history. It will be written.

So I have thought and acted. This book is the first-fruits of my conviction.

Nevertheless, my conviction once formed, I was not at the end of my doubts. When I had decided to attempt special dissertations and treatises, I found myself stopped by another grave difficulty, which is this: I asked myself if all these monographs were independent of each other; if I could commence with this or that one indifferently; if there was any connection between them by any certain logical order or fixed dependence, so that it was necessary to begin with that, which was the key of all the others, under penalty of plunging into labors, not only long but useless. Such a question could only be solved by experiment. So I attempted the study of the first specialty, which presented itself, the history of law.

Scarce entered upon the history of law, I discovered that all laws were fundamentally divided into two groups—feudal laws and civil laws; and that these were based on two classes of men, historically distinct and separated — the nobles and the common people. It was thus clearly demonstrated for me, from the first steps, that this history of law should be preceded by another, which is the history of the noble and of the freed races.

Once convinced that the history of law was not the point of departure, nor the key of the system, I undertook another specialty, the history of the family. Here the first facts observed showed me the existence of two species of families: one, in which the paternal authority was more or less absolute, and property entailed; another, in which the paternal authority was scarcely perceptible and property was movable and alienable. The first of these two species of families belonged to the nobles, the second to the common people. Thus the history of the family, like the history of law, brought me back to the noble and freed races.

I made the same experiments on the greater part of the historic specialties of some elevation and extent, and I was always brought back to this result: that the primitive part of history, that which is nearest the root, that, on which all others depend, that, from the foot of which all others start, as streams of water from their head-springs, is the fact of the noble races and the slave races.

This result once reached, the great primordial fact of the noble races and the slave races became for me the object of constant and continued study. I searched into its origin, its development, its character, and I remained entirely convinced that it was like a high mountain with two water-sheds, from the top of which all the secondary chains of history started out, to flow down and be lost in the infinite.

In my view, the noble and the slave races are the two moieties of human history, which make it up faithfully and entirely, whether we consider them in their highest generality or most local specialty. By taking this fact as a base and following it up through all its radiations, we arrive at the rapid, comprehensive, and complete intelligence of all the details of the life of peoples; — laws, family, politics, art; — we see the birth, the growth, the development of all.

What, then, is this fact of the noble and slave races? This is the secret of this book. However, the volume now published contains only half of the subject. It contains the history of the slave races, taken from their point of departure, and followed through all the phases of their social fortune. I will soon give to the public the history of the noble races, and until then, I ought to add that many of my thoughts will naturally appear obscure and incomplete, because the members are only thoroughly explained by a study of the whole body.

The historic method, which I have just explained and which I have followed, and especially the point of view, which has given me the idea of this book, have thrown me entirely out of the ordinary paths of science. I do not conceal, then, the strangeness of the principles, which I have sought to establish, and the many repugnances, which I run the risk of exciting. I accept with confidence the hazards of the public judgment, for truth can always defend itself. If, perchance, I may have been mistaken in one or other of my convictions, I may give them up for others that are better.

The only thing, that could be painful and sad to me, would be that any one should doubt the perfect sincerity of my ideas, from any paradoxical taint, that might at first glance be seen. I have not labored for seven successive years, without a day's intermission, to mystify the public or deceive myself.

However, I have not wished to be believed on my word in a matter so novel, and therefore so open to discussion. It will be seen that I have quoted literally all the essential evidences, which have served to form my opinion and support my doctrine. It was necessary, first, to justify the entirely new historic path, which I have ventured upon, and secondly, because, as many of my ideas were based on my own interpretation of certain ancient texts, it was important to show what I had done in this critical part of my work.

I have already given the reasons for my belief that this is at this day the best, the only good, manner of writing history. If God permits me to follow the bent of my studies and tastes, I will thus take up, in succession, the historic specialties, which seem to me indicated by the logic, which connects facts with each other, and will work patiently to quarry out some stones, which some future architect will one day cement into a general monument, erected to human traditions.

Moreover, it is a profound conviction of my soul that politics will only cease to be a dangerous empiricism, and become a calm and serene science, when it takes history for its point of departure. For half a century it has felt the want of a base, and has sought one in abstract theories about the rights of man and other metaphysical entities, which have no reality except in the belief of those, who accept them, and which all the world can deny. These theories are to-day worn out and abandoned, without results; we can rely on that. Now that experience has brought reflection, it may well be said that man is neither a triangle nor an idea, but a complex being, having a history, which must be studied and known, to appreciate his social nature, his character, and his wants. The first condition required for finding out the laws of the future, is to know those of the past.

ADOLPHE GRANIER DE CASSAGNAC.

PARIS, 10*th December*, 1837.

# HISTORY

## OF THE

# WORKING AND BURGHER CLASSES.

---

## CHAPTER I.

### GENERAL IDEA OF THE PROLETARIAT.

THE working classes constitute one of the elements of European society in particular, and of all civilized societies in general. We add this qualification, because there are societies, in which the laboring classes do not exist. For example, they are a fact almost entirely unknown among the Arabs of Africa, and they have but little development, and, if we may so speak, little spread in Russia and Greece, in Turkey, and in all the East.

Few among those, who have undertaken to speak of the working classes, have remarked in them this strange characteristic, of existing among certain people, and not existing among others; of not reproducing themselves at all epochs, but of waiting certain moments and in some sort certain historic seasons to germinate and flourish. On the whole, there are in the newspapers, in books, and in the public mind, few clear and fixed ideas as to working-men. No one has ever thought, for example, of asking whether or not they constitute a race apart among the peoples, where they are found, or what cause produces them at certain times and in certain countries more than in others; what cause scatters them thinly in one country, thick and swarming in another. In a word, no one has yet seriously concerned himself about their history; more than that, and what is worthy of note, no one has been curious to know whether the working-men had a history, a separate history of their own, a history actually unknown, but which, if written, would bring the minds of economists and statesmen on the track of possible, easy, and immediate ameliorations.

The publicists of the present time, who have treated of the working classes, have done so without any clear, proper, and special idea. They have taken them in their present condition, without even asking if they were always what they are to-day. They have no key, which opens their historic nature and their social signification, and they move around without being able to seize them with the slippery tweezers of their ideology. They know not, therefore, whence they came; and hence they know not whither they go.

Yes, indeed, the working classes have a separate history, or rather they have in the general life of nations a peculiar and distinct destiny, the recital of which constitutes a separate history, and shows under what conditions and at what epochs the working-men appeared, united, worked, lived, were perpetuated. This history has not yet been composed and written for two reasons: First, because Europe has only to-day reached that period of the social revolution, when the working classes have acquired sufficient development and importance for governments to trouble themselves and for publicists to occupy themselves with them. Second, because history is now only emerging from the condition of the epics and chronicles, in which the ancients placed and our fathers left it, to that of criticism, to be studied, known, completed, to find out the reason of its poesy and the reflection of its action. Thus, on the one side, governments begin to note that there is in their mechanism a grit, which stops its movements, and which has been accumulated grain by grain; on the other, historians begin to observe that we have upon our hands an immense social fact, which they have forgotten to notice in the books, which they call history, and which are filled almost exclusively with the names of battles, emperors, and captains; so that the working classes are now rapping at the doors of the learned and of kings, and say to the first, "We want a history;" and to the latter, "We want bread."

The principal reason why the publicists of our time have only half succeeded, when they have treated of what relates to the working classes, is, as we have said, because they have not approached them from the side of history. The men, who are now at the head of affairs, and those, who have filled the last twenty years with their ideas or with their reputation, all belong by education to the philosophic school of the eighteenth century. This is the school whose theories are found most clearly and eloquently summed up and related in the *Social Contract*, and in the *Discourse on the Inequality of Conditions*, and from its time critical history has not been attempted except by Vico, whom France did not recognize; which has led all the publicists, since the Revolution of 1789, to enter upon the question of the working-men and the poor — of the *people*, in short — from the side of abstractions, of those *rights of men* in general, which the eighteenth century made the fundamental axiom of political science.

Nevertheless, there were two great inconveniences in this mode of proceeding. To draw to and absorb in the great abstraction contained in the word *man*, the working-men and the poor, that is to say, the *people*, and to assume as a principle the absolute unity and identity of the rights and duties of all, was to prejudge the question, whether there are in the history of mankind different races suited to different political functions, of different social destinies, and who, having thus different duties, should therefore have different rights. We don't say positively that these races exist, which would upset the axiom of the *rights of man*, but when the eighteenth century asserted that they did not exist, it manifestly begged the question, that is to say, it answered the question by the question.

Then to make of the working-men and the poor ciphers contained and added up in the grand total *man*, is to launch out upon a series of operations perfectly strict in themselves, but entirely barren of results. In effect, if a working-man is only an abstract citizen, a human unity equal to every other human unity, we make of him a quotient of the sovereignty, which is the grand social dividend. Now this method only ends in giving to the citizen-quotient a share in the ballot. If the citizen has the wherewith to live, he may discharge his arithmetical function as a pastime; but if he is poor, if this abstraction of a citizen covers some reality like the working class, which has neither bread for the table nor clothing for the body, the ballot will certainly not give him either the one or the other, and all imaginable contrivances of abstract citizens, attempted after the manner of the ideologists, only lead to a complete mystification in politics and in industry.

For fifty years this abstract idea of the man and the citizen has been discussed over and over, without arriving at any but a logical though barren solution; and the question remains still and will always remain where Rousseau placed it, and at the point to which he brought it, without being able, whatever one may do, either to advance or recede; which shows that it was inexpediently carried into ideology, which is the domain of pure ideas, instead of being carried into history, which is the place for the positive and complex facts of politics.

Now, then, to be wise, we must profit by the faults of the ideologists, not obstinately to take men for triangles, not imprudently to mix politics and geometry; to distinguish the mathematical from the social question, which for our part we will take care to do. Thus, instead of saying that a working-man is a citizen, a member of the sovereignty, which is obvious and proper, but leads to nothing useful, we will search in history for what the working-man really is, what is his origin, what causes produce him here, exclude him there, and multiply him elsewhere, in order that, his social nature being known, his propensities studied, it may become possible and easy to draw from the knowledge of his past and present the formula of his future.

The working classes, however general and widespread this element of society may be, proceed nevertheless from another social element much more widespread and general still. This great historic fact, simple, primordial, which precedes the working classes, and of which they are a branch, a subdivision, and a fragment, is the proletariat.

The proletariat is thus, according to our ideas, a primitive and general element of society, in which the working classes take their origin.

In a work so difficult and delicate as this, we need, first, that the reader shall accord to us his good-will; second, that he shall have patience with our reasoning, and wait, sometimes for a page, sometimes for two, the slow and tardy proofs, which often perhaps it may be difficult to produce, to test, to classify and put in line; third, that he will permit us to advance certain general assertions, which we will afterward establish, but which it will be more convenient for us first to throw out without demonstration; fourth and lastly, that he will not dispute everything with us step by step, but give us a little free scope and let us tell all, that he may judge of what we have done.

We do not concern ourselves with the meaning, which the word *proletary* derives from its Latin etymology. Proletarius designated a thing peculiar to the constitution of Rome; the word, *proletary*, denotes, according to our ideas, a thing common to all societies.

Thus, for example, there is among the peoples of modern Europe, and there has been among the peoples of ancient Europe, a mass, more or less considerable, of families and individuals, forming the lowest position, the lowest stratum of society. Ordinarily these families and individuals live by the painful and daily labor of their hands; the wages of the day before is all they have for the morrow, and landed property, when they succeed in obtaining it, is for them much less the rule than the exception. These men, who are not landed proprietors, who never have been, and whom one cannot venture to promise that they ever will be; these poor men, obscure, without fortune accumulated and transmitted from father to son, and for whom all the domestic traditions are reduced to the necessity of gaining their daily bread; these men are the PROLETARIES — the condition to which they belong is the PROLETARIAT.

This being established, see what the proletariat embraces: 1st, working-men; 2d, mendicants; 3d, thieves; 4th, women of the town.

A working-man is a proletary who works and gains wages for a living.

A mendicant is a proletary who will not or cannot work, and who begs for a living.

A thief is a proletary who will neither work nor beg, and who steals for a living.

A woman of the town is a proletary, who will neither work, nor beg, nor steal, and who prostitutes herself for a living.

The absence of all acquired property, of all accumulated fortune, is then, as we have said, what constitutes the proletariat; and the necessity, when one has nothing but his or her body, either to work, to beg, to steal, or to prostitute for a living, naturally divides the proletaries into four great categories, which we have mentioned; categories in which they range themselves according to their education, their character, their physical and moral force, the particular condition of the family to which they belong, or the general conditions of the society which surrounds them — sometimes by their own faults, sometimes from the faults of others, often by accident.

---

## CHAPTER II.

### ORIGIN OF THE PROLETARIAT.

WE have already shown that the question of the working classes cannot be logically and effectually treated, without treating at the same time of beggars, of thieves, and of prostitutes; and we have also explained how these four great social facts, which encumber all civilized nations, viz., working-men, the poor, malefactors, and prostitutes, are the four branches of one and the same trunk, which is the proletariat. It is then, necessarily, with the proletariat that we should commence, to arrive afterward at the history of the working classes; and by so doing we have the advantage of explaining the end by the beginning, and effects by their causes.

Nevertheless, many, who will read this, will perhaps ask why we do not come at once to our ideas of the organization of the working classes, and why, being master of our conclusions, as we ought to be, we laboriously search for our premises two or three thousand years back, among the Greeks and Romans, instead of at once laying hold of, classifying, and arranging the facts which we have before our eyes; for after all, it is about her own working-men, mendicants, thieves, and prostitutes, and not those of Rome, of Athens, or of Argos, that France is troubled. The history of the proletariat may therefore appear to some a digression on this occasion, and the appearances will be to some extent with those, who would wish to dispense with the history of the working classes, and to enter at once upon the data, which lead to their organization.

These are the reasons, which decide us. It is not enough to wish to organize the working classes; it is also necessary that the working classes themselves should wish to be organized. Above all, it is necessary that they should recognize that the condition of the working-man is a natural and normal condition, and consequently, one to be maintained, ameliorated, cherished, and not destroyed; that, if there be rich and poor, the rich have not amassed their fortunes at the expense of the poor,(*a*) and that those, who have an in-

(*a*) Our author starts out with the declaration that his book is one of history, and not of politics. Yet it is very evident that he writes with a very strong political bias in favor of the old nobility, to which class the *de* before his patronymic indicates that he claims to belong. The inexorable logic of historical facts, forces him to contradict all that he here says, when he comes to treat, in his fourteenth chapter, of the Ancient Trades' Unions and their Fall. There, after speaking of the prodigalities of Caligula, Claudius, Nero, Heliogabalus, and others, he says: "Alas, it was the labor unions, which had to pay the greatest part for these feasts, this profusion, these follies! It was they (the working classes) who had to support the emperors, their mistresses, their eunuchs, their minions, their lackeys, their lions and their panthers, their paroquets and their monkeys; and if we bear in mind that between Augustus and Constantine there were fifty-two emperors, that is to say, nearly fifty-two prodigals, and that one of them alone, who died at eighteen years of age, spent in a single day more than all the others together, in having the court of his palace paved with all the diamonds, all the emeralds, all the precious stones of Italy, we can, without difficulty, account for the exhaustion of the Empire in the fourth century, and for the tyrannical laws against the labor unions, (and the working classes,) for which the people and the government are both to blame. This explains how these tyrants, these fools, these ambitious men, who passed away so quickly, each took away some part of the wealth of the people; how the most frightful exactions were practised to obtain money, how all the statues of the gods, and even the household gods (penates) of Rome, were melted down by Nero; how the ancient subsidies paid by the state to the priests and the vestals were suppressed; how, in fine, to the great scandal of the idolatrous devotees, the immense revenues of the pagan clergy were confiscated and sold throughout the Empire for the benefit of the public treasury, which was the burden of the lamentable epistles of the Prefect Symmachus to the Emperor Valentinian the Second!"

The facts and philosophy of history were much more truthfully and clearly stated by Calhoun, in 1837, before De Cassagnac's book was ready for the printer. Calhoun was the great tribune of the industrial and productive classes — of labor in all its forms; the inflexible opponent of monopolies and special class legislation — of all taxation by government that tended to reduce the wages of labor, and increase the cost of living. In his speech on Abolition petitions, February, 1837, he said:

"I hold, then, that there never has yet existed a wealthy and civilized society, in which one portion of the community did not, in point of fact, live on the labor

come of a hundred thousand livres, have had nothing to do with the misfortunes of those, who die of hunger; that the *people,* consisting principally of the working classes, have not been reduced to the condition, in which they find themselves, by the cupidity of the *great;* and that the crimes of priests and kings, if priests and kings have committed crimes, have not been to rivet the chains of any one; that there are simple, logical, visible causes for everything — for the evil as for the good — and that the poor have never had any other *tyrants* than the imbeciles, who have filled their hearts with unjust hatred, and have thus led them astray from making the most of the destiny, which God has given them; that, if it is good, moral, and right that working-men, as intelligent men capable of improvement, should have their ambition, they should take care that that ambition should not err in its object, and that it does not seek to *retake* violently or legally, by riot or by universal suffrage, the wealth, consideration, and authority, which no one ever *took from* them; that the welfare of the working classes ought to be sought in the amelioration of the condition, which is proper for them, and not in the barren pursuit of a condition, which is inappropriate to them; in fine, that the object of every apprentice, in commencing his career, should be to become the best workman in the shop, and not the first consul of a republic.

Thus, before addressing ourselves to the good sense of the working classes, it seemed to us logical to address their prejudices and passions. The most formidable evil, in fact, under which working-men have labored for the last forty years, is their repugnance to being only working-men, and the belief, which bad historians, bad publicists, bad revolutionary orators have instilled into them, that the condition of a hireling is a degrading and anomalous one, which the violence and avarice of the great have for a long time imposed

of the other. Broad and general as is this assertion, it is fully borne out by history. This is not the proper occasion, but if it were, it would not be difficult to trace the various devices, by which the wealth of all civilized communities has been so unequally divided, and to show by what means so small a share has been allotted to those, by whose labor it was produced, and so large a share given to the non-producing class. The devices are almost innumerable, from the brute force and gross superstition of ancient times, to the subtle and artful fiscal contrivances of modern."

upon the people, and which, so far from there being any morality in accepting or profit in regulating, they should throw off, cost what it may. The example of the Constituent Assembly in abolishing liveries, that of the Convention in abolishing the domestic relations, and all those souvenirs of popular *fraternity*, which gave for the first time indiscriminately the name of a citizen to the rich and the poor, to the duke and to the lackey, and which, for all that, really only concealed the inequality of the thing under the equality of the name, have left to the working classes this movement of feverish restlessness, which follows hopes deceived and ambition misled, and which is complicated with a desire to be what they are not, and disgust at what they are.

We would wish therefore, if possible, to make the working classes understand that they have no cause for social vengeance; that the question for them is not to break their chains, nor escape from slavery, nor to punish tyrants; that their slavery and oppression have never existed except in melodramas, comic operas, and drinking songs; that history shows that the working classes were formed, like all the others, freely and progressively; that in time they have had, like all other social facts, their bright and dark hours, their good and bad years; but that their condition, as that of all others, has been improving from century to century; that the working classes of the middle ages were incomparably more happy than the working classes of antiquity, and those of to-day are incomparably more happy than those of the middle ages; in fine, that the condition of the working-men, as we have already said, is regular, moral, natural, legitimate; a condition which has arisen of itself, spontaneously, without constraint or violence; a condition, which has been developed in history according to appropriate laws, which had nothing harsh, cruel, or tyrannical in them; a condition, which is shown, by its origin, its duration, by the evidences of its present and the indications of its future state, to be an essential part of the general system of human societies, forming a harmonious note in the general concert of the wants, griefs, pleasures, and destinies of all.

This was our object in wishing to write the history of the working classes. The difficulty of their association is, as we think, less perhaps in the discovery of a logical and apposite mechanism than in

7

the obstacles to every simple, natural, and peaceful solution of the great social difficulties of our times, caused by the false political ideas, the ridiculous learning, and the pseudo-Lacedemonian fraternity, with which the working classes have been infected for the last forty years. One will never answer satisfactorily all the objections of those, who think themselves interested in making them, and whatever he may say, he will with difficulty persuade a working-man, who aspires to be a triumvir, to become some day a boss mechanic. It is not in a few years that the political prejudices of the working classes can be reformed; but history applied to their social condition seemed to us one of the surest and shortest ways to its accomplishment.

The proletariat may, perhaps, be compared to a river, which always has its principal and original source and its tributaries. The difficulty in its history consists in separating its accidental and relative from its general and absolute causes, or, as we may say, its tributaries from its head-springs.

The first general, universal, absolute cause, the original source of pauperism, is the *emancipation of slaves*. Pauperism and its four subdivisions — hirelings, (that is to say, those who work for wages,) mendicants, thieves, and prostitutes — cannot exist in a slave country, unless emancipation has been there already begun. It is not difficult to comprehend how the want of food and clothing — the necessity of living, in a word — being the motive that impels the hireling to work, the mendicant to beg, the thief to steal, and girls of the town to prostitution — all to do what they do with a view to a necessary gain — these four conditions could not exist under the slave system, under which all have naturally the necessaries of life; the master because he is master, and the slave because he is a slave. Thus there are neither hirelings, nor mendicants, nor thieves, nor prostitutes among the Arab tribes who inhabit the desert, because slavery is there almost in its primitive entirety.

We hope hereafter to say with accuracy when that emancipation of slaves, which produced the first proletaries, commenced among the people of the West; but first we must notice two important facts regarding this emancipation.

The first is, that before the Christian era there was no instance of a systematic emancipation, in mass, among the ancients, in the name of any philosophic or philanthropic system, and that all emancipations among them were accidental and individual. We may even say that all the pagan philosophers, without exception, were unanimous in considering slavery as a legitimate and normal condition of society, from Aristotle, who called children "the animated instruments of their parents," to Plato, who cites in his treatise on law two verses of Homer, from the 17th book of the Odyssey, in which it is said that "slaves have only the half of a human soul." There is perhaps only one exception to this unanimity of the ancient philosophers as to the legitimacy of slavery; and even that exception is taken from the history of the Jews, who had in the Law and the Prophets the germ and rudiments of the Gospel. Flavius Josephus relates in the 13th book of his ancient history of the Jews, that there were in his nation three great philosophic sects outside of the precise text of the Law, the Pharisees, the Sadducees, and the Essenians;[1] and he gives many details in regard to this last-mentioned sect in his 18th book, where he says the Essenians recognized a community of goods, that they did their own work, and had no servants, because they considered men as being equal by nature;[2] but the Essenians in antiquity were only a small obscure sect, numbering scarcely four thousand, toward the end of the reign of Augustus, that is to say, in the dawn of Christianity, and the doctrine of equality was mixed up with other dogmas, which injured them greatly in the opinion of the Jews, as, for example, the doctrine of celibacy.

We state rapidly the principal opinions of the ancient philosophers in regard to slavery, (intending to recur to the subject hereafter,) only to explain how, public opinion never having been excited by any precept or doctrine whatever in favor of slaves, there was never in antiquity any systematic emancipations in mass. In fact, we do not wish to give the name of systematic emancipation to the enrolment of slaves in the time of civil troubles.

The second fact, of which we have spoken, and which is a consequence of the first, is that in ancient times there was never any of those trying times among the working classes such as we have

[1] See Flav. Joseph., Antiq. Hæbr., lib. xiii., cap. x.
[2] Ibid., lib. xviii., cap. ii.

in our manufacturing cities, nor any such distress among the poor as now in certain localities in France at the approach of winter, and in Ireland at all seasons. It is easy to conceive how the individual cases of emancipation turning out proletaries only drop by drop, so to speak, the soil of ancient society had time to absorb before being overrun and wasted by them. The free working population before the Christian era was very small, and the thirty-five labor unions enumerated in the law of Constantine of the year 337, contained in the 8th book of the Code of Theodosius, had their work done by slaves.[1]

The number of proletaries was therefore very limited before the Christian era, and even in the three following centuries, because of the small number of freedmen that emancipation had cast upon society.

First, as to the working-men, they were, as we have said, nearly all slaves. The treasury, or, as we would say, the domain, had slaves of all trades, by whom the public works were executed. Contractors even made large fortunes by the daily hire of workmen, and the labor unions themselves turned the privileges they obtained to the profit of a few, and had their shops filled with slave workmen.

As to mendicants, they were very rare; so rare that there is not one example in all antiquity of a city, which founded a hospital to feed the poor or to cure the needy sick. A law of the Emperor Justinian of the year 530, given in the code, is on this point a very valuable document, inasmuch as it enumerates all the public expenditures of the municipalities, and it makes not the slightest mention of a hospital or house of refuge of any kind, either for mendicants, or for the infirm, or for wounded or sick laborers.[2] We must not lose sight of the fact that, in the organization of ancient society, every owner of slaves had in his own house an infirmary for taking care of, and a prison for punishing them. Now, as emancipation did not entirely destroy all ties between the slave and the master, and the latter had still a right to the inheritance of the freedman, so the freedman could on occasion have recourse to the munificence

[1] This appears from many passages relating to the Roman labor unions. See Cod. Theod., lib. xiv., tit. iii., leg. 7.

[2] See Cod. Justin., lib. i., tit. iv., leg. 26.

of his old master, and ask it with confidence, either in case of sickness or of destitution. All mendicants or infirm laborers, proceeding necessarily from the emancipation of slaves, returned to the care of individuals, and did not necessitate the system of public provision of modern societies, of the formation of which we will hereafter give an account. We find that private prisons were abolished in the Empire of the East by a law of Theodosius and Arcadius of the year 388, (Cod. Theod., lib ix., tit. xi., lex unica,) and in the Empire of the West by a law of Justinian of the year 529, (see Cod. Just., lib. i., tit. iv., leg. 26,) which authorizes us to believe that the private infirmaries lasted as long.

Thieves were also very rare in ancient society; but on this point it is necessary to make a distinction. Highway robbers, those who lived in caves, bandits, men commanding troops more or less considerable and taking the field, were very numerous, as were corsairs and sea-rovers; but the profession of a bandit or of a corsair, which requires skill, courage, and some fortune, was never considered infamous by the ancients. Thucydides, lib. i., cap. 5, informs us of the high estimation, in which the profession of corsair was held by the ancient Greeks; and even in his time, Polybius informs us, that Teuta, Queen of Illyria, replied to the Roman ambassadors that the laws made by the kings, her predecessors, never forbade piracy, (Polyb. Hist., lib. ii., cap. 8,) but the contrary, although it was recruited from among the runaway slaves and adventurers of all parts of Europe. The thieves, who were scarce and almost unknown, were those of the cities, pickpockets, sharpers, *la haute et la basse pegre*, to use the low vocabulary of the police; the picklocks, the handkerchief-stealers; in fine, all those mean scamps, who hide in our cities, instead of arming themselves like the brave bandits, who boldly confronted a Roman army commanded by Pompey.

Prostitutes, who are the fourth and lowest degree of the proletariat, had not in ancient society the frightful development they have attained in modern society. That is easily understood, when we bear in mind that every slave woman could be a concubine, and that the passions of the master had with them enough, wherewith to be satisfied. Besides, we see in the comedies of Plautus and Terence that the bad places were kept by slave-merchants, which shows how limited the number of free prostitutes must have been. There were some, however; but these were pretty freedwomen, such as Pompey's Flora, the Lesbia of Catullus, the Delia of Tigranes, the Corinne, Lydia, and Chloe of Horace; the Marion de l'Ormes of their time, at whose houses fashionable young idlers and poets met to make love.

There remains a great question, new and difficult: to ascertain what is the origin of that universal slavery, which is invariably found in the commencement of all nations, and how those primitive slaves, who are the ancestors of the proletaries, found themselves in slavery. On that question depends this other, viz.: Is slavery of violent or peaceful origin, and have the proletaries been unjustly despoiled, in the persons of the primitive slaves, their forefathers, of the social advantages possessed by the rich?

Without wishing to give in this chapter to this question all the importance and all the development, which it would perhaps demand, we can say that proofs abound to solve it negatively. Thus innumerable proofs concur to establish that slavery was not originally *instituted*, *established*, *created*, voluntarily and of set purpose, as, for example, the *communes* of the middle ages were established and instituted. In fine, everything leads in the most positive manner to the belief that slavery had no other commencement than the commencement of the human family, of which it constituted an integrant part; of which it formed a natural, essential, and constitutive law. That being so; that is to say, slavery not having been established all at once, much less did it commence violently, by reducing to slavery men originally free and the equals of other men. We are not ignorant that there is an axiom at the present day generally received among civilized nations, which says that all men are naturally equal. That may be true morally, but it is false historically; and besides, this axiom, which is of Christian origin, proves just the contrary of what is sought to be proved by it. For when St. Paul, in his Epistle to the Galatians, said, (ch. iii., v. 28,) "there is neither Jew nor Greek, there is neither bond nor free, there is neither male nor female, for ye are all one in Christ Jesus," he evidently preached this language of his Divine Master to show how noble, liberal, and civilizing this doctrine was, which called to it all human infirmities, which raised the humble and exalted the low, and before which there was no longer what had up to that time been seen in the world, that is, societies filled with contrasts: the Jews, who had the word of God, the Greeks who had not; slaves, who were sold, and free men, who bought them; men, who had authority in the family, women, who were crowded in harems, repined, obeyed, and were silent.

Christianity has positively no social signification or progressive value, except this, that it brought to society the doctrine of equality, which before had never existed anywhere, neither among the Jews, nor among the Gentiles.

In studying carefully the books and primitive writings in reference to slavery, we very soon find that it arose in the family. In all the books and in all the old manuscripts the fathers of families had an absolute right of life and death over their children. This requires to be explained more at length.

---

## CHAPTER III.

### OF THE ORIGIN OF SLAVERY.

BY a long and laborious route, we have reached a result, which may appear singular, but of which we will submit the proofs to the reader. Taking history at its sources, before they have been stirred and muddled by theories, we have found numerous, deep, conspicuous, and unexceptionable traces of two classes of men, (we do not say of two races,) who have universally in all countries abounded in the commencement of all societies. One of these classes were MASTERS, the other SLAVES. The first own, the second are owned. This fact, we say, is universal. There were masters and slaves among the Hebrews; [1] among the Greeks; [2] among the Romans;[3] among the Germans;[4] among the Gauls;[5] in France in the

[1] See legislation of Moses, concerning slaves, and especially Leviticus, ch. xxv., v. 40, 41, 44, 47, 48.

[2] See numerous passages in the Iliad and Odyssey, especially the Iliad, book xii., where Achilles says to Lycaon, "I have taken and sold many living;" and in the Odyssey, book xxii., where Euriclea, governess of the slaves of Ulysses, says to him, "You have in your house fifty slave women, whom I have taught to work, to spin, and to endure servitude."

[3] See, among a thousand other proofs, tit. v., lib. 1, of the Institutes of Justinian, de *Libertinis*.

[4] Tacitus, de Moribus Germanorum.

[5] See Cæsar's Commentaries.

twelfth century;[1] in Prussia in 1750;[2] they exist still in the United States of America; in all Mohammedan countries, and in all the kingdoms and empires of India.

We will not longer insist on this great historic fact, the proofs of which are everywhere, in all books, in the poets, historians, in the codes, before our eyes. We proceed to the examination of their character.

First, it is clear from all the concurring testimony, that this fact is very ancient; so ancient that we can nowhere find its commencement. When the institutions of all peoples began, slavery was already established. Moses founded the institutions of the Hebrews, and slavery is found in the books of Moses. Homer was many centuries anterior to the historic times of Greece, and slavery is found in the books of Homer. The Twelve Tables were the basis of Roman institutions, and Romulus, long anterior to the Twelve Tables, opened at Rome an asylum for the fugitive slaves at Latium.[3] The Salic law, the law of the Saxons, of the Thuringians, of the Germans, and of the Angles, are the points of departure of the institutions of all modern peoples, and slavery is found in all the codes of the invasion.[4] We add another very important consideration, which is, that in all the legislative, poetic, and historical monuments which we have mentioned, slavery is not instituted for the first time, but is mentioned as a fact, existing, known, accepted, fixed. Neither Moses, nor Homer, nor the Twelve Tables, nor the laws of the invasion founded slavery. They mention and regulate it. It was, before they existed.

Next — and what we are about to say is, as it were, the consequence of what we have said — it nowhere appears by the study of all traditions that slavery was ever instituted, founded, created, or that it was enacted by statute, to use the expression of the jurists. The statute law took hold of the fact of slavery, as it did of all other social facts, when it regulated society; it has taken it, in its turn, under its control; it has shaped and defined it, and so entirely taken it under its power, that when the institutions of nations began,

[1] See the Assises de Jerusalem, Court of Burghers, art. 32, copied from the manuscript of Venise, in the Royal Library.

[2] See General Code of the Prussian States, published in 1794, vol. ii., part 2, tit. v., art. 196–197.

[3] Plutarch, Romulus.

[4] See the salic, riparian, and other laws, *passim*.

slavery had become a part of the statute law; but it had a proper, and, so to speak, personal existence, before falling under the action of the civil and political law; and it is this primitive existence, of which we say that it does not appear to have been the handiwork of man. More than that: Returning hereafter to the Hebrew, Greek, Roman, and barbarian legislation, which mention slavery and evidently do not create it, we believe we can say that we have in reserve irresistible mathematical considerations, which will be produced in their place, and which will establish in a manner that admits of no doubt, not only that slavery, in Leviticus, in the Iliad, in the laws of the Twelve Tables, and in the codes of the invasion, was not a thing actually or even newly created; but that it was an old thing, a decrepit thing, a wornout thing, a decaying thing, already past the half of its time, halfway to a great social metamorphosis and to its own annihilation; so that, far from owing its existence to human institutions, slavery was already greatly shaken, and declining, when the most ancient institutions saw the light.

If the language of the politics of these latter years had not given a reactionary and ridiculous signification to the words *divine right*, we would readily say that slavery is of divine right; but we fear to be misunderstood. We prefer to use other words, and to say that, from all traditional appearances and all historic realities, slavery universally presents itself, in the primitive times of all nations, as a fact, spontaneous, natural, autochthon; a fact which is connate with nations, without their direct assent or deliberate concurrence; a principle mixed by God himself with the thousand principles of human society; a kind of absolute evil, wounding the logic of civilization, destined to be a relative good, and to satisfy the primordial instincts of incipient society; a thing, in fine, which has the appearance of a monstrosity, but which finds its natural explanation and legitimate place in given places and times of history. This is the sense, in which we would have said, that slavery was of divine right; only to make it understood that it was anterior to human institutions — that it came from higher and farther back.

Nevertheless, though the proofs, which we have already deduced, must necessarily have some value in the eyes of every man of intelligence and good faith, it is not our intention to rest only upon them, in what we have said of the spontaneous, and in some sort providential nature of slavery. This opinion, which as yet we have only suggested, will hereafter be justified ; at least, we shall attempt it. Our arguments hitherto offered are of that class called negative in the exact sciences ; that is to say, that we, proposing to establish a certain general conviction, produced in us by a comparison of a great number of facts, viz., that slavery is a spontaneous and primitive element of society, have set ourselves first to show that man did not establish it of deliberate purpose, and that it was not the result of human institutions. It remains for us to give the positive and direct arguments ; that is to say, to show by what natural, simple, logical, successive process, slavery was found already established at the same time that all peoples were formed.

Perhaps it may be thought at first sight that we take hold of our subject very far back. We take it at its root, at its first rudiment, at its embryo, at the mathematical point whence all its lines start. We have already forewarned the reader of the historic novelties, upon which we venture. This is one of them, an important one, which perhaps will furnish a key to many problems hitherto obscure, and which merits at least the good-will, which every just man accords to every earnest man. See then what, as we believe, was the origin of slavery.

We cannot enter directly upon the history of slavery, because slavery is the negation of liberty and of property, and a negation cannot exist of itself. It becomes necessary, then, to turn to liberty and property, the absence of which constitutes slavery, just as the absence of light constitutes darkness ; but the strength of our theory will lose nothing, because we will know certainly the slaves by knowing the masters. Whence, then, came the masters ?

After much thought, and especially much reading, undertaken in view of the problem we attempt to solve, it seems to us that primitively, and going back to the first glimmerings of historic times, the idea of master and the idea of father are entirely confounded. In general, at the commencement of the formation of all peoples, the father is master, absolute master. We should say, what is very important, that it was not sufficient to be father according to the flesh ; certain conditions of tradition, duration, family, and ancestors were also required. In Homer, the fathers, who are masters, are all sons of the gods. They are called *divine*, *sons of the gods*, *nurselings of the gods.*[1] More than that: the great families ranked according to the order of the gods, their ancestors. In the twentieth book of the Iliad, Apollo says to Æneas that he was much above Achilles, because Achilles was born of Thetis, and he was the son of Venus. In the twenty-first, Achilles says to Asteropæus that he was very bold, being only the son of a river, to come and attack him, who descended from Jupiter;[2] and he adds that there was as much distance between them as between their ancestors. The same thing is remarked in the Latin traditions. We know that Romulus was the son of Mars, and Plutarch says that the first master of the house of the Fabii passed for the son of Hercules.[3] In the life of Cæsar, Suetonius relates that Cæsar, pronouncing the funeral eulogy of his aunt Julia, recalls the origin of his family, which descended from Jupiter by Venus, the mother of Æneas.[4] Behold why he was called *divine*, like Achilles, that is to say, *son of Jupiter*, which is the true meaning of *divus* and of *dios*.[5] Before flattery interposed to trouble the hierarchy, only the members of the Julian family at Rome were called *divine*.

There was still another name, by which the ancient Latin families, who were descended from the gods, were designated, that of *pius*, which has been wrongly translated *pious*. Virgil constantly calls Æneas *pius*, that is to say, *son of Jupiter*, a signification, which many successive translators have generally ignored.

The proofs of what we say are easy and conclusive, and we take some pleasure in presenting them, because it is a question of a very curious historical point, and at the same time of a very piquant literary point.

First, Suetonius relates that, after the victories of Tiberius in Illyria, the senate wished to give him immediately the surname of *Pius*,[6] which should have a signification more honorable than that of *Augustus*, which was his signature, and hereditary in the Claudian house.[7]

[1] Iliad, lib. i., v. 7; lib. ii., v. 98; lib. xxii., v. 320; lib. xxiii., v. 293.
[2] Iliad, lib. xxi., v. 186–7.
[3] Plutarch, Fab. Maximus.
[4] Suet. Tranq., Jul. Cæsar, cap. vi.
[5] Cæsar, divi genus. (Æneid, lib. vi., v. 793.)
[6] Suet. Tranq., Tiber. Nero, cap. xx.
[7] Suet. Tranq., Tiber. Nero, cap. xxx.

Next, Virgil habitually alternates the surname of *Pius* with many others, which signify *sons of gods.* In the third and fifth books of the Æneid, he calls Anchises and Æneas sons of a goddess.[1] In the sixth book, Æneas himself tells the sibyl that he is son of Jupiter;[2] in the tenth book he is spoken of as of *race divine.*[3] On the other hand, the word *pius* is found explained in the same book, where Juno, after having said that it would be a grievous necessity, if Turnus must shed his *pious* blood, adds, *he is of our race.*[4] Finally, there are three passages, one in Tertullian, another in Papinianus, and a third in the Pandects, which leave no sort of doubt relative to the signification of *pius.* In these three passages, the question is of a word derived from *pius* — of the word *pietas* — which there serves to designate the parental power, that is to say, the power attached to a descent from ancestors. "Piety," says Tertullian, "is sweeter than paternity."[5] The passage of Papinianus is still more explicit, but the difficulty of translating it exactly in French (or English) words forces us to give it in the original in a note.[6] Finally, see the passage in the Pandects, which removes all doubt: "The parental power consists in PIETY."[7]

Thus it is evident, both from the meaning that the different passages of Virgil give to the word *pius*, and from the strict signification of *pietas*, that *pius* designates the relations of filiation, and in the special case of its application to Æneas it means *son of Jupiter*, as does DIVUS, of which we have shown that DIVI GENUS was the paraphrase.

[1] Æneid, lib. iii., v. 374. Ibid., lib. v., v. 383.

[2] Ibid., lib. vi., v. 123.

[3] Ibid., lib. x., v. 228.

[4] Ibid., lib. x., v. 618.

[5] *Gratius nomen est pietatis quam potestatis.* We have translated *potestatis* by *paternity*, because that is the sense indicated, first, by the very phrase of Tertullian, and, next, by the passage which follows *potestatis*, and which is, *etiam familia magis patresquam domini vocantur.* (Tertull., Apologet., cap. xxxiv.)

[6] Divus Trajanus filium, quem pater male contra *pietatem* afficiebat, coegit emancipare; quo postea defuncto, pater ut manumisso bonorum possessionem sibi competere dicebat. Sed concilio Neratii Prisci et Aristonis ei propter necessitatem *solvendæ pietatis* denegata est. (Papinian. Quæstion., lib. xi., lex ult.)

And that nothing may be wanting as to the meaning of "solvendæ pietatis," we note that Cujas comments on these words as follows: *Quia dissoluerat patriam potestatem: because* it *would abolish the parental power.* (Cujas in lib. xi., quæst., Papinian. Commentar.)

[7] Patria potestas in pietate consistit. (Digest., lib. xlviii., lib. ix., leg. v.)

We have said that the comparison of a great amount of testimony leads us to think that, in the primitive times of all people, the idea of authority is intimately connected with the idea of paternity, and we have added that this did not apply to every paternity, but only to that connected with a certain series of *divine* ancestors. What is the meaning of this word *divine?* We know not. Perhaps it signifies *master*, and was given to the primitive chiefs of families, precisely because they were powerful. In the present state of historical studies, there is something mysterious in this; but what great question has not its mysteries? It appears certain, moreover, that the greater part of the facts relative to the ancient family were regulated by religious dogmas. There is an example of this in the right of primogeniture, which already existed among the great families of Greece from the time of Homer. Thus, in the fifteenth book of the Iliad, Iris says to Neptune, "You know that the Furies are favorable to the first-born."[1] So, also, in the sixth book of the Odyssey, Nausicaa says to Ulysses that "guests and the poor are under the protection of Jupiter."[2] When we come to treat of the poor, perhaps we will show that Jupiter was favorable to them, precisely for the reason that he was the distant ancestor of the great families, with whom travelling guests and the poor found refuge.

Moreover, there is nothing strange in that the ancient family should lean upon mystic traditions and religious dogmas. The modern, that is to say, the Christian family has analogous bases in another order of ideas. When Jesus Christ said to the multitude which followed Him beyond the Jordan, that He had abolished divorces, He gave no other reason except that God so willed it;[3] and when St. Paul wrote to the churches of Asia Minor that the domestic relations were thereafter modified, that the wife and the son were no longer subject to the father of the family, he gave no other authority for this doctrine — then so strange — but that of his Divine Master: "You are all equal before God."[4]

Whatever may have been the cause — hitherto unknown, and

[1] Iliad, lib. xv., v. 204.
[2] Odyss., lib. vi., v. 207, 208.
[3] What therefore God hath joined together, let not man put asunder. (Matt. xix. 6.)
[4] Omnes enim vos unum estis in Christo Jesu: for ye are all one in Christ Jesus. (Galatians iii. 28.)

which history will perhaps some day discover — why certain ancient great families were called *divine*, it is certain that the chiefs — the fathers — in those families had absolute power, and that they possessed that power, by virtue of their character, as fathers.

The grave question, which occupies us, now enters upon historic times, and we proceed, surrounded by the most precise and clear proofs.

The absolute powers of fathers of families is a universal fact of primitive history, which has left its traces everywhere. The evidences are at hand, in the Bible, in the Greek tragedies, in the Roman legislation, in Asiatic traditions. We cannot doubt that in ancient times this power was unlimited. The pagans, to give the highest idea of the power of Jupiter, called him the Father of the Gods.[1] It is because the parental power is a universal and human fact that the Jews and Greeks have both named God the Omnipotent Father. The parental power was primitively so extended that it admitted of no other, and completely absorbed the existence of wife and children. The effect of civilization has been to diminish it, and almost to equalize the father with the other members of the family. This is what all legislation shows, when studied in this point of view.

In the time of the Patriarchs, the parental power over children was still absolute. The sacrifice of Abraham is a proof. It is clear the God would not have commanded what was against the positive law.

Moreover, different passages of Flavius Josephus establish, in the most clear and positive manner, that the absolute power of fathers in their families was maintained among the Jews, at least up to the time of Herod the Great, which corresponds to the reign of Augustus in the Roman Empire. We cite for example the trial, by Herod, of his two sons, Alexander and Aristobulus. In the accusation, which Herod brought against them before Augustus, he says that in this he had used excessive moderation, since, having the power, as a father, to kill them, he had brought them before the emperor.[2] In the reply of Alexander, the first-born, to the accusation of Herod, he formally recognized the right which the character of father gave to take his life and that of his brother.[3] But what is more clear and

[1] Virgil, Æneid, lib. v., v. 358.
[2] Flav. Joseph., Antiquit. Hæbreor., lib. xvi., cap. vii.
[3] Ibid., lib. xvi., cap. viii.

formal is another speech, made by Herod five years afterward, at Beryta, before a great assembly of illustrious persons, against these same children, whom he had already pardoned. This is one passage of that speech: Herod said that "nature gave him full power over his children; that a law of his nation was express upon the subject, which commanded that when the father and mother brought an accusation against their children and placed their hands upon their heads, all present were obliged to stone them; that thus he might, without any other form of process, have taken the lives of his children in his own country and kingdom; but that he desired to have the advice of that great assembly; that nevertheless he had not brought his sons to them because they were the judges of the case, since their crime was manifest; but only that they might enter into his just resentments."[1] Thus we have what formally establishes, first, that among the Jews the authority of fathers over their children was absolute; next, that that authority was maintained intact, at least up to the first century of the Christian era; finally, that there was a law which sanctioned it and regulated its exercise. Besides, we will find this jurisdiction among the Romans at a period still more recent.

It is not more difficult to establish that the absolute right of fathers over their children likewise existed among the Greeks, although at a more remote period, because Greece was one of the countries of the West, which sooner passed from the aristocratic to the popular form of government. Now, we have already said that it was only the aristocratic fathers, noble fathers, fathers who were *sons of the gods*, who enjoyed this absolute authority over their children. It existed fully in the time of the Trojan war, as is clearly proved by the sacrifice of Iphigenia, which is a fact completely identical with the sacrifice of Abraham. Nevertheless, at Sparta, a city of nobles, a city of gentlemen, a city where there was no burgher class, as we will show hereafter, the power of life and death over children seems to have been maintained up to a late period. It was in full force at the time of Lycurgus. Plutarch relates that at that time, at the birth of a child, a kind of family council was held, in which it was decided whether the newly born should be saved or killed.[2] Even at Athens,

[1] Flav. Joseph., Antiquit. Hæbr., lib. xvi., cap. xvii.
[2] Plutarch, Lycurgus, cap. xvi.

a democratic city, where the civil law early replaced the seignorial and domestic law, the absolute authority of fathers ended so recently that in the time of Solon, many Athenians sold their children, which, Plutarch says, no law forbade.[1] It was during the Homeric period that the absolute authority of fathers of families was in full vigor among the people of Greece. This period corresponds exactly, in the comparative history of legislation, to the epoch of the Patriarchs among the Jews.

For example, at each of these two epochs, daughters were still the property of their fathers, and it was necessary to pay a certain price to marry and take them away. Thus Jacob served Laban seven years to obtain his daughter Rachel;[2] and Othryon engaged to serve Priam during the siege of Troy to obtain his daughter Cassandra, *without dowry*, that is to say, without other consideration than his services. After using the expression, "*without dowry*," Homer immediately adds that her lover promised to buy her by the expulsion of the Greeks.[3] This will be further established below. *Dowry*, as we understand it, belongs to a much later epoch, when the existence of children in the family was established, and when they not only no longer depended absolutely upon the father, but even had a fixed part, a right, in his inheritance. It is because of their not having clear ideas of the family relations that all the translators of the primitive poets committed monstrous errors, and disfigure their models. We stop midway in our proofs relative to the analogy of the Greek and Hebrew legislation, at two epochs, of which we are about to speak. We say here only what is indispensable; the rest will come in its place.

The Roman legislation is very rich in souvenirs of the ancient parental authority, and their chronicles amply confirm what their legislation says. In his history of Roman antiquities, Dionysius of Halicarnassus recites the old law of the Papirian Code, which authorized fathers to kill and sell their children;[4] the Code of Justinian likewise mentions it,[5] as does also the Digest.[6] Dionysius of

[1] Plutarch, Solon, cap. xiii. [2] Genesis xxix. 18.
[3] Iliad, lib. xiii, v. 367.
[4] Dion. Halicar. Antiq., lib. ii., cap. xxvi.
[5] Cod., lib. viii., tit. xlvii., leg. x.
[6] Digest, lib. xxviii., tit. ii., leg. xi.

Halicarnassus, who had no critical understanding of the fact, which he relates, says that this law was made by Romulus, and that the decemvirs transferred it to the Twelve Tables.[1] This fact of the absolute power of fathers among the Romans is surrounded by so many proofs, that we give a few of the most curious. Plutarch relates that, Rhea being delivered of Romulus and Remus, Amulius, her uncle, ordered them to be cast away.[2] This recalls to mind that Moses was similarly exposed, and that Œdipus was suspended by the feet from a tree. Dionysius of Halicarnassus, in relating the well-known history of the Horatii, says that the old Horatius, defending his son, the murderer of his sister, claimed jurisdiction of the case; because *in his character of father he was the natural judge of his own children.*[3] Plutarch, in his life of Publicola, relates that in the conspiracy of the Aquilians in favor of the Tarquins, Junius Brutus likewise claimed jurisdiction of the case of his son; and that he tried, condemned, and had him executed, by virtue of his parental authority, without observing the judicial formalities followed in the cases of the other conspirators.[4]

This absolute parental power was slightly limited by the law of Sylla, known to jurisconsults by the name of *Cornelia de Sicariis;* but we find, even under the emperors, examples of domestic jurisdiction, which prove that the sovereign parental authority extended over the whole duration of the civil law. Seneca relates the trial, by a great personage named Titus Arrius of his son, of his own authority in his domestic tribunal, at which Augustus assisted, simply as a spectator. The statement of Seneca is very precise and clear. He says:

"Titus Arrius, wishing to try his son, invited Augustus to his domestic court. The emperor came to the home of the citizen; he sat down as a simple spectator of an affair, with which he had no concern. He did not say, Let the accused come to my palace! which would have been to assume to himself the cognizance of the trial and to take it away from the father. The cause having been heard, for the prosecution and for the defence, Titus Arrius asked that each one should write out his judgment."[5] Tacitus also relates

[1] Dion. Halicar. Antiq., lib. ii., cap. xxvii.
[2] Plutarch, Romulus, cap. iii.
[3] Dion. Halicar. Antiq., lib. iii., cap. xiii.
[4] Plutarch, Publicola, cap. vii.
[5] Seneca de Clement., lib. i., cap. xv.

that a senator named Plautius, under the reign of Nero, himself before his whole assembled family and according to ancient usage, passed judgment on Pomponia Græcina, his wife, accused of being given over to superstitions;[1] and Tertullian mentions, in the introduction to his Apology, domestic trials, which had recently taken place at Rome, and which, like that of Plautius, appear to have been directed against the Christians.[2] Many documents authorize the belief that this absolute parental authority did not disappear before the end of the third century; and the first law, which positively forbade fathers to give, sell, or pawn their children, was that of Diocletian and Maximian.[3] Nevertheless a law of Constantine permits the sale of children in case of great poverty, and their abandonment was legally permitted under Diocletian and under Constantine.[4]

Now it would be very easy to collect analogous facts in the history of other ancient peoples, besides the Jews, Greeks, and Romans. The history of the different nations, that inhabited Asia Minor, is full of testimony, which proves that the authority of fathers over their children was absolute among them down to a period nearly approaching the Christian era. Xenophon relates, in his Anabasis, that a Thracian king, named Teutes, offered to give him his daughter and to buy his, if he had one. The barbarian added, This is the law of the Thracians.[5] There is in Plutarch still another fact of the same kind. This chronicler relates that in the distress of the proprietors of Asia Minor, after the defeat of Tygranes and the arrival of Lucullus, the fathers of families, who could not pay the tax to the Roman collectors, sold their young children and their daughters in marriage.[6] We will recur to other analogous and conclusive examples in the chapter, in which we treat of the origin of pauperism.

We have dwelt upon the history of fathers of families and of the ancient parental authority, because fathers were the first masters, and the well-established history of the first masters naturally gives the history of the first slaves.

[1] Tacit. Annal., lib. xiii., cap. xxxii.
[2] Tertull. Apologet., cap. i.
[3] Cod. Justin., lib. iv.; tit. xliii.; leg. 1.
[4] Ibid., lib. iv.; tit. xliii.; leg. 2.
[5] Xenophon, Anab., lib. vii., cap. ii.
[6] Plutarch, Lucullus, cap. xx.

Thus, according to our ideas — ideas which are our own, which some may perhaps think bold and very strange, for which we ask indulgence, and which we present in all humility, but in all sincerity — the first slavery, which was seen on this earth, was nothing but a subjection to the ancient and primitive paternity.

In admitting this idea, which we have supported by some proofs, which has been strengthened in our mind as we have pursued our studies, to which we do not know of one important fact to the contrary, and which we are convinced cannot fail to be established immovably by greater and more unremitting study and labor than our own; with this idea, we say, we can solve, with wonderful exactness and ease, a great number of questions hitherto unanswerable, relative to slavery. We explain how it was anterior to all written constitutions; how it was mentioned, not instituted, in Genesis, in the Iliad, in the Papyrian law, and in the Twelve Tables; how it was, as we have said above, a natural, primordial, simple, logical fact; how it did not make masters proud; how it did not lower the slaves; how it was not established of deliberate purpose; how there remains no souvenir in the tradition of any people of any violence, which it has done suddenly to any part of the human race; how, finally, being one of the conditions of the family, it did not wound the moral ideas of the ancients, which were derived from the actual condition of the ancient family.

Thus we can now say that we have found out who were the first slaves. They were the children.

By a singular coincidence, which shows that, when a social fact is realized, it is surrounded by Providence with all the circumstances necessary to its development, the epoch of history, in which the parental authority was absolute, was that, in which polygamy prevailed. In reflecting a little on this point we realize that the one is the consequence of the other. The ancient fathers of families had a great number of children. The Greek traditions have preserved the memory of the fifty daughters of Danaus. In Homer, Priam says to Achilles that he had fifty children, nineteen by the same mother, Hecuba, and the rest by different concubines.[1] Plutarch relates that in the early wars of the republic, in a battle

[1] Iliad, lib. xxiv., v. 495-7.

with the Tuscans, three hundred Fabii were killed;[1] and he mentions, in the Life of Theseus, a personage named Pallas, who had fifty children.[2] In the history of the Jews, families of fifty children were very common. Flavius Josephus relates that Gideon had seventy sons,[3] Jair thirty,[4] Apson thirty sons and thirty daughters,[5] Abdon forty sons, who were all living at his death, and also thirty grandsons.[6] On the other hand, the Bible is full of proofs of the multitude of children born to the ancient patriarchs, even at so recent a period as theirs, when concubinage, if not precisely prohibited, was already notably weakened. We thence conceive that the great number of women possessed by the first fathers gave rise to families much more numerous than ours; small tribes or clans, in which the children and grandchildren were servants, and the father was master.

---

## CHAPTER IV.

### OF THE ORGANIZATION OF SLAVERY BY POSITIVE LAW.

AS we have said, by all sorts of testimony, which we have abridged, by all sorts of proofs, which we have collected, slavery appears to have been born in the family. It originated there, spontaneously, without reflection, without law, without written decree, accepted or imposed. But it came; and facts attest that, when families began to have relations with each other, when they met and mingled, that is to say, when that generalization of individuals in one body, which we call society, took place, this primitive fact of slavery, growing out of the absolute power of the father in, and till then confined exclusively to, the family, extended beyond it; was regulated and generalized by the first intervening law; and new sources of slavery arose. For example, it was an occasion of slavery to be captured in war, to take refuge in the house of another,

[1] Plutarch, Fur. Camillus, cap. xix. [2] Ibid., Theseus, cap. iii.
[3] Flav. Joseph. Antiq. Hæbreor., lib. v., cap. ix.
[4] Ibid. [5] Ibid. [6] Ibid.

to fail to pay one's debts, and for daughters to be married out of their families or tribes.

The right of war over men, in primitive times, came from this, that, by *mancipation*, as the Roman jurisconsults say — by *seisin*, as ours express it — the conqueror was substituted to the rights of the father of the vanquished. What appears to prove this clearly is that, according to the remark of Vico, among the ancients the vanquished were considered as men without gods;[1] and that, as we have shown, in the language of the primitive poets, the gods and the ancestors of great families were absolutely the same thing. This explains why the ancients so carefully hid their gods in their citadels, and why enemies besieging a city sought above all things to seize these gods. The Trojan Pallas, the Juno of Argos, and the Sacred Shield of Rome are monuments of these primitive notions; and the grammarian Macrobius has preserved the very curious formula, with which the ancient Romans besought the gods to leave the cities, which they were about to assault.[2] The vanquished without gods were what the jurisconsults express by *ex lex*, out of the pale of the law.

Places of refuge, or asylum, were still another source of slavery;[3] the man who had recourse to them became the *thing* of his protector. These asylums, which are found in all the early epochs, in all those moments of confusion, when there were no social guarantees, drew to them the maltreated slaves, malefactors, and that always notable mass of inquiet and turbulent men, who had occasion to fly and take the chances. History bears witness that all founders of cities thus opened asylums. Moses determined the cities, in which murderers could take refuge.[4] Theseus opened a refuge at

[1] The conquered were considered as *men without a god;* slaves were called in Latin *mancipia*, as if they were inanimate things, and they were placed *loco rerum* in jurisprudence. (Vico, Science Nouvelle, translated by Michelet, lib. iv., ch. iv.) (*a*)

(*a*) Notwithstanding all we have suffered in the South from military governors, carpet-baggers, and scalawags, our conquerors have treated us magnanimously; for, according to ancient law and usage, they might have treated us as *men without a God* — as inanimate things — and sold us into slavery, by right of conquest. Perhaps, then, it is, after all, fortunate for us that they had accepted the doctrine that "*free labor is cheaper than slave labor*," because it does not carry with it the corresponding obligation of taking care of infancy, sickness, and old age.

[2] Macrob. Saturnal., lib. iii., cap. ix.

[3] Leviticus xxv. 45, 46.

[4] Numbers xxxv. 11, 14, 15.

Athens, and the recollection of it was preserved so faithfully that Plutarch thinks that the language of the public criers of his time, "All people, come here," were the exact words of Theseus.[1] Finally, Romulus opened another at Rome, to which all the serfs of Latium withdrew.[2] The asylum of Romulus even remained open during the whole time of the republic, for we read in Suetonius that Tiberius closed it.[3]

There is this general remark to be made on asylums: that, primitively — (and the proofs of this would not be difficult) — the men, who repaired to them, became the clients, the subjects of their protector, and that, consequently, these places of refuge became the opposite of places of social safeguard and franchise. This radical difference is explained in a word: Asylums were the occasions of slavery, when they were opened by the fathers, the masters; and that was the case of the more ancient; they were the occasions of enfranchisement, when they were opened by cities within their walls, or by the priests in their temples, and this was the case of the more recent.

It was in the middle ages, that is to say, at a time when the general guarantees had ceased, that asylums reappeared. There were certain territories, where a sojourn imposed slavery, and the jurisconsults called "the advowry of free persons not noble" the declaration of freedom, which every free person, entering those territories, prudently was required to make.[4]

The common law, or rather the generality of the local laws — for there was no common law in France in the middle ages — was then that masters or lords had the right to pursue their slaves or serfs, as we read in many customs.[5]

[1] Plutarch, Theseus, ch. xxv.

[2] Æneid, lib. viii., v. 342.

[3] Sueton. Tranquil., T. Nero Cæsar, cap. xxxix.

[4] This declaration is still called *adveu de bourgeois*. It should be made within a year and a day from the settlement. (La Thomassiere, Local Customs of Berry, etc., chap. xiii.)

[5] See in the Coutumier General the customs of Vitry, article 145; the customs of Chatelet, article 10; the customs of Chateauneuf, article 14; the customs of Chateau-Meillan, article 29.

"What we have said," adds La Thomassiere, "that the lord has a right to follow his serfs, wherever they may flee, ceases when the serfs take refuge in the places of asylum and cities, in which, by privilege, there is no right of pursuit." (La Thomassiere, Local Customs of Berry, chap. 5.)

Moreover, this right of pursuit over slaves and serfs is found naturally established among all peoples during the period of slavery. It was established

Nevertheless, there were many cities in France, which had the right of asylum, and in which masters and lords lost all their rights over slaves and serfs, who took refuge in them. Of this number was, first, Toulouse, on which Chopin recalls that many Moorish slaves of Spain, having taken refuge there and invoked the liberty of the Christians, were admitted to the enjoyment of municipal rights.[1] To Toulouse, we must add, according to Chopin and La Thomassiere, Bourges, Issoudun, Duns-le-Roi, Meun, Vierzon, Concorsault in Berry, St. Malo in Bretagne, and Valenciennes, in Hainault. Paris was not a city of refuge, as Dumoulin observes in his remarks on the first article of the customs of Berry. Also, the lord of Chateau-Roux, in Berry, was permitted (Chopin does not say at what epoch) to follow his fugitive slave at Paris, in spite of the Abbé of St. Genevieve, in whose court he had taken refuge.[2] Neither had Lyons the right of asylum; and La Thomassiere cites a decree of the year 1559, in favor of Hugues de Nagu, commander of Echelles, in Savoy, for the body of his fugitive slave at Lyons.[3] Nevertheless things changed, as to Paris at least, toward the middle of the eighteenth century; for, by the intervention of the city in the trial, the Marquis de la Tournelle was denied a right to take his fugitive slave at Paris, by a decree of 17th June, 1760, and the city of Paris thus obtained the right of asylum, twenty-nine years before the time, when the whole of France became an asylum for all the serfs and slaves of the universe.[4]

Debt also was another source of slavery. This is not doubtful,

throughout the whole Roman Empire since the third century, as is proved by the following law of Gratian:

"Omnes omnino fugitivos adscriptitios, colonos vel inquilinos, sine ullo sexus, muneris, conditionisque discrimine, ad antiquos penates, ubi censiti atque educati, natique sunt, provinciis præsidentes redire compellant."

All rulers of provinces everywhere shall compel the return of fugitive slaves, whether agricultural or domestic, to their old homes, where they were enrolled and educated and born, without regard to sex, reward, or condition. (Code of Justinian, lib. xi., tit. xlvii., leg. vi.) (*a*)

(*a*) This is curiously interesting to the historian as precedents for the contract between the States, contained in second and third paragraphs, sec. 2, art. iv., of the Constitution of the United States.

[1] Renat. Chopin, de Doman. Gallic., lib. i., cap. xiii., No. xxiii. See, also, as to other cities we have named, La Thomassiere, Local Customs, cap. xiii.

[2] Renat. Chopin, quoted above. [3] La Thomassiere, Local Customs, cap. xiii.

[4] Renauldon, Dict. des Fiefs, word *serfs*.

so far as relates to Roman and Greek history. We even read in Tacitus that the Germans sometimes lost at play even the liberties of their persons, and in that case resigned themselves very quietly to slavery.[1] Among the Jews, the legislation of Moses, which, it is true, is comparatively recent, speaks only of the case where a Jew is forced by poverty to sell himself to another;[2] but Flavius Josephus relates that at a much later period, under King Joram, the son of Josaphat, the widow of Obdias, steward of King Achad, went to find the prophet Elias, and told him that, not having wherewith to pay the money, which her husband had borrowed to feed the hundred prophets, whom he had saved from the persecutions of Jezebel, *his creditors claimed to have her and her children for slaves.*[3] Plutarch relates that Solon, on his accession to the government, found a great number of citizens, who were slaves of their creditors.[4] Samuel Petit also mentions the ancient Athenian law, which gave to lenders the liberty of the borrowers in pledge;[5] and Aulus Gellius cites the terms of the law of the third table, which established an analogous legislation among the Romans. The severity of the law was even such that, if there were many creditors, they could, at their choice, sell the debtor to strangers, or they could cut his body in pieces and divide it among them.[6] We add that for such facts we need authorities, such as Aulus Gellius, Tertullian,[7] and Quintilian.[8]

As to the marriage of daughters, we have few documents, except for the epoch when the fusion of the primitive families in the common or civil life commenced to operate, and the authority of the fathers began to be limited. We have, therefore, souvenirs rather than proofs of the enslavement of girls by marriage. The legislation of Moses as to daughters is much advanced, and furnishes us almost nothing for our subject. All that we see in Numbers, on the occasion of the immense step made in the law by the demand

[1] C. Tacit. de Germania, cap. xxiv.
[2] Leviticus xxv. 39, 40.
[3] Flav. Joseph., lib. ix., cap. ii.
[4] Plutarch, Solon, cap. xv.
[5] Samuel Petit, in *Leges Atticas Commentar.*, tit. iv. It should be remarked that the right of exposing infants was considered by the jurisconsults as equivalent to the right of killing them. See Digest., lib. xxv., tit. iii., leg. iv.
[6] Aulus Gellius, *Noct. Attic.*, lib. xx., cap. i.
[7] Tertullian, Apologet., cap. iv.
[8] Quintilian, *Institut.*, lib. iii., cap. vi.

of the daughters of Zelophehad, is that a daughter, who marries out of her tribe, breaks all the bonds of parentage.[1]

This is certainly a trace of the much more complete solution of continuity, which marriage worked in more ancient epochs. For example, in the Iliad, which is, relative to the developments of the family, much more ancient and primordial than the Bible, the evidences abound as to the slavery, to which marriage reduced daughters and wives. We have already cited the example of Cassandra, whom Othryon bought of Priam, as Jacob bought Leah and Rachel of Laban, their father; but there are many others that are neither less clear nor less conclusive. In the ninth book, Agamemnon, regretting having occasioned the wrath of Achilles, to appease him, offers to give him magnificent presents; first, seven Lesbian slaves, with Briseis; then, when Troy shall be taken, twenty captives, the most beautiful after Helen; then finally, as the capstone of his generosity, one of his own three daughters, at his choice and *without dowry*, as the translators have it, or rather *without his paying any price for her*,[2] as it ought to be translated. It is evident that if the rule had been to give a *dowry* to daughters, Agamemnon would not have boasted of offering his for nothing, as of a very magnificent proceeding. Besides, it is so certain that in the mouth of Agamemnon, the word ANAEDNON means "*without his having to purchase her*," and not "*without my giving her a dowry*," that he immediately adds: "for my part, on the contrary, I will give him gifts, such as fathers do not give with their daughters; I will give him seven superb cities."[3] Besides, there is in the 16th book an example, which leaves no reply. Homer says of Polydora, mother of Menestheus, that her husband espoused her, *buying* her with many riches.[4]

The evidences are not more rare in Roman history as to the slavery, to which marriage reduced women. Virgil, who was a man of profound knowledge of ancient Italian usages, has touched

[1] And if they be married to any of the sons of the other tribes of the children of Israel, then shall their inheritance be taken from the inheritance of our fathers, and shall be put to the inheritance of the tribe whereunto they are received; so shall it be taken from the lot of our inheritance. Num., chap. xxxvi. (*a*)

(*a*) See also the reply of Moses in the verses which follow.

[2] Iliad, lib. ix., v. 144–146.

[3] Ibid. ix., v. 147–149.

[4] Ibid., lib. xvi., v. 178.

this matter two or three times in his poems. In the Æneid, Juno proposes to Venus to be reconciled to, and accept, Dido as the spouse and *slave* of her son Æneas.[1] Servius, in his commentary on Virgil, adds on this passage, "the author here refers to marriage *by purchase*."[2] The Georgics contain another analogous fact, not less curious. Virgil wishes for Cæsar that Thetis should *buy* him for a son-in-law.[3] Only, there is this peculiarity that Thetis is considered as the father of a family marrying his children. We know, moreover, to finish this subject, that there were in the ancient Roman jurisprudence three kinds of marriages, one of which had the name of *purchase, coemptio.* In the ceremony, the man gave a piece of money, which was the symbol that he had succeeded to a real purchase. Pierre Pithou calls to mind that by the marriage *coemptio,* as well as by another, which was called *confarreatio,* the woman fell under the power of the husband, or of him, to whom the husband belonged.

We have, then, independently of the paternal power, four great sources of slavery among the ancients. The slaves, who successively sprang from them, had this special feature: that they were not slaves of their fathers; and began the long chain of stranger slaves. At first no one was master without being the father, nor did the master own any but his own children. As soon as these four sources were opened, one could be master without being father, and own the children of another. The absolute power thus extended beyond the circle of the family, to which it was primitively confined, and acquired from without subjects, which blood had not given.

It is evident that, although there were many differences between slavery applied to children, and slavery applied to strangers, the one naturally proceeded from the other. The authority of the master proceeded from the authority of the father. Long time after slavery in the family had existed as a fact, laws and institutions came, which fixed its theory and erected it into a right. In this state we find it established in history, and it is only by the souvenirs, scattered through the primitive traditions and collected by the heroic poets, that we go back by induction to its original situation and its nature. It was necessary that slavery should have become

[1] Æneid, lib. iv., v. 103. [2] Servius, in Æneid. [3] Georg., lib. i., v. 3.

a fact before becoming a right, without which the past of nations would be an absurd enigma; without which we cannot explain what is observed in all legislation relative to the family, namely, that the farther we go back, the more the authority of the father absorbs and swallows up the personality of mother and children; without which it will be impossible to account for the moral conviction, which makes slaves, who are twenty times more numerous than their masters, consent to remain slaves; without which we can not comprehend how, among the hundreds of millions of men sold in the Jewish, Greek, Roman, and Gallic markets, none were found, who rose in their dignity and strength to buy their buyers; without which it would be monstrous, incredible, unheard of, that so many great geniuses of antiquity, who were slaves, or sons of slaves — that Æsop, who was the preceptor of Greece; Phædon, the disciple of Socrates; Terence, the most elegant writer of Italy — that Plautus, Phædrus, Horace, the poets, the immortal poets, who had reason and poesy, the ideas and the form, who comprehended and could speak — never cried out once, not once, in favor of the slaves, their brothers; without which, finally, there would have remained in the memory of the peoples, in legends, in songs, in poems, something of that terrible, sacrilegious, and abominable time, when men had, of deliberate purpose, enslaved other men, had taken from them not only their liberty, but, much more than that, their families, their rights, their personality, their name; more than that still, their faith in themselves, their consciousness of the nobility and sanctity of their nature.

Now, admitting the theory, which we have deduced and facts justify; all is explained, all becomes simple, easy, and natural. The different legislations and the passages of the poets, which unite to bear witness to the primitive absolute authority of the fathers of families, give us a knowledge of the spontaneous formation of slavery, which is thus found to have been contemporary with liberty; that is, it had no beginning, and dates from the very birth of men. Once accepted without hesitation in the family, we comprehend easily how slavery passed beyond the family, and how a son, sold, given, contracted for or lost by his father, became the servant of a stranger, without any change in his condition, and without his having anything to regret or to fear; he continued a slave, which he was before. Things being at this point, then came the generalization of families, their reunion in the city or the state, and then the facts already existing were fixed, regulated, and sanctioned; manners became laws, customs were written, the slave remained still a slave. There was nothing in all these changes to wound him, or to revolt at. Society was for him only the continuation of the family; he is what he was, and the laws do not add a single strand to the lash of the father.

Behold an explanation, which we are the first to propose, and of which we are forced to restrict the proofs. We are convinced that there is no grave objection to be made to it, and we will certainly find insuperable difficulties to every theory, which is not in the sense of this.

In following the thread of our ideas, we explain how, in the history of all peoples, there are always two inimical races in presence of each other;[1] the patricians and the plebeians, as they said at Rome; the nobles and the roturiers, (common people,) as we say. The nobles are the historic prolongation of the ancient fathers of families; the roturiers, or burghers, are the prolongation of slaves. We give our thoughts in bulk; we will give them soon in detail; the affirmation first, the proofs afterward.

The history of the nobles and that of the slaves or burghers contain the history of humanity itself. All comes from that; all is explained by it. The nobles are a magnificent subject for study, full of things fruitful, new, curious in the highest degree. We will treat of them in another volume, because the ideas which we present as to slaves will be conclusive evidence, when completed by the ideas we will present as to the masters. Now we must pass on. We cut one of the branches of our historic theory, to take it up again, to readjust it, to graft it again in its place. We will now follow the slaves in all the accidents of their fortune and social changes, and show by what road the sons and slaves of the heroes of primitive times have become the sovereign people of the present.

[1] Plato de Legibus, lib. vi.

# CHAPTER V.

## OF THE EMANCIPATION OF SLAVES AND FORMATION OF THE BURGHER CLASSES.

IT is easy to conceive how slaves multiplied from the first ages of history, until they became much more than three-fourths of all populations. Taking slavery in the family, we find that there was but one master, the father, while he might have in his children fifty slaves. Hence the limited number of men of the noble race, and the infinite number of the slave race. We make use of these words, free race and slave race, although the human species evidently sprang from the same bed; because once seized upon by slavery, the slaves have really lived and multiplied apart, marked among every nation with an indelible seal, which has resisted every habilitation. Always, everywhere, not only the freedmen, but those, who have been ennobled, have been pointed out and mocked. The language of Horace to Menas, the opulent freedman of Pompey, is a profound historic truth: "Fortune does not change the race."[1] This is not, however, the moment to dwell upon this.

From the earliest times, as we have said, the slaves found themselves separated from the free men, and constituted a race apart. They were fed and clothed in a special manner proper to them. The Jews pierced their ears,[2] the Greeks and Romans marked them on their faces,[3] whence the name *stichus* has remained a common and general name for slaves. From the time of Homer their food was regulated, and they did not eat wheat bread. In the Odyssey, wheat bread is mentioned as the food of the sons of Jupiter, that is to say, of the nobles;[4] and there is a passage where Ulysses boasts of being, after Ajax, the most remarkable of

[1] Horat. Epod., lib. od. iv. [2] Exodus xxi. 6.

[3] In his treatise on the *Revenues of Attica*, Xenophon advises the city of Athens to buy slaves with the public funds, and hire them to individuals, as contractors did. He adds that, to prevent their running away, the slaves should have some particular mark. (Xenoph. de Vect., cap. iv.)

[4] Odys., lib. iii., v. 479, 480.

the men, who ate of this bread.[1] (*a*) The exclusive use of wheat bread by the nobles, is confirmed by a passage of Lucan, and established in a general and peremptory manner by Pliny, the elder, in his histories.[2] It appears, moreover, that slaves were fed in Italy and Greece with pork,[3] garlic, parsley,[4] and onions. The fact of the onions corresponds with what Herodotus says, in the twelfth book of his history, that Cheops expended sixteen hundred talents of silver for horseradish, onions, and garlic, to feed the workmen, who built the great Pyramid of Egypt.[5] A verse of the *Ars Poetica* of Horace seems to establish that the slaves and poor of Rome also lived on peas and nuts.[6] We thus readily explain how the slave races, separated from the free races by moral ideas, by physical labor, by their clothing, which was miserable, by their food, which was unwholesome, in reproducing among themselves, in their lowliness and poverty, should end by degenerating, by decreasing, carried off by the maladies which were peculiar to them, as Titus Livius and Pliny the elder testify, and which have disappeared, to the great astonishment of medicine, in proportion as slavery has given way before liberty.[7]

We have no means of estimating how long in history pure slavery, that is, slavery without emancipation, existed. There were already freedmen in the Bible and in the Odyssey. Before reaching the period when emancipations began to multiply, we must be permitted some important reflections upon the state of primitive society, when all were still either masters or slaves.

One thing, which throws great light upon the study of the forma-

[1] Odys., lib. viii., v. 221, 222.

(*a*) See King James's translation of the Bible, Psalm lxxxi. 16: "He should have fed them also with the *finest of the wheat;* and with honey out of the rock should I have satisfied thee."

Compare with Psalter for the sixteenth day, morning prayer, Psalm lxxxi. 17: "He should have fed them also with the *finest wheat flour:* and with honey out of the stony rock should I have satisfied thee."

[2] Plin. Nat. Hist., lib. xviii., cap. xiv.; Ibid., lib. xix.

[3] Odys., lib. xiv., v. 414–416.

[4] Virgil, Eclog. ii., v. 9, 10.

[5] Herodot. Euterp., cap. cxxv.

[6] Horat. ad Pison., v. 249.

[7] Pliny mentions a malady, which first appeared in Italy, in the time of Claudius. This malady did not attack the nobility. Subsequently he mentions another, which attacked the lower classes and the slaves. (Plin. Hist. Nat., lib. xxvi., cap. iii.)

tion of societies, is that, during the primitive period of pure slavery, there were no beggars. In effect, one is not a beggar, as long as he has wherewith to live; and the slave is fed by his master. There were no beggars in our colonies during the first years of their existence, and there are none still, notwithstanding the emancipation of a great number of negroes. (*a*)

Blackstone judiciously remarks in his Commentaries on the English law,[1] without at all suspecting the general and human value of the local fact, which he reports, that the great number of paupers, who already covered England in his time, and for the support of whom the government found it necessary to provide, ever since the reign of Henry IV., by alms raised with the regularity and permanence of a normal tax, came principally from the many freedmen, emancipated without precaution during the middle ages, and cast without prevision upon society. The monasteries, with their magnificent organization of free hostelries and infirmaries, fed and supported them as best they could for a long time. But the Reformation pitilessly closed the monasteries, and changed laborers into paupers, and paupers into thieves. England, in her civil history,

(*a*) In this, our author, generally so accurate in his statement of facts, is sadly in error. In 1849–50, the translator visited the West Indies, and found pauperism and mendicity frightfully abundant. It is true that they did not reach the extremity of starvation, as in more Northern and inhospitable climes; because, in the luxurious vegetation of the tropics, the spontaneous products of the forest furnished an abundance of the wherewith to live, without other labor than to gather and eat. But even this labor of gathering the fruits, which bountiful nature provides in that latitude, was too much for the "great number of freedmen of the colored race," and their children, who, rather than labor for a half hour in gathering in the woods the fruits, which would support a family for a week, took to mendicity and thieving.

It may be said, that our author's book was published at Paris, in 1838, and that we did not visit the French colonies until 1849–50. But Edwards and McKenzie, who visited them long before — (if our memory serves us, McKenzie's report was laid before Parliament, and given to the public in 1822 or 1824) — found the same condition of things then prevailing. McKenzie not only dwells upon the pauperism and mendicity, which confronted him at every turn, but notices the fact that a very few short years of liberty had carried the negro freedmen back to the worship of Obeah, and to the revolting superstitions and practices of Africa.

[1] Blackstone, vol. ii., chap. i.

presents this character, which is peculiar to her, that there, more than anywhere else, emancipations have operated in a manner prompt, immediate, at a single blow, so to speak, and without causing the slaves to pass through the intermediary preparation of apprenticeship. In other countries, for example in France, (and the many charters entered upon the catalogue of Brequigny prove this,) the emancipations of the middle ages produced fewer paupers; because, without any premeditation certainly, and solely through the effects of a happy, and, we may say, providential inspiration, they were made gradually and by means of a preparatory apprenticeship. Thus it appears that in England slaves were all at once set at liberty, pure and simple.

In France they were only half set free, and were placed in an apprenticeship, which was the novitiate of liberty. Reserving to ourselves to treat more at length hereafter of the history of the emancipation of slaves in France, we propose now to state rapidly what is indispensable to the proper understanding of the matters touched upon in this chapter. A piece of land was given to the slave to cultivate, at an annual rent. This kind of lease, made by the master to the slave, which was not according to the civil law, but formed one of the elements of the subsequent *customary* law, was extended more or less according to the activity and probity of the slave. They were made for ten, twenty, or thirty years, for one generation, for two, sometimes for three. We do not know that any of these contracts made by the masters with their slaves now exist, except in the ancient archives of notaries, that fruitful mine for the study of civil history, where it is not rare to find documents of the thirteenth century, which no one has yet thought of searching; but the leases made to slaves were made upon the system of long leases, (*emphyteotiques*,) of which the first elements exist in the code of Theodosius, which was followed up regularly through the middle ages, arrived at its greatest development in the thirteenth century, and on which there are, in ancient charters, explicit and numberless documents. This kind of contracts had this advantage, that when they were for a long term, as, for example, for three generations, a century passed, during which the action of the master upon the slave was restrained and weakened; while the slave, almost free in fact, acquired the manners and customs of the father of a family, became industrious, economical, settled, prudent, accumulated small profits, and left them to his children. At the end of a century, when three generations had passed away, the master was much less a master, the slave much less a slave. Both had forgotten whence they came, by only seeing where they stood. A singular thing! Since the thirteenth century, we can see, as it were, an immense reconciliation of men and things kept apart by Providence for five thousand years. While the sons of the ancient slaves took courage to approach less cringingly the sons of the ancient masters, a similar phenomenon was taking place around them. Little cabins, small houses, small hamlets, and small towns began to venture, little by little, upon the plains, in the face of the strong castles standing still on the summit of the hills, like black sentinels, which guarded feudal France, and which, with feet booted and spurred with sally-ports, and heads armed with battlements, let their new, timid, and wondering neighbors approach, as a relief, one might say, to their solitary majesty.

It was not from the agricultural slaves, nearly all of whom became small proprietors, that the paupers, who are seen in France, originally sprang, but from the slaves of the workshops, the industrial slaves, who could not from the nature of their labor be comprised in the system of long leases. This is one reason why there are fewer paupers in France than in England; but in bulk and generally, whether in France, or England, or elsewhere, whether in modern or ancient history, everywhere and always the emancipation of slaves is the first and universal cause of pauperism and mendicity.

For many years, the economists have written on the causes of pauperism, without having found out this one, which is the first of all, the most general, the most real, the most permanent. It is true that the science, called political economy, until now in its positive part has been nothing but a great heap of facts without connection, and in its theory a great crowd of ideas more or less crude. Having studied nothing seriously, it knows nothing positively, which seems to have been one reason for calling it a science. But what is required to ascertain and prove that the emancipation of slaves is the general cause of mendicity? We should remark, first, that pauperism seems to be a social human fact, since it shows itself among all peoples; that it is only slaveholding peoples, who are not infested with it; that is to say, only slaveholding peoples before the period of numerous emancipations; and that, as soon as emancipations become frequent, beggars make their appearance. Next we should remark that the great irruption of beggars in Europe took place, as we will hereafter show more at length, from the second to the sixth century of the Christian era; that is, when to the mass of pagan freedmen the mass of Christian freedmen were added; and that this irruption manifested itself in a very striking manner in the regular organization of hospitals, which were unknown to the ancients, among whom there were only private infirmaries, where each one took care of and fed his own slaves. History thus observed can furnish certain data to the science of the economists; but it has seemed to them a much shorter process to pass over facts than to understand them.

Whenever, therefore, we find beggars mentioned in ancient books, we can be certain that they belong to an epoch, when a large number of slaves had already been emancipated; that is to say, to a secondary epoch. It is the same with books, where we find hirelings mentioned; for the ancient hireling was nothing else than a slave become entirely free, and from whom one bought his labor by contract. Hirelings are spoken of in Leviticus[1] and in the Odyssey.[2] Plutarch, in his Life of Theseus, cites a verse of Hesiod, taken from his poem on *Labor and the Day*, where mention is also made of hirelings.[3] There is also another passage in the same poem, where mendicants are spoken of, which brings us back precisely to the same point.[4] We conclude from these evidences that the books of Moses, the Odyssey, and the poems of Hesiod form a synchronism in the development of the civil history of the Jews and the Greeks. We have read the Iliad word for word, deeply impressed with the ideas we have here advanced, and we can say that there is not a line in it, where there is any mention of paupers; which is not the only reason, which we could allege, to show that it is historically impossible that this poem should not be somewhat older than the Odyssey.

The only means of establishing with exactness the remote epoch,

[1] Leviticus xxv. 6.
[2] Odys., lib. xi., v. 489.
[3] Hesiod, Oper. et Dies, v. 340.
[4] Ibid., v. 365.

when the first emancipations took place, is to find out when paupers and hirelings made their appearance in history; for, as we have already said, there could not be either paupers or hirelings in the epochs of pure slavery, which were the primitive epochs. It does not appear that in remote times emancipations were made rapidly and with profusion. Slaves were set free one by one, according to their merits, and when it pleased their masters. As we have said, we do not find anywhere among any ancient people any burdensome accumulation of paupers or hirelings, or even, what is a symptom of a nature entirely identical, any association of thieves in great cities. In fact, the great cities, as will be explained and proved in its place, were never infested with thieves until the epoch, when the system of houses in blocks — *insulas*, as the Roman architecture styled it — succeeded to the system of isolated houses. The aggregation of houses in the cities not having begun, as we will hereafter show, until the formation of the burgher classes, to find thieves organized into secret and nocturnal companies in a city, is to prove that it was built under the system of houses in blocks; consequently that its population was organized by the burgher classes, and that a great number of emancipations had previously taken place; since, as we will prove, it was from the freedmen that the burghers arose. Besides, it is certain that thieves were first produced from hirelings without work, and the hirelings themselves were produced by emancipation; whence it follows, as we have said, that the existence of thieves proves the same fact as the existence of paupers and hirelings. The first thieves met in history were, as we have already explained, the pirates; because the banks of rivers and the coasts of the sea were the first frequented places: and there is a passage in the sixth book of Plato's treatise on *The Laws*, where he says positively that the pirates, who covered the coasts of Greece, were fugitive slaves.[1]

It was then individually that emancipations were made in ancient times, and this explains the tardy coming of the burghers, and the advantage, which ancient peoples enjoyed, of not being encumbered with beggars and thieves, two social plagues, which emancipation has caused. When we approach the Christian era, we meet some

[1] Plato de Legibus, lib. vi.

examples of general emancipations made by party chiefs in times of civil war, or by some general of an army in extremities.

Mithridates employed a corps of 15,000 slaves against the Romans.[1] Marius, in his contest with Sylla, published, by sound of trumpet, that he would give freedom to the slaves who enrolled; but only three presented themselves.[2] During the campaign of Sicilius against Sextus Pompeius, Augustus set free 20,000 slaves, to make sailors of them.[3] These are some examples of emancipation *en masse*, to which we might add others; but when paganism turned over the ancient world to Christianity, freedmen were not numerous.

It was principally the spirit of Christianity which has multiplied emancipations. Add to that, that the disorder, which pervaded all the known world by the dismemberment of the Roman Empire, singularly favored the escape of slaves. Nevertheless, the system of emancipation in mass did not prevail; they continued to be made one by one, but were more frequent and more continuous. In four thousand years ancient civilization had not cast upon society enough freedmen to clog and obstruct it; while in less than three centuries Christianity had multiplied them, with so much political improvidence and such charitable profusion, that these poor people, turned over prematurely to themselves, in the midst of a disordered and selfish world, of which they had no experience, found themselves in their isolation in a frightful misery. It was, in fact, from the three first centuries of the Christian era that beggars abounded in Europe, a phenomenon until then unseen and full of fearful menaces, which, alas! have been too fully realized. From that moment individual charity was recognized as insufficient. The intervention of the entire society became necessary, and we find in the code of Theodosius two rescripts of Constantine, of the years 315 and 322, which are the first public acts in relation to paupers, which we meet with in the legislation of the West. The second, which is addressed to Menander, prefect of the prætor's tribunal, proves that, as we have said, emancipation having produced paupers, the paupers became thieves.[4]

1 Plutarch, Sylla, cap. xviii.

2 Ibid., Marius, cap. xxxv.

3 Sueton., Oct. Cæs. August., cap. xvi.

4 Cod. Theod., lib. xi., tit. xxvii., leg. 2.

Besides, whatever may have been the epoch or the number of emancipations in primitive times, their history leads us to lay down this principle, which this book will demonstrate, namely, that the emancipation of slaves has produced the proletariat. This mass of men, as we have said, is common to all peoples, since all peoples have had slaves; but it was singularly swollen by the spirit of Christianity, and it presses upon modern society with all the weight of six thousand years.

The proletaries then are the children of the ancient slaves, the ancient children of families, given, traded, or sold by their fathers of the heroic period. This great, active, terrible, poetic, and unhappy race tramps, since the beginning of the world, toward the conquest of repose, like Ahasuerus, and perhaps like him will never reach it. It has also upon its head an old curse, which commands it incessantly to tramp.

All that it has gained by *tramping*, is what Homer and Plato said to it: "Tramp; you will not reach it in this world;" and what Paul said: "Tramp; you will reach it in the next." It tramps then since sixty centuries, all covered over with raillery and opprobrium, and without any one taking account of its virtues or its griefs. It is no more beautiful for having produced Aspasia; no more illustrious for having produced Phaedon; no more brave for having produced Spartacus. Whatever may have been its patience, intelligence, and wisdom, it has never been called child of the gods, like the race of nobles; and Plato himself, notwithstanding he was the slave of King Dionysius, cast at it those verses of the poet, which say that a slave has only half of a human soul.[1] Singular fatality! Emancipation came to break the chains of the slaves; their necks remained with the hair rubbed off, like the dog in the fable; and one of themselves, the son of a freedman, Horace,[2] in the most brilliant epoch of ancient philosophy and civilization, cast in their faces this eternal stain: "Money does not change the race!" Whether they gained that money by fatigue of the body or of the mind; with the hand or with the head; whether they were merchants or soldiers, senators or philosophers, they were told that "money does not change the race!" This curse of blood is implacable. Ventidius

[1] Odys., lib. xvii., v. 322, 323; Plato de Legibus, lib. vi.
[2] Horat. Sermon., lib. i., Satyr. vi., v. 6.

Bassus had the good fortune to become consul. They said to him: "You were a boot-black and a groom."[1] Galerius, Diocletian, Probus, Pertinax, Vitellius, Augustus himself, had the good fortune to become emperors. They said to Galerius: "You were a swineherd;" to Diocletian: "You were a slave;" to Probus: "Your father was a gardener;" to Pertinax: "Your father was a freedman;" to Vitellius: "Your father was a cobbler;" and they went so far as to write on the marble of the statue of Augustus, in the lifetime of this master of the world: "Your grandfather was a merchant, and your father a usurer."

If this eternal and universal contempt of the freedmen does not respect the highest and most illustrious heads, judge whether it will do reverence to the humble, poor, and degraded proletary. The noble family keeps them away from its hearthstone; civil society denies him its prerogatives. He is born, lives, and dies apart from other men, and as is said of certain rivers, which flow together in the same bed without mixing their waters, the proletariat and the nobility, the freedman and the gentleman, touch, elbow each other, travel the same road, without ever combining or mingling with each other.

Thus the proletaries, driven from the families and cities of the nobles, repulsed from the social circle and the senate, should naturally and providentially be led to some other society, where they could rest their heads. God gave them that society—a society new in fact, unknown to the ancient fathers of families, to the ancient heroes, to the *divine* men of primitive times; a society timid, submissive, degraded like them, cursed like them—the commune! Yes! Everywhere, always, in antiquity, in the middle ages, among the Hebrews, the Greeks, the Romans, the French, the freedmen were organized into a society proper to the slave races, which is the commune; the commune, which has been developed like all other things that are born; the commune, poor little nest of owls, which has grown great enough for the outstretched wings of the eagle. (*a*)

[1] Aul. Gell. Noct. Attic., lib. xv., cap. iv.

(*a*) The majority report of the H. R. Committee on Education and Labor, (Forty-first Congress, second session, Report No. 121,) intended to *whitewash* General O. O. Howard, Commissioner of the Freedmen's Bureau, on the charges brought against him by the Hon. Fernando Wood, contains the following (see pp. 18 and 19):

"FRENCH EMANCIPATION IN THE ANTILLES.

"The French Government, in a fit of enthusiasm over liberty, declared emancipation in all her colonial dependencies. This occurred in 1794. It brought only confusion and collision in the different islands. To proclaim liberty was one thing; but to maintain it under proper restraints of law, and to allow emancipation to bring forth its legitimate fruits, was another and quite a different problem, and one which the wisdom of France could not solve. True, 250,000 slaves had been freed; but war, insurrections, jealousies, and race hatreds arose and bore their natural fruits. Emancipation seemed to be only a consuming curse to these islands, and France, wearied out by the heart-sickening condition of her colonies, in the year 1802, the year of the Peace of Amiens and of the Consulate, solemnly decreed re-enslavement.

"BRITISH EMANCIPATION.

"In abolishing slavery, the English Government found itself beset with difficulties, which it attempted to overcome by adopting a system of semi-slavery or apprenticeship. It is generally understood that this was the scheme of Lord Brougham. Wilberforce, Clarkson, and others had given sixteen years of thought and effort to the abolition of the slave trade; and now that emancipation itself was a fixed fact, the combined wisdom of English statesmen, Pitt, Fox, Burke, and others, agreed upon apprenticeship: it exploded, however, before the prescribed term of years, which it was to run, had expired. In other words, the entire scheme was a failure.

"Such were the lights General Howard had before him for his guidance."

If the Freedmen's Bureau had had competent and honest administrators, it might have been of incalculable benefit to both races in the South, and could have done much to relieve the "frightful misery" resulting from throwing a large number of slaves, without prevision or preparation, on their own resources for support. It in fact exerted a very beneficial influence in some few localities, where the officers of the Bureau happened to be competent and honest. This, however, was unfortunately very rare; and for some reason or other, such men were dismissed, as soon as it could be reported to headquarters in Washington that they were giving general satisfaction to the people where they were stationed. Why this was, I do not stop to inquire; but only refer those, who feel an interest in the subject, to the minority report, (same document, page 25,) by which it clearly appears that, however incompetent General Howard was to carry out the benevolent and beneficent designs, contemplated by the honest supporters of that institution, he was very competent to make out of it, for himself and his brothers, gigantic fortunes in an incredibly short space of time.

The actual results of his administration soon brought so many complaints from both races, that President Johnson found it necessary in 1866, within twelve months from its establishment, to send a commission, consisting of Major-General J. B. Steadman and Brigadier-General J. S. Fullerton, to report the true state of facts. (See their report.)

The New York Herald also sent special correspondents. The result of their inquiries, subsequently fully confirmed by the official report of Generals Steadman and Fullerton, is thus summed up in an editorial of the New York Herald of the 9th May, 1866:

"The Northern humanitarian has taken the place of the Southern nigger-driver of other days, only to show that he can be the more cruel of the two, and outdo all that maudlin fiction imputed to the other. Our correspondence on this subject, yesterday, showed how a reverend humanitarian from Massachusetts, attached to the Freedmen's Bureau and managing a plantation on his own account, actually shot a negro for attempting to "run away," and this when slavery has been abolished. This establishment (the Freedmen's Bureau) is the parent of untold evils in every part of the Southern States.

"All the idleness, misunderstandings, and cases of bad treatment are traceable directly to this Bureau and its agents. It is corrupt through and through. It sells negroes to planters at so much per head, and, following the plan of the bounty-brokers, sells the same negro over and over to different men.

"It is undeniable that the operation of this Bureau is identical with slavery; that it treats the negro just as slavery did, only that it gives the preference in possession to another class of men."

At the anniversary meeting of the Anti-slavery Society in New York city, on the 9th May, 1866, (see New York Tribune, 10th May,) "Mr. Calvin Pepper denounced the Freedmen's Bureau. It was the curse of the South, and was used for the purposes of private speculation, selling the labor of the negroes. He could show twenty affidavits to prove his statements, extraordinary and startling as they may appear. He was not in favor of the military occupation of the South. He did not want the *habeas corpus* eternally suspended there, nor a military despotism. General Howard was doing his duty, but as a general thing the action of the Freedmen's Bureau was disastrous in its effects."

An editorial in the New York Herald, 10th May, 1866, quotes "a colored correspondent of a journal in the South owned and edited by negroes, who says of the Bureau: 'A thousand times better far would it be for the colored man were it abolished; for instead of being a safeguard or protection for the freedmen, it is only a place, in which freedmen's rights are bartered away. The sooner it is out of the way the better.'" The Herald editor adds:

"This is the opinion of one likely to be informed of the practical workings of the system. Accounts of official malfeasance in the Bureau multiply with every day's mail. At one time we hear of some swindling or oppressive operation in Louisiana, next in North Carolina, again in South Carolina, Georgia, and other Southern States. It is an iniquitous, expensive, and altogether unnecessary establishment, and should be abolished."

May 16th, 1866, the Herald says:

"It will be seen that General Howard admits one of the main accusations; that is, that the chief and subordinates and representatives of the Bureau were 'running plantations,' and furnishing rations to their negro hands at Government expense, for their own personal benefit. Nor does he deny or explain the charge that the same officers were bartering away the services of the freed negroes, and allowing them to be sent away from home associations and separated from family ties, under circumstances of as much cruelty as ever characterized the late rebellious slaveholders."

Mr. Pepper wished to believe, and to make the world believe, that "General Howard was doing his duty," and that the fault was in his subordinates. But General Howard would not permit this; for the very men, who were making the Bureau a gigantic nigger-trading monopoly, supported by Government, were General Howard's special pets and favorites; men altogether after his own heart, and, in their aptitude for hypocrisy and acquisitiveness, fashioned after his own image.

To break the force of the official confirmation, by the report of Generals Steadman and Fullerton, of the Herald's disclosures, he hastened to make himself conspicuous in the religious and humanitarian anniversaries in New York city. There, relying on his sanctimonious reputation, backed by the usual mixture of slanderous abuse of the Southern whites, he boldly took upon himself the responsibility for the atrocious practices of his subordinates, admitting that he had "*urged* (upon them) *the renting and running of plantations, to afford practical examples, to encourage joint-stock companies.*" (See his letter to the Rev. George Whipple, of 8th May, 1866, published in the New York Tribune, of 14th May.) His excuse was that the Southern whites were indolent, and required to be stimulated into industry by practical examples of the rapidity, with which the Bureau officials could grow rich, on the labor of the negroes and at the expense of the Government. But aware that this explanation would hardly be sufficient even at the North, without an appeal to their sectional hatred of the South, he sought to divert just indignation from himself and his subordinates, by exciting an unjust indignation against the Southern whites. He therefore added, in his Whipple letter: "The Bureau does not do enough to secure the rights of the negroes, I will admit; but *it does not burn negro churches and school-houses; it does not reject negro testimony.*" In his speeches, not fully reported and therefore not of record, this idea was carried out, with amplifications. By this means, and by party influences, General Howard escaped a just responsibility for the infamous atrocities of the Freedmen's Bureau; but its "disastrous action" was too manifest even for the Radicals to continue it, and it was abolished.

Since the religious anniversaries of May, 1866, in which General Howard played so conspicuous a part, his tactics have been crystallized down to a single word, *Ku-Klux;* and now, whenever the Radical party wish to defend or excuse any outrage on the States, or any violation of the Constitution, all they have to do is to cry out, *Ku-Klux!*

The practical action of the Freedmen's Bureau, while it lasted, was threefold:

First, to stimulate *acquisitiveness*, by showing what sudden and enormous fortunes its officials could gather together in the South.

Second, to organize the negroes into loyal leagues, all bound by secret oaths to vote as the Radical party, through Bureau officials, should direct.

Third, to excite *race hatred* between the Southern whites and the freedmen.

Since the discontinuance of the Bureau, the "race hatred," which it had succeeded in exciting to a considerable extent, has nearly entirely disappeared. Mutual dependence on each other — the necessity for employment or protection on the one hand, and for labor on the other — has brought the old masters and the old slaves again into kindly contact, and revived the old attachments and mutual fidelity, so strikingly manifested throughout the whole war, and in thousands of instances continued uninterrupted long after the war, in spite of the mischief-making tendencies of the Bureau. A mutual interchange of the offices of good neighborhood is every day strengthening this good understanding between the freedmen and their old masters. A single incident of the last election in Georgia, which happened in my own town of Dalton, will illustrate how these influences are working, generally, throughout the South.

We have at Dalton a freedman, named Bill Wilson, by trade a blacksmith, very hardworking and honest, and much respected by all the whites. He is moreover a very zealous Presbyterian. Of course the Bureau carried him into the Loyal League, and he was a leading member. No Democrat ever thought of approaching him on the subject of voting a Democratic ticket. But at the last election, to the surprise of everybody, he not only voted the straight-out Democratic ticket, without a scratch, but quit his work for the three days of the election, and exerted himself actively to persuade other freedmen to do the same. Being told of this, I asked him if it was true, and why he had left his friends, the Radicals? His answer was: "I have found out that these Radicals, who pretend to be such great friends to us colored people, are very willing to let us do their work, but very unwilling to pay us for it. I have been working for them till I am tired of it; for I can't get a dollar out of them. I find that all those gentlemen, who give me work and pay me, are Democrats. Besides, last summer we colored people were trying to build our church. We could not get ten cents out of the whole Radical party. We went to you, and you let us have a lot, and gave us fifty dollars. Every other Democrat, that we applied to, gave us something, and liberally, according to his means. So some of us just concluded that hereafter we will vote with those, who give us work and pay us for it, and who helped us to build our church."

This explains the object of, and the necessity for, the Shellabarger Ku-Klux Bill. Similar influences are producing like results all over the South. The freedmen are quitting the Loyal Leagues and the Radical party, going back to their old and true friends, and voting, with them, the Democratic ticket. Something must be done to force them back under the control of the "carpet-baggers and scalawags," or their votes will be cast in 1872 for the Democratic nominees. The Freedmen's Bureau, under General Howard's administration, became so infamous and so odious, at the North as well as at the South, that its re-establishment is out of the question. Hence the necessity and the purpose of the Shellabarger Bill; to enable General Grant, by martial law, suspension of *habeas corpus*, and such other instrumentalities as may hereafter be devised, to force the freedmen to vote in 1872 for the candidates of the *cheap labor* and imperial party.

## CHAPTER VI.

### GENERAL IDEA OF THE COMMUNE — TWO KINDS.

THE commune, then, is that special association, to which emancipated races have tended, universally, among all nations, without exception. In it the slave has found himself redeemed from what may be called social damnation. In it he became completely a man. By it he has taken rank among those other men, who had never been enslaved, whom poetry called divine, and history called noble. Thus, in the fact of the commune, there is nothing accidental or local, as we will show hereafter. It belongs to no chance of time or country. It has no predilection for the East or the West, for India, Greece, Italy, or France. It is a phase of the life and development of the slave races. On the one hand, as there has never been one single nation, among whom slavery has not at one time existed, it is a universal fact; on the other, as there is no nation from among whom slavery has not disappeared, it is a necessary fact. Universal and necessary, it is thus bound up with the very destinies of society, of which it is an element, a form, an inevitable law. In other words, it is human.

Evidently it is not the word, the name of commune, of which we say that it is universal and necessary, but the fact, which that name designates. In other words, we hope to establish that this association, which was produced in France, for example, in the twelfth century, and which we call commune, is absolutely of the same nature as the association of the freed races of all antiquity; — reciprocally that the association of the freed races of all antiquity has had absolutely the same form as the commune. Thus the commune of the middle ages was this human fact of the association of slave races; this fact, which, in its form and substance, is found in the Bible, in the Odyssey, in the Papyrian Code, and in ancient charters. As we think, one may follow and study it with the same results in all its successive manifestations, and rely with as much reason for its repetition on a text from Moses as on one from Dumoulin.

Perhaps this is the time for us to say to our readers that, in the subject of this chapter, we will notably cut loose from the opinions of some men of great historic value, to whose talents we have always been one of the first to render justice. Also, it is because of the esteem and respect, which we have always professed for their learning, that we feel the necessity of justifying ourselves in some manner for daring to think differently from them. But the liberty of science is something so inviolable, and they have had to claim it for themselves so haughtily, so justly, of their predecessors, that they will find it quite simple and proper that we demand it after them. Nevertheless, although we find their works on this subject either incomplete or erroneous, we recognize in them too much patience, merit, and true wisdom, to pass on to the exposition of our own ideas, without giving theirs this mark of deference, to mention and examine them.

There are principally three men, who have treated the matter of the commune, with more or less profundity: M. Raynouard, M. Augustin Thierry, and M. Guizot. We ask pardon of the reader for the intentional omission of a fourth name; but we cannot regard M. de Sismondi as a critical historian of any serious value. Nevertheless, we do not mean to condemn absolutely and brutally his very numerous works; for we recognize a certain merit in collecting ancient traditions without altering their signification. But we are convinced that M. de Sismondi has left pending all the great questions of the middle ages and of the formation of modern nations; and if it is true that he has taken nothing from the science of history, it is true that he has added nothing to it.

The opinion of M. Raynouard is that the communes had no proper existence, and that they were only the prolongation and complement of the municipal system of the Romans applied to Gaul. Wherever there was a commune, M. Raynouard seeks to show that there a municipality pre-existed. As to the municipalities themselves, he sees in them cities, conquered by policy or force, and admitted to enjoyment of Roman rights. These notions are taken from a chapter of the Attic Nights of Aulus Gellius;[1] which

[1] See this passage: "Municipes et municipia verba sunt dictu facilia et usu obvia; et neutiquam reperias, qui hæc dicat, quin scire se planè putet, quid dicat; sed profectò aliud est, aliud dicitur. . . . Municipes ergò sunt cives Romani ex municipiis, LEGIBUS SUIS ET SUO JURE UTENTES, muneris tantum cum populo Romano honorarii participes, à quo munere capessendo appellati videntur, nullis aliis necessitatibus, NEQUE ULLA POPULI ROMANI LEGE ASTRICTO, cum numquam populus eorum fundus factus esset." (Aul. Gell. Noct. Attic., liber xvi., cap. xiii.)

we will hereafter show that he has not understood. Besides, M. Raynouard finds in the municipalities only a certain form of administration invented by the Romans, and applied by them to all of Europe, and particularly to Gaul, of which the communes were the continuation, and which would never have existed, if Rome had not created them.

M. Thierry finds that the communes are a fact *sui generis*, spontaneous, proper to France, the same in the centre and at the north of France. He thinks that this fact is properly the first form, which the democratic and revolutionary principle has assumed in modern history, and he gives insurrection as the point of departure and origin of every commune. The importance which he attributes to insurrection in the formation of communes is so exaggerated and radical, that he goes so far as to say that the conspiracy (*conjuration*) organized to establish the communes has given the name of *jurés* to their members and magistrates, while the magistrates of the municipal towns were called consuls. We already see that the theories of M. Raynouard and of M. Augustin Thierry are nearly contradictory of each other, and we will see that both are disproved by the facts.

M. Guizot, with that profound sagacity, which characterizes his mind, has not failed to recognize that the communes were not a simple fact, and all of a piece; but that they were formed generally and in varying proportions of Roman and indigenous elements. He admits at the same time, in the organization of the towns of the middle ages, the Roman municipality and the commune, of which he comprehends the mechanism in the same manner as M. Raynouard and M. Thierry. Further, and this is the most important point in the question, he penetrates to the very origin of the commune, of which M. Raynouard has not spoken, and of which M. Thierry only says vaguely, that it was the democratic and revolutionary element; and he thinks that the origin of the communes was the slaves of the lords and convents, set free in mass by numerous and successive emancipations. We will have occasion to show, in the course of this book, how searching was this glance at the formation of the communes. Only, and this seems strange after a first observation so suggestive, M. Guizot stops short at the commune of the middle ages, and does not inquire whether this commune might not be, in form and substance, the continuation of an analogous fact, of which the history of ancient peoples offers a thousand proofs. This, perhaps, is all that is wanting to his theory; but it must be said that it is a great want. Moreover, M. Guizot not only does not say that the commune may be anything more than an accident proper to modern history; but what he does say does not indicate that he had that idea. It is singular that he, who has so clearly explained the municipal system of the Romans, being halfway on the road to a great idea, should not follow it to the end. Has he not observed that the communal system of France has no other origin, or nature, or form?

We hope to show clearly, in the course of this book, what is erroneous in the first two of these theories, and what is incomplete in the third. We think that we will not be supposed to be inspired by a desire to find errors in the works of another. We have an object much less personal and much more worthy. It is not our fault, if human science is a fully sown field, where it is impossible to plant one idea without digging up another. We are under this necessity. Perhaps we may pull up a stalk of wheat to plant a thistle. Let the reader judge. We only desire to show our intention in all its disinterestedness and purity. Besides, we will only combat the theories we have just mentioned, as we complete our own. The best and most sincere way to criticize an idea is to replace it by another.

We have reached the point, in our subject, to say that the commune, among all peoples, is the political and administrative association of slaves. We have prepared and announced this fact rather than proved it. What we have said shows that it is possible and even probable. It remains for us to produce what will render it certain.

Before entering upon the detail of the formation of communes, and to remove some difficulties, which spring up from the development of our subject, we should say that there are in history two kinds of communes, of which the difference is perhaps more apparent than real; but it is necessary to distinguish and characterize them, so that their juxtaposition may create no mistake or confusion. We will call one the spontaneous commune, and the other the artificial commune; and these are the ideas we attach to these two designations.

We call a spontaneous commune, that which was originally formed spontaneously, naturally, by the sole fact of the agglomeration on one spot of a certain number of freedmen, who had obtained or assumed the right to govern themselves. We call an artificial commune that, of which the mechanism has been intentionally imitated from another, and which was not produced, like the first, without a model or premeditated design.

It is very important to make the distinction between these two communes, for this reason: Wherever a commune was formed of itself, without reference to any theory and without being the work of any legislator, we may be certain that those, who composed it, were freedmen; because, as we will hereafter establish, the commune is the government, to which the slave races invariably come. But when, on the contrary, a commune was imported into any place, of deliberate purpose, by a conqueror or legislator, it may very well have been that those, to whom it was applied, or who adopted it, were not freedmen, or even they may have been people of noble blood. For example, when the Romans, having conquered Europe, had applied to the smallest boroughs of Gaul or Greece their form of government, which was the communal or municipal, it often happened that the families, which accepted or submitted to this government, were rich, ancient, powerful, glorious. Thus in the first years of the empire, the decurions, that is to say, the municipal officers, were persons of great distinction. This came from the fact that all Europe was brought under the form of the Roman government, without regard to its origin, taking it as it was without reference to the past. Nevertheless, this government, which then suited the greatest, proudest, and most illustrious people of the world, commenced by a collection of fugitive slaves on Mount Palatine.

When then we say, that every commune invariably corresponds with a population of the slave race, we speak of communes, which were originally formed spontaneously, and not of those, which, after having been slowly modified, corrected, ameliorated gradually, by revolution after revolution, came at last some fine day to be applied, as a model government, to a free people. Certainly the Roman government was not formed of slaves under Julius Cæsar; but it was under Romulus.

Ancient history is full of instances of certain cities, which have been suddenly struck with admiration for the government of some other city, and were not satisfied until it was given to them. They did not ask from what point this government started, but what point it had reached; not what it had been formerly, but what it was then. They took no account of its first trials, its experiments, its revolutions. They regarded only its last phase and its great progress. Thus Aulus Gellius relates that the little city of Ceres, toward the end of the last invasions of the Gauls into Italy, full of admiration for the mechanism of the Roman Republic, asked of the senate permission to adopt it.[1] The city of Ceres did not inquire as to the successive changes this government had gone through. It did not dream of the seven kings of Rome, nor of the revolution, which drove them out, nor of the mutinies of the people, nor of the aggrandizement and ennobling of the senate. It saw a government well understood, at the same time active and conservative, multiplicate and consolidated, and it desired to have one on the same plan. Thenceforward the commune of Ceres was not a commune of freedmen, since the Roman government, which it imitated, was applied without distinction to its entire population; but its ancient government, its primitive commune, which had been spontaneous in its origin, and the customs of which it preserved in taking the Roman form, had been a commune of freedmen.

Aulus Gellius says in effect, in a passage which we have quoted above, that the cities, which, like Ceres, had adopted the form of the Roman government and become *municipia*, preserved nevertheless their own laws, which can only be understood of the civil, criminal, and commercial laws, which were applied by their municipal councils or by their magistrates.[2] This proves that the *municipia*, before existing as an imitation of Rome, had existed in their own name and according to their special form. Aulus Gellius adds that from his time the Roman scabbard had used the national sword, and that the *municipia* had forgotten their own ancient customs, so far as not to know how to use them.[3] They had become, as Aulus Gellius expresses it, little Romes, after the likeness of the great Rome.[4]

We can now see, by this analysis of the passage from Aulus

1 Primos autem municipes sine suffragii jure Cerites esse factos accepimus. (Aul. Gell., lib. xvi., cap. xiii.)

2 Legibus suis et suo jure utentes. (Aul. Gel., lib. xvi., cap. xiii.)

3 Obscura obliterataque sunt municipiorum jura, quibus uti jam per ignorantiam non queunt. (Aul. Gell., lib. xvi., cap. xiii.)

4 Quasi effigies parvæ simulacraque Romæ esse quædam videntur. (Aul. Gell., lib. xvi., cap. xiii.)

Later, Justinian justified in these terms that imitation of the Roman form, which was imposed on all the cities of the empire: "Secundum Salvii Juliani scripturam, quæ indicat debere omnes civitates consuetudines Romæ sequi, quæ est caput orbis terrarum, non ipsam alias civitates." (Prefat. Prim. de Concept. Digestor, ad Tribonian.)

Gellius, quoted by M. Raynouard, that he has not been well understood. In effect, the theory drawn by M. Raynouard from this passage rests on the idea, that the communes of the middle ages did not exist of themselves, and that they were only the continuation and revival of the ancient Roman *municipia.* Now M. Raynouard has not observed that the cities, which, like Ceres, became *municipia* in taking the Roman form, were previously communes, on their own account, with their own special and national form, and using their own ancient laws, even after they had adopted that form; whence it evidently follows that it was not impossible for communes to be spontaneously organized in the middle ages, without reviving the ancient *municipia,* since they were organized in the cities of primitive Italy, before they had the idea of grafting the Roman government on the trunk of their own history.

What has been seen in Italy of fancies, which certain cities have taken for another, had also been seen in Greece, and instances can be cited of *municipia* organized with the form of the Athenian government. In the discourse, which Thucydides makes Pericles pronounce, at the funeral solemnities celebrated by the Athenians in honor of the soldiers, who fell in the first year of the Peloponnesian war, it is formally said that the government of Athens served as a model for other cities.[1] Some years before that war, and in the height of the power of the Athenians, they went to Samos, and there established, as conquerors, the form of their own republic.[2] Besides, it suffices to recall the custom of the ancient cities of Greece of having their laws made by a philosopher, or of sending to search for them in some neighboring city, to comprehend how there must have been among them artificial communes, which were superimposed on the spontaneous communes.

We have now said enough about each of these two kinds of communes, to pass on to the development of our subject, without fear of confusion.

[1] *Χρώμεθα γαρ πολιτειᾳ οὐ ζηλουση τοὺς τῶν πέλας νομους, παραδειγμα δὲ αὐτοὶ μαλλον ὄντες τισὶν, ἤ μιμουμενοι ετερους.* (Thucyd. Hist., lib. ii., cap. xxxvii.)

[2] *Πλεύσαντες οὐν Αθηναῖοι ες Σάμον ναυσὶ τεσσαρακοντα, δημοκρατίαν κατεστησαν.* (Thucyd. Hist., lib. i., cap. cxv.)

# CHAPTER VII.

## THE FRENCH COMMUNE.

IT is of the greatest importance, for the proper understanding of the matter to be treated of in this chapter, to understand exactly, first, what constitutes a commune, and then the different names by which the communes are designated by the charters and by historians.

The right of *commune* consisted in the privilege granted to the inhabitants of a borough or city to govern themselves, instead of being governed by the officers of a lord, lay or ecclesiastic, baron or abbé.

The confirmation of the charter of commune granted by Hugo, Count de la Marche et d'Angoulême, to the inhabitants of Ahun, in the year 1268, expresses exactly in three words in what a commune consisted.

"*Approbamus*, said the count, *consulatum*, sigillum, et communitatem."[1] *Consulatum*, that is to say, administration; *sigillum*, that is to say, the dispensation of justice; *communitatem*, that is to say, the public treasury, the *arca communis*. The inhabitants of a city, who obtained or took these three things, had, properly speaking, a commune. So, to take away from a city the right of having a public seal and magistrates, or the consulate, was to take away its commune. This was done to the commune of Laon, by decree of the Parliament of La Toussaint, in the year 1295,[2] and to the city of Paris by King Charles VI., in the year 1382, after the sedition of the Maillotins.

If a city had the right of self-government, it had a commune. It may be said that certain cities had a commune, more or less than others, in this sense, that their right of dispensing justice, for example, was more or less extensive. One city had only civil jurisdic-

[1] Approbamus expresse et confirmamus hominibus villæ nostræ Agedunensis ... consulatem, sigillum et communitatem. (Charter of Hugo, Count de la Marche, for the franchise of Ahun. La Thomassiere, Local Customs, ch. cvi.)

[2] Olim., vol. ii., fol. 108.

tion. Another had the right to take cognizance of affairs both civil and criminal. This was the case with most of the great cities of the kingdom, at least until the Edict of Moulins, which left the cognizance of civil affairs only to the municipalities of Toulouse, Rheims, Boulogne, and Angoulême, which proved that they had possessed this right since the time of the Romans.[1]

The name, designating this privilege, granted or taken by a city, of governing itself and being perfectly independent, within the terms of its charter, varied in different localities. Sometimes it was *communio;*[2] sometimes *communia;*[3] sometimes *communitas;*[4] sometimes *franchisia;*[5] sometimes *consuetudines;*[6] sometimes *libertas;*[7] sometimes *burgesia.*[8] Nevertheless, whatever the difference in name, the substance of the thing remained the same. It was the right of self-government, or, as the charter of Ahun says, *consulatum, sigillum* et *communitas.*

On the other hand, whatever may have been the source of the right of self-government possessed by a city, this right was none the less a right of commune, whether it came from a lord, or from the king; whether it was a grant or a purchase; whether obtained by humble remonstrances or by open rebellion.

It is thus seen that M. Augustin Thierry has committed two great errors in what he has written about the communes: first, in

[1] The Edict of Moulins, issued by Charles IX. in 1556, was intended to restrict the rights of the municipal magistrates, for the profit of the royal magistrates. The Chancellor de l'Hospital was the promoter of it. This edict, the meaning of which was afterward greatly extended, was one of the most powerful causes, which more lately produced the consolidation of the administration of the kingdom.

[2] *Communio* autem, novum ac pessimum nomen. (Guib. abb. de Novigent, lib. iii., cap. vii., apud Script. rer. Franc., t. xii.)

[3] Concessimus *communiam* habendam. (Charter of the commune of Cerny. La Thomassiere, Local Customs, chap. civ.)

[4] *Communitas* habitatorum villæ Parisiensis. (Decree of Parliament of 1 June, 1316. Olim., vol. iii., folio 154, cited by De la Mare in his treatise on Civil Government, t. i., p. 149.)

[5] Frater meus *franchisiam* voluit et concessit. (Charter of the city of Lury. La Thomass., Local Customs, chap. lvi.)

[6] Subscriptas *consuetudines* habendas in perpetuum concedimus. (Charter of the city of Duns le Roi. La Thomass., Local Customs, chap. xlviii.)

[7] Hominibus commorantibus apud Cellas talem concessi *libertatem.* (Privileges of the inhabitants of Celles. Charter of Robert de Courtenay, 1216. La Thomass., Local Customs, chap. lviii.)

[8] In conservationem jurium *burgesiæ* hujusmodi. (Chapter of the borough of Aigues-Mortes. La Thomass., Local Customs, chap. cv.)

refusing to recognize a commune where the name of *communia* was not to be found; secondly, in asserting that every *commune* sprang from a rebellion. First, the commune of Aigues-Mortes, established by Charles V., in 1373, was as complete a commune as could be,[1] and nevertheless it was not called communia, but burgesia. Next, the commune of Cerny, which was called communia, did not spring from a rebellion, and its members were called *jurati*, although they had never conspired.[2] Besides, as La Thomassiere observes, the name of *juratus* or *jurat* was universally given to the magistrates of the communes of La Guienne.[3]

It is important again to notice an historical error very common among those, who have treated of the communes. We refer to the common opinion as to the date of their institution. M. Augustin Thierry has with much reason reproved the authors of the Charter of 1814, who in the preamble have attributed the establishment of communes to Louis the Fat. Perhaps we should now reprove M. Augustin Thierry himself for having believed, with so many others, that the formation of communes dated from the twelfth century. The formation of communes, as we believe, does not date precisely from any century, because it dates from all. It is a permanent fact of the history of all peoples, and for this reason: The commune, as we have already said and will presently clearly establish, is the government, to which the emancipated slaves in every country attain. Now in Europe, from the commencement of society to the 15th century, slaves have been constantly obtaining their liberty, and consequently, communes have been constantly forming, under one of the names mentioned above. We find in every century of the history of the middle ages privileges more or less extensive accorded to different cities, that is to say, a self-government of com-

[1] The charter of Charles V. says expressly that the city of Aigues-Mortes should have the same privileges and franchises as the city of Montpelier: "Statuimus edicto irrevocabili . . . burgenses predictos . . . vocari burgenses Aquarum Mortuarum, prout burgenses Montispessulani anteà vocabantur; volentes ut universi et singuli cujuscumque conditionis et status qui voluerint se burgenses nostros constituere, modo et forma consuetis et debitis, hoc facere possint in dicta villa Aquarum Mortuarum, prout in dicto loco Montispessulani." (La Thomass., Local Customs, ch. cv.)

[2] Majori et juratis . . . satisfactionem faciet. (Charter of the commune of Cerny. La Thomass., Local Customs, ch. civ.)

[3] The *jurats*, which is the ordinary name in the province of La Guienne of the magistrates of the people. (La Thomass., Local Customs, ch. xix.)

munes confirmed or established. For example, a letter of Theodoric, King of Italy, in the year 510, confirms the immunities previously granted to the city of Marseilles.[1] A formula of Marculfus speaks of *communal* property, and thus proves that the word *commune* itself existed toward the end of the sixth century.[2] An act of sale of the year 877 mentions a *communal* way, and proves that the word *commune* was likewise used in the ninth.[3] A diploma of Charlemagne, of the year 777, confirms the privileges of a place called Salona, in the bishopric of Metz.[4] A charter of Pons, Count d'Alby, of the year 797, declares free a borough called Viancium.[5] Lastly, a charter of the 30th of March, 1068, mentions Jane, wife of Pierre de Coq, *burgher* of Pontoise.[6] The establishment of communes, that is to say, of the self-government of freedmen, is then, as we have said, a permanent fact of history. All that can be said of the twelfth century, is that it was the precise moment when the greater part of the populations passing from slavery found themselves organized for self-government; a commune formed then set the example for a crowd of others. Thus there was a time in the history of Greece, when all the cities wished for a commune like that of Athens, and another time in the history of Italy, when all the cities desired a commune like that of Rome.

We repeat, the commune is nothing else than the self-government of the freed races, whatever may have been, in other respects, the origin, extent, or name of that government; whether it was taken by force, granted, or purchased; whether absolute or limited; whether called communio, or communia, or communitas, or libertas, or consuetudines, or franchisia, or burgesia. Communes were formed all along the history of peoples, as slaves attained their liberty, and the grave question of knowing to what precise epoch the establishment of communes dates back, whether to Louis the Fat,

1 Cassiodori variar., lib. iv., epist. xxvi.

2 Cum terris, silvis, campis, pratis, pascuis, communiis, necnon et mancipiis. (Formul. Marculf., a Lindenbrogio edit., No. 58.)

3 Speaking of the boundaries of a piece of land: De uno fronte *centerius communalis* pergit; de alio vero fronte strada publica pergit. (Perard. Recueil de pièces curieuses, p. 155, 156.)

4 D. Calmet, History of Lorraine, t. i. 287.

5 Catel., Counts of Toulouse, p. 100.

6 History of the Curacy of Pontoise à Venin, p. 22.

or Philip the First, is a scientific puerility, into which the critic of our day should take care not to fall.

The communes, which were formed, confirmed, or extended in France, in all the course of our history, were of two kinds. One, the least numerous, were a remnant of the Roman communes, or of the Roman municipia, (for these two expressions are identical,) with which Gaul was covered during the golden era of the empire. The other was the aboriginal, national communes, which sprang up spontaneously upon the soil, and were formed little by little, year by year, as the slaves attained their liberty.

The communes of Roman origin were themselves of two kinds: one entire, having resisted, without dissolution, all the waves of invasion, and having preserved intact their primitive and original form; the others, mutilated, defaced, scarce recognizable, being nothing more than a ruin marked only by some remnant of an inscription, rising pitifully to the surface of new manners, like a half-buried stone of a monument which has long since disappeared.

As is well believed, the Roman communes, which passed through the middle ages, were few in number. But few suspect that when, in the year 1556, the Edict of Moulins came to take away from the magistrates the right of civil jurisdiction, on the ground that they held it by grant, and that the king could take away what the king had given, some of them resisted the edict, replying and proving that they were more ancient than the French monarchy. The commune of Rheims was the first which ventured upon this memorable struggle. The Parliament of Paris recognized the legitimacy of their pretensions by decree of the 25th May, 1568.[1] Boulogne and Angoulême followed the example of Rheims. The pretensions of Boulogne were recognized to be founded in right by the decree of parliament of January, 1571. Those of Angoulême by decree of the year 1572, which, however, did not prevent the execution of the Edict of Moulins,[2] by letters-patent. Toulouse was treated in the same way, that is to say, deprived by letters-patent of the right of civil jurisdiction, although she proved that her magistracy, or capitoulat, was anterior to Clovis.[3]

[1] Borgies, Discourse on the Antiquity of the Magistracy of the City of Rheims.

[2] Dubos, History of the Establishment of the French Monarchy in Gaul, lib. vi., ch. xii.

[3] La Faille, Annals of Toulouse, t. i., p. 55.

The communes, that were only a debris of the Roman municipalities, and in which a young and vigorous franchise of the middle ages was grafted on the old trunk of a curia, were very numerous. M. Raynouard cites nearly a hundred in two chapters only of his History of Municipal Rights;[1] and M. de Savigny, in his curious and patient work on the History of the Roman Law in the middle ages, cites many examples of ancient Roman cities becoming French communes. We refer, on this point, to the two books we have mentioned, having no taste for treating questions which have been already treated, and well treated, and we pass on to the communes of purely French origin, and which arose as the freedmen accumulated on some point of territory.

Nothing is more frequent in the history of the middle ages than the formation of communes with men recently emerged from slavery. We have, therefore, plenty of examples to choose from. The revolt of the burghers of Bruges, and the assassination of Charles the Good, Count of Flanders, in 1127, was one of the events of democratic nature and intent, which resounded most in the twelfth century. Now, the prévôt of the Chapter of Bruges, the first and richest of their burghers, the author and instigator of the sedition, Bertulphe, was claimed by the count as a slave, enjoying, it is true, a kind of liberty, but only by favor and complaisance. It is certain, on the one hand, by the inquest, which the count caused to be made, that Bertulphe could not produce any act of emancipation, and it is true, on the other, that he was so much a slave, although he had become prévôt, that is, grand judge in all the extent of the jurisdiction of the chapter, that a cavalier, who had married one of his nieces, had himself declared a slave at the end of a year and a day, following the custom of the country.[2] The great revolt of the inhabitants of Véselay against the Abbé and Chapter of St. Marie Madeleine de Véselay, in 1152, also offers the spectacle of a tumultuous association of serfs and slaves, who wished to obtain the legal association of a commune; and, in the insurrectionary and provisional municipality which was formed, the prévôt Simon was reclaimed by the chapter as a slave.[3]

[1] Book 3, chap. viii., xi.

[2] Vita Caroli Boni, auctor Galbert. Brugens. notar. Apud Script. rer. Franc., t. xiii., p. 347.

[3] Hugues de Poitiers, Chronicles of Véselay.

La Thomassiere says: There are few cities in the kingdom that do not bear the marks of this servitude, and that have not been redeemed from it by the grant of privileges, which conferred citizenship upon them. It is especially in the customs established among the freedmen, who, having long had to contend with family interests and the rentage of land, before being completely free, had need of a special law, not being able to take advantage of the civil law;—it is especially in the customs, we say, that we find numberless and undeniable traces of the ancient slavery of the burghers, who constituted the communes. Thus, the communal charter granted by Philip Augustus to the inhabitants of St. Jean d'Angely, in 1204, accords to them the right of giving their children in marriage, and of making a will, which clearly proves that they did not previously have this right, and that they had been slaves.[1] And thus another charter, granted by Philip Augustus to the burghers of the city of Bourges, in 1197, also gives to them the right of devising by will, which ranks them in the same category with those of St. Jean d'Angely.[2] Likewise, a charter granted to the inhabitants of Chateau Roux, on the 15th November, 1370, by Guy II., Lord of Chauvigny and Chateauroux, concedes to them the rights of inheritance;[3] and even the burghers of Paris themselves could only have the guardianship of their children and parents, by special grant recorded in the book of royal ordinances in the office of the Prévôt of Merchants.[4] So, the inhabitants of the faubourg St. Germain, who made part of the ancient commune of Paris, *communitas habitatorum villæ Parisiensis*, in the words of a decree of parliament of the 1st June, 1316, which we have quoted, were set free by Frère Thomas de Mauleon, Abbé of St. Germain, in consideration of the sum of two hundred Paris livres.[5] So, the plebeians, *roturiers*, in mass, were degraded by certain customs, as for example, the custom of Bretagne, which denied them the right

[1] Cartul. de Philippe Auguste, p. 998.

[2] ... Noverint universi præsentes ... nos bene velle ut quando aliquis ex burgensibus nostris Biturigensibus moriens legatum suum fecerit, ipse, si voluerit, partem suam et partem puerorum suorum in manibus alicujus amicorum suorum mittat. (Cited by La Thomassiere, Local Customs, chap. xlviii.)

[3] Item, que les dits habitans pourraint et pourront succeder l'un à l'autre, en quelque degré, ordonner de leur biens, meubles, heritages, à leur pure et liberale volonté. (Cited by La Thomassiere, Local Customs, chap. lxxv.)

[4] Bacquet, Des Francs Fiefs, part. i., chap. x., No. 6.

[5] Renat. Chopin. De Moribus Parisiens, lib. ii., tit. viii., where he quotes the charter.

of testifying on certain occasions.[1] So a clause of the charter accorded by the Bishop Geoffroy to the city of Amiens, under penalty of a fine, forbids calling the burghers *serfs;* whence it follows that they had only recently ceased to be such.[2] So, Roger de Rosoy, having become Bishop of Laon, in 1177, applied to Louis VII., praying him to have pity on his church, by abolishing the commune of Laon, which he calls the commune of his serfs.[3]

Behold a last example of what we have said in relation to the formation of communes by slaves, and we limit ourselves to this, among many others, because it generalizes our principle, and confirms it theoretically. It is a passage of Guibert, Abbé of Nogent, quoted and translated by M. Thierry, in his fourteenth letter on the History of France, but translated with an essential omission, which we are going to supply: "Commune, new and execrable word, signifies that *all those, who are subject to poll tax*, shall only pay once a year, to their masters, the customary dues of serfdom; and as to the other arbitrary taxes customarily inflicted upon serfs, they are altogether exempt."[4] We see clearly by this passage, applicable to all the communes, that those, who formed them, were previously *subjected to a poll tax*, were *serfs*, and had *masters*.

It now remains for us to show rapidly, and as a matter of secondary importance, the form of the communes.

We distinguish in the communes two sorts of persons, the *burghers* and the dwellers (*manants*). The burghers were members of the

[1] Nul roturier doit-être reçu en temoignage pour fait de noblesse, de personne, ni de fiefs. (Cout. Nouv. de Bretagne, art. 152.)

[2] Guibert. Abbat. de Novigent., de Vita sua. Apud Script. rer. Franc., t. xii.

[3] It was, in fact, a commune formed by the serfs of the Bishop of Laon. "Homines de Lauduno... communiam ordinarunt habere, et sic perperam cogitantes a jugo servitutis cervices suas et suorum heredum excutere arbitrati sunt. At Rogerius, egregius Laudanensis episcopus regis presentiam adiit, et ecclesiæ suæ misereretur, *communiam servorum suorum delendo*, omnibus modis exoravit. (Chronic. anonym. Canonici. Laudurens. Apud Script. rer. Franc., t. xiii., p. 677.)

[4] Communio autem, novum ac pessimum nomen, sic se habet, ut capita censi omnes *solitum servitutis debitum* dominis semel in anno solvant... cæteræ censuum exactiones, quæ servis infligi solent, omnibus modis vacent. (Guibert. Abbat. de Vita sua, lib. iii., cap. vii., Apud Script. rer. Franc. t. xii.)

See the translation of M. Thierry, which will explain our idea perfectly by the omission found there. "Commune is a word, etc., which signifies that taxable people paid only once a year to their lord the dues which they owed him." It is to be remarked, that *taxable people* is not a proper translation of *capite censi*, which signifies *slave*, or *serf of the body;* and that these words of Guibert, *solitum servitutis debitum*, which confirms this meaning, are omitted.

commune; that is to say, those, who were inscribed on the registers of the municipality, and who had sworn to observe its laws. The dwellers were simply people from without, who had their domicile in the city erected into a commune, without participating in its privileges, or even natives, whom low birth made yet unworthy of the immunities of the borough.

This distinction between burghers and dwellers is remarked in the communes of antiquity, as well as in the communes of the middle ages. A passage of Thucydides shows that the burghers of Athens were called πολῖται, *cives, citizens*, and the dwellers μετοίκοι, *manentes, inhabitants*. The Roman laws also make a great distinction between the burghers, whom they called *cives*, and the dwellers, whom they called *incolæ*.[1] Besides, without having the right of burghership by birth, it could be acquired, as we have said, by an inscription on the municipal registers. Plutarch relates an inscription made at Rome, under the censorship of T. Quintius Flaminius, in favor of a great number of individuals born of free parents.[2] Thucydides also speaks, in the history of the Peloponnesian war, of many foreigners, whom the Leontines inscribed on their registers as burghers.[3] An ordinance of Philip IV., of the year 1302, likewise mentions burghers, whom it calls *recepti et annotati, received* and *inscribed;*[4] and we read in a very remarkable dissertation, introductory to the History of Paris by Felibien, that foreigners, who wished to become burghers of Paris, caused themselves to be registered at the Hotel de Ville.[5]

The inhabitants of a city, who obtained or purchased their liberty, the right of commune, organized for themselves a government at their pleasure. In general it is to be remarked that the cities, which obtained the right of commune, copied voluntarily one from another. The charter of Laon, for example, had as many imitators

[1] Cives quidem origo . . . incolas vero . . . domicilium facit. (Code of Justinian, lib. x., tit. xxxix., law vii.)

[2] Προσεδεξαντο δε πολίτας ἀπογραφὲνους παντας ὅσοι γονέων ἔλευθερων ἦσαν. (Plutarch, Flaminius, chap. xviii.)

[3] Λεοντίνοι γὰρ, ἀπελθοντων Αθηναίων ἐκ Σικελίας . . . πολίτας ἐπεγραψαντο πολλους. (Thucyd., lib. v., cap. iv.)

[4] Est enim ordonnatum quod nullus vel nulla Burgensis recipiatur aut defendatur in aliqua Burgensi, quamdiu tenebit primam in qua receptus fuit et advocatus, seu annotatus. (Ord. of Philip IV., of the year 1302, in the collection of ordinances of the kings of France. La Thomassiere, Local Customs, chap. xix.)

[5] Dissertation of M. le Roi, on the origin of the Hotel de Ville, § 9.

in the twelfth century as the English institutions in the nineteenth. This government of the communes consisted of a municipal council, in imitation of the ancient senates and areopagi. The number and names of the members of this council were very various. Peronne had twenty-two *cossors*. Tournay had thirty *jurats*. Chateauneuf, in Touraine, had ten *burghers*. The officers of the commune of Verdun were called *li communs de la ville;* those of Boussac *consuls;* those of the city of Aix selectmen, *elects;* those of Issoudun *governors;* those of Nancy *free burghers*.

At the head of this council was a magistrate differently called in different cities. Sometimes he was called the *maire*, sometimes the *maïeur*, sometimes the *prévôt*. Ordinarily there was at the head of these councils only one magistrate; sometimes, however, there were two—for example, at Tournay. The functions, as well of the councilmen as of the mayor, were generally annual and always elective. The election generally took place on the Monday after Easter, or on the feast of St. John the Baptist. Bapaume re-elected its officers every fourteen months.

The municipal magistrates took cognizance of all the affairs of the commune, administrative, civil, criminal, commercial, and police. A commune was, as we see, a complete state. It was what the small republics of antiquity were, and what the free cities of Germany are at this day. We have already said how the Edict of Moulins began the demolition of the communes by despoiling them of jurisdiction in civil matters. Half a century ago the communes perished altogether in the general shipwreck of the institutions of old France. There only remain three stones of this great edifice erected by the hands of the freed races. These are the tribunals of municipal police, the obscure jurisdiction of the *prudhommes*, (*a*) and the tribunals of commerce.

We conclude by calling attention to the singular blunder committed by the legislators of the Revolution, when they abolished the ancient division of France into parishes, to establish the division by communes. These brave men, whose great patriotism must excuse their little learning, did not remark that the commune was not an extent of territory, but a right of self-government, which certain

(*a*) These were men chosen by the fishermen of the French seaports, to have authority over the rest and keep good order among them.

cities enjoyed, and that a commune being thus a moral thing, inscribed in a charter, might very well serve as a bond of union for men, but not as the type of a geographical limit. The commune of a city was contained in a record, and not in its walls, and the grandeur of this commune depended, not on the size of the city, but upon the extent of the privileges which it enjoyed.

The legislators of the Revolution, therefore, showed themselves, perhaps, to be very good statesmen, but assuredly very poor historians, when they made of the commune, which is an idea, a territorial limit. (*a*)

(*a*) Our author's very clear and precise explanation of the French commune throws a flood of light on the present condition of France. The general, almost universal, idea in this country, which has confounded the French commune with what is understood by the English word, *communism* or *socialism*, is a great error. It is a great mistake also to confound it with *agrarianism*. It is nothing more nor less than the right of local self-government; the right of the inhabitants of a city to raise and expend their own local revenues, and to regulate their own local matters, by officers chosen by themselves from among themselves, instead of being governed by some "carpet-bagger" or "scalawag," appointed over them by some lay or ecclesiastical lord, or by some centralized despotism, called king, or emperor, or president.

M. Guizot, in his Lectures on the History of Civilization, draws a glowing picture of the advantages of centralization and monarchy over republicanism, and explains how, by a "silent and hidden process," the right of local self-government was taken from the cities and centred in the crown. Our author explains, in a note, that the object of the Edict of Moulins was to restrict the rights of the municipal judges, *for the profit* of the appointees of the king. The Bonapartists and the Legitimists, or advocates of the old Bourbon dynasty, agree with M. Guizot (who wrote in the interests of the Orleans dynasty) in his admiration for a centralized despotism. The only difference between them is, as to who shall exercise that power "*for the profit*" of his favorites — a Bonaparte, a Bourbon, or one of the house of Orleans?

The communists, on the other hand, seek to take advantage of the fall of Louis Napoleon, to *decentralize* the government into a republic, and to recover the right of local self-government, of which the "silent and hidden" process of centralization had robbed them. They are tired of "carpet-bag" and "scalawag" rule, and wish to get rid of it. We know in the South what that is. To those, who suffer under and are impoverished by it, it is equally grievous, whether inflicted by an emperor or king, through the instrumentality of a standing army, or by a radical Congress and a President, who wants to be an emperor, through the instrumentality of a Freedmen's Bureau or a Ku-Klux Bill.

The recent act of Congress, taking away the *commune* of the cities of Washington and Georgetown, *for the profit* of the appointees of the President of the United States, is another "*Edict of Moulins*" for those cities. The Ku-Klux law, which has just passed Congress, taking away the *commune* from the States, *for the profit* of the "carpet-baggers" and "scalawags," is another "*Edict of Moulins*" for the States.

This process of centralization would seem to be what our author would call a human, because universal, fact; confined to no time or country. We are beginning what republican France is seeking to put an end to. There the effort is to recover the right of local self-government; here the effort is to suppress it. Here the process is open as day, and is made noisy with the cry of *Ku-Klux!* There, though M. Guizot says it "was silent and hidden," the cities of Toulouse, Rheims, Boulogne, and Angoulême made such a noise, in defence of their rights of *commune*, that Charles IX. did not dare to do to those cities what a Radical Congress has done to what were sovereign States before there was any Congress. The difference is that here the noise is made by those, who are seeking to suppress the right of local self-government; there it was made by those, who were defending that right. In the sixteenth century that right prevailed in France; in the nineteenth, it was trodden under the foot of centralism in the United States.

Yet, after all, there must be something silent and hidden in the process; or surely the people of the North would not be so deaf as not to hear, nor so blind as not to see that, as the South is impoverished, *they* will *lose profitable customers*, and when the South is stripped of all rights of local self-government, their turn will come next.

If the right of local self-government enjoyed by a city or State, makes their inhabitants *free*, *e converso*, the negation of that right makes them *slaves*.

The enslavement of the inhabitants of the cities of Washington and Georgetown, in the *now* Territory of Columbia, "*for the profit*" of the appointees of the President, furnishes a remarkable illustration of the truth enunciated by M. Guizot, in the passages which we have quoted in our preface. Men may become "the free and intelligent artificers of a work, the plan of which they do not perceive or comprehend." The Democrats in Congress, who voted for that law, did not see that they were taking a long, long step in the process of centralization. The citizens of Washington and Georgetown, who urged it upon Congress, did not see that, in seeking to get rid of one swarm of half-gorged flies, they were exposing themselves to another more thirsty and of greater suctorial powers. Their purpose was to get relief from the burdens imposed by the corrupt officials foisted upon them by negroes, imported periodically, for the occasion, from the adjoining States of Maryland and Virginia and the fish-landings of the Potomac. But have they not mistaken the remedy? Have they not made too much haste to get well? It is sometimes better to bear the ills we have, than fly to others that we know not of. It is an old, old adage that "power is always stealing from the many to the few." And it is no less true, that as the power of the few increases, their capacity of absorption from the public treasury is magnified a thousand-fold.

This enslavement of the inhabitants of the cities of Washington and Georgetown is also an exemplification of the idea, (attributed by the old Federalists (monarchists) to Mr. John Quincy Adams,) that the only way to disgust the people of the United States with republican government, and prepare them for a transition to a monarchy, or a despotism, was to join in with the ideas of democracy, and run them to extremes. On this principle the imperialists, commonly called Radicals — those who, like Governor Holden of North Carolina, "want to see General Grant an emperor, and his son succeed him as emperor"* — have acted; and already we see the cities of the District of Columbia asking to be disenfranchised, and voluntarily surrendering that right of local self-government, which the cities of Toulouse, Rheims, Boulogne, and Angoulême successfully asserted against Charles IX. in the sixteenth century.

The people of the District have mistaken their remedy, and have swallowed an overdose of mercury, the tendency of which is to corrupt and undermine the whole constitution of republican government. They should have waited, bearing with silent and dignified endurance — as the South have borne the corrupt and infamous rulers forced upon them, through the instrumentality of the Freedmen's Bureau and martial law — until reason can regain its throne at the North, and hurl the authors of their troubles from power.

Then the freedmen will settle down to some regular labor; and range themselves in one or the other of De Cassagnac's four classes of the proletariat. They will become hirelings, beggars, prostitutes, or thieves, and will cease to be six-barrelled voting-machines, by which bad and corrupt men can climb into office, and by office put money in their purses. Then, without in any way infringing on any of the rights secured to them by the constitutional amendments, they can easily be brought to abandon the idea that less than 4,000,000 of negroes, lately slaves, can govern more than 30,000,000 of free-born whites. Then the necessity for employment or protection on the one hand, and for labor on the other, will again bring the freedmen and their late masters into kindly relations. Then the freedmen will cease to be the means of creating a disgust for democratic principles, and by fair and just treatment may in time be educated to exercise honestly and intelligently their right of suffrage.

* See testimony of Rev. J. B. Smith, principal of the normal school for the education of colored teachers, at Raleigh, N. Carolina. Sen. Doc., 42d Cong., 1st Sess., Report No. 1, page 221.

# CHAPTER VIII.

## SYMPTOMS OF THE ANCIENT COMMUNE — HIRELINGS AND BEGGARS.

TO repeat one of the principal ideas, on which the economy of this book rests, the commune is not, as now and in the present state of historic study is generally believed, a fact of modern times and Western kingdoms. It is also an error to believe that the first formation of communes dates only from the twelfth century. As we think, the commune is a general fact, universal, human, belonging to all countries and to all times; a fact, developed under the certain circumstances, which we have shown, among the Hebrews, Greeks, and Romans, as well as among us, absolutely by the same causes, and almost in the same form. There is among all peoples an element — we have said what it is — which undergoes a certain fermentation, a certain secular preparation, and when the moment arrives, is regularly, infallibly metamorphosed, and becomes the commune. This metamorphosis, we say, takes place in every country, because it operates on a human element; but it is not always taking place, because it is the supreme effect of many successive causes, which must have the natural delay of their gestation. Admitting this, it follows then that at a given time every people have their communes.

Our intention, in a matter so grave, is not only to make an assertion, but to prove it. We do not shrink from the necessity of establishing the existence of communes among the ancients. Nevertheless the reader must find it very natural that we should make the conditions of our labor as little arduous as possible, leaving to him the sincerity and strictness which it is our desire to give him. Thus we have commenced by re-establishing, as exactly as we knew how, the French commune in all the truth of its principles and in all the fidelity of its form. We have given the first place to modern, before ancient, times, because the latter are less under our hands, and are more concealed from our knowledge. In this we have had no other object than to proceed from the more known to the less known; to spare the reader the prolonged and fatiguing effort of the analysis, which we must make, to rebuild the ancient commune directly, without any point of comparison, without looking elsewhere, and collecting one by one the debris, which it has left in history; and, on the contrary, to give him the easy and complete view of the commune at an epoch near to us, in which it appears well determined and plain, to aid us afterward to recognize its principle and form at an epoch remote from us, in which it only appears, especially at the first glance, uncertain, undetermined, and doubtful.

But we must premise that we shall not be so categorical in regard to the ancient communes as we have been in reference to the French commune, or, better said, we will not be so systematic and complete. First, the important thing for us in this book is less to fix the form and mechanism of the commune among the ancients, than to remove all doubt of its existence. It is especially to this last point that we direct our efforts. Besides, we have been so explicit in everything relating to the French commune, only that we might not have to be so again in what relates to the ancient commune, which is in our opinion an historic fact exactly similar. We will, therefore, confine ourselves to presenting the different order of symptoms, which attest in the most formal manner the existence of the ancient commune, leaving the reader free to fix more or less its form, after the complete type, which we have placed before his eyes.

When we speak of the antique commune, we wish to designate the Hebrew, Greek, and Roman.

We have not yet found a natural occasion for saying why we have introduced the Jewish municipality. It is nevertheless an explanation necessary for us, and which we are going to venture here, in the form of parenthesis, without knowing precisely whether we have selected the best or the worst moment for it. We have placed, or rather we wish to place, the Jewish commune alongside of the Greek, Roman, and French; because the Jews, who are the trunk and centre of all Semitic people, may be considered as representing the East; and we desire, in the universal, human, and absolute explanation, which we wish to give of the commune, to show it always identical in the most opposite circumstances; for example, among the peoples of the East and among the peoples of the West.

The testimony which we have sought, and are going still to seek, in the Bible, is not then an effect of the desire to display our erudition, but makes an integral part of our thoughts, and is the natural stay of our subject. We resume.

We said that there are symptoms, the presence of which, sufficiently established, always infallibly certify the formation of communes. It is by the aid of these symptoms that we proceed to re-establish the ancient commune.

The first of these signs is the existence of hirelings and beggars. Without wishing to repeat on this subject what we have already said at the commencement of this book, it is evident, that in the primitive periods, that is to say, during the periods of pure slavery, there were no beggars, because each master supported his slaves. Even now, notwithstanding the very considerable decline of their primitive institutions, the European colonies of the Antilles (*a*) and of the Indian Sea have not one single beggar; and for some years, we have a sort of likeness, sufficiently faithful, of people under their primitive constitution, in the Arabs of Atlas and the Desert, where mendicity is a thing perfectly unknown, and unheard of; for this reason, that there the masters are above want, because they are masters, and the slaves also, because they are slaves; the former having all they want, since they are able to give, and the latter also, as they receive what they need from their masters. The first paupers seen since the formation of great peoples, thus come from the hireling freedmen, who, having been turned over to themselves, with little property or industry, that is to say, in the language of the economists, with a capital and a credit naturally very inconsiderable, run the risk of spending the one, and losing the other, and of being reduced to beggary for their support. Now, as the fewer hireling laborers there are in a country, the greater the chances of making a living, to find beggars among a people is a sign that the hirelings, that is to say, the freedmen, are already there in great number; and, on the other hand, as the freedmen have always and everywhere been repelled with disdain from the government, (*b*) and

(*a*) How different the condition of the West Indies, now that pauperism and beggary have become, by emancipation, the normal condition of three-fourths of the freedmen!

(*b*) The only exception, and a very notable one it is, to the general rule here laid

from the alliances of noble families, to find the freedmen numerous among any people, furnishes a strong presumption, is almost a positive indication that they form a separate association, fraternity, corporation, or commune, which are all more or less the same thing.

Here we have a sign, on the faith of which we are disposed to believe, in presence of texts from the Odyssey, from Leviticus and Deuteronomy, that there had been enfranchisements of communes among the Greeks, and among the Jews, at the time of the dispersion of the chiefs, and at the epoch of the sojourn in the desert. We have above indicated our proofs, which are the existence of hirelings and beggars. Beggars are mentioned in the Odyssey, in Hesiod, and in Leviticus. We have already said that they are not to be found in the Iliad; and in the primitive poets, above all in Homer, silence as to a great fact is almost equivalent to an affirmation, because of the scrupulous exactness with which all realities, historic, political, and even scientific, moral, and religious, are there always set forth. We say that there is no mention of paupers in

down by our author, is to be found in the condition of the Southern States, since the late war. There the freedmen now fill the legislative halls, and control the government, while their former masters, the once free citizens of a State, have been deprived of their commune, or right of self-government. This remarkable phenomenon is not without a cause, which is this: all other emancipations, of which we read in history, were made by the masters themselves, either from good-will to their slaves, or to rid themselves of the burden of their support. But in this instance, emancipation was forced upon the masters by their conquerors; and, as the avowed object of those conquerors was *to make free labor cheaper than slave labor*, that is to say, "*to reduce the wages of labor below the cost of feeding and clothing a slave and taking care of him in infancy, sickness and old age*," the war was not made upon the slaveholders because they held slaves, so much as because they voted, with the working classes of the North, to shape the legislation of the country so as to keep up the wages of labor, and keep down the cost of living. Therefore, the late masters have, since the war, been as much as possible excluded from all participation in the government; while the late slaves have been placed in power by the bayonets of the conquerors, for an additional reason, namely, because the natural tendency of the European immigrants, Germans and Irish especially, is toward the Democratic party, because of its proclivities for high wages and cheap living. Therefore, the monarchists, who despise democracy, and the capitalists, who seek to reduce wages, have sought to use the freed negro in the Southern States as a counterpoise to the Irish and Germans in the North and West.

the Iliad; but we must add, that there is in the Odyssey, a poem which we consider as a little posterior; for there is a passage in the fourth book, which says that there were no paupers in the Greek camp.[1]

Moreover, other reasons, for we give them all, those that are against us, as sincerely as those for us — other reasons cause us to affirm that, although there is no mention of paupers in the Iliad, the Trojan population must have been organized as a commune. First, mention is made of hirelings in the twenty-first book;[2] and as to the establishment of municipalities, the existence of hirelings is a sign almost as certain as the existence of paupers, as it presupposes, though in a less degree, the operation of manumissions. In the second place, in a passage of the ninth book, mention is plainly made of an association, which could be no other than a communal association, or an industrial corporation. Achilles says to Ajax, that he had been treated by Agamemnon like a wretch driven from his fraternity.[3] This passage is literally repeated in the sixteenth book, verse 59. The word *μεταναστης* by itself only signifies one banished from an association, a body, a city; but the word of contempt, *ἀτίμητος*, evidently indicates that the question was of an association much below Achilles, who was a gentleman, and often boasted of it. Finally, and we only come to proof by words, after having given the proof by facts, the expression, burgher or citizen, formally appears in the Iliad, book twenty-second.[4] We have seen, in the preceding chapter, that the word *πολίτης* expressly signifies burgher, in Thucydides. Besides, we must not forget how precise, particular, and of exact meaning the primitive writings are. Moreover, there are so many passages in Homer that establish the elevated position of the Trojan nobility, that it is not possible to ap-

[1] Αὐτὸν φωτι κατακρυπτων ἠΐσκεν
Δέκτῃ, ὃς ουδεν τοῖος ἔην ἐπι νηυσὶν 'Αχαιῶν.
(Homer. Odyssey, lib. iv., v. 247, 248.)

[2] Τότε νῶι βιησατα μισθον απαντα
Ακομὲδων ἔκπλαγος απειλησας δ'απεπεμπεν.
(Iliad, lib. xxi., v. 451, 452.)

[3] Μνησομαι, ῶς μ'ασυφηλον εν Αργειοισιν ερεξεν
Ατρειδης, ῶσει τιν' ατιμητον μεταναστην.
(Iliad, lib. ix., v. 647, 648.)

[4] Ως ἐφατο κλαίων' ἐπι δε στενὰχοντο πολιται.
(Iliad, lib. xxii., v. 429.)

ply the word πολῖται to others than the burghers. Finally, there are many other reasons, which we will present hereafter, why we do not hesitate to affirm that Troy had a commune.

---

## CHAPTER IX.

### SYMPTOMS OF THE ANCIENT COMMUNE — ARCHITECTURE.

THE second sign by which, among ancient peoples, the formation of communes is infallibly recognized, is the existence of walled cities.

We hasten to resume, and make this observation: it is a great error to imagine, without having closely examined, that the construction of houses or of cities has always been a matter of indifference, caprice, or whim, and that it would be impossible to draw from it any instruction. It is true that at present the history of architecture proves nothing, for the simple reason that there is no history of architecture. But if that history were written, we would very soon realize that architecture has its laws like every other order of facts; that intimately connected with the nature of families and their developments, it always receives a counterblow from social revolutions, and that such and such form of habitations in a country may, after thousands of years, aid the historian to recognize such or such species of inhabitants, as the shells that the laborer's plough raises to the surface cause us to say, with certainty, The sea has been here.

On our own account, and only as far as the exposition of our ideas about the ancient commune requires, we will essay to write a chapter of the history of architecture. We must be permitted meanwhile to point out the singular position of every historian of the present day, on account of the disorder, incoherence, and, above all, the insufficiency of their studies. Having ventured to describe the communal and burgher life of antiquity, it happens that we have occasion to consult on one point the history of architecture; but this history has not been written. We will have need to consult in the next chapter the history of ancient law; but that too has not been written. Whenever, then, we wish to penetrate into the critical history of an order of facts other than the list of kings, cities, and battles, we are arrested constantly by the want of certain preparatory and necessary works. Thus, having now undertaken to write the history of the ancient communes, we are forced to leave that subject, and first, for our own special use, write a small chapter of the history of architecture; like a woodman, who had started to cut down a forest, and finds it necessary to retrace his steps to forge an axe.

We were just saying that the existence of walled cities proves among ancient peoples the existence of communes. We will, in fact, show that whenever a city was enclosed with a wall, it is a proof that its houses were constructed in blocks, *en pâtés*, as we say in our language, *insulas*, as would be said in the Latin tongue. Now, on the other hand, we will show that in the commencement of all peoples, the noble families always inhabited isolated houses, and the burgher families houses built together and associated; so that a castle invariably corresponds to a gentleman, as a partition wall infallibly corresponds to two burghers.

Without going farther, we can say in two words, reserving all the developments and proof, that noble families must naturally have inhabited houses differently constructed from those of the burgher families. We have already shown that, in the first ages of every people, every chief of a family had jurisdiction. Now in all times, in antiquity as in the middle ages, the centre of the jurisdiction was the seignorial tower. For example, all the territory of the ancient Viscount of Paris was held in fee from the Tower of the Louvre. It must necessarily then have been that the residence of every noble family stood alone, because every seigniory was indivisible. In a word, architecture always represents the organization of society; for the nobles it built isolated houses; for the associated burghers, associated houses.

We regret to enter now, ever so little, on the history of the noble races, which we purpose to treat separately; but the noble races and the slave races are two great facts so intimately connected that in a multitude of cases it is impossible to speak of one without touching upon the other. There are some occasions, when they are so evidently the counterparts, the cause or the effect, the limitation or the generalization of each other, that it becomes indispensable to study them together to fully comprehend them separately. We will therefore briefly explain what the isolated houses were, to explain fully what the associated houses were.

Primitively, that is to say, before the time of emancipations — for it is necessary to go back so far, that the two histories, of the noble races, and of the slave races, may be distinct, and not encroach upon each other — primitively, an isolated house, a castle, always belonged to a gentleman, to one of the nobles, to one of the fathers, whom the poets call divine, and to this castle a tower was essential. This is fundamental and universal, and nothing is more historically correct than the expression of Horace in the ode, where he says that "death strikes equally the huts of the poor and the towers of the princely races." [1] *Turris* means strictly DONJON in this passage, and we will tell why.

In the first ode of Horace, in which the poet dedicates his verses to Mæcenas, he calls him, in his language, *atavis edite regibus*,[2] *issue of the blood of kings*, as the translators say; which, in our opinion, is a wrong construction. The difficulty of the passage is in the word *regibus*, which is erroneously translated *king*, which is the modern meaning, and not the true one in this case. First, it should be remarked that the ode of Horace is dedicatory, and consequently Mæcenas ought to be designated in it by the titles which he bore officially. He is, in fact, designated in it by the title of *rex*, which is in the ode a word of strict sense, belonging to the heraldic vocabulary of the Roman nobility, and ought to be translated in French *prince*, equally in the strict sense, and signifying what this word signifies in a name like that of M. le Prince d'Henin, or M. le Prince de la Tremoille. Mæcenas, in fact, took in the public acts the title of rex, which proves very clearly that it does not signify king, as the translators of Horace think. Besides, a passage of Plutarch is very explicit on this point, for he

[1] Pallida mors æquo pulsat pede pauperum tabernas
*Regumque turres.* (Horat. Carmin., lib. i., od. iv.)

[2] Mæcenas, atavis edite regibus. (Horat. Carmin., lib. i., od. i., v. 1.)

says that there were at Rome four families, the Mamerci, the Calpurnii, the Pomponii, and the Pinarii, who alone had the right of signing and taking the title of *reges*. Plutarch adds that these four families justified this title, in saying that they were descended from Numa.[1] Now, Mæcenas was of one of these families. It results from this passage of Plutarch that the explanation, true or false, of the origin of the title of *prince*, given by the four families which bore it, was invented too late. It is thus that the first-born of the house of Rohan also justify their title of prince, by saying that they were descended from the dukes of Brittany, which is only half true; for they are descended from them, but only through the females. All that we have said of the princely title of Mæcenas will be strengthened by the evidence in the second volume of this work, which will treat of the noble races, and in which we will essay to revive the principles which regulated proper names, the blazon, the titling, in fine, all the heraldic ceremonial of the Greek and the Roman nobility.

We have then shown that in the verse of Horace, of which we speak, the word *rex* signifies prince. Now this signification, which is the true one, reacts upon that of the word *turris*, in the same verse, which does not mean simply *tower*, but *seignorial tower*, *donjon*. In its character of a seignorial house, the house of a gentleman, that of a Mæcenas, ought to have had a *donjon*. It, in fact, had one. Horace mentions it in an ode, in which he writes to Mæcenas that he will be happy to drink with him under his roof.[2]

[1] Οι δε προς ταύτη τεσσαρας ὑιοὺς αναγραφουσιν αυτοὺ (Νουμας), Πομπωνα, Πινον, Καλπον, Μαμερκον, ὧν ἕκαστον οἰκου διαδοχην και γενους ἐντίμου καταλεπειν· είναι γαρ ἀπὸ μεν τοὺ Πομπωνος τους Πομπωνίους, ἀπὸ δέ Πινου τους Πίναρίους, ἀπὸ δέ Καλπου τους Καλπουρνίους, απο δε Μαμερκου τους Μαμερκίους· οἱς διὰ τοῦτο και ρηγας γενεσθαι παρανύμιον, ὅπερ ἐστι βασιλέας. (Plutarch, Numa, ch. xxi.)

The text of this passage proves very clearly that *reges*, in the present case, was a technical word, and did not signify *king*, since Plutarch, who could not translate it strictly into Greek, *Grecianizes* it, and renders it by ρηγας, adding only for his Greek readers that this word means to say, in their language, βασιλέας; but that was only the approximative and derivative sense, since the primitive and proper sense had no corresponding word in the Greek language, unless ρηγας, which is a barbarism.

[2] Quando
Tecum sub *alta*, sic quando Jovi gratum *domo*,
Beate Mæcenas, bibam? (Horat. Epod., lib. od. 9.)

Besides, this tower is expressly named by Suetonius, who says that Nero went up into it to see the burning of Rome.[1]

The characteristic of all the houses of the nobles was, as we have said, to have a tower, and to be isolated. It is a principle, which has no exception among any people in the primitive times. Thus, in the Iliad, Patroclus and Hector are mentioned as having a high house,[2] and, in the Æneid, Turnus also has one.[3]

More than that. We may descend from the Homeric times to those nearer the Christian era, without ceasing to find isolation and the tower the characteristic signs of seignorial houses. In the Anabasis, Xenophon cites a village without walls, and consequently, as we will show, a village of nobles, whose houses were surmounted by towers,[4] and a little farther on he also mentions a chief of a tribe of Asia Minor, who lived in a tower.[5]

The history of the Jews is full of analogous facts. To limit our examples, we will cite Demetrius, King of Syria, who inhabited, at some distance from Antioch, a castle with four great towers,[6] and Herod the Great, who built, sixty stadii from Jerusalem, a pleasure castle, which also had towers at its extremities.[7]

As to the Romans, Suetonius relates that Augustus, being still an infant, disappeared one day from the family country-seat, where he was raised, and that the women, after a long search, found him at the top of the tower.[8] As to the form of these towers, it appears that they were round, and that they were at the angles of the building. This, at least, is what is proved by a tower almost entire in a Roman wall, which may be seen in the curious *Pelasgian Museum*

[1] Hoc incendium e turri Mæceatiana prospectans. (Sueton. Tranquil., Nero, Claudius Cæsar. cap. xxxvi.)

[2] Ὑψερεφὲς μέγα δῶμα. (Hom. Iliad., lib. xix., v. 333.)
Δόμου ὑψηλοῖο. (Hom. Iliad., lib. xxii., v. 440.)

[3] Tectis hic Turnus in *altis*. (Virg. Æneid., lib. vii., v. 443.)

[4] Εἰς δὲ ἣν ἀφίκοντο κώμην, μεγάλη τε ἦν, και Βασίλειον τε εἶχε τῷ σατράπῃ, και ἐπὶ ταῖς πλείσταις οἰκίαις τύρσεις ἐπῆσαν. (Xenophon, Anabasis, lib. iv., ch. iv., § 2.)

[5] 'Ο δ' ἦν εν τύρσεί μάλα φυλαττόμενος. (Xenophon, Anabasis, lib. vii., cap. ii., § 21.)

[6] 'Αποκλείσας γὰρ αὐτὸν εἰς τετραπύργιον τί Βασιλειον, ὁ κατεσκεὐασεν ἀυτός οὐκ ἄποχεν τῆς Αντιοχείας, οὐδένα πρυσίετο. (Flavius Josephus, Antiq. Judæorum, lib. xiii., cap. iii.)

[7] Προσκατεσκευάσατο φρούριον ἐπί τόπον . . . φύσει δε ἰσχυρὸν . . . διείλεπται δέ κυκλωτερέσι πυργοις. (Flav. Joseph., Antiq. Jud., lib. xv., cap. xii.)

[8] Diu quæsitus, tandem in altissima turre repertus est. (Sueton. Tranquil., Oct. Cæsar Aug., c. 114.)

of M. Petit-Radel. The houses of the German nobles made no exception to this rule of seignorial houses. Tacitus relates that the Roman ambassadors sent to Velleda found her in a tower, which she made her habitual residence.[1]

Moreover, it is certain that the towers of these castles were intended for defence, for they were fortified in the country, and in the cities they stood apart by themselves. In the Odyssey, the house of Ulysses, which likewise had its tower, on which the eagles perched,[2] was girt by a wall, and its entrance was closed by a solid double door.[3] Within this enclosure were kept the greyhounds of the chatelain,[4] and, what will perhaps surprise, the geese raised by the chatelainess.[5] This house, then, nearly resembled those castles of the fourteenth century, which are still to be seen in Bourbonnais and Quercy. Homer adds that only the house of Ulysses, among all those of the neighborhood, was thus constructed.

In the history of Greece and Asia Minor we frequently find these fortified castles, even at epochs much later than Homeric times. Alcibiades had one in Chersonesus.[6] These castles in the Greek chronicles bore the name of τεῖχος or that of βασίλειον, as one would say *chateau-fort*, or Palais-Royal; but a great number of texts establish that, whatever their name, they were always provided with towers. In the Anabasis, Xenophon speaks of a castle of King

[1] Legati ad... Velledam missi cum donis... ipsa edita in turre. (Tacitus, lib. iv., cap. lxv.)

[2] . . . Ὅ μοι αἰετὸς ἔκτανε χῆνας,
Ἀψ δ' ἐλθων κατ' ἄρ' ἕξετ' ἐπὶ προὔχοντι μελάθρῳ.
(Odys., lib. xix., v. 543, 544.)

[3] . . . Ἐπήσκηται δέ οἱ αὐλὴ
Τοίχω και θριγκοῖσι, θύραι δ' εὐερκέες εἰσίν
Δικλίδες.
(Odys., lib. xvii., v. 266–268.)

[4] Ἂν δὰ κύων κεφαλήν τε καὶ οὔατα κείμενος ἔσχεν
Ἄργος, Ὀδυσσῆος ταλασίφρονος, ὅν ῥά ποτ' αὐτὸς
Θρέψε μεν.
(Odys., lib. xvii., v. 291–293.)

[5] . . . Χῆνας ἐνὶ μεγάροισι νόησα,
Πυρὸν ἐρεπτομένους παρὰ πύελον.
(Odys., lib. xix., v. 552, 553.)

[6] Λαβὼν τειήρη μίαν, ἀπέπλευσεν ἐς Χεῤῥονήσον, ἐς τὰ ἑαυτοῦ τείχη. (Xenophon, Hellenic., lib. i., ch. v.)

Asidates, which had a tower with ramparts,[1] and contained a strong garrison. A little lower he adds that after having undermined this castle, they found the walls to be eight bricks in thickness.[2] In the Cyropedia, Xenophon mentions the castle of a chief named Gobryas. He adds that this castle was strong.[3] It results from another passage that the tower of this castle must have had a platform with battlements, for it was furnished with machines of war.[4]

In Virgil we find this kind of fortified castles very positively mentioned in two places, in the Æneid[5] and in the Georgics.[6] As to seignorial houses in enclosed cities, they stood apart and on an elevation. Those of Priam, Hector, and Paris were all three separated, as Homer relates.[7] Virgil says as much of that of Anchises, and of that of King Latinus.[8]

All the testimony, which we have collected, in relation to the houses of the nobles in primitive times, are then unanimous on these two points, that they had a tower, and that they were isolated. The tower was a sign of seignorial jurisdiction, and the isolation was a consequence of the paternal jurisdiction. We have already observed

[1] Πυργομαχοῦντες δ'επεὶ οὐκ ἐδύναντο λαβεῖν τὴν τύρσιν, ὑψηλὴ γὰρ ἦν, καί μεγάλη, καί προμαχεῶνας, καὶ ἄνδρας πολλοὺς, καὶ μαχίμους ἔχουσα, διορύττειν ἐπεχείρησαν τὸν πύργον. (Xenophon, Anab., lib. vii., cap. viii., § 13.)

[2] 'Ο δε τοῖχος ἦν ἐπὶ ὀκτὼ πλίνθων γηίνων τὸ εὖρος. (Xenophon, Anab., lib. vii., cap. viii., § 14.)

[3] "Εχω δὲ καὶ τεῖχος ἰσχυρὸν, καὶ χώρας ἐπάρχω πολλῆς. (Xenophon, Cyrop., lib. iv., cap. vi., § 2.)

[4] . . . γίγνονται πρὸς τῷ Γωβρύου χωρίῳ, καὶ ὁρῶσιν ὑπερισχυρὸν τε τὸ ἔρυμα, καὶ ἐπὶ τῶν τειχῶν πάντα παρεσκευάσμένα, ὡς ἂν κράτιστα ἀπομάχοιτο. (Xenophon, Cyrop., lib. v., cap. ii., § 2.)

[5] Aut montana sedet circum castella sub armis.
(Virgil, Æneid, lib. v., v. 440.)

[6] . . . Norica si quis
Castella in tumulis.
(Virgil, Georg., lib. iii., v. 473, 474.)

[7] "Εκτωρ δὲ πρὸς δῶματ' 'Αλεξάνδροιο Βεβήκει
Καλὰ, τὰ ῥ αὐτὸς ἔτευξε σύν ἀνδράσιν, οἵ τότ' ἄριστοι
Ησαν ἐνί Τροίῃ ἐριβώλακι τέκτονες ἄνδρες·
Οἵ οἱ ἐποίησαν θάλαμον καί δῶμα, καί αὐλήν,
Εγγύθι τε Πριάμοιο, καί "Ερτορος, ἐν πόλει ἄρκῃ.
(Iliad, lib. vi., 313–317.)

[8] Anchisæ domus arboribus obtecta recessit. (Æneid., lib. ii., v. 300.) Tectum augustum, horrendum sylvis. (Æneid., lib. vii., v. 313–317.)

that it is not difficult to give the reasons for this latter fact. The general and primitive fact, on which the historic value of families rests, is the paternal power, and the paternal power itself rests on an uninterrupted succession of noble ancestors. Now, this paternal power, exercised in the name of ancestors, had its seat by the hearth, which was, in some sort, the sanctuary of domestic justice. Coriolanus, banished from Rome, went to seat himself by the hearth of Tullus, King of the Volscians. It was precisely there, that the fathers of families offered sacrifices to the gods of their houses, who were called the gods of parents, *divi parentum*,[1] in the same manner as the Bible says: *the God of our fathers, the God of Abraham, of Isaac, and of Jacob.* Now, as in a whole noble family there was but one father, in a noble house there could be but one hearth, but one sanctuary, but one tribunal; and, as a stranger could not participate in the paternal power of a noble, so a house near to the house of a noble did not participate in the sanctity of its hearth. The paternal authority of a noble was a perfect whole; the house of a noble was another.

The association of houses, that is to say, the creation of the party wall, is contemporaneous with the association of the freedmen, and the creation of burghers. It is a very difficult history, but one very important, and which we can only sketch.

And, first, it is a general fact for all the primitive cities, that they were formed by the accumulation of houses built around a castle.

The birth of cities, and the epoch of their infancy, when they were still in the condition of feudal villages, is one of the most curious spectacles in history. The Greek chronicles furnish abundant examples of these primitive boroughs, the houses of which were grouped around a seignorial castle. Xenophon mentions the castle of the satrap Pharnabases, around which villages were built.[2] Elsewhere, he also mentions the castle of the King of the Mossynæcians, situated also in the centre of a village; and what he says of it is very conclusive of the general principle, which we have laid down; for he

[1] Sei. Parentum. puer. verberit. Ast. oloe. plora. Sit. *diveis parentum*. Sacer. Estod. (Codex Papyrian., leg. 30. Terrass., History of Roman Jurisprudence.)

[2] Xenophon, Hellenic., lib. iv., cap. i., § 15.

relates that this king or this seignior protected the village, and that its inhabitants paid him, for so doing, an annual tribute.[1]

Asia Minor does not present the only examples of this accumulation of men of the slave race around a seignorial castle. The same fact is found in what Plutarch relates of the foundation of Athens by Theseus, and of Rome by Romulus. There was this peculiarity of certain cities of ancient Greece, that, instead of being formed around a castle, they were founded around a temple. It was always a vassalage and a seigniory. Such were the cities of Delphos and Olympia. They were sacred cities, to which the temple, which was in the centre, served as a safeguard; and became free early, governing themselves and having jurisdiction.[2] This explains how these two cities were almost the only ones of Greece, which were at the same time cities having a commune and not having walls.[3]

In our middle ages, this phenomenon of little cities founded under the protection of a seignior, baron, or abbé, is presented with exactly the same characteristics as in Asia Minor, Greece, and ancient Italy. A chronicler of the twelfth century relates that Louis VII. founded, under his protection, a multitude of *new cities*, which did great wrong to the monasteries and seigniors of their vicinity, whose slaves came thither for refuge.[4] As we go back in the history of France, analogous examples multiply. In 1118, a charter permitted the monks of Machecoul to build a free borough.[5] On the 28th July, 1100, another charter determined and sanctioned the enclosure of the borough of Nogaro, in the territory of the church of Sainte Marie d'Auch, which is at this day a principal town of the canton.[6] In 1080, one Archambaud de Liriac, near Ancenis, gave to a monastery lands, on which to build a borough.[7]

When these nascent cities were thus founded around a castle or a temple, the castle or the temple always occupied the high ground, and the houses were extended *en échelon* on the plain.

[1] Xenophon, Anabasis., lib. v., cap. iv., § 26.
[2] Thucydides, lib. v., chap. xviii.
[3] Xenophon, Hellenic., lib. iii., ch. ii., § 27.
[4] Quasdam villas novas ædificabit, per quas plures ecclesias et milites de propriis suis hominibus ad eas confugientibus, exhæredasse non est dubium. (Apud Script. rer. Franc. t. xii., p. 286.)
[5] D. Morice, Preuve de l'Hist. de Bretagne, t. i., col. 541.
[6] Chroniq. eccles. d'Auch., part iii., preuve, p. 62.
[7] D. Morice, Preuve de l'Histoire de Bretagne, t. i., col. 451.

For example, as to Troy, Homer relates that Dardanus, son of Jupiter, built his castle upon a height, and that long afterward he built in the plain the sacred city of Ilium, for men speaking different languages, who had till then lived at the foot of Mount Ida.[1] It is evident on the one hand, that the city of Ilium was called *sacred* because it served as an asylum; and on the other, that these men, speaking different languages, and consequently belonging to different nations, who lived at the foot of Mount Ida, and came together in the city, were slaves or freedmen; because it is not to be supposed that free men, nobles of different nations, should naturally be found brought together at the foot of Mount Ida. Plato, in his treatise on the laws, speaks of the advantage which he had of possessing only slaves speaking different languages, to avoid complots by the difficulty of communication.[2]

To the example of Troy, we should add, among many others, that of Athens. Thucydides says expressly that Athens was commenced by the citadel, which at first was all the city.[3] Those, who are familiar with the Greek history and language, know that nearly all the cities had then within their enclosure a castle situated on a height, and bearing at Athens the name of Acropolis, at Corinth the name of Acrocorinthus, and so of others. Thucydides adds that the circumference of the citadel, which had been formerly all of primitive Athens, still bore in his time the name of πολις, that is to say *city*,[4] (πολίτης, *burgher*,) a word which must not be confounded with ἄστυ, which designated the modern city. All the important cities of Europe at this day, and among others Paris and London, have thus two names, like Athens. They are called *city* (*cité*) in their ancient part, where was, at London the seignorial tower of the kings of England, at Paris the palace of the kings of France; and *town* (*ville*) in their modern part.

Moreover, the building of seignorial residences on the heights and of the houses of the freedmen on the plain, was a thing so noticed by the ancients that to designate a noble, they almost always said, "*a man born in a high place*," and to designate a burgher, one of the commonalty, they said, "a man born in a low place." The examples of this sort of speech are so numerous that we find

[1] Iliad, lib. xx., v. 216–218.

[2] Plato de Legibus, lib. vi.

[3] Thucydides, lib. ii., ch. xv.

[4] Ibid.

some embarrassment in choosing from them. They are found in Titus Livius,[1] in Cicero,[2] in Valerius Maximus,[3] in the treatise on illustrious men attributed to Pliny,[4] and in a hundred other places, into the detail of which we think it useless to enter. This mode of speech of the ancients even remains in our language, for we say, "a high-born man," "low-born man."

Thus we are now certain that the houses of the nobles had the several characteristics, which we have attributed to them, viz.: that they were isolated and had a tower; the isolation to mark the seignorial authority; the tower to mark the military authority. We pass on now to the houses of the burghers, and will show that they were grouped together in masses, in blocks, as we have said, and then, for their common defence, they were enclosed by a wall of circumvallation, and formed the walled cities.

There were among the ancients two kinds of cities: some, which may be called cities of nobles and which were open; others, which we may call cities of burghers, and which were walled.

The cities of nobles, were found among the peoples, with whom emancipations, still restricted, had not produced a great mass of freedmen, and consequently had not necessitated the establishment of communes. In general, the peoples, among whom emancipations were slow, were mediterranean and agricultural, while the islanders and inhabitants of the coasts, addicted to piracy and commerce, arrived much sooner at the communal and democratic life.[5] The cities of the agricultural peoples were open, because they were composed of isolated houses, or rather because they were only an assemblage of some strong castles, having the dwellings of the serfs or vassals around them.

The ancient Sabines were of these pastoral and aristocratic peoples, who inhabited open cities.[6] The Cisalpine Gauls were a nation of the same kind, and their cities had no walls.[7] This fact

[1] . . . Tanaquil summo loco nata. (Titus Livius, decad. i., lib. i., ch. xxxiv.)

[2] . . . Sed tamen tres fratres, summo loco natos. (Cicero, Epist., lib. ii., epistle 18.)

[3] Lucius Petronius . . . admodum humili loco natus, ad equestrem ordinem pervenerat. (Val. Max. Hist., lib. iv., ch. vii., § 5.)

[4] Caius Marius septies consul, Harpinas, humili loco natus. (De Vir. Illust., incert. auctor., cap. lxvii., § 1., Apud Aurel. Victor.)

[5] Thucydides, lib. i., cap. viii.

[6] Plutarch, Romulus, ch. xvi.

[7] Polybius, lib. ii., ch. xvii., § 9.

relative to the Gauls is all the more characteristic, since Polybius adds that they lived in seignorial state and had vassals.[1] Neither had the Germans of the time of Tacitus, in their towns, houses, united by a party wall,[2] and we know that it was only a little before the middle of the fourth century, about 330, that the Emperor Henri l'Oiseleur caused the cities of Germany to be walled. Thucydides represents the Etolians, the Acarnanians, and the Locrians as people who were at the same time agricultural and warlike, always with sword in hand, like the barons of the middle ages.[3] Afterward he adds that they all inhabited castles in the centre of different boroughs, without walls of enclosure, according to the primitive usage of Greece.[4] The noble and open city most curious to study of all antiquity was Sparta. Xenophon says formally, in two places, in the Life of Agesilaus,[5] and in the Hellenics,[6] that Sparta had no walls. Thucydides affirms the same fact, and explains it by saying that the city occupied a great extent of territory, being composed of isolated houses, surrounded by cultivated fields.[7] It elsewhere appears that the isolated houses were seignorial residences, castles more or less fortified ; for Xenophon relates that, during an incursion of the Thebans into the territory of Sparta, the Lacedemonians placed an ambuscade of three hundred hoplites in the castle of the Tyndarides, which made part of the city.[8] Plutarch likewise says that Sparta had no walls, and he explains the fact in another manner, in saying that there was in the city no company of tradesmen, no trades' union, and consequently no communal association.[9] Thus, in recapitulating these three equally formal testimonies, we arrive at this striking result: First, Xenophon testifies that Sparta had no outer walls; secondly, Thucydides testifies that she had no party walls ; thirdly, Plutarch testifies that she had no corporation of working-men, and consequently no commune.

[1] Polybius, lib. ii., ch. xvii., § 12.

[2] Ne pati quidem inter se junctas sedes. Colunt discreti ac diversi, ut fons, ut campus, ut nemus placuit. Vicos locant, non in nostrum morem, *connexis* et *cohærentibus* edificiis: suam quique domum *spatio circumdat.* (Tacitus, Germania, cap. xvi.)

[3] Thucydides, lib. i., ch. v.

[4] Thucydides, lib. iii., ch. xciv.

[5] Xenophon, Agesilaus, ch. ii., § 24.

[6] Xenophon, Hellenics, lib. vi., ch. v., § 28.

[7] Thucydides, lib. i., ch. x.

[8] Xenophon, Hellenics, lib. vi., ch. v., § 31.

[9] Plutarch, Lycurgus, ch. xxiv.

Nevertheless, as the theory which we develop in this chapter will gain nothing by being specious, if it is not solid, and we desire to reply not only to the objections of others, but to our own, we must confess that these three imposing witnesses, whom we have just cited, appear to be formally contradicted by a fourth of great weight in history. Polybius affirms in two places that Sparta had walls.[1]

We hasten to say that the contradiction is only apparent. Xenophon and Thucydides speak of Sparta as she was in their time, more than 400 years before the Christian era. Polybius speaks of Sparta as she was in his, only 30 years before the Christian era. The walls of Sparta, then, were only an accident, since Polybius speaks expressly of their demolition, and Plutarch, posterior by more than a century to Polybius, has no account of them. We add some details, which confirm instead of attacking our theory.

In the mutilated state, in which the Greek chronicles have reached us, the history of Sparta is very incomplete. At the epoch of which the fragments of Polybius speak, Sparta had undergone a popular revolution; the seignorial population of the city had been banished, their property confiscated, and a kind of insurrectional commune, of which a person named Chæron appears to have been the soul,[2] had been installed, and had surrounded the city with walls, which were afterward destroyed by the Acheans. Thus — and this fact seems to us very remarkable — as long as Sparta was a city of nobles, she was open, and when she became a communal city she was walled.

Moreover, there are in the Greek history of the fourth and fifth centuries before the Christian era, two conclusive examples, which establish, as we have said, that every walled city was a communal city. First, Thucydides relates that the people of Samos, having massacred a part of the noble population, and driven out the rest, immediately erected themselves into a commune, at the instigation of the Athenians,[3] and immediately afterward surrounded with walls the city, which until then had been open.[4] Secondly, Xenophon

[1] Polybius, lib. xxii., fragm. iii., ch. xii., § 3; vii. § 6.
[2] Polybius, lib. xxv., fragm. v., ch. vii., § 1.
[3] Thucydides, lib. viii., ch. xxi.
[4] Thucydides, lib. viii., ch. iv.

relates that the Spartans, wishing to revenge themselves on the Mantineans, decided to take from them the popular or communal government, and for that reason ordered them to demolish their walls, which had been recently built.[1] The Mantineans having resisted this injunction, the Spartans forced them to resume the government of the nobles; that is, they pulled down the walls of the city, and re-established the burgher population in villages around the castles, *according to ancient usage.*[2]

Thus, when the city of Samos obtained a commune, she was enclosed by walls; and when the city of Mantinea lost her commune, she saw her walls destroyed. Walls of enclosure are, then, among the ancients, as we have said, a certain sign of the formation of a commune.

Thus, the walled cities were those burgher cities, of which we have spoken above. They were inhabited by freedmen, they had a municipal government, and their houses were contiguous. We have already seen that in the open cities generally, and especially in Sparta, the houses were isolated.[3] We can show that in the walled cities, on the contrary, the houses were contiguous. For example, as to Platea, which was a walled city, Thucydides gives the details of a siege by the Thebans, from which it results that the houses had party walls.[4] On the other hand, every kind of association which accompanies the commune, is found in the walled cities, and wanting in the open cities. Thus all the closed cities of Greece had a public treasury; Sparta, which was an open city, had none.[5] Thus again, Thucydides mentions a city of Bœotia, named Mycalessa, which had a public school,[6] an infallible sign of a commune, because noble families have all their children educated by private tutors. Now, he immediately adds that the city was walled.[7] Finally, Xenophon speaks of Tegea, a city which had a *communal house*, town hall, (hotel de ville,) and Tegea was enclosed with walls.[8]

At first, however, the burgher houses were not built in blocks,

[1] Thucydides, lib. viii., ch. li.; Xenoph., Hellen., lib. v., ch. ii., § 1.

[2] Xenophon, Hellen., lib. v., ch. ii., § 7.

[3] Thucydides, lib. i., ch. iii.

[4] Thucydides, lib. ii., ch. iii.

[5] Thucydides, lib. i., ch. lxxx.

[6] Thucydides, lib. vii., ch. xxix.

[7] Thucydides, lib. vii., ch. xxix.

[8] There is a passage which says that the Thebans, having taken Tegea and many prisoners, filled the city prison and the *town hall* with them; and a passage in the same chapter proves that Tegea had walls. (Xenoph., Hellen., lib. vii., ch. iv., § 36.

12

neither had they a party wall. The first freedmen and fugitives were too poor to build houses of stone; and, strictly speaking, it was not until a large number of them had been brought together at one point and had somewhat improved their primitive settlements, that street and road laws came into existence and introduced some regularity into what may be called the police of houses. In taking for example the history of the Roman road laws, all these ideas come to light and are wonderfully strengthened. Thus, although Rome had a species of commune from her foundation, this commune did not take the essential characteristics of a municipality until toward the year of Rome 260, at the time of the creation of the tribunes and ædiles, a creation which established a burgher magistracy with a civil jurisdiction, analogous to the right of magistracy established in the communes of France, until the Edict of Moulins, under Charles IX. Also we find that before the complete formation of the Roman commune, that is to say, before the creation of ædiles, the regularly built houses, which all belonged to the nobility, were isolated one from the other.[1] Tacitus also testifies that after the burning of Rome by the Gauls, in the year 390 B. C., and consequently fifty-three years before the entry of the burghers into the prætorship, which took place in the year of Rome 416, and which was the veritable sanction of the communal institution, the houses were separated from each other within the enclosure of the city.[2] This state of ancient Rome may be compared to the state of ancient Paris, filled with mansions with battlemented towers, and where even the burgher houses were mostly separated, because they were built on small lands held by feudal tenure.

It was by degrees, and principally toward the time of the emperors, that the burgher houses of Rome were grouped in blocks, always excepting the dwellings of the nobles, which remained for a long time still separated. With Augustus commenced the urban *services*, which were the result of this new order of things. He fixed the height of houses, so that one should not intercept the light of the other.[3] Under Nero appeared the laws produced by

[1] This results from the terms of the law of the Twelve Tables relative to buildings, and which is thus mentioned by Varro: Ambitus, iter quod circumeundo teritur; nam ambitus circumitus, ab eoque Duodecim Tabularum interpretes ambitus parietis circumitum esse describunt. (Varro, de Lingua Latina, lib. iv.)

[2] Tacitus, Annals, lib. xv., cap. xliii. [3] Strabo, Geograph., lib. v., cap. iii.

the party wall, and which, in the laws upon *services*, bear the names of *oneris ferendi, tigni immittendi, non officiendi luminibus*, and some others. Thus houses required nearly eight centuries in passing from the system of isolation to that of association, just the time required for the freedmen to enter the senate, and to conquer without dispute a participation in political affairs. Plutarch, recounting the privilege granted by the Roman senate to Valerius Publicola for his great services, of opening the door of his house outward, adds that anciently all the doors of Greece opened in this way.[1] This independence of the houses and the species of seigniory which they exercised around them, even on the public highway, is the characteristic of the epoch anterior to the establishment of the freedom of cities, and the point of departure for architecture; the *urban services*, commencing under Augustus and completed under Nero, are the characteristics of the epoch essentially municipal, and the point of arrival for architecture.[2] She has for *alpha* the door opening outward and the tower; for *omega*, the door opening inward and the party wall.

Now it must be comprehended that the wall of enclosure is the natural and necessary complement of burgher houses, constructed *en pâté*, that is, associated, and that it is to a commune what a line of circumvallation is to a camp. The wall is in effect the unity of defence applied to the multiplied interests drawn together, combined and united. Generally, the isolated house, the castle, has no wall of enclosure, being itself a sort of citadel with its tower. The burgher house, on the contrary, is much too poor to have its own tower; it is united to its equals in blocks, and all together, as one and the same corporation, are surrounded by one and the same wall, which is their common defence. It is to be remarked in history that as soon as a slave, in consequence of some political revolution, becomes ennobled, or even a burgher, he at once hastens to give to his poor house the distinctive sign of no-

[1] Plutarch, Publicola, ch. xx.

[2] This distinction between doors opening outward and doors opening inward was profound in the ideas of the Romans. The former were called *fores*, and the latter *janua*. It results from a passage of Tertullian that Janus was the god who presided over the latter, and Foreculus the god who presided over the former. See this passage: At enim Christianus nec januam suam laureis infamabit, si novit quantos deos etiam ostiis diabolus affixerit, Janum a Janua . . . Foreculum a foribus. (Tertul. de Corona, cap. xiii.)

bility, which is the battlemented tower. The serf of the church of Veselay, who showed himself the boldest in the revolt against the abbé, during the insurrection, and the attempt to establish a commune, built a superb tower to his hut, and certainly one of his greatest griefs must have been to see it fall under the victorious hammer of the chapter.[1] (*a*)

The wall of enclosure is not the only monument of unity which the communal association has produced. There is the town hall, the hotel de ville, which is to the civil side of the commune what the wall of enclosure is to the military. Considered in its unity, the commune has a seignorial existence; it has its law, its judge, its gallows, its hangman. Being thus sovereign, it gives place for an architecture, which enters into the conditions of the architecture of the nobility, that is to say, which ends in an isolated house with its tower; with this difference, nevertheless, that it in a manner divides up this house, only preserving at the centre its hearth, which is the seat of justice in the town hall, and moving its tower, which is the symbol of its power, to the ramparts.

We believe that we have now sufficiently established by all the considerations we have presented, that a city has walls of enclosure only when the houses have not towers, when they are not isolated; that is, when they are built in blocks and with party walls, and that these two last characteristics are an infallible sign of a free borough. Whence we conclude that whenever we find a walled city in the primitive books, it is a proof that they were composed at an epoch when a communal institution existed.

Thus the Hebrews had communes from the time of Moses, since mention is made of walled cities in many places of Leviticus; and the Greeks from the time of Homer, since the city of Troy was enclosed by a wall. It is to be remarked that among the large

[1] Hugues de Poitiers, Chron. de Veselay, liv. iv.

(*a*) This remark of our author calls to mind the fact, that Senator Wilson, of Massachusetts, originally a shoemaker, having grown rich by politics, now belongs to, and is a leader of, that party, which carried fire and sword through the Southern States, in order to "*make free labor cheaper than slave labor;*" to reduce the wages of white shoemakers below the cost of feeding and clothing a negro; and whose whole legislation is intended, and tends, to cheapen labor and enrich capital.

number of cities named in the Iliad and the Odyssey, Homer mentions with great care those that had walls, and that the number was very inconsiderable as compared to the number of those that had none. There are near a hundred cities, at least, cited by Homer, and of this number four only had walls, including Troy, namely, Thyrintha, Gortyna, and Calydon.[1]

We would not insist longer on this point, if the matter of which we treat was not so new and unusual, and if the historic theory, which we present, had not so many chances of passing for strange and paradoxical. We do not attach too much importance to the serious difficulties, which may be opposed to what we have said. Nevertheless, we do not wish to seem to advance lightly opinions on such grave matters. We therefore present another kind and series of proofs establishing beyond reply, as it seems to us, that walled cities are really burgher or communal cities.

---

## CHAPTER X.

### SYMPTOMS OF THE ANCIENT COMMUNE—JURISPRUDENCE.

THE new proofs by which we have to establish the existence of the ancient communes, belong to the history of jurisprudence, and are drawn from the fundamental difference to be observed between property within the enclosure of a city, and property without its walls.

As in the preceding chapter, we are forced again for a moment to leave our subject and make a digression before pursuing our route. We are convinced that the history of property would aid us to prove that with the ancients walled cities were always, as we have said, municipal cities; but the history of property has not been written any more than the history of architecture. We will therefore essay to sketch it, but only within the limits that the necessity of the subject imposes, and will give to it only that just degree of importance necessary to present its results.

[1] Iliad, lib. ii., v. 559, v. 646; lib. ix., v. 552.

Taking property in its most general aspects and in its most summary history, we find that it is always constituted from the same point of view as the family; and this is what we understand by these words.

There is an order of families which are, if we may so speak, constituted to last always, and always in the same condition; in which the son is the exact continuation of the father in his rights, in his prerogatives, and in his actions; and in which the first and most sacred of all duties is to maintain and leave after him all things in the state, in which they were maintained and left by his ancestors. These are the noble families.

There is another order of families, of which it may be said that they recommence with every generation; in which there is no precise domestic tradition necessary to be observed under penalty of historic loss, and in which the sons are much more occupied in establishing and building up themselves than in continuing their ancestors. These are the burgher families.

Now history proves that in these two orders of families, property is constituted like the families themselves; that is, it is perpetual and entailed in the first, movable and alienable in the second.

What we have said of property in the two kinds of families which fill history, and which are the family of the man of noble race, and the family of the man of slave race, is fully confirmed by the property of another species of family, which is, if one may so speak, the third of the genus, the corporation. The corporation, in effect, whether religious, commercial, or communal, constitutes in a measure a family, in that it is reproduced. Now the corporation is not only reproduced, but it is reproduced perpetually. Its members die, but it is renewed and lives always. Well, the property of the corporation, which has the characteristic of the noble family in that it is perpetual, is always entailed and inalienable, like the property of the noble family. We will return to this subject.

Property, we have said, is always constituted like the family. We have added to these words the explanation they require. The family is constituted in two ways, according to the nature of the noble races and according to the nature of the slave races; or rather there are two sorts of families. There are, then, two sorts of property. Let us take first noble property.

Noble property corresponds to the noble family, and undergoes the same number of revolutions. Now the noble family has two ways of being successive. Primitively, as we have established, all the noble family was in the father, and was summed up in him. The father absorbed the wife, the son, the daughter, the servant, all persons that had neither right nor individuality outside of his will, who were less persons than things. In this state of the noble family the property in land resided in the father as absolutely as the property in the persons and life of the wife, son, daughter, and servant. In this first period, therefore, noble property was alienable: the father could sell his land as he could sell his posterity.

But little by little — and what we call civilization consists in this — the wife, son, daughter, and servant, withdrew from the paternal restraint, acquired a personality at first doubtful, then more complete and solid, and ended by existing in their own proper names. Then the rights of the fathers were no longer sole, absolute, and without limits in the family; on the contrary, they ended where those of the wife, son, daughter, and servants began. This new state of the noble family is developed in history, as to the wife by the establishment of dower; as to the son and daughter, by the establishment of the child's portion; as to the servants, by the establishment of wages. In this second period, noble property ceases to depend absolutely upon the father, becomes inalienable and entailed, and passes to his descendants in spite of him.

We add that when democracy dominates society and absorbs the nobility, noble families are dissolved and noble property disappears. Thus there have been years when entailed and inalienable property came to be destroyed in France.

The proofs of what we have said are easy and numerous. But as this matter belongs more especially to the history of the noble races, we ask permission to give here only those indispensable to an understanding of the subject.

The first period of noble property, that is to say, of property dependent on the absolute will of the father, is so ancient that it had even disappeared when the primitive books commenced, and can only be established by induction. The second period of noble property, that is to say, the period of entailed property, belongs to historic times.

Among the Hebrews, entailed property existed fully for the sacerdotal races from the time of Moses, as we will see presently; and it had not long ceased to exist for the noble races; for the law of jubilee, by which all property necessarily returned to the family after seven times seven years of alienation, evidently succeeded to entails, by which no property ever left these families.

Among the Greeks, entails were abolished from the time of Solon, according to Plutarch, who expressly says that up to that time fathers of families had not the right of making a will.[1]

Among the Romans, a people having communal institutions, entails disappeared very early. But we find a first trace of them in the sacred, that is to say, noble (the nobles being the sons of the gods) character of the *Ager Romanus*,[2] and a second in the judicial action for the sale of lands, which was introduced very tardily, only in the 648th year of Rome, by the prætor Publius Rutilius.[3]

In France, the two periods of noble property were developed successively and established under our eyes. Down to an epoch, which we will not undertake to fix precisely, but which must have been near the eighth century, fathers had the absolute right to give away or sell their lands. By degrees came restrictions, which limited their authority. Thus, toward the ninth century we find a multitude of public acts, in which fathers made their wives and even the infant at the breast parties, to have the power of selling or giving away. We do not now cite any of these acts because of the difficulty of choosing one rather than another.

At that time entails, then, were progressing toward their establishment; and what is singularly curious, we find how they progressed toward their fall. At the end of the twelfth century came other laws, providing that, if a noble wished to sell his land,

[1] Plutarch, Solon, ch. xxi.

[2] We will treat, in the history of the noble races, of the nature of the *Ager Romanus*, which was a noble property, and could not be held by freedmen. We limit ourselves to giving its exterior characteristics. Limites sunt in *agris* limitatis, qui populo iter præbent, ex lege Sempronia. . . . Ex eis alii sunt Decumani Maximi, qui fiunt ab oriente in occidentem, alii Cardines Maximi, qui ex transverso currunt, alii Actuarii, alii Subruncivi. Decumani . . . pedes xl., Cardines pedes xx., Actuarii pedes xii., Subruncivi pedes viii. habent. (Jacob. Cujac. Observat., lib. ii., cap. ix.)

[3] Quæ species actionis appellatur Rutiliana, quia a prætore Publio Rutilio, qui et bonorum venditionem introduxisse dicitur, comparata est. (Gaii Instit., lib. iv., § 35.)

the next of blood should buy it; if the next of blood could not, then the next after him, and so on; if none of the blood could buy it, then, when it was well established that it could not remain in the family, the father was free to sell it to a stranger. These laws add that, even in that case, the relatives have seven days to annul the sale.[1]

We have assimilated corporations to noble families. It was their nature to last always, and, on the other hand, it is certain that their property was entailed. As to the property of commercial or industrial corporations, we will establish their entailed character in the chapters, in which we will treat of the trades' unions. We will only say two words as to the property of the religious corporations of Christendom. Pope Urban VIII. was the first, who departed from the jurisprudence of the canons, which sanctioned the perpetual inalienability of the property of the Church;[2] to which we should add that the beginning of the departure goes back to Paul II., who permitted alienations for three years by papal authority.[3]

The burgher family commences precisely where the noble family ends. When the father has lost all his primitive authority over his wife and children; when the latter acquire a distinct individuality and personal rights well established; when the son and the daughter, detached from their ancestors, go where their own will leads them; when there is no longer a first-born, who represents and sums up in himself the traditions of the family; when the whole family crumbles and falls apart, like a too-ripened head of grain; then the noble family ends, and the burgher family begins.

Thus burgher property is essentially movable, like the species of family, of which it forms the material side. In all legislations it has always preserved its special character of alienability, and the power of entailment has never been given to it. It even appears certain, judging at least from past history, without occupying ourselves with what the future may produce, that it is in the nature of property to escape from the immobility, which attaches to it in the first ages of history, and that progress consists for it, as for the children and wives of the heroic and divine fathers, in withdrawing

[1] Assis. de Jerusal., Cour des Bourg., ch. xxviii., copie de manuscrit de Venise, biblioth. du roi.

[2] Bull. Magn. Constitut. Urban VIII., 715, § 1.

[3] Bull. Magn. Pauli II., Constit. 2, § 1.

itself from the absorbent action of the primitive family, to acquire a value of its own, individual, distinct, and, as it were, a sort of personality. At this day, France is the country of the world, in which property has gone through the most successive evolutions, and in which it is completely detached from the family, or rather individualized and mobilized, like the family. The law in relation to entails upon the eldest son was the last blow struck at the old immovable and entailed property; and probably those, who were its promoters, little dreamed of the species of necessary and providential functions, which they filled at that moment.

Whenever, then, we meet in the ancient books a movable and alienable property, we cannot avoid recognizing in it a burgher property, for the reason that the ancient books are not so old as to show us noble property, before it entered upon the immobility of entails, or are too old to show it, after it had escaped from it. The mobility of property in the ancient books is therefore as certain an index of the existence of free boroughs, as mendicancy is of the existence of emancipations.

In the Bible, for example, movable and alienable property is only found in the walled cities. In the first place, Moses, when he speaks of cities, always takes great care to indicate whether they were open or walled. Thus, when he sent twelve commissioners to spy out the promised land, he instructed them to examine the fertility of the land, what cities there were, whether they had walls or not.[1] In Leviticus, property was entailed and alienable only for forty-nine years, (*a*) after which the first possessors retook it,[2] which was, as we have said, an improvement on the primitive epoch, when it was absolutely inalienable; but this property was noble property, because burgher property is movable and alienable. The proof of this is found in chapter xxv., where it is said that if a house is sold in a walled city and the owner shall not have redeemed it within a year,

[1] And see the land . . . and what the land is that they dwell in, whether it be good or bad, and what cities they be that they dwell in, whether in tents or in strongholds. (Numb., ch. xiii., verses 18 and 19, as published by the American Bible Society, 1850.)

(*a*) In the original there is a misprint of seven for seven times seven, or forty-nine, years.

[2] Levit. xxxv. 8, 11, 13.

it was aliened forever;[1] and the thirty-first verse adds, that if this house was in a village without walls, it was subject to the law that governed lands, that is to say, to the law of the nobles, to the law of entails, and the first possessor should retake it in the fiftieth, or year of jubilee. A last very characteristic trait to be added to all this is that verse fifty-four expressly forbids the sale of anything in the suburbs, that is to say, without the walls, where all was entailed, lands and houses. (*a*)

There were, therefore, among the Jews, two different civil laws, which governed property, according as it was found within or without the walls of a city; and such was the importance of these walls of enclosure, that is to say, such was the difference between the two sorts of society, which they separated, that on one side, property had a certain nature, on the other, an opposite nature; on one side, it was alienable and commercial; on the other, immovable and entailed.

Now the history of property, which we have only sketched, but which will be fully treated in the volume on the noble classes, proves that salable or alienable lands are always either a burgher property, or a noble property in its first or last degree of development. It is to be remarked, that neither of these two latter cases could be that spoken of in Leviticus, not only because noble property was then entailed, but also because it was still when the book of Ruth[2] was composed, and even when Jeremiah wrote.[3] We must therefore necessarily conclude that the alienable property of walled cities was

[1] Levit. xxv. 29–31.

(*a*) And if a man sell a dwelling house in a walled city, then he may redeem it within a whole year after it is sold; within a full year may he redeem it. And if it be not redeemed within the space of a full year, then the house that is in the walled city shall be established forever to him that bought it, throughout his generations; it shall not go out in the jubilee. But the houses of the villages, which have no walls round about them, shall be counted as the fields of the country; they may be redeemed, and they shall go out in the jubilee. Notwithstanding the cities of the Levites and the houses of the cities of their possession may the Levites redeem at any time. And if a man purchase of the Levites, then the house that was sold and the city of his possession shall go out in the year of jubilee; for the houses of the cities of the Levites are their possession among the children of Israel. But the field of the suburbs of their cities may not be sold, for it is their perpetual possession. (Levit. xxv. 29–34.)

[2] Ruth iv. 3, 4.

[3] Jeremiah xxxii. 7, 8.

a burgher property, which establishes that there was a free government in those cities, a thing already proved by the very fact of their walls.

We are thus brought back to what we have already said at the beginning of our two chapters on the history of architecture and the history of property, viz., that all the walled cities mentioned in the primitive books were burgher cities, in which there already was a commune. And as, if that were not true, many things in relation to houses and property, otherwise undeniable, must be false, we do not think it possible to dispute with us this result. We should, nevertheless, here again repeat that all this history of the slave races will be otherwise clear, plain, and evident, after our history of the noble races; so that if we cannot now remove every mist from our ideas, that mist will be certainly dissipated, we hope, as we shall sufficiently develop and support those views. The commentary will be found in the whole.

Meanwhile — and we think we have done enough to be pardoned for this boldness, if it is one — we lay it down as an established principle that communes existed among the Jews from the time of Moses, and among the Greeks from the time of Homer, and we draw this certainty from the walled cities mentioned in the Pentateuch and in the Iliad.

We should say, without more delay, that we do not pretend that the communes of Jericho and of Troy exactly resembled those of the thirteenth century — for example, those of Soissons and of Rheims; that is to say, that they had exactly the same administrative forms and the same number of magistrates. We have already shown that the details of the administrative organization are not what constitute essentially the commune; and that the number, the functions, and the names of the administrators amount to nothing; but what we firmly believe is that there was in Jericho, Troy, Calydon, and Gortina, in the small number of walled cities mentioned by Moses and Homer, an association of men of the freed races, living apart from the noble races, having their own statutes, their own distinct civil law, their own separate administration; and it is in this association of organized freedmen that we make the commune to consist, whatever may otherwise have been the mechanism of that organization; whether there was one chief, or two; whether he was called consul, mayor, prévôt, or échevin. We believe, moreover, that these primitive communes were organized spontaneously, gradually, day by day a little, without premeditated agreement, without precise purpose, without a plan for the future, without any preconceived political theory; and that, nevertheless, for having been thus formed peaceably, insensibly, without noise, revolt, or massacre, they were none the less communes, as well as completely, as those of Laon and Cambray, in which rebellion and murder were, in our opinion, only local circumstances and fortuitous accidents, without general value or human signification.

To sum up the progress of this book to the point to which we have brought it, we have taken the slave races in the bosom of the primitive family, and have followed them up to the moment, when, being sufficiently numerous, they have obtained from their masters, their seigniors, the faculty of living apart, of organizing, of creating for themselves a government humble, lowly, obscure, despised — the *commune*. We have shown the communal government forming, little by little, in every country, in the East and in the West, as slaves were emancipated.

Nevertheless, the freedmen, who organized into communes, who were grouped around some seignorial castle, temple, or church, and who thus, in building poor villages, laid the foundations of future great cities, did not constitute all the freedmen. Independently of those, whom a professional industry permitted to choose a residence at their pleasure, and to shut themselves up within walls, there were still those, whom agricultural or pastoral life retained forcibly in the fields. By the side of the burghers were the peasants.

Thus we have another moiety of the freed races, of whose mode of administrative association we should give some account. The peasants did not have the commune: what, then, had they?

# CHAPTER XI.

## THE PEASANTS.

AMONG the innumerable writers who have treated of the ancients, none have dreamed of sketching the history of the peasants. They have mentioned the cities and their inhabitants, for a thousand different reasons: because they were the residences of princes; because they were the schools of philosophy and literature; because they sustained sieges; in fine, because they were the cause, the victim, or the theatre of some great fact of a nature to resound among men; but for the peasants, who were dispersed through the country, poor, ignorant, obscure, powerless, no one has thought of them. Nevertheless, the order of peasants made part of the whole body of the ancient peoples, as well as the order of senators. Although the peasants were in some sort hidden in the political life of antiquity, though they were not prominent, though they did not strike the eye, they were none the less there. Neither do we see the roots of trees nor the foundations of walls; but for all that there is no wall without a foundation, no tree without roots. But in reading the history of the ancient peoples, one is almost authorized to believe that there were no peasants among them. The historians, who are guilty of this forgetfulness, who pass over with this indifference the moiety of the human kind, should observe, in their own interest, that this gap makes an irreparable break in the middle of their books, and that this great fact forgotten, must leave a multitude of historic ideas incomplete, and many problems without a solution. It is now for the young critic, born in this century, to make the tour through the historic edifice left to us by our fathers, to visit its holes and crevices, and to at least repair, if not to rebuild it.

This history of the peasants among the ancient peoples is preceded by another, which we are not now free to undertake, but of which it is necessary that we should say something. This other history is that of the landed proprietors, whose laborers were the peasants. The history of the landed proprietors, which also has not been written, would require a book. It will therefore be found very natural that we should say of it what it is impossible for us to omit here.

We believe — and this firm belief, which we announce here, will be discussed, and, we hope, justified in the second volume of this work — that the most remote historic times of ancient peoples, of which we have any knowledge, were nevertheless, for them, very secondary. For example, we are convinced that in Italy before Romulus, and in Greece before Theseus, there was a long historic epoch, corresponding in its character to what the middle ages were to us. The existence of a *middle age*, but of a *feudal middle age*, in the history of ancient Greece and ancient Italy is, to our eyes, and in the present state of our historic studies, a fact completely demonstrated. The foundation of Rome, and the establishment of the first municipalities, like that of Ceres in Italy, the foundation of Athens, and the establishment of the small republics of Peloponnesus, in Greece, ended, according to our ideas, that ancient feudality, and are in ancient history what the enfranchisement of the communes was in modern history. It is not our intention to prove this, in this chapter; but we give some detached observations on this general opinion.

The existence of this antique middle age once admitted — and it is for us completely — we can, if we wish, follow its traces through history. For example, and to limit ourselves to Italy, a system of vassalage and suzerainty was still completely organized in all the extent of the Roman Empire in the times of Marius and Sylla. On this point may be cited among other testimony the efforts of Marius to withdraw himself from the vassalage, in which he was, and his ancestors always had been, to the house of Herennius, a house whose seignorial rights the judges maintained, although Marius alleged that having been elected prætor, that rank was for him equivalent to a title of freedom and nobility.[1]

Besides, it is not doubtful that the expression *vassal* (*vasallus*, *vassus*, *vas*, in the language of the jurists of the middle age) belonged to the most remote Roman legislation. Aulus Gellius, who contains on this point very precise and clear documents, asked a lawyer, in an interview which took place, he says, in the market-place at Rome on a festival day, what was the meaning of some terms found

[1] Plutarch, Marius, ch. xxii.

in the third book of the Annals of Ennius, which some one had read. The lawyer excused himself, saying that he knew the law very well, but not the philology; but when it was answered that he ought to be competent to explain these terms, since they were found in the Twelve Tables, he again excused himself, saying that he could not, because he had not studied the laws of the Aborigines and the Fauns.[1]

Now among these terms, of the signification of which the lawyer acknowledged himself ignorant, were *vas* and *subvas*, *vassal* and *arrière vassal;* and this primitive legislation of the Aborigines and Fauns, which the jurists of the time of Aulus Gellius had not studied, because it no longer entered into the practice of the civil law, and which they left as a curiosity of learning to the historians and poets, (for a poet explained the terms which the lawyer did not understand;[2]) this legislation of the Aborigines and Fauns was the old feudal jurisprudence of Italy. More than that, and singular to have to say at this day! the expression *serf of the glebe* in so many words belonged to the Roman law, and is formally found, as we will hereafter show, in a constitution of Honorius and Theodosius.

Thus ancient Italy was feudal, like modern Europe from the fifth to the fifteenth century.

This feudal Italy contained seigniors, (lords) who inhabited the country; for the cities only began to have importance, when the nobility had decayed and the free boroughs were formed. These seigniors had, to work their lands, slaves, who later became *serfs of the glebe*, who still later became the *peasants*.

Perhaps it may be well to say here in a few words that the men, who in the ancient Roman legislation bore the name of *proletaries*, *proletarii*, were precisely these serfs of the glebe of primitive feudal Italy. It results from the chapter of Aulus Gellius, of which we have just now spoken, that the expression *proletary* had become very difficult to understand, and had entirely dropped out of the language of the law, to which it belonged, toward the twelfth century of the Christian era. The poet, who undertook to explain the terms taken from the laws of the Aborigines and Fauns, in default

[1] Aul. Gell., lib. xvi., cap. x., § 7.

[2] Tum forte quadam Julium Paulum, poetam memoriæ nostræ doctissimum prætereuntem conspeximus. Is a nobis salutatus rogatusque uti de sententia deque ratione istius vocabuli nos doceret. (Aul. Gell. xvi.; cap. x., § 9, 10.)

of the lawyer, who never had studied them, said that in the ancient jurisprudence, the proletaries were the serfs, who came immediately above the *capite censi*.[1] Now the *capite censi* were properly serfs of the body, paying, according to the ancient custom of Italy, three hundred and seventy-five pennies tax; the proletaries paid fifteen hundred.[2] We see by this that the Saint Simonian school, which has latterly put in circulation the word proletary as signifying a free man possessing nothing, and which has undertaken to base the sense, which it gives, upon Roman history, was not very sure of the erudition, which it displays on this point.

This being well understood and established, viz., that the country of ancient Italy was inhabited by rich and lordly families, and that there were great domains belonging to the temples, of which the pagan clergy, as proprietors, superintended the culture and received the revenues, we may ask what became of the numberless slaves, laborers, vintners, gardeners, shepherds, who cultivated the lands and tended the flocks, and of whom a certain number from time to time attained to freedom. The masters always, for a thousand different causes, set free some of their slaves in the cities: why should they not have set free some in the country? Besides, the fact of a rural population, attached only to the soil, but possessing a property of their own, sometimes even of a rural population entirely free, is so evident in ancient history that we will presently take a rapid notice of them.

We may then ask, we say, what became of the serfs and freedmen of the country? Did they remain isolated? Did they live in communities? Did they possess an administration of their own? Did they have judges taken from among themselves in their disputes?

And what we have said of the rural serfs and freedmen of Italy, we may equally say of the serfs and freedmen of France. What became of those so numerous serfs, who were primitively slaves, whether of lords, or of monasteries, or of chapters, and who, notwithstanding their number, being separated in little groups or scattered in hamlets through the country, were never expressly erected

[1] Extremus autem census capite censorum æris fuit trecenti septuaginta quinque. (Aul. Gell., lib. xvi., cap. x., § 10.)

[2] Qui in plebe Romana tenuissimi pauperrimique erant, neque amplius quam mille quingentum æris in censum defuebant, proletarii appellati sunt. (Aul. Gell., lib. xvi., cap. x., § 10.)

into communes? Nearly all the agricultural population of the kingdom, and a considerable multitude of burghs and villages, whose inhabitants, first slaves, then serfs, then freedmen, were finally brought into the common mass of the *tiers-état*, have never passed through the form of municipal association. Now, what was the domestic and civil state of these rural populations? Who took care of them? Who judged them? All these are difficult but very important questions, on the solution of which must evidently depend the general and superior signification of the history of the peoples of the West.

It appears certain, as far as it is possible to have certainty and precision in a study attempted for the first time, on facts so distant and obscure, that the slave population of the country, as they were set free, resolved themselves into little villages, little burghs, and hamlets. It should be remarked that these primitive little villages became the germ of communes that were formed later, when they had acquired some development. Besides, these villages always had for their centre a castle or a temple in ancient times; a castle, a church, or a monastery, in the middle ages. The castle or the temple, the church or the monastery were the safeguard, to which the serfs, feeble, naked, disarmed, came for shelter. It was thus, in every country, in all times, the boroughs and cities commenced. This perhaps would require some examples, which it would be easy to give; but we limit ourselves to Rome, commenced by a castle on Mount Palatine, and Athens, by a castle on the Acropolis. We must except from this general rule only those cities, which have been founded all at once by colonies or by peoples emigrating; but it must not be lost sight of that we speak of cities and boroughs founded by nascent, not by old, populations.

These open boroughs, having a castle in the centre, and formed by the accumulated houses of the serfs of the seignior, were frequent in primitive Italy. Plutarch testifies in the Life of Romulus that the ancient Sabines lived thus. The Cisalpine Gauls, according to Polybius, and the Ætolians, according to Thucydides, also led this feudal life. There still remained in Greece some of these burghs in the time of Pericles; and Thucydides mentions four or five; but the greater part of them had at that epoch acquired sufficient importance, either by the number of their inhabitants or by the extent of the franchises which they enjoyed, to be erected into communes; and, besides, some of them were surrounded with walls and changed into strongholds by the Athenians or the Lacedemonians, during the Peloponnesian war.[1]

In the middle ages, open burghs, having a castle or a monastery in the centre, were innumerable. Although the greater part of them have since become cities, it is very easy to recognize some of them at this day by their names, in which is mentioned the castle, to which they owe their origin, as Chateau-roux, Chateau-Meillan, Chateau-neuf, Castelnau, and the other cities, in whose names appear the word *ferté*, which also signifies strong castle; *firmitas*, as the ancient charters express it.

The slave population of the country, we say, flowed into these thousand small burghs, of which some became cities and others have disappeared. In fact, it must be remarked that isolated houses in the country belong to modern times; in primitive times, we have shown, there were none isolated but the castles.

At the time when these burghs were formed, they were inhabited by populations in a state of slavery. Italy was still covered with them toward the first century of the Christian era. For example, there were few grand Roman lords, who did not possess many villages, and they were masters of them as absolutely as the French lords of the middle ages were of theirs.

The lords, who owned these villages, had them governed by officers, whose functions nearly corresponded to those of our *baillis*. Suetonius expressly relates that the Emperor Claudius had thus on his domains officers, who administered justice to his vassals, not in his name as emperor, but in his name of seignior.[2] There were laws of Gordian, Diocletian, Maximian, Julian, and Zeno,[3] which instituted in the empire judges called *pedanês*, (*a*) who by the nature of their attributes, were exactly what in the fourteenth century were our village judges, who were called, says Loyseau, *juges sous l'orme*, judges under the elm.[4] Finally, a constitution of Justinian, of the

[1] See the speech addressed to an assembly of the people, at the commencement of the Peloponnesian war, by Pericles, as to the disposition of the Athenians and Lacedemonians to fortify different points of territory. (Thucydides, lib. i., cap. cxlii.)

[2] Suetonius, Tib. Claud. Cæsar, ch. xiii.

[3] Cod. Justin., lib. iii., title iii., leg. 2, 4, 5.

(*a*) So called because they had no bench, but judged cases standing.

[4] Loyseau, on the abuses of village judges, p. 21.

year 539, established, or rather regulated, the jurisdiction of lords over their vassals, or of *masters* over their *laborers*, as in the Latin tongue it is expressed.[1] Moreover, we should never hesitate to employ, on occasion, the terms of heraldry in treating Roman history. We will show summarily hereafter that the titles of prince, duke, marquis, count, baron, chevalier, belong to the Latin tongue.

It is easily understood that it is difficult to say with precision up to what time the villages of Italy remained thus the property of the lords. There were some still in the fifth century. We know that moral revolutions never have any precise date. Otherwise, the laws of Theodosius, Arcadius, Valentinian II., Diocletian, Leo, and Anthemius contained most precise indications as to the state of the peasants of the empire.

The most precise idea, that can be formed of the peasants of antiquity, is this: they were slave agriculturists, slave laborers, slave vintners, slave shepherds, to whom their masters, in pursuance of a new system of management applied to their property, no longer gave lodging, clothes, and food, as in the past; but accorded to them the faculty of managing, at their pleasure, but under their responsibility, either the cultivation of a certain extent of land or the care of the flocks, on condition of paying annually to the master a certain portion of the revenues of the flocks or land, and to keep the rest for themselves, as an equivalent for food, clothing, and lodging, which they no longer received.

This general idea, which we express, as to the peasants of antiquity, results from a comparative study of the mode of emancipation of agricultural slaves in antiquity and in the middle ages; and, as regards the Roman Empire, it rests on the formal text of a law of the Emperor Anastasius, which dates from the first years of the sixth century.[2] This law, as may be seen, is important on three points: first, in that it announces the fact generally; second, in that it shows that it was ordinarily after thirty years of trial that the masters intrusted the cultivation of the lands to the discretion of

[1] Si vero forsan cum instituerint auditores litis, aut agricolarum domini, qui a nobis sunt judices statuti. (Anth. Coll. vi., tit. ix., novel. lxxx., cap. iii.)

[2] Agricolarum alii quidem sunt adscriptitii, et eorum peculia dominis competent; alii vero tempore annorum triginta coloni fiunt, liberati manentes cum rebus suis; et ii etiam coguntur terram colere et canonem prestare. Hoc et domino et agricolis utilius est. (Cod. Just., lib. xi., tit. xlvii., leg. 18.)

their slaves; third, and finally, in that it says that this new mode of cultivation was at the same time more advantageous to the slaves and to the masters.

This law, well interpreted, explains with admirable simplicity and rigor the nature and condition of the peasants in the Roman Empire.

The masters, we have said, in place of lodging, feeding, and clothing their slaves, as they had done in more remote times, found it more convenient to get rid of this care, and to leave them free to cultivate the lands at their discretion, and to give to them from the fruits of their labor all beyond a certain fixed rent, called *canon*, that is to say, *custom*.

It is very evident that the masters did not grant this favor, for it was a very great one, to all their slaves, but only to those, who evinced regular habits of intelligence and industry, and in whose hands they could be certain that the lands would not lie fallow. Hence we have two species of peasants; those, who were still under the hand of the master, and those, who had deserved to be intrusted with the cultivation of the lands and the care of the flocks. The former were called *coloni adscriptitii*, and were veritable slaves; the latter were called *coloni originarii*, *inquilini*, *censiti*, or simply *coloni*, and were what serfs of the glebe were in the middle ages.

The *coloni adscriptitii* were, we say, veritable slaves;[1] the master could sell them at his pleasure. The *coloni censiti*, *originarii*, or *inquilini* were no longer slaves; all personal action of the master over them had ceased, and he could no longer sell them except by selling the lands to which they were attached.[2]

This latter species of peasants, after thirty years' evidence of an active and regular life, became then, by the terms of the law of Anastasius, entirely free in their persons. Nevertheless, even in this freedom, which they had acquired, they were bound to work the grant, the *fief*, and to pay rent, *cogentur terram colere et canonem prestare*. A law of Theodosius and Valentinian calls them serfs of

[1] Quæ enim differéntia inter servos et adscriptitios intelligatur, cum uterque in domini sui positus sit potestate. (Cod. Just., lib. xi., tit. xlvii., leg. 21.)

[2] Quemadmodum originarios absque terra ita rusticos censitosque servos vendi omnifariam non licebit. (Cod. Just., lib. xi., tit. xlvii., leg. 7.) Si quis prædium vendere voluerit vel donare; retinere sibi transferendos ad alia loca colonos privata pactione non possit. (Cod. Just., lib. xi., tit. xlii., leg. 2.)

the land,[1] and a law of Honorius and Theodosius says that they were *attached to the glebe.*[2] These laws consider slavery as if it ought to be eternal;[3] but it results from the terms of a constitution of Theodosius and Valentinian that there were degrees in this slavery; for example, there might be exemptions from the poll tax, which the *coloni censiti*, inscribed in the public register of rents,[4] generally paid.[5]

The law of Anastasius teaches us, we have seen, that the serfs of the glebe paid annually to the master a part of the revenues to represent his right of property, and kept the other part to represent their food, lodging, clothing, and profits. All this is elsewhere found formally expressed in a constitution of Valentinian and Valens.[6] Another constitution of the same emperors provides that this rent should be paid in kind, unless the custom of the land otherwise prescribed.[7]

Once free in their persons by the expiration of thirty years, the serfs of the glebe, provided they were faithful to the terms of their feudal compact, acquired a moral value and a civil capacity in the sphere of their own interests. Public officers could not, under heavy penalties, impose upon them menial labor,[8] and if their lord exacted

[1] Servi tamen *terræ* ipsius, cui nati sunt, existimentur. (Cod. Just., lib. xi., tit. li., leg. 1.)

[2] Quos ita *glebis inhærere* præcipimus, ut ne puncto quidem temporis debeant amoveri. (Cod. Just., lib. xi., tit. xlvii., leg. 15.)

[3] Cum... lex... colonos quodam æternitatis jure detineat, ita ut illis non liceat ex his locis, quorum fructu relevantur, abscedere. (Cod. Just., lib. xi., tit. l., leg. 1.)

[4] Qui in suis conscripti locis proprio nomine libris censualibus detinentur. (Cod. Just., lib. xi., tit. xlvii., leg. 4.)

[5] Sublato in perpetuum humanæ capitationis censu, jugatio tantum terrena solvatur. Et ne forte colonis tributariæ sortis nexibus absolutis, vagandi, et quo libuerit recedendi facultas permissa videatur, ipsi quidem originario jure teneantur. (Cod. Just., lib. xi., tit. li., leg. 1.)

[6] Cæterum si profugi, quod alieni esse viderentur, quasi sui arbitrii ac liberi apud aliquem se collocaverunt, aut *excolentes terras partem fructuum pro solo debitam dominis præstiterunt, cætera proprio peculio reservantes, vel quibuscumque operis impensis mercedam placitam consecuti sunt.* (Cod. Just., lib. xi., tit. xlvii., leg. 8.)

[7] Domini prædiorum id, quod terra præstat, accipiant, pecuniam non requirant, . . . nisi consuetudo prædii hoc exigat. (Idem, lib. xi., tit. xlvii., leg. 5.)

[8] Si quis eorum, qui . . . sub quocumque pretextu publici muneris possunt esse terribiles . . . rusticano cuipiam necessitatem obsequii . . . imponant, aut servum ejus, vel forte bovem in usus proprios . . . converterint, . . . ablatis omnibus facultatibus, perpetuo subjugantur exilio. (Idem, lib. xi., tit. liv., leg. 2.)

a greater rent than was the custom of the domain, the serfs could reclaim it before the judge.[1]

These two, or rather three, species of peasants, those who were purely slaves, those who were serfs paying a poll tax, and those who were serfs paying only rent, habitually collected in little villages, and bore the name *villagers, vicani*. It appears that toward the middle of the fifth century these villagers were already preparing the way for a political result, which was completed in the compulsory feudality of the middle ages, by placing themselves under the safeguard of a powerful lord, who granted them his protection in consideration of a tribute paid to him, that is to say, by creating a voluntary feudality.[2] The law of Leo and Anthemius, which signalizes this fact, forbids it under severe penalty; but it prevailed later, as we know, and gave birth to the whole system of feudal dependencies.[3]

We thus come to see that ancient Italy was fundamentally feudal: we will show that it was feudal even in its language. With very little more trouble we could show that feudality was Greek, next that it was Jewish, and finally that it is, like the commune in another order of facts, a phase of the history of humanity.

Without wishing to set forth here all the facts and ideas, by which we will establish, in the volume on the history of the nobility, that the nomenclature of the nobility of the middle ages belonged to the ceremonial of the Roman Empire, we can nevertheless show, as we have announced, that the titles *gentleman, chevalier, baron, count, marquis, duke*, and *prince*, are taken from the Latin language.

Gentleman (*gentilhomme*) is the literal translation of *gentis homo*, and designates exactly the same thing, viz., *a man of free race*, one who counts no freedman among his ancestors. This is the sense given to gentilhomme and gentis homo by the French and Latin jurists.[4] Moreover, if we consider the word *gentilhomme* at the moment when it first entered into the French language, we again

[1] Quisquis colonus plus a domino exigitur quam ante consueverat . . . adeat judicem, cujus primum poterit habere presentiam. (Idem., lib. xi., tit. xlix., leg. 1.)

[2] Ne quis vicanis patrocinium polliceatur vel agricolas in clientelam suscipiat, redituum, alteriusve lucri promissione recepta. (Cod. Just., lib. xi., tit. liii., leg. 1.)

[3] Præterea ut vicani, si servi sint, dominis castigati reddantur; si liberi xx. libris multentur. (Idem, leg. 2.)

[4] Servi genus vel gentem non habent; liberti, vel ab iis orti, gentem non

find its form purely Latin; for example, we read *gentis hons* in the romance of *Bertha with the Big Feet*, which was of the year 1240, or very nearly;[1] and *gentil'homo* in a charter of 1228, cited by Adrian de Valois in his Notice of the Gauls.[2]

*Chevalier* is the translation into the Celtic idiom of the Latin *eques*. Already in the time of Nero the barbarian word *caballus*, to signify horse, had entered into the Latin language. It is found in Perseus.[3] In following the charters of the middle age, we trace all the successive transformations, by which *caballus* became *cheval*;[4] and the grade of nobility, designated by *eques* among the Romans, very nearly corresponds to the grade of nobility designated by *chevalier* in France.

We find *baron* in so many letters in the Commentaries of Cæsar, or rather in the continuation of the Commentaries by Hirtius, the friend and colleague of Cæsar;[5] and again *baron* is expressly given in four places by Cicero; first, in his book *De Finibus*;[6] secondly, on his treatise on Divination;[7] third, in his letters to Atticus;[8] fourth in his letters to his friends.[9] Finally, we find *baron* in the Satires of Perseus.[10]

It must be admitted that *baron*, in the authors we have just mentioned, does not signify precisely what it signifies in the history of

habent; nam gentem habent soli, quorum parentes nemini servierunt. (Jacob. Cujas, in lib. iii., quæst. Papinian. Comment. ad leg. 1, de probat.)

1 Moult ot el roy Pepins très gentis hons. (Le Romans de Berte aus grans piés, verset. cxxxix.)

2 Hadrian. Vales. Notit. Gall., p. 333.

3 Nec fonte labra prolui *caballino*. (Perseus, Prolog., v. 1.)

4 Caballus is found in most of the laws of the seventh century. (Lex Salic., tit. xxvii., § 9;) in a record of 1275 we read *cavalcata*, (Ordon. du Louv., t. iii., p. 58;) in a charter of 1224 we read *chevalcata* (Carpent. Gloss. Med. Æv.;) finally, *cheval* is found in Villehardouin.

5 Concurritur ad Cassium defendendum: semper enim *barones* compluresque evocatos cum telis secum habere consueverat. (A. Hirtii de Bell. Alexand., cap. liii.)

6 Hæc cum loqueris, nos *barones* stupemus: tu videlicet tecum ipse rides. (Cicero de Fin., lib. ii., cap. xxiii., § 77.)

7 Huic quidem Antipho, *Baro*, inquit, te victum esse non vides? (Cicero de Divinat., lib. ii., cap. lxx., § 144.)

8 Apud patronem et reliquos *barones* te in maxima gratia posui, et hercule merito tuo feci. (Cicero, Epis. ad Atticum, lib. v., epis. xi., § 5.)

9 Ille *baro* te putabat quæsiturum, unum cælum esset, an innumerabilia. (Cicero, epist. ad divers., lib. ix., epist. xxvi.)

10 . . . Eheu!
Baro, regustatum digito terebrare salinum
Contentus perages, si vivere cum Jove tendis.
(Pers. Satyr., v. 137–139.)

the French nobility; but we do not hesitate to affirm that its modern is derived from its ancient sense. In Perseus, and in some passages of Cicero, and notably in the two first and in the fourth of the passages quoted, it appears to signify something like *rustic;* but in the third, taken from his letters to Atticus, baron has evidently an honorable signification. In the Commentaries of Cæsar, *baron* designates a certain kind of soldier. As the word baron is Celtic, we are authorized to believe that it was applied to the Gauls in the Roman service. The passage from Hirtius completely justifies this opinion. Once admitted that the barons were barbarian soldiers, it is easy to conceive how baron might equally mean rustic. In the middle ages, before the noble hierarchy was completely organized, baron signified simply *seignior* or *gentleman.* We find the epithet baron given to St. Peter in two passages of the Romance of Bertha;[1] and we read in a third place that King Pepin was "très gentis hons et *ber.*"[2] Besides, it results from a great number of texts that *ber* and *baron* meant the same thing in the middle ages. As to the etymological meaning of the word, the glossarists pretend that *baron* or *ber* signified a brave man, *vir.*[3]

*Count* is the translation of *comes.* Many witnesses establish that the eminent persons of the Roman nobility had always around them men, who were attached to them by some bond little known, and who were called counts, *comites.* Cicero speaks of his counts in a letter to Atticus;[4] he also mentions the counts of Verres.[5] Suetonius, in his Life of Claudius, speaks of the counts, who followed the young Roman gentlemen to the schools of rhetoric.[6] In the Life of Cæsar he also mentions the counts of the magistrates, and what he says of them necessarily attributes to them public functions, by virtue of their title of count, since in determining the persons, who had authority to be absent from Rome for three years, Cæsar ex-

[1] A Dieu s'est commandée (Berte) et au baron St. Pierre. (Le Roman de Berte aus grans piés. (Vers. xl.; ibid., vers. cxxx.)

[2] Moult ot el roy Pepin très gentis hons et ber. (Ibid., vers. cxxxix.)

[3] Porro quod in quibusdam glossariis exponerentur *Baro,* ἀνὴρ et vir fortis in laboribus, putarunt quidam *baronem* vocabulum et dignitatis et honoris. (Forcel. Lexic., verb. Barb.)

[4] Hominem certum misi de comitibus meis. (Cicero ad Atticum, lib. viii. I.)

[5] Comites illi tui dilecti manus erant tuæ. (Cic. in Verrem., Act. ii., lib. ii., cap. 10.)

[6] Vix remisit (Claudius) ne cuivis comiti calamariæ adimerentur. (Suet., Tib. Claud. Cæsar, cap. xxxvi.)

cepts only the military and the counts of the magistrates.[1] In the Life of Adrian, Spartian speaks of the counts of the emperor, and distinguishes them from his friends.[2] Moreover, it is certain that *comes*, as employed in these passages of the different authors we have mentioned, does not simply mean *companion*. This word had already received, from the usages of society and the language of ceremony, a special signification; for the Greeks, as we will show presently, translated this word in the cases cited by κομης, which was a barbarism; when, moreover, they had the word ακολουτος, if *comes* had meant *companion*.

When the emperors had abolished the last remnants of the republican form of the Roman government and become absolute in fact and by law, they made their counts so many public officers, without ceasing by that to keep them attached to their persons. In absolute governments, the magistrates are always the familiars of the prince. Thus the grand chamberlain and the grand pantler of the kings of France were at the same time officers clothed with immense powers.

It was about the time of Constantine that the counts of the emperor became public officers. The first count of the sacred largesses was of the year 340, under Constant;[3] the first count of the privy purse was of the year 342;[4] the first count of the domestics was of the year 367;[5] the first count of the Orient is of the year 342;[6] the first count of Egypt was of the year 391;[7] the first count of Macedonia in 327;[8] the first count of Africa in 326;[9] the first count of Spain in 317;[10] the first count of the Gauls in 367.[11] The counts mentioned are the most ancient whose names are known; but nothing authorizes us to believe that they were the first that existed with like functions.

The title of count was common to the Empires of the East and

[1] Sanxit (Cæsar) neu quis senatoris filius, nisi contubernalis aut comes magistratuum, peregre proficisceretur. (Suet. Tranquil., C. Jul. Cæsar, cap. xliii.)

[2] Cum judicaret, in concilio habuit non amicos suos et comites tantum, sed jurisconsultos. (Spartian. in Hadrian.)

[3] Zosim. Hist., lib. ii., cap. 42.

[4] Cod. Theod., lib. x., tit. x., leg. 6.

[5] Ammian. Marcel. Hist., lib. xxvii., cap. 8.

[6] Cod. Theod., lib. xii., tit. i., leg. 33.

[7] Cod. Theod., lib. xvi., tit. x., leg. 11.

[8] Cod. Theod., lib. xi., tit. iii., leg. 2.

[9] Cod. Theod., lib. xii., tit. i., leg. 15.

[10] Cod. Theod., lib. xii., tit. i., leg. 4.

[11] Cod. Theod., lib. vii., tit. i., leg. 9.

of the West. We have said that the Greek writers called them κομητες. The word is found in a great number of authors; among others, in Constantine Porphyrogenitus,[1] in Leo,[2] and in Pachymerus.[3]

In France, under the kings of the first race, there were magistrates representing the government in the provinces, who bore the title of count.[4]

The Latin expression signifying *marquis* was *comes limitis, count of the frontiers.* The word *limes* was rendered in the Celtic language by *marca,* whence was first derived the false Latin word *marchio,* signifying *marquis,* and thence was afterward derived the French word *marche,*[5] signifying *frontier.* This is expressly shown in a letter of Pope John VIII., written between the years 872 and 882, which were the two limits of his pontificate.[6] Moreover, the counts of the frontiers are named in a law of Valentinian and of Valens of the year 367, and in a law of Honorius and Theodosius of the year 417.[7]

The title of duke is also Roman, and comes from *dux.* Before passing into the language of ceremony, *dux* meant general. The word had, however, a meaning sufficiently precise; for example, *dux* was next below *imperator.* Pompey received the title of *imperator* after having long commanded the Roman armies, and Metellus after a victory gained in Portugal over the army of Sertorius.[8] Cicero very clearly distinguishes these two titles.[9] Phædrus gives to the Emperor Tiberius the title of dux.[10] In the fourth century

1 Const. Porphyrog., lib. i. de them., cap. 1.

2 Leo in tact., cap. iii., § 10.

3 Pachymer., lib. i., cap. 11.

4 Si quis judicem fiscalem, quem comitem vocant, interfecerint. (Lex ripuar., tit. lv.)

5 Si quis alterum ligat et foris *marcha* eum vendiderit. (Lex Allaman., tit. xxxiv.)

6 Marca dicitur comitatus terræ alicujus, unde ipse comes marchio dicitur. (Joan. Pap. VIII., epist. ii.)

7 Comites . . . quibus Rheni est mandata custodia. (Cod. Theod., lib. vii., tit. i., leg. 9.)

Lege dudum latu, quæ licentiam exigendi . . . comitibus inferioribus denegavit, duci limitis Eufratensis. (Cod. Theod., lib. viii., tit. xi., leg. 2.)

8 Plutarch, Sertorius, ch. xxii.

9 M. Attilius Regulus, quum consul iterum in Africa ex insidiis captus est, *duce* Xantipo Lacedæmonio, *imperatore* autem patre Hannibalis, Hamilcare. (Cicero de Off., lib. iii., cap. xxvi.)

10 Tum sic jocata est tanti majestas ducis. (Phæd. Fabul., lib. ii., fabula v.)

the dukes are found among the officers of the emperors, and in the hierarchy next below the counts.[1] The first Duke of Egypt was of the year 364, under Valens.[2] There was a Duke of Mesopotamia in 349.[3] A law of Valentinian, of the year 367, mentions the dukes, who were in Gaul and who guarded the passages of the Rhine.[4] We find in Cassiodorus the terms, in which the investiture of the dukes was made by the emperors.[5]

As for the title of *prince*, we have already shown in the ninth chapter that it corresponds to the character expressed by the word *rex*.

It results from this rapid glance at the origin of the feudal titles of the middle ages, that their roots extend far into Roman history. As we have said, we do not wish to conclude from that, that they had in the Latin of the age of Augustus exactly the same meaning as with us, but only that our feudalism was not an isolated fact in the history of the West; that it was immediately preceded by the feudalism of ancient Italy, a feudalism identical in substance and like enough in form to have given to ours some of the principal terms of the heraldic vocabulary.

Another order of facts, which serve to prove the state of feudal subjection of ancient Italy, is the fairs, which the seigniors had the right of establishing in the villages; which proves that these villages belonged to them. In the second Philippic, Cicero reproaches Anthony with having defrauded the state of its rights by establishing, on his own private authority, fairs in the villages situated on his lands.[6] On the other hand, Suetonius relates that the Emperor Claudius, wishing to establish them on his private domains, asked authority for so doing from the senate.[7] It appears by a letter of the younger Pliny to Valerius, that the villages, which had fairs, sometimes made remonstrances to the senate against the neighboring

[1] Emensa ad magistros militum, et comites et duces omnes. (Cod. Theod., lib. viii., tit. xii., leg. 11.) Dukes are called inferior counts in law 2, tit. xi., book vii.

[2] Cod. Theod., lib. xii., tit. xii., leg. 5.

[3] Cod. Theod., lib. viii., tit. iv., leg. 4.

[4] . . . Duces . . . quibus Rheni est mandata custodia. (Cod. Theod., lib. vii., tit. i., leg. 9.)

[5] Ducatum tibi credidimus Retiarum, ut milites et in pace regas, et cum eis fines nostros solemni alacritate circumeas. (Cassiod. Var., lib. vii., cap. iv.)

[6] Imperium populi Romani hujus domesticis nundinis diminutum est. (Cicero, Philipp. ii., ch. xxxvi.)

[7] Jus nundinarum in privata prædia a consulibus petiit. (Suet. Tranquil., Tib. Claud. Cæsar, cap. xiii.)

lords, who wished to establish them on their lands.[1] A fragment of Modestin, in the Digest, testifies that from the time of Justinian it was the emperor, who authorized the creation of fairs in the villages,[2] and a law of Valentinian and Valens makes known that all, who attended them, were inviolable during their continuance.[3]

The establishment of these fairs in the villages belonging to the lords had a double object. First, they facilitated the sale of the slender productions of the soil, and procured for the peasants a small income. Next, they created for the lords an annual revenue from the various taxes, which they did not fail to establish, on the merchandise and provisions brought thither. This, the law of Valentinian and Valens just cited very expressly mentions.[4] Moreover, if we descend to the middle ages, we find innumerable examples of lords, who gave away or sold the fairs established on their domains; that is, the annual revenues those fairs produced. La Thomassiere relates, in his treatise on the local customs of Berry and Loris, that Geoffroy the Noble, Viscount of Bourges, gave, in 1012, two fairs on his domains to the monks of St. Ambrose.[5]

By force of time these boroughs of ancient France grew and became free: their lords accorded to them, little by little, the right of governing themselves, and the peasants who inhabited them, once subject to poll tax and bodily service, after having become proprietors of the lands, on which their fathers were slaves and they were serfs, now are the equals of their ancient masters, and send representatives to the king, who is the master of their masters.

[1] Vir prætorius Solers a senatu petiit ut sibi instituere in agris suis nundinas permittetur. Contradixerunt Vicentinorum legati. (Plin., lib. v., epist. iv.)

[2] Nundinis impetratis a principe. (Digest., lib. l., tit. xi.)

[3] . . . Nullum in mercatibus atque nundinis ex negociatorum mercibus conveniant . . . vel sub prætextu privati debiti aliquam ibidem concurrentibus molestiam possint inferre. (Cod. Justin., lib. iv., tit. lx., leg 1.)

[4] . . . Vel in venalitiis aut locorum temporali quæstu et commodo privata exactione sectentur. (Cod. Justin., lib. iv., tit. lx., leg. 1.)

[5] Dono etiam ex mea proprietate duas nundinas; unam scilicet in festivitate S. Petri de mense Junio; alteram in natale S. Ambrosii, et unamquamque per Septenos dies totidemque noctes. (La Thomas. Cout. Locales, ch. xxx.)

## CHAPTER XII.

### THE TRADES' UNIONS OF ANTIQUITY — THEIR FORMATION.

WE have now the slaves set free; some in the commune, as burghers; others under the feudal system, as peasants.

What will they become?

Some will labor, economize, amass, and become, in the commune, the body of artisans and merchants; under the feudal system, the class of small proprietors, farmers, and day-laborers.

Others, betrayed by physical and moral forces, by sickness, by revolutions, by the thousand disappointments, which attend man at every turn of his life, will not labor, will not economize, will not amass, and will form the hideous mass of paupers, thieves, and prostitutes.

Sometimes from this mire some pellets of gold will rise, as if to show that, wherever man is, intelligence, courage, and beauty, which are three gifts of God, are never entirely effaced; and we will see that the paupers are a tree which bears for fruit poets; robbers became conquerors, and prostitutes queens.

In general, then, the emancipated slaves, whether in the commune or in feudalism, divide into two branches: those who labor, and those who do not labor. We must now sketch the history of both. We commence with the history of those who labor.

Although beggars were not the objects of general attention and sympathy, and only received a sort of organization, by the foundation of establishments of public charity, about the beginning of the fourth century, we must not thence conclude that the number, more or less considerable, of laborers, produced by the emancipation of slaves, waited until that epoch to receive their organization through the trades' unions. The creation of trades' unions was anterior, by at least a thousand years, to the creation of houses of refuge. The reason of this fact is very simple. It is clear that the first emancipated slaves having necessarily become laborers, in order to live, these laborers were only transformed into beggars when the expenses of the family, the inadequacy of compensation, the suspension of industry or other analogous causes, rendered the wages of labor insufficient. In historic order, then, laborers naturally precede beggars; which explains why establishments of public charity only come a long time after the trades' unions, of which they are in some sort auxiliary, since the only resource of the laborer, in time of want, is to have recourse to charity, and to ask of the poorhouse what the workshop refuses. . We should here remark, before going farther, that to the number of causes, which we have already deduced to explain the rarity of beggars, thieves, and public women, in the times anterior to the fourth century, we should add the organization of labor, and the system of industrial and mercantile corporations among the ancients, of which we are going to indicate the formation, recount the development, and explain the fall.

The system adopted by the ancients for the organization of labor would be impracticable and odious to our customs and ideas; nevertheless, it had among them, and notably in the Roman Empire, the inappreciable advantage of changing every laborer into a public functionary, in attaching him and his indissolubly to the trade, which he had chosen, and of guaranteeing to him and his always all the necessaries, and sometimes all the commodities of life. It was by means of this provident organization that the laboring classes of antiquity so energetically resisted the causes of dissolution, abasement, and misery, which oppress the laboring classes of modern times, and were more than a thousand years in being transformed, in part, into beggars, thieves, and prostitutes.

Corporations or trades' unions—for we will use these two terms indifferently, although the latter is more particularly applicable to the corporations formed in the middle ages; the corporations, of all times and of all countries, having a common nature, differing but little in form, and not at all in their object—corporations or trades' unions existed among the Jews since the time of Solomon; among the Greeks from the time of Theseus, and among the Romans from the time of Numa.

We would remark—and the principles above established justify us—that the Jewish trades' unions go back even to the time of Joshua, since we have established that there were communes in Syria at that epoch. Now there is this connection between communes and trades' unions, that communes were the association of freedmen with a view to government, and trades' unions were the association of freedmen with a view to industry or commerce.

Communes, therefore, never existed without trades' unions; first, because their elements are the same; and next, because the freedmen, not being originally landed proprietors, were forced to become artisans or merchants. Wherever, therefore, we find a commune, we may be certain of the existence of a trades' union. More than that, we have a hundred examples of communes, which were formed with a trades' union already existing, and whose municipal charter was nothing but a statute law for a commercial corporation. The commune of Paris is an example.[1] We are therefore authorized to date the Jewish trades' unions as far back as Joshua, because we have shown the establishment of communes in Syria at the epoch of the egress of the Israelites from the desert.

The Jewish trades' unions are seen in the different corps of workmen employed to build the temple of Solomon, of which Flavius Josephus, in the eighth book of his history, gives abundant indications.[2] The Greek trades' unions, which bore the name of *fellowships*, *ἑταιρεία*, are clearly indicated by Plutarch in what he has written of the division of the citizens of Athens made by Theseus,[3] and

[1] We will hereafter show how the commune of Paris had, as the germ of its formation, a company or union of watermen, making part of the general organization of the trades of the empire, under the name of *Nautæ Parisiaci*.

[2] What Flavius Josephus relates of the works executed at different times at Jerusalem, in building, rebuilding, and repairing the temple, leaves no doubt that the workmen employed, both Jews and Sidonians, were organized in trades' unions. Besides, every scintilla of doubt is removed by the following passage, which clearly speaks of the hierarchy, which prevailed among the workmen, and of the thirty-two hundred *masters*, who had forty thousand masons employed on the walls of the temple. *Ησαν δ' εκ των παροίκων οὒς Δαυιδης καταλελοιπει, . . . τῶν δὲ λατομουντων ὀκτάκις μυριοι τουτων δ' επιραται τριχιλιοι καὶ τριακόσιοι.* (Flavii Josephi, Ant. Jud., lib. vii., cap. ii.)

[3] Plutarch thus expresses himself in the Life of Theseus, on the separation made by the founder of Athens of the nobility and the corps of artisans: "*Ου μὴν ἀτακτον, οὐδὲ μεμιγμένην περιειδεν υπο πληθους ἐπιχυθεντος ἀκρίτου γενομενην την δημοκρατιαν· ἀλλὰ πρωτος αποκρινας χωρις Ευπατριδας και Γεωμορους και Δημιουργους, Ευπατριδαις γινῶσκειν τα θεῖα, και παρέχειν αρχοντας ἀποδοὺς, και νόμων διδασκαλους είναι.*" (Plutarch, Theseus, ch. xxv.)

A little above, he mentions a feast, which was held in honor of the pilots, which establishes the existence of confraternities among the Athenian workmen. This feast was called *κυβερνησια*. "*Μαρτυρει δε τουτοις ἡρῶα Ναυσιθοου και Φαιακος εισαμενου Θησεως Φαληροι προς τὼ του Σχιρου ἱερῷ, και την ἑορτην τα κυβερνησια φησιν ἐκεῖνοις τελεισθαι.*" (Plutarch, Theseus, cap. xvii.)

Moreover, if the text of Plutarch could leave any doubt as to the fact of the Athenian trades' unions, a fragment of Gaius on the Twelve Tables, preserved in

the Roman trades' unions were, if not instituted, at least regulated by Numa, according to Dionysius of Halicarnassus, and all who have written on Roman antiquities.[1]

It would not be easy to reconstruct the Jewish trades' unions established in different cities, as Jerusalem, Samaria, Bethsura, Jericho, Tarshish, Sephŏris,(*a*) and others; first, because we have very few documents on the interior history of the Jews, and next because a great number of the laws of their interior administration were preserved only by tradition, like the customs of France, of which no general digest was made until the time of Charles V.; and lastly, because Flavius Josephus cites, in the 17th chapter, book xvi., of his Ancient History of the Jews, a law in relation to the paternal power,[2] which is not found in the Bible; whence we are authorized to believe that the Sacred Scriptures do not contain a complete collection of the Hebrew institutions down to the Christian era. The documents relative to the Greek trades' unions are a little more numerous, and although of all the ancient legislation of the Greeks there remain only the few fragments contained in the compilations of John Meursius and Samuel Petit,[3] it would not be impossible,

the Digest, says that the law on the corps of craftsmen would seem to have been borrowed from the laws of Solon on the same matter; and below Gaius cites the very text of the laws of Solon, in which it is decreed that the members of the crafts may organize themselves into trades' unions respecting the laws of the state. See the passage of Gaius and the text of Solon: "Sodales sunt qui ejusdem collegii sunt; quam Græci εταιρειαν vocant. His autem potestatem facit lex pactionem quam velint sibi ferre, dum ne quid ex publica lege corrumpant. Sed *hæc lex videtur ex lege Solonis translata esse;* nam illuc ita est: "Σὰν δε δημος, ἡ φρατορες, ἢ ἱερῶν ὀργίων, ἡ ναυται, ἡ συνσιτοι, ἡ ομοταφοι, ἡ θίασωται, ἢ ἐπι λιαν οιχομενοι, ἢ εἰς ἐμποριαν. Οτι ἂν τουτων διαδῶνται προς ἀλλήλους, κυριον ειναι, ἐὰν μη απαγορευση δημόσια γραμματα." (Digest, lib. xlvii., tit. xxii., leg. 4.)

1 Plutarch, in his Life of Numa, does not limit himself to saying that this king regulated the constitution of the Roman trades' unions, but names the corps of craftsmen, who made part of them. See what he says: "Των δε ἀλλων αυτου πολιτευματων ἡ κατα τεχνας διανομὴ του πλήθους μαλιστα θαυμαζεται." And a little farther on: "Ην δε ἡ διανομὴ κατα τας τεχνας, αὐλητων, χρυσοχόων, τέκτονων, βαφέων, σκυτοτομων, σκυτοδεψων, χαλκεων, κεραμεων." (Plutarch, Numa, cap. xvii.)

(*a*) Probably Sardis. See Dictionary of the Bible, by Dr. William Smith: "Sardis was a commercial mart of importance; the art of dyeing wool is said by Pliny to have been invented there; and at any rate, Sardis was the entrepôt of the dyed woollen manufactures. Sardis *recovered the privilege of municipal government* upon its surrender to Alexander the Great.

2 This is the law mentioned by Herod the Great in the assembly held at Beryta, giving to fathers an absolute right of life and death over their children. We have already spoken of this law in our third chapter.

3 Joannis Meursii Themis Attica, 1685, in 4to. Samuel Petit, Leges Atticæ, 1635, in folio.

with an attentive reading of their comedians, orators, and historians, to reproduce nearly all the essential features of the trades' unions of Athens or of Argos. We have not thought it necessary to undertake this labor; first, because we can fall back upon the Roman trades' unions, in relation to which the evidences abound, and next, because the trades' unions of all antiquity, we might almost say of all times, are very nearly cast in the same mould.

Plutarch relates in the Life of Numa, that this prince established at Rome the corps of craftsmen.[1] In the mouth of ancient chroniclers, who rarely criticized the facts they reported, such a fact should signify that Numa made some regulations relative to the confraternities and fellowships, which already existed at Rome, just as King John regulated the different corps of craftsmen, which existed in his time at Paris. In fact, it would be difficult to believe that, Rome having formed a species of commune from the day of its foundation,

[1] We do not know whether it is necessary that we should here give an opinion on the modern theories applied to the origin of Roman history, which consider all the royal period, which precedes the Twelve Tables, as a long myth, in which Romulus, Numa, Tullus Hostilius, and the other kings were symbols, and not men who really existed. This theory, imagined by the late Niebuhr and imported into France by M. Michelet, derives from the authority of these two names, eminent for historic learning, a solidity, which is proof against a mere note. We limit ourselves to saying of this theory what is necessary to show that it is not without premeditation that we have not accepted it.

In our opinion, to explain the origin of Rome by supposing that the kings of Rome were but symbols, is to create difficulties ten times greater than to follow the beaten track and suppose that these kings really existed. It is well understood that we content ourselves with expressing our opinion, without pretending to justify it, which would carry us too far from our subject. We would only remark that Niebuhr, who applied himself principally to the history of the Etruscan antiquities, may have had his reasons for belittling as much as possible all nationalities except that, of which he was the renovator and apologist. Moreover, without entering fully into the discussion, it is well to observe that Plutarch, writing, as he says in the Life of Theseus, on the faith of a considerable number of very ancient chronicles, was much nearer to Romulus and to Numa than we are to Charlemagne, and that the idea never occurred to us to take Charlemagne for a myth. Finally, to see only abstractions and allegories in the (to us) very real and plastic rudiments of ancient histories, is to fall into the same idea (it seems to us) which suggested to Dupuis his famous explanation of Christianity by the solar mythology.

Nevertheless, we accord full liberty to those, who have an opinion made up on these matters. We accept the scientific worth of Niebuhr with too much sincerity to suppose that we had refuted him in a few lines, and we have personally known too much of the strength of mind and immense acquirements of M. Michelet not to recognize that his excellent book would at least require another.

But we are convinced that the royal period of Roman history, excepting some details introduced by the chroniclers, was a reality and not a symbol, and we cite the acts of Romulus, Numa, Tarquin, and the other kings as of persons as real as Dagobert, Charlemagne, and Hugh Capet.

the emancipated, and consequently industrial and commercial, class should have waited until the time of Numa to create an association, that is to say, to fix the rule of their daily labor and transactions. However that may have been, it is under King Numa that the Roman trades' unions enter into history.

From that epoch the Roman corporations passed through three successive periods, each of which marked them with a particular stamp. The first period commenced with King Numa, and ended near about the time of the Emperor Vespasian; the second commenced with Vespasian, and ended near about the time of the Emperor Constantine; the third commenced with Constantine, and ended with the empire.

The first period comprises the formation of the trades' unions. That formation was spontaneous. Workmen of the same craft, traders in the same line of business, masons with masons, watermen with watermen, came together, united, agreed upon certain fixed points to regulate their relations, elected certain of them to judge the cases and apply the accepted rules. Such were the first trades' unions. And there could be as many of them as there were trades.

It appears that the number of those established at Rome under the kings was considerable, and also that their regulations were sometimes from a point of view so circumscribed, that they conflicted with the general spirit of the public laws. Then the control of the government commenced over the trades' unions, and they entered upon a new period, on which it will not be useless to give some explanations.

We have mentioned above, and the fragment of Gaius proves, that the Twelve Tables prescribed that the trades' unions should conform to the general laws of the state; and the fragment of Solon establishes that a like regulation was applied to the Athenian trades' unions, which shows that the corps of craftsmen have had, in every country, nearly the same destiny. We will show, when we come to treat of the trades' unions of the middle ages, that after having commenced by the good will of the workmen and merchants themselves, they have equally ended by receiving their institution from the good will of kings.

To comprehend well this new situation of the trades' unions under the republic, that is to say, at an epoch when the liberty of industry ought, it seems, to have been enlarged instead of being repressed, we must take into account some facts, which explain how the restrictions applied to their primitive liberty were nevertheless more favorable than hurtful to the unions.

At whose service could the workmen of Rome place themselves? Was it in the service of rich individuals? Never. The rich each possessed a great number of slaves,[1] of nearly all professions, by whom they had their work done. There were capitalists, who bought children of ten to twelve years of age, had them brought up and taught different professions, and reimbursed themselves for their advances by the product of their daily hire, when they were grown up and instructed. Thus people went to them to hire a slave tailor, shoemaker, musician, mason, grammarian, dancing-master, or philosopher; and these, who returned to the capitalist in the evening, brought back to him the price of their day's labor. Thus Crassus maintained, for profit by hiring them, readers, scribes, goldsmiths, silversmiths, stewards, housekeepers, and carvers.[2] This is true of all the people of antiquity, the Greeks as well as the Romans. For example, we find in the treatise of Xenophon on the *Revenues of Attica* the most circumstantial details as to the hirers of slaves, and as to the profit of their industry. Xenophon cites, among others, one named Nicias, who had a thousand slaves, whom he hired to a contractor for working mines, for an obolus a day per head.[3]

[1] Among the ancients, when they wanted to know a man's fortune, they asked him how many working slaves he had; that is, how many exercising a profession, whose wages constituted a fixed income for the master. Socrates having at Athens called to see a pretty freedwoman, called Theodota, holding the position of what we call in Paris a kept-woman, asked her, in admiration of the luxury of her house and her numerous domestics, if she had many slave workmen. (Xenophon, Memorabilia, lib. iii., cap. xi., § 4.)

[2] Plutarch, M. Crassus, cap. ii.

[3] Xenophon, De Vectegal., cap. iv., §§ 14, 15.

It results clearly from two passages of the same treatise that the senate, or rather the state, bought a great number of slaves, who were made to labor in their different professions, either on hire to individuals, or in the cultivation of lands, which they (the senate or state) took on lease; as, for example, in the cultivation of thc lands of the clergy, in keeping their houses, or in receiving the offerings, alms, or rent for seats in the pagan temples.

§§ 23, 24 of the same book prove that the state bought slaves to draw a revenue from their labor, and § 19 establishes that the state took the lands of the pagan clergy on lease. In a preceding and subsequent passage, Xenophon proposes to the Athenians to create a sort of bank, the capital of which, consisting of slaves, should be applied to the development of private industry for a certain consideration. (*a*) Finally, as to the small receipts of the temples, for example, from the rent of seats, we limit ourselves to citing from among other authorities this passage of Tertullian. "Exigitis mercedem pro solo templi, pro aditu sacri; non licet deos nosce gratis: venales sunt." (Tertul. Apologet., cap. xiii.)

**(*a*) Did General Howard get his ideas of the administration of the Freedmen's Bureau, from Xenophon's Treatise on the Revenues of Attica?**

So it was among the Romans. Thus Cato the elder had a number of slave workmen, according to Plutarch. He even lent money to his own slaves, with which to buy others still young, to whom they taught trades, and resold at a great profit, in which Cato participated.[1]

Crassus also had a battalion of five hundred slaves, of all trades connected with architecture. When he learned that a house was on fire, he hastened to offer to buy it. It is easy to comprehend that at such a moment the price would be greatly diminished. The purchase concluded, Crassus set his five hundred slaves to work, who put out the fire and repaired the house. It was thus that he became the owner of an entire quarter of Rome.[2]

It was not, then, to the rich that working-men united in trades' unions could offer their labor. Was it to the poor? But even among these, the trades' unions were met by the competition of the hirers of slaves. And such competition! As we have already said, the competition of such capitalists as Crassus, who often repeated — it was his favorite saying — that no man could boast of being rich without having the means of keeping in pay an army of 40,000 men.[3]

There remained only the government, which was the true patron of the trades' unions, and the works undertaken by it formed the only permanent workshop where labor could gain its daily wages.

On its side, the government needed always a number and variety of workmen sufficient to execute its works, and how great were the works executed by the Roman government! How many and such temples! So many and such aqueducts! So many and such bridges! Here the numerous workmen of Cato, the five hundred of Crassus could do nothing; corporations, associations of working-men, were needed; and it was because of being always their patrons and employers, that the senate and the emperors interfered to legislate for them. The law of the Twelve Tables, which ordains that every corporation shall conform to the general laws of the state, is then in reality the first privilege established in favor of the laboring classes already regularly organized at that epoch; since it to a certain extent created a monopoly in their favor, prevented

1 Plutarch, Marcus Cato, cap. xxi.
2 Plutarch, M. Crassus, cap. ii.
3 Plutarch, M. Crassus, cap. ii.

interference and loss to industry by prohibiting an unrestrained competition, and enriched all the existing trades' unions at the expense of all those, who could not organize into unions.

From the establishment of the republic to its fall, the Roman government never ceased to interfere by legislation with the trades' unions, to consolidate them, to simplify them, above all to render them in a measure sole collectors of the public revenues, and to make them the instruments and interior organs of the administrative life. See, in few words, how the trades' unions drew near to the state, and ended by becoming an integrant part of it.

As the republic extended her conquests, she successively increased her public domains and her armies; that is to say, her revenues and expenditures. For a government, which had neither our centralization, nor our hierarchy of functionaries, nor our rapid means of transportation, nor our banks, nor our system of credit, which improvises in twenty-four hours as many contractors as needed, it was very difficult to regulate and collect the revenues, not only from the Roman citizens and the conquered provinces, but principally from the immense and innumerable possessions belonging to the public domain, and from the extensive lands of the pagan clergy, which had to be let out on leases more or less long.

The taxes under the Roman Empire had not the unity and simplicity of modern states. To obtain an idea of them, we must go back to the taxes of every kind that existed in the middle ages. But it may be said that the Roman taxes were of two great classes. The first comprised the taxes assessed on persons and paid in money; the second the taxes paid in kind by the farmers of the public domain. The taxes in money were collected under the emperors by the prætorian prefects, with the aid of inferior officers, and were applied to feeding and paying the troops, as Zosimus relates in what he says of Constantine;[1] the taxes in kind were ordinarily received by farmers-general and by the trades' unions, as is proved by the laws on master butchers and pork butchers, which we will cite below.

The history of the possessions of the pagan clergy would be very curious and ample. We are forced to leave it for the volume in

[1] Zosim. Hist. Rom., lib. ii., in Constantin. See also a law of Valentinian cited in note 3 of page 209.

which we will treat of the history of the noble classes. Meanwhile we limit ourselves to saying that the lands of the clergy were enfeoffed, or, which comes to the same thing, let out on long leases, and the rents, paid in kind, were generally received by the trades' unions; for example, by the decurions, who formed a veritable union, and who had the right of farming out the lands of the public domain and of the temples, at least from the end of the fourth century, as is proved by a law of Arcadius and Honorius of the first of December, 400.[1] A passage of the treatise of Xenophon on the Revenues of Attica proves that the property of the pagan clergy was farmed out in the same way among the Greeks.[2]

Add to this the care of transporting to Rome the public revenues, or of having them at certain points for the support of the armies, that of provisioning the city, that of having ready in the most distant and desert localities those legions of marvellous workmen, who have covered Spain, Gaul, Germany, England, Greece, Asia Minor, Egypt, Syria, and the north of Africa, the whole known universe, with indestructible monuments.

It was by the aid of the trades' unions that the government organized its administrative service, its distribution of military forces, and the development of its architectural splendor. There were trades' unions charged with the collection of the revenues; others that supplied Rome with provisions; others that fed it; others that took care of the edifices; others that clothed the soldiers; others that armed them; others that supplied the interior and domestic wants of a city full of riches and devoted to all kinds of pleasures. The trades' unions then were the framework of bone that supported this great Roman body. It was by them that the senate and the emperors acted after having spoken; it was by them that so many different provinces, nations, tongues, and religions were held together; it was by them that the material acts conceived by the sovereign people were put into operation; finally, it was they that executed all those minute details of daily labor, for which we have

1 Ædificia, ... et reipublicæ loca ... vel ea quæ de jure templorum aut per diversos petita, aut æternabili domui fuerint congregata, vel civitatum territoriis ambiuntur, sub perpetua conductione, salvo dumtaxat canone, quem sub examine habitæ discussionis constitit adscriptum, penes municipes, collegiatos, corporatos urbium singularum conlocata permaneant. (Cod. Theod., lib. x., tit. iii., leg. 5.)

2 ... *Μισθοῦνται γοῦν καὶ τεμένη, καὶ ἱερὰ.* (Xenophon, De Vectigal., cap. iv., § 19.)

that crowd of contractors, private workshops, and free laborers, who are the active part of modern states, but were completely unknown to the empires of antiquity.

The Roman trades' unions were naturally of two sorts, although at bottom they had the same regulations, the same privileges, the same duties, and the same object. They were divided, or may be divided, into commercial and industrial unions. In the law they bear the name of colleges, *collegia*, or of corporations, *corpus*. A law of Honorius and Arcadius, of the year 412, calls the members of the trades' unions indifferently *collegiati* or *corporati*.[1]

The principal commercial corporations of the empire were the sailors' union, *navicularii;* that of the bakers, *pistores;* butchers, *suarii;* limeburners, *calcis coctores;* weavers, *linteones;* tailors, *gynæceiarii;* the shell-fish gatherers and silk-dyers, *murileguli;* carriers, *bastagarii;* wine merchants, *vini susceptores;* lumbermen, *dendrophori;* and a crowd of others, not omitting the respectable corps of sworn measurers of grain at the warehouses of the port of Ostia, *mensores portuenses*.[2]

We must now give an idea of the manner in which all these corporations worked and were connected. We will take, for example, the bakers and butchers.

The port of Ostia was the great entrepôt of Rome. Thither the corporation of watermen were required to bring the revenues of the lands of the public domain, which were immense. Almost always the revenues of the domain were in kind, which would prove that the lands were held under leases by the farmers, who paid half the product, or a third, according to their fertility. Moreover, we are authorized to believe that each commercial union, as we have said, collected the tax in kind, which appertained to its specialty; that is to say, the bakers received from the lands of the domain the rent in grain; the wine merchants the rent in wine; and so of the rest. The fact is that the butchers, by agents, collected the rents in hogs

[1] *Collegiatos*, et vituarios, et nemesiacos, signiferos, cantabrarios, et singularum urbium *corporatos*. (Cod. Theod., lib. xiv., tit. vii., leg. 2.)

[2] Navicularii, Cod. Theod., lib. xiii., tit. v. — Pistores, lib. xiv., tit. iii. — Suarii, *ibid.*, tit. iv.— Calcis coctores, *ibid.*, tit. vi. — Linteones, lib. x., tit. xx., leg. 6, 8, 9, 16, et passim. — Gynæceiarii, *ibid.*, leg. 2, 3, 7, et passim. — Murileguli, *ibid.*, leg. 5, 12, et passim.— Bastagarii, *ibid.*, leg. 4, 11.— Vini susceptores, lib. xiv., tit. iv., leg. 4. — Dendrophori, lib. xiv., tit. vii., leg. 1. — Mensores portuenses, lib. xiv., tit. iv., leg. 9.

and cattle from the farmers of certain provinces, as in Lucania, Campania, Brutium, and Samnium. We find this much in detail in a law of Constantine of the year 326,[1] in a constitution of Julian of the year 363,[2] and especially in a law of Valentinian and Marcian of the year 452.[3]

The sailors' union, then, for a fixed charge for freight, transported the revenues in kind to the warehouses of the port of Ostia.[4] The bakers' union, located at Rome, became in a measure responsible for the grain as soon as it was in the warehouses.[5] They had it measured before admitting it into the warehouses by the experts of the measurers' union,[6] and they had it transported to Rome by another union of the coasters of the Tiber, distinct from the great union of navicularii, and called *corpus caudicarium*, as appears from a law of Honorius of the year 417.[7]

The caudicarii, on arriving at Rome, distributed the grain among

[1] Ea prætia, quæ in Campania per singulos annos reperiuntur, suariis urbis Romæ debent solvi, ita ut periculo suariorum populo porcinæ species adfatim præbeatur. (Cod. Theod., lib. xiv., tit. iv., leg. 3.)

[2] . . . Lucanus possessor et Bruttius, quos longæ subvectionis damna quatiebant, possint, si velint, speciem moderatam . . . dissolvere. (Cod. Theod., lib. xiv., tit. iv., leg. 4, § 2.)

[3] Nec ante quidquam de Lucania Samnioque provinciis arca prætoriana deposcat, quam suariis exigentibus debitum omne solvatur. (Cod. Theod., leg. novell. Theod. lib., tit. xxix.)

[4] Ex quocumque Hispaniæ littore portum urbis Romæ navicularii navis intraverit. (Cod. Theod., lib. xiii., tit. v., leg. 4.) Patronos horreorum portuensium. (Cod. Theod., lib. xiv., tit. xxiii., leg. 1.)

Cassiodorus reports at length the instructions given by the emperor to the prefect of subsistence, to the end that he should oversee the bakers. We read as follows: . . . Si querela panis, ut assolet, concitetur, tu promissor ubertatis seditiones civicas momentanea satisfactione dissolvis. . . . In fraudulentos distringe; panis pondera æquus examinator intende; sollicitius auro pensetur. (Cassiodor. Variar., lib. vi., formul. xviii.)

[5] Ἠσαν ἐξ ἀρχαὶου κατα την μεγιστην Ρωμην οικοι παμμεγεθεις, εν οις ὁ τη πολει χορηγουμενους ἄρτος εγίνετο. (Socrat. Hist. Ecclesiast., lib. v., cap. 8.)

[6] Ad excludendas fraudes . . . *portuensium mensorum*. (Cod. Theod., lib. xiv., tit. iv., leg. 9.)

[7] Qui navem Tiberinam habere fuerit ostensus, onus reipublicæ necessarium agnoscat. (Cod. Theod., lib. xiv., tit. xxi., leg. 1.)

Besides, these boatmen of the Tiber, *nautæ Tiberni*, were identically the same as those designated in law 9, title 4, of lib. xiv., and in law 2, title 3, of the same book, under the name of caudicarii, as is established by this passage from Seneca: "Et naves nunc quoque, quæ ex antiqua consuetudine per Tiberim commeatus subvehunt, *caudicariæ* vocantur." (Seneca, De Brevit. Vit., cap. 13.)

On the other hand, Varro thus explains the signification of *caudicarius*: Quod antiqui plures tabulas conjunctas codices dicebant, a quo in Tiberi naves *codicarias* appellamus. (Varro apud Nonium, cap. xiii., num. 12.)

the bakeries, which were situated very nearly one in each quarter, that is to say, to the number of fourteen for the whole city.[1] These bakeries, which had a separate accountability, and were directed by three master bakers, of whom one filled the office of dean[2] for five years, and all were elected, were so many members and branches of the Roman bakery. The grain was then ground in hand-mills,[3] and the bread baked there,[4] and sold for the consumption of all. It appears by a law of Honorius, of the year 398, that the custom was to make bread of three qualities.[5]

The butchers at Rome were divided into two unions, that of the pork butchers, *suarii*, and that of the mutton and beef butchers, *pecuarii*. Butcher's meat was never used except by slaves and poor people. The rich ate fish, poultry, and fat venison. Pork, as we have said, was used exclusively for slaves. The beef and mutton butchers' union declined very much, and a law of Honorius of the year 419 reunited them to their fortunate rivals, the pork butchers' union.[6] The butchers were charged with going personally into the stock-raising provinces to collect the taxes in kind from the Roman citizens, and the rents, which were also in kind, of the lands of the public domain, which were either enfeoffed or leased out. A law of Constantine, of the year 326, nevertheless shows that the proprietors or tenants had the option of paying the tax in money.[7]

[1] Septem cohortes opportunis locis constituit (Cæsar), ut binas regiones urbis unaquæque cohors tueatur. (Cod. Justin., lib. i., tit. xv., leg. 3, in proem.)

[2] These master bakers, who administered the branch bakeries, are designated by the name of patroni pistorum, in laws 2, 7, and 12 of tit. iii., book xiv., of the Theodosian Code. Law 7, in reference to the dean, says: Post quinquennii tempus emensum, unus prior e patronis pistorum otio donetur.

[3] Cum servis, *molis*. (Cod. Theod., lib. xiv., tit. iii., leg. 7.)

[4] Annona in pane cocto domibus exhibenda. (Cod. Theod., lib. xiv., tit. xvi., leg. 2.)

[5] Horace mentions bread, which he calls *second quality:*

Vivit siliquis et *pane secundo*. (Horat. Epis., lib. ii., epis. 1., v. 123.)

It remains to be ascertained whether this was better than that which Suetonius calls *black bread.* Panem sordidum oblatum aspernatus est. (Suet. Tranq., Tib. Claud. Nero, cap. xlviii.)

Galen mentions four kinds of bread; the first, which he calls σιλιγνίτης, of the finest flour; the second, σεμιδαλίτης, made of shorts; the third, συγκομιστικος, of unbolted flour; the fourth, ῥυπαρος, that is to say black, of which one variety, the most inferior, was called ὁ ἄρτος πιτυριας, bran bread.

[6] Suariis pecuarii jungantur. (Cod. Theod., lib. xiv., tit. iv., leg. 10.)

[7] In arbitrio suo possessor habeat, ne suario pecuniam solvat; quod ideo permissum est ne in æstimando porcorum pondere licentia suariis præbeatur. (Cod. Theod., lib. xiv., tit. iv., leg. 2.)

Generally, as we have said, they paid in kind, and the rent of a forest or of a heath was fixed at so many pounds of pork. The animals were then weighed before delivery to the butchers,[1] and, the law adds, after having passed a night without food. A law of Julian, of the year 363, to obviate the fluctuations in the price of animals, ordains that they shall be appraised at least in Campania; that the butchers shall receive the taxes or revenues in money, and that they should buy the hogs wherever they wished, as the union might find to their advantage.[2] When purchased, the hogs were taken to Rome, killed, cut up, and sold in the different quarters of the city, exactly as the bakers did with the bread.

The interior organization of the Roman trades' unions appears to have been very simple. Those of the same trade, for example the bakers, who were scattered throughout the empire, were divided into groups in the different provinces and cities. A law of Honorius and Theodosius fixes the maximum of each of these local unions at 563 members.[3] Every five years these members elected a dean and two assessors. We will see hereafter that Pliny the younger asked of Trajan permission to establish a union of 150 members.

Each of these unions elected annually officers, who bore the name of *patrons*. This is seen specially in the imperial laws for bakers,[4] boatmen of the Tiber, and measurers of grain at the port of Ostia.[5] These *patrons* were also called *syndics* in all the unions generally,[6] and there were at least four for each local union. A law of Hono-

[1] Pondus porcorum trutinæ examine, non oculorum libertate quæratur . . . animal vero a possessore tradendum, ob digeriem, prius unius noctis tantum jejunitate vacuetur. (Cod. Theod., lib. xiv., tit. iv., leg. 4.)

[2] Per singulos itaque annos juxta prætia quæ reperiuntur in publica conversatione, per Campaniam habitentes pecuniam pro singulis libris porcinæ præcipiantur exsolvere; ita ut, non ad prætia quæ in urbe Roma reperiuntur, sed quæ apud Campanos in publicis ruribus habentur, nummariæ exactionis facultas denegetur. (Cod. Theod., lib. xiv., tit. iv., leg. 3.)

[3] Cessante omni ambitione, omni licentia, quingentorum sexaginta trium collegiatorum numerus maneat, nullique his addendi mutandive, vel in defuncti locum substituendi pateat copia, ita ut judicio tuæ sedis (Præf. Pret.) sub ipsorum presentia corporatorum, in eorum locum quos humani subtraxerint casus, ex eodem quo illi fuerant, corpore, subrogentur; nulli alii corporatorum præter dictum numerum per patrocinia immunitate concessa. (Cod. Just., lib. iv., tit. lxiii., leg. 5.)

[4] Unus prior e *patronis* pistorum. (Cod. Theod., lib. xiv., tit. iii., leg. 7.)

[5] Ad excludendas *patronorum* fraudes. (Cod. Theod., lib. xiv., tit. iv., leg. 9.)

[6] In communi totius corporis causa, *syndico* ordinato. (Cod. Theod., lib. xiv., tit. ii., leg. 42.)

rius and Theodosius, of the year 417,[1] speaks of *the three first patrons*, which must be understood without prejudice to the dean, of whom we are about to speak. One of these patrons or syndics was named for five years, by the whole entire corporation, administrator-general of the interests of the society,[2] who bore the title of *prior*, and he had charge of all the property, movable and immovable.[3] All the trades' unions were organized after this general plan.

The industrial unions, in relation to which the documents are not always so clear nor so abundant, were formed after the same model. A law of Constantine of the year 337 mentions thirty-five of them. There were others, which are mentioned by authors, and also in later laws. Behold the thirty-five mentioned in the law of Constantine, some of which it is not easy to recognize, either because the texts have been altered, or because their specialties have perished in the wreck of ancient civilization!

There were unions of the following trades: architects, *architecti;* carvers in plaster, *laquearii;* a kind of roofers, of whom Tertullian speaks in his treatise on idolatry, and whom he, like Constantine, calls *albarii;*[4] carpenters, *tignarii;* doctors, *medici;* lapidaries, *lapidarii;* chasers in silver, *argentarii;* masons, *structores;* veterinarians, *mulo medici;* stonecutters, *quadratarii;* furbishers, *barbaricarii;* a union, which Cujas believes to have been that of the pavers, and whose name, probably corrupted, is in the law of Constantine *scasores;* painters, *pictores;* sculptors, *sculptores;* pearl-dressers, *diatritarii;* joiners, *intestinarii;* statuaries, *statuarii;* decorative painters, *musivarii;* gravers on copper, *ærarii;* blacksmiths, *ferrarii;* marble-cutters, *marmorarii;* gilders, *deauratores;* founders, *fusores;* dyers in purple, *blatiarii;* pavers in mosaic, *tessellarii;* goldsmiths, *aurifices;* looking-glass makers, *specularii;*

[1] . . . Decernimus ne in singulis tres primos patronos corporum singulorum. (Cod. Theod., lib. xiv., tit. iv., leg. 9.)

[2] Unus e patronis totius consensu corporis eligatur, qui per quinquennium custodiam . . . suscipiat. (Cod. Theod., lib. xiv., tit. iv., leg. 9.)

[3] Post quinquennii tempus emensum, unus *prior* e patronis . . . ei qui sequitur, officinam cum animalibus, servis, molis, fundis dotalibus, pistrinorum postremo omnem enthecam tradat atque consignet. (Cod. Theod., lib. xiv., tit. iii., leg. 7.)

[4] Scit albarius tector et tecta sarsire, et tectoria inducere, et cisternam liare, et cimatia distendere, et multa alia ornamenta præter simulacra parietibus inscrispare. (Tertul. de Idol., cap. viii.)

wheelwrights, *carpentarii*; water-carriers, *aquæ libratores*; glaziers, *vitriarii*; workers in ivory, *eburarii*; fullers, *fullones*; potters, *figuli*; plumbers, *plumbarii*; furriers, *pelliones*.[1]

The law of Constantine only mentions these trades' unions, although there were many others. It suffices to say that every profession had its laws; that there was a fortune-tellers' union, mentioned in a law of Honorius and Arcadius of the year 412, under the name of *corpus nemesiacorum*,[2] and that the same emperors did not disdain to occupy themselves with regulations for the venerable master-banner-bearers-at-feasts,[3] and with their numerous varieties, from the *signiferi*, who were the genus, to the *cantabrarii*, who were the species.

---

## CHAPTER XIII.

### ANCIENT TRADES' UNIONS — THEIR DEVELOPMENT.

TO comprehend fully the revolution, which took place in the trades' unions toward the commencement of the fourth century, it is necessary to retrace our steps, and elucidate a fact, which we have only intimated: we speak of the passage of the trades' unions from the free to the obligatory state.

The point of departure of the trades' unions is clearly characterized in the law of Solon, on the Greek fraternities, which has been preserved in the Basilicon, and in the Digest, and which we have already cited from the latter compilation.[4] By the terms of that law all working-men, all merchants, all of the same industry or trade, had the right to unite, organize, and form a society, *provided that the public laws* did not forbid it;[5] or, in other words, provided

1 Cod. Theod. de Excusationib. artific., lib. xiii., tit. iv., leg. 2.)

2 Nemesiaci, a dea Nemesi, quæ eadem est cum bona Fortuna. (Cod. Theod. Notul. Gothof. ad leg. 2, tit. vii., lib. xiv.)

3 Signiferi, . . . qui scilicet signa, et in his deorum, ferebant in pompis, festis, ludicris gentilitiis. (Ibid.)

4 See note 3, page 200.

5 *Εαν μὴ απαγορευση δημοσια πραγματα*, according to the Basilicon (vide Cujac., observat., lib. vii., cap. xxx. in fine; or *ἐάν μὴ ἀπαγορευση δημοσια γραμματα*, according to the Digest. (Vide Digest., lib. xlvii., tit. xxii., leg. 4.)

that the association formed did not infringe the common law. We have elsewhere shown that the Roman law of the Twelve Tables on corporations contained the same provisions as the Greek law, so much so that one appeared to Gaius to be the translation of the other.

Thus the first thing to be established relative to trades' unions, Greek or Roman, is that they commenced by being free, by having the right of the initiative in their formation, in conformity to the law. This is what we call their point of departure.

History proves that the Roman unions preserved this right of initiative first under the kings, then under the consular government, and lastly under the imperial government, nearly up to the time of Trajan.

During this period of more than seven centuries, counting from Numa, unions were formed, subject to be suppressed when they violated the general regulations of the state; but it is very clear that those, which were destroyed during this interval as *illegal*, were created without authorization, since an authorization would have rendered them legal. Besides, it is not less clear that there could be no clandestine unions, since the effect of every union was to confer privileges, and, consequently, to produce civil effects.

The first act of reform, which modified the Roman unions, was that of Tarquin the Proud. This king made a general revision of them, maintained those of Numa, and dissolved some of the others.[1] It appears that when these purgations had been made, fraud recommenced, and that it was necessary at long intervals to proceed to new revisions. But it was not until nearly four and a half centuries after Tarquin the Proud that we find another purgation of the unions. It took place, according to a senatus consultum reported by Barnaby Brisson,[2] under the consulate of L. Cæcilius Creticus and Q. Martius Rex; that is to say, according to the consular registers, sixty-six years before the Christian era. We find another, eleven years afterward, in the consulate of P. Lentulus Spinther and Q. Cæcilius Metellus Nepos, which is mentioned by Cicero in a letter to Quintus, his brother.[3]

[1] Dion. Halicarn., lib. iv., cap. xliii.

[2] Barnabe Brisson. Selectæ antiquitatis juris, lib. i., cap. xiv.

[3] Eodem die senatus-consultum factus est, ut sodalitates decuriatique discederent, lexque de iis ferretur, ut qui non discessissent, ea pœna, quæ est de vi, tenerentur. (Cic. Epist. ad Quint. Frat., lib. ii., epist. 3.)

Under the emperors the reforms of the unions were very numerous. Cæsar made one,[1] Augustus another,[2] Nero a third.[3] We can see by the texts of the authors that these three, like the previous reforms, were undertaken with a view of bringing back anarchical associations within the general spirit of the Roman law.

After Nero, we find no reforms in the unions. Maximin[4] plundered them, but did not reform them. Zeno forbade monopolies and clandestine coalitions, but he did not reform them.[5] There is for this change a very simple reason, which is this:

Between Nero and Trajan, nearly thirty years, there was a revolution in the unions, which consisted in taking away from them the initiative of their formation, and subjecting them to a previous authorization. We readily conceive that thereafter there could be no more illegal unions, since none existed except on condition of having been authorized.

Under Nero this revolution had not taken place, since this emperor reformed some unions. Under Trajan it had, since Pliny asked permission of him to establish a union of blacksmiths in Nicomedia, which that emperor refused.[6]

All that we find new respecting the unions before Constantine is, toward the end of the second century, some edicts of Severus, authorizing slaves to organize in fraternities with the consent of their masters; but on condition of having a curator, who should act for them, and of not meeting oftener than once a month;[7] and, at

[1] Cuncta collegia, præter antiquitus constituta, distraxit. (Suetonius Tranq., C. Jul. Cæsar, cap. xlii.)

[2] . . . Collegia, præter antiqua et ligitima, dissolvit. (Suetonius Tranq., C. Jul. Cæsar. Octav., cap. xxxii.)

[3] . . . Collegiaque, quæ contra leges instituerant, dissoluta. (Corn. Tacitus, Annal., lib. xiv., cap. xvii.)

[4] Zosim. Hist. Rom., lib. i., in Maximin.

[5] Jubemus, ne quis . . . monopolium audeat exercere; neve quis illicitis habitis conventionibus, conjuret aut paciscatur, ut species diversorum corporum negotiationis, non minoris quam inter se statuerint, venundentur. (Cod. Just., lib. iv., tit. lix., leg. unica.)

[6] . . . Tu, domine, dispice, an instituendum putes collegium fabrorum, duntaxat hominum CL; ego attendam ne quis, nisi faber, accipiatur, neve jure concesso in aliud utatur. (C. Plin. Epist., lib. x., epist. xxxiv.)

Trajan refused in these terms: Tibi quidem secundum exempla complurium in mentem venit posse collegium fabrorum apud Nicomedenses constitui; sed meminerimus provinciam istam et præcipue eas civitates ab ejusmodi factionibus esse vexatas. (Ibid., epist. xxxv.)

[7] Sed permittitur tenuioribus stipem menstruam conferre, dum tamen semel in

the commencement of the third century, an edict of Alexander, creating in certain unions, under the name of *defender*, an officer, who already existed in most of them under the name of *syndic*.[1]

With Constantine commenced, as we have said, a new era for the unions. It was then that their bonds were tightened; that a kind of fatality weighed upon those, who composed them, and that they became a *necessary body*, according to the language of the Roman laws.[2]

At the point, to which we have now brought them, they had a strong and complete organization, formed by the laboring, industrial, and commercial classes, for the benefit of the government. We must now show them, constituting a normal, permanent, and hierarchical association, sanctioned by the government for the profit of the laboring, industrial, and commercial classes, up to the moment, when causes, arising outside of their organization, nature, laws, and object, made them parties to, and responsible for, all the misfortunes of the empire, its disorders, its enslavement, and its fall.

It was toward the commencement of the fourth century, as we have said, that this change took place in the institution of the trades' unions, which was truly an entire revolution. Until then the different corps of craftsmen had been absolutely under the direction of, and dependent on, the government. In Africa they were subject to the jurisdiction of the vicar of the province;[3] in Italy, of the prefect of subsistence, or of the prefect of Rome;[4] in the East, of the proconsul, or other dignitaries of the palace.[5] They were, as to their duties, subject entirely to the discretion of the emperors. The bakers' union was required to furnish bread to the cities; the sailors' and wagoners' to furnish transportation; the masons' to fur-

mense coeant, ne sub prætextu hujusmodi illicitum collegium coeat. Quod non tantum in urbe, sed et in Italia et in provinciis, locum habere, Divus quoque Severus rescripsit. (Digest., lib. xlvii., tit. xxi., leg. 1., in proem.)

Servos quoque licet in collegio tenuiorum recipi volentibus dominis, ut curatores horum corporum sciant, ne invito aut ignorante domino in collegium tenuiorum reciperent. (Digest., lib. xlvii., tit. xxi., leg. 3, § 2.)

[1] Lamprid. in Alexand.

[2] Et quoniam necessarium corpus fovendum est. (Cod. Theod., lib. xiv., tit. iii. leg. 2.)

[3] See Cod. Theod., lib. xiii., tit. v., leg 36, *navicularii.*

[4] See Cod. Theod., lib. xiii., tit. v., leg. 2, as to the *navicularii;* as to the unions generally, ibid., lib. xiv., tit. ii., leg. 1.

[5] See Cod. Theod., lib. x., tit. xix., leg. 2, and tit. xx., leg. 11.

nish a sufficient number of hands for the public works; in a word, the corps of craftsmen were strictly instruments of the administration, and in many respects even the administration itself. But, at least, the different members of these corps were perfectly at liberty to enter or leave them, to pass from one to the other at will, and in all cases to keep their patrimony entirely free, separate, and per sonal, carrying it with them into any union, with which they might affiliate, and with power to will, give away, or sell it. This is expressly stated in a law of Constantine of the year 319, relative to the bakers' union.[1]

Well! forty-five years later, in 364, the right, which members of the unions had to sell, give away, or bequeath their patrimony, like other citizens, was taken from them by a law of Valentinian II., and of Valens, addressed to Symmachus, prefect of Rome.[2] This law only permitted gifts to sons and grandsons; but even this favor was not of long duration; for a new law of Valentinian, of the year 369, forbids absolutely the alienation of the patrimony of members of the unions.[3]

Thus, toward the middle of the fourth century, the position of the members of all the unions was entirely changed. The unions held to the government the same relations; but the individuals, who composed them, contracted new and unheard-of obligations. In fact, from this epoch no member of a union could leave it and pass to another under any excuse whatever. This is declared, for all the unions generally, in a novel of Valentinian, of the year 445, which ordains that all those, who had quitted a union, should be brought back to it, although they had become soldiers, or even clergymen up to the grade of deacon;[4] and we find this established for sailors,

[1] Cunctis pistoribus intimari oportet quod si quis forte possessiones suas ideo putaverit in alios transferendas, ut postea se, rebus in abdito conlocatis, minus idoneum adseveret. (Cod. Theod., lib. xiv., tit. iii., leg 1.)

[2] Prædia rustica vel urbana, quæ possident privato jure pistores, nec senatorem, nec officialem comparare permittimus (contractu pari cum aliis non interdicto), quippe mercantes ad venditoris officium vocabantur. . . . In donationibus vero filii excepti sunt et nepotes. (Cod. Theod., lib. xiv., tit. iii., leg. 3.)

[3] . . . Sciat corpori obnoxium vendere et alienare non posse, sed in sua causa et pistorum nomine ac jure residere. (Cod. Theod., lib. xiv., tit. iii., leg. 13.)

[4] . . . Oportet revocari, sive etiam in clericorum numero reperitur, usque ad diaconis locum. (Cod. Theod., leg. novel. lib., tit. xxvi.)

15

especially in a law of Valentinian and Valens, of the year 365;[1] for bakers, by another law of Valentinian and Valens, of the same year;[2] for butchers, by a law of Arcadius and Honorius, of the year 408;[3] for tailors, by a law of Theodosius and Valentinian, of the year 426;[4] and so of all the other unions. From the middle, then, of the fourth century, that is, at least from the year 364, the general institution of the trades of the empire became like the orders in the Church; it stamped them with a character, so that death itself could not loosen their bonds; and the son or legatee of a working-man, the former for having taken his name, the latter for having taken his estate, were forced to choose the same trade, and enter into the same fraternity.[5]

Perhaps it would be interesting to trace the successive encroachments of the trades' unions upon the persons, the families, and the property of those, who composed them. First, we have seen, and this is the point of departure, every member of a union indissolubly attached to it till death, so that neither flight, nor the military, nor the clerical, character, nor anything else, could withdraw them from it. Then, the children and grand-children were forced to adopt the profession of the father and grandfather; to enter into their union, and fulfil its duties. This is decreed by a law of Valentinian and Valens, of the year 364, relative to bakers,[6] and by a law of Valentinian, Theodosius, and Arcadius, of the year 389, relative to butchers.[7]

After the sons and grandsons came the sons-in-law. They too

[1] Quisquis ex naviculariorum corpore, defugiens solita munia, ad honores indebitos venit, in corporis sui consortia revertatur. (Cod. Theod., lib. xiii., tit. v., leg. 11.)

[2] . . . Ne illud quidem cuiquam concedi oportet, ut e officina ad aliam possit transitum facere. (Cod. Theod., lib. xiv., tit. iii., leg. 8.)

[3] Quicumque de suariorum corpore originariam functionem . . . declinasse noscuntur . . . ad munus pristinum revocentur. (Cod. Theod., lib. xiv., tit. iv., leg. 6.)

[4] Si quis de corpore gynæceiariorum . . . voluerit de suo collegio liberari . . . universam generis sui prosapiam . . . obnoxiam largitionibus sacris futuram esse non dubitet. (Cod. Theod., lib. x., tit. xx., leg. 16.)

[5] This absolute subjection of craftsmen to the service of their union explains this passage of Herodotus on the Egyptians, so often thought strange, in which he says that sons were required to follow the profession of their fathers: . . . παῖς παρὰ πατρὸς ἐδεκόμενος. (Herodot., lib. ii., cap. 166.)

[6] Filios pistorum . . . post emensum vicesimum annum ætatis, paterni muneris necessitatem subire cogantur. (Cod. Theod., lib. xiv., tit. iii., leg. 5.)

[7] . . . Consanguineos quoque eorum (suariorum) . . . functionibus jubeas adjungi, plenum et æquitatis et juris est. (Cod. Theod., lib. xiv., tit. iv., leg. 5.)

were attached, they and their posterity, fatally to the trades' union of their fathers-in-law by a law of Constantine II., of the year 355, relative to bakers.[1] After the sons-in-law came all the descendants generally, who were claimed by the union of their ancestors; as is provided by a law of Valentinian and Valens, of the year 365, relative to bakers.[2] After the descendants came all, who were named in the will of a member of a union; as was sanctioned by a law of Valentinian, Theodosius, and Arcadius, of the year 390, relative to sailors.[3] In fine, and this is the extreme point, to which the spirit of absorption was carried, the trades' unions imperatively claimed all, who, by whatever title, whether by gift or purchase, were found in possession of property, that had belonged to a member of the union, and a *pro rata* of the property; which was established by a law of Constantius, of the year 319, relative to sailors,[4] by a law of Valentinian and Valens, of the year 397, relative to butchers,[5] and by a law of Valentinian and Valens, of the year 364, relative to bakers.[6]

All these persons, who were seized by the trades' union — son, grandson, son-in-law, descendant, heir, possessor of property, which had belonged to a member of the union — were forced, as we have said, to take a place in the union. Whether they had become soldiers by deceiving the military tribune, or clergymen by deceiving the bishop, the novel of Valentinian II., of the year 445,[7] returned them to the union; and if they fled from the duties of their

[1] Si quis pistoris filiam suo conjugio crediderit esse sociandam, pistrini consortio teneatur obnoxius. (Cod. Theod., lib xiv., tit. iii., leg. 2.)

[2] Prædia rustica . . . quæ possident privato jure pistores . . . nec officialem comparare permittimus. . . . Filii vero excepti sunt . . . eodem loco positis omnibus qui qualibet proximitate junguntur, quibus ideo non dempsimus beneficium largitatis, quia et paneficii necessitatem suscipere successiones jure coguntur. (Cod. Theod., lib. xiv., tit. iii., leg. 3.)

[3] Si, cum obierint (navicularii), sobolem non relinquent, quique ille in eorum facultatibus qualibet ratione successerit, auctoris sui munus agnoscet. (Cod. Theod., lib. xiii., tit. v., leg. 19.)

[4] . . . Si quis patrimonium naviculario muneri obnoxium possidet, licet altioris sit dignitatis, nihil ei honoris privilegia, in hac parte dumtaxat opitulentur; sed, sive pro solido, sive pro portione, huic muneri teneantur. (Cod. Theod., lib. xiii., tit. v., leg. 3.)

[5] . . . Non minus habeatur obnoxius quem possessio tenet, quam quem successio generis adstringit. (Cod. Theod., lib. xiv., tit. iv., leg. 7.)

[6] . . . Quippe mercantes ad venditoris officium vocabuntur, super hac emptione P. F. annonæ testatiore deposita. (Cod. Theod., lib. xiv., tit. iii., leg. 3.)

[7] See note 4, page 217.

condition, the governors of the provinces were required to arrest and send them to Rome, in obedience to a law of Honorius and Theodosius of the year 391,[1] and another law of Honorius and Arcadius of the year 412.[2]

This rigor of the trades' unions was only relaxed in one single case. When a member of a union had become a priest, he could break the tie, which bound him to the union, by surrendering to it his patrimony, according to a law of Arcadius and Honorius of the year 408, relative to butchers.[3]

All, but priests, had to live and die in the union, unless they furnished substitutes, who were acceptable; that is to say, equal in fortune. This exception is provided for in a law of Constantine, of the year 324, relative to butchers,[4] and in a law of Valentinian and Valens, of the year 364, relative to bakers.[5]

We have said that this revolution, which entirely changed the nature of the trades' unions, and made them obligatory instead of voluntary, took place toward the commencement of the fourth century. This date, however, must not be taken rigorously; because moral revolutions neither commence nor end at precise moments of history. All that we can say is, that the most ancient law on this point is that of Constantius, of the year 319, relative to those in possession of property, which had belonged to members of the unions.

At first sight, it must appear to us of modern times, accustomed to the liberty of the professions and trades, that there was a very hard necessity in this absolute obligation to live and die in a trade, without the possibility of quitting it or going into another; and especially, that that was a very subtle and odious tyranny, which

[1] . . . Cura autem rectorum provinciarum corporati urbis Romæ, qui in peregrina transgressi sunt, redire cogantur; ut servire possint functionibus, quas imposuit antiqua solennitas. (Cod. Justin., lib. xi., tit. xiv., leg. unica.)

[2] This law was a reproduction of the exact terms of the former. (Cod. Theod., lib. xiv., tit. ii., leg. 4.)

[3] . . . Eos etiam qui ad clericatus se privilegia contulerunt, aut agnoscere oportet propriam functionem, aut ei corpori, quod declinant, proprii patrimonii facere cessionem. (Cod. Theod., lib. xiv., tit. iv., leg. 8.)

[4] . . . De duobus alterum eligant, aut retineant bona quæ suariæ functioni destricta sunt, ipsique suario teneantur obsequio, aut idoneos quos volunt, nominent. (Cod. Theod., lib. xiv., tit. iv., leg. 1.)

[5] . . . Quod si fuerint cupidi dignitatis, in tantam paneficii substantiam idoneos de suis subrogare cogantur, quantum ipsi exhibuere pistores. (Cod. Theod., lib. xiv., tit. iii., leg. 4.)

threw around the working, industrial, and commercial classes so many snares, into which the imprudent might fall, either by marrying the daughters of working-men, or by buying their property, or by receiving, by testamentary gift, ever so small a part of the property of one of them. Nevertheless, if we go back to their times, places, and ideas, and seek for the compensations, which the working classes found in the trades' unions, we will recognize that such an institution was for them, after all, a great good.

First, by the side of this necessity of remaining in an union all their lives, the working-men had a guarantee of never wanting their wages; of being subsisted and supported always and under all circumstances out of the social funds of the union. Now, this seems to us a great advantage; a position, in which many working-men would perhaps to-day be most happy to find themselves. To be entirely free is without doubt much; but this freedom really profits only those, who possess the activity, industry, and patience to make it available; while there are many people of moderate ability, and these, are the great majority, who derive no benefit from this freedom so precious to others; who succumb in the contests of competition, and who, crushed by the necessity of taking care of themselves, never succeed in doing so, and remain always a prey to the wants of the day, and have to seek by beggary — from the poor-house — sometimes by crime instigated by misery — the necessary supplement to the product of their free labor, that they may not die of hunger.

We have spoken of the *social funds* of the unions. These consisted of immense domains, inalienable and constantly added to, which served for the support of the members, as the property of the monasteries in the middle ages served for the support of the monks.

The sources of the wealth of the unions were various: the first and most important consisted in an endowment granted to them by the government. If we suppose that there was a similitude of development and of fortune among all the unions, we would be tempted to believe that this patrimonial endowment was very ancient; for we find that from the time of Numa the state granted one to the priests' *union*.[1] However, it is certain that these endowments,

[1] Plutarch relates in many places in the Life of Numa, that this king instituted the college of pontiffs, and some other priests' unions. But he only speaks expressly of the endowment made to the temple of the Muses.

which are formally stated and defined only in the laws of the end of the fourth century, existed under the first emperors; for we read in Zosimus that Maximin confiscated them.[1]

The first law, which expressly mentions the endowment of the Roman trades' unions, is that of Valentinian and Valens, of the year 364, relative to bakers, which speaks of their *endowment fund.*[2] A second law of the same emperors, of the year 369, says expressly, in naming the endowment, that it had been attached to the unions since their origin;[3] and a third law, of Arcadius and Honorius, relative to the same union, again mentions their endowment, specifies that it was in lands, and adds that it was originally granted as a guarantee and encouragement.[4]

The endowment of the unions consisted of real estate. If any doubt could remain after the law of Arcadius and Honorius, which we have just cited, it would be completely removed by a novel of Theodosius, of the year 440, relative to limeburners, in which their endowment is expressly designated under the name of *cespes;* that is to say, land.[5] This novel is elsewhere fortified and explained by a law of Constantius, of the year 359, in which it is said that the endowment of the limeburners ought to produce annually a certain quantity of wine and three hundred oxen.[6] The novel of Theodosius also mentions two other endowments of land, belonging to two other trades' unions; but the text, evidently altered,[7] does not permit us to know exactly which they were. Godfrey thinks that one had charge of the aqueducts, and the other of the sewers of Rome.[8]

The second source of the wealth of the trades' unions was the

[1] Zosim. Hist. Rom., lib. i., in Maximin.

[2] . . . Officinam cum servis, molis, fundis dotalibus . . . tradat. (Cod. Theod., lib. xiv., tit. iii., leg. 7.)

[3] Non ea sola pistrini sunt, . . . quæ in originem adscripta corporis dotis nomen . . . retentant. (Cod. Theod., lib. xiv., tit. iii., leg. 13.)

[4] Pistores urbis æternæ, prætermissa veteri consuetudine, fundis vel prædiis ad nihilum redactis, quæ eorum corporis solatia certa præhebant. (Cod. Theod., lib. xiv., tit. iii., leg. 19.)

[5] . . . Cespes calcarius. (Cod. Theod., leg. novellar. lib. Theod. novell. 43.)

[6] . . . Coctoribus calcis per ternas vehes singulæ amphoræ vini præbeantur . . . vectuarios etiam . . . trecentos boves præcipimus dari. (Cod. Theod., lib. xiv., tit. vi., leg. 1.)

[7] . . . Cespes formensis, aetrinsis.

[8] Cespitem formensem existimat (Gothofredus) esse possessionem per quam formæ, sive aqueductus transeunt. — Cespitem aeriensem (sive aetrinsem) cloacario, sive tributo, quod cloacarum purgandarum causa infertur. (Cod. Theod.; notul. ad novell. Theodos., 43.)

profits from the state and from individuals. It is certain that the trades' unions undertook the works of the government and of individuals; but by a law of Valentinian, of the year 382, relative to limeburners, the works and wants of the state took precedence of all others.[1]

The third source of the wealth of the unions was the inheritances of their members, who died intestate, on which it is proper to make one remark. The property of each member of a union was of two kinds. First, the member had his proportional part in the endowment fund of the association; and this part the association managed. He had his share of the income, but not the capital. Second, he had his patrimony, his peculium, his personal fortune. Of this second portion of the fortunes of their members, the trades' unions indirectly got possession under the law of Valentinian II. and of Valens, of the year 364, which we have cited; by forcing all, who possessed them, to enter into their association; and they seized it entirely by the novel of Theodosius and Valentinian, of the year 438, which declared every union the universal legatee of its members dying intestate.[2]

Moreover, once in the hands of the unions, their wealth never passed from them. Their property was inalienable, as was that of every industrial, municipal, or religious corporation, by virtue of the principles we have established in the tenth chapter of this work. The inalienability of the property of the trades' unions is established by a great number of laws; among others, by a law of Valentinian and Valens, of the month of June, 365,[3] and by a law of Valentinian, Valens, and Gratian, of April, 372.[4] The property of the Roman trades' unions, therefore, was so constituted that it could always increase and never diminish.

Finally, the Roman trades' unions were, in regard to their social

[1] Quisquis ex his (calcibus) nihil accipiat, nisi quod cunctis mœnibus fabricationique Romanæ superfluere ac redundare constiterit. (Cod. Theod., lib. xiv., tit. vi., leg. 4.)

[2] Ut quisquis fabricensium sine liberis, vel legitimo hærede decesserit non condito testamento, ejus bona cujusque summæ sint. (Cod. Theod., leg. novellar. lib. Theodos. novell. 13.)

[3] Patrimonia naviculariorum, quæ, quolibet genere, in extraneorum dominia demigrarunt, in corporis sui jus proprietatemque remeent. (Cod. Theod., lib. xiii., tit. vi., leg. 2.)

[4] Fundi omnes, ad naviculariorum dominium pertinentes, et ad aliorum jura translati . . . reddantur dominis. (Cod. Theod., lib. xiii., tit. vi., leg. 6.)

endowment, like so many tontines, in which the last survivors profited by the spoils of those, who died first. It is easy to conceive how these endowments, being inalienable, never diminishing and always accumulating, ended by acquiring an immense development. Thus the property of the laboring and industrial unions, in Roman history, may be compared with the wealth of ecclesiastical corporations in modern history. This property, accumulating from man to man, from century to century, increased prodigiously in the lapse of years. But as certain religious orders were richer than others, so some of the Roman trades' unions eclipsed their rivals by the display of their strength and grandeur. For example, it may be said that the sailors' union under the empire was what the order of St. Benedict were in Christianity,[1] and the former has furnished as many senators and knights as the latter has illustrious abbés, cardinals and popes.

Notwithstanding the appearance of excessive tyranny in the statutes, relative to the Roman trades' unions, we can nevertheless easily conceive why the members of the unions were well satisfied with them. It was always for the ultimate advantage of the unions that these rigorous laws were instituted. Who profits by the members of a fraternity not being allowed to quit it? The fraternity, which thus is always and uniformly recruited with skilled men. Who profits by requiring the son, grandson, all the descendants, to follow the profession of their ancestor? The fraternity, which is thus composed of permanent families of workmen or artists, in which the traditions of industry or art are perpetuated from age to age, and which acquire, by the lapse of time, a generic eminence, of which they are proud; a sort of dynasty of labor, like the Aldes, the Etiennes, and some others in the history of the free industry of modern times. Finally, who profits by the return to the union of the estates of intestate members? The fraternity, whose wealth is increased, and who are thus enabled at the same time to extend their operations, ameliorate the condition of their members, and provide for the chances of the future.

[1] The sailors' and bakers' unions were the most powerful of the empire. The bakers furnished many senators. (Optio concessa est his, qui e pistoribus facti sunt senatores. Cod. Theod., lib. xiv., tit. iii., leg. 4.) A law of Valentinian and Valens, of the year 371, and another of Gratian, of the year 379, show that a great number of sailors were made senators and knights. (Cod. Theod., lib. xiii., tit. x., leg. 14, 15.)

Now, if the result of these rigorous laws was to the profit of the trades' unions, was it not an advantage to those, who composed them? Does not the monk rejoice in the prosperity of the convent? Well, just as the best and most active portion of Europe, in the sixth century, pressed into the cloisters, which, like the Roman unions, they could not leave; where they lost their civil rights, and could neither give, nor sell, nor bequeath, nor receive by way of gift or legacy; so, as long as the good times of the trades' unions lasted, they did not want proselytes, who were ready to give to them their own bodies, and the bodies of all their posterity.

This was, we say, so long as the good times of the trades' unions lasted; for there came a time, when their prosperity declined; when their glory disappeared; when it was necessary to bring back their fugitive members by force, as appears from the laws of Honorius and Arcadius, of the year 412, and the novel of Theodosius and Valentinian, of the year 445; when, to complete their reproach, it was necessary to seek recruits among the Jews and Samaritans, as appears from the law of Gratian, Valentinian, and Theodosius, of the year 390.[1] But these misfortunes belonged to an order of facts, foreign, as we have said, to the nature and object of the trades' unions, and of which we must make the lamentable recital.

---

# CHAPTER XIV.

## ANCIENT TRADES' UNIONS — THEIR FALL.

AT the commencement of the fourth century, the Roman trades' unions had long been secretly laboring under a malady, which was to ruin them at a later period.

Generally it is with peoples as with men, who are not aware of their disease until its progress has undermined their organization. It was very nearly under the reign of Constantine that the internal

[1] Judæorum corpus ac Samaritanorum ad naviculariam functionem non jure vocari cognoscitur . . . inopes, vilibusque commerciis occupati naviculariæ translationis munus obire non debent. (Cod. Theod., lib. xiii., tit. v., leg. 18.)

disease of the trades' unions began to make itself felt by all that series of coercive and tyrannical laws, which we have mentioned, and which prove that the unions no longer attracted, as they once did, the laboring, industrial, and commercial classes; since it was necessary to strengthen them with recruits from without, by all sorts of legislative contrivances, and to oppose multiplied and arbitrary obstacles to the withdrawal of those, who no longer found any advantages in the community of the fraternities. Now, more than fifty reigns had passed by since the first blow was struck at the prosperity of the unions; and their decay, always increasing, was the work of the emperors, and dates, if not from the first years of Augustus, at least from the disorganizing and destructive reign of Caligula. The causes of the gradual decay of this great institution should be studied one by one, and related separately.

We have already explained how the unions were, properly speaking, the administrative corps of the Roman Empire. The public revenues were not derived, as among modern peoples, from an impost regularly distributed; they consisted, in the greater and better part, of the rents of the public domain. This domain, known in the law by the name of *reipublicæ loca*, was leased to individuals, who paid an annual rent, generally in kind; this rent, which was a veritable feudal service, bore, like the feudal services of the middle ages, the name of *canon*. When it was in grain, it was called *canon frumentarius;* and so of the rest.[1] Now, it was in the warehouses of the trades' unions that these rents in kind were received annually. We have already seen that the butchers' union collected the rents in hogs in Brutium and Samnium. The bakers received the rents in grain, which the wagoners and sailors' unions deposited in the warehouses of the port of Ostia. The wine-measurers' union received the rents of the vineyards; and, all together, they took care of, manipulated, and disposed of for consumption, all these raw materials, which came crude into their hands.

Well! the unions were responsible for the revenues of the empire, of which they had the administration; and when the annual rents of the domain were insufficient for the consumption, the government seized upon their property.

[1] De canone frumentario. (Cod. Theod., lib. xiv., tit. xv.)

Here we have, in two words, the explanation of many things, until now somewhat obscure. Here we find the reason for all those laws, which declared the property of the unions inalienable; which required the descendants of members of a union to remain in it forever; which ordained that whoever received any portion of the private fortune of a member of a trades' union, either by legacy or purchase, or even as marriage dowry, should contribute to the expenses of the union, *pro rata*, for that portion. The government, which had need of certain revenues, thus accumulated the guarantees it wanted in the trades' unions; so that, if its resources were deficient on one hand, it was always certain of finding them elsewhere.

Unhappily those resources were, to the detriment of the unions, often deficient, from causes both natural and frequent. Vessels loaded with provisions were wrecked. Now, the sailors' union was responsible for all wrecks, at least up to the time of Claudius, who, as related by Suetonius, placed the losses to account of the government.[1] Subsequent laws, for three centuries — and among others a law of Valentinian, Valens, and Gratian, of the year 372, in relation to the sailors' union — prove that the regulation of Claudius did not remain unrestricted, and that the republic only became responsible for wrecks and losses by sea, when it was clearly proved that there was no fault of the agents of the company.[2]

Again, sterile years doubtless were no more rare in the times of the Roman emperors than now. If we refer to the testimony of history, we find that they were even more frequent. That is easily conceived, when we consider the progress of agriculture and metallurgy in two thousand years, and their want of artificial means of contending most advantageously against the sterility of the times and the disorder of the seasons. Thus, under Claudius, there was a violent tumult at Rome, caused by the want of breadstuffs, which forced him to grant to the sailors' union the indemnity just mentioned.[3] Ammienus Marcellinus relates, in the fourteenth book of his history, that a frightful sedition also took place under Constantius the Second, in the year 353, because of the total want of wine;

1 Suet. Tranquil., Tiber. Claud., cap. xxi.
2 Cod. Theod., lib. xiii., tit. ix., leg. 1.
3 Suet. Tranquil., Tiber. Claud., cap. xxi.

and it is impossible to count the passages, in St. Ambrose, Symmachus, Libanius, and even in the laws of the emperors, in which it is related that the magistrates repeatedly drove off without pity the fugitive slaves and beggars, who flocked to Rome from all points of the empire, when famine invaded Italy, and surprised the capital of the world in the midst of the ruinous luxury, feasts, and fancies of her emperors.[1] We readily conceive that, before resorting to these terrible extremes, the treasury of the unions was first exhausted, and that when senators had one plate less at their tables, the members of the trades' unions did not dine at all.

There was a third cause, equally natural and not less frequent, which was long preparing the ruin of the trades' unions — the bad faith or insolvency of the farmers of the domain. The unions, the *corporati*, were required to have in store each year a sufficient quantity of products; but who was to guarantee to them that the possessors of the public lands should faithfully perform the conditions of their ancient leases? If we refer to the successive laws for the regulation of this matter, it appears that there was no kind of ruse or expedient, to which the vassals and arrière vassals of the empire did not resort, to avoid paying the annual rent, or to diminish the amount. This became all the more easy for them to do, when the lands of the domain, at least from the middle of the fourth century, were enfeoffed to them in perpetuity, as appears by a law of Arcadius and Honorius, of the 1st December, 400.[2] Now, when three or four generations had rolled by, after the first enfeoffment, it became very difficult to prevent the violation of its stipulations by the vassals for their own profit. This they in fact did, as shown by a law of Gratian, Valentinian, and Theodosius, of the 1st February, 383, by refusing to cultivate second quality lands included in their grants, and by reducing, in proportion to the lesser extent cultivated, the rent payable to the treasury;[3] that is to say, by thus subordinating the revenues of the empire to the discretion of the farmers, who had taken the lands of the state in vassalage. The unions, thus pressed by the exigencies of the government on one side, and the indolence or bad faith of the farmers on the other, used great severity to collect the rents.

[1] Cod. Theod., lib. xiv., cap. xviii., lex unica.

[2] Cod. Theod., lib. x., tit. iii., leg. 5. [3] Cod. Theod., lib. x., tit. iii., leg. 4.

Plutarch relates, in the Life of Lucullus, that after the war with Tigranes, who had ravaged Asia Minor, the Roman collectors sold at the market-place the marriageable daughters of the farmers, who had not paid their rents;[1] and without speaking of other passages in the homilies of St. Basil, or in the letters of Libanius, which bear witness to the same severity, see the terrible recital, in St. Jerome's Life of Paphnuca, by a poor woman, whose husband and children had been carried off: "I had a husband," she said, "whom the tax-collectors had often hung, whipped, tortured, and imprisoned. We had three sons, whom they have taken from us, and sold for the same debt."[2] If any one should think that there must be some exaggeration, (*a*) in what these writers and holy per-

[1] See Plutarch's Life of Lucullus. [2] See St. Jerome's Life of Paphnuca.

(*a*) If any one should find it difficult to believe that such things could be done, in the days of St. Jerome, in the dawn of Christianity, let him read the testimony in the pending impeachment trial of Governor Holden, of North Carolina:

"Lucien H. Murray, being duly sworn, testified: I live in Alamance County, and am a merchant; on the 27th of July last I was arrested by Colonel Bergen, and carried to his camp. That night he came to my tent with a light, touched me on the foot, and asked, 'Is that you, Murray?' I told him it was. He told me to get up and go with him. I asked him to wait until I could put on my shoes. He replied: 'No, you won't have any use for shoes long.' After I had gone out with him, he told me to confess, or he would blow my heart out. I said I knew nothing to confess. Said he knew a way to make me tell; carried me a short distance, and put a rope around my neck, tied my hands, and threw the rope over a limb. There were four soldiers with him. He asked me again to confess. I said I knew nothing. He pulled me up, then let me down, and commanded me to confess. I knew nothing to confess. He then pulled me up twice more, the third time letting me stay *until I became unconscious.* I don't know how long I was kept up. When *I came to,* I was sitting by a tree, and the men were rubbing me. He then put the pistol to my breast, and told me if I did not confess he would kill me. I again told him I knew nothing. He then said to the sergeant, 'Hang him to that limb, and let him hang until 8 in the morning; then *bury him under this tree.*' I said, 'If you hang me until I am dead, your time will come in three days, if not before.' After this I was ordered back to camp, and told not to speak of this, and if I did not confess by 10 o'clock to-morrow night I would be hung. I was finally released by Judge Brooks, of the United States District Court, and no charge was made against me.

"William Patton being sworn, testified: I was arrested by Bergen in July last; he asked me about the murder of Outlaw; I told him I knew nothing about it; he then put a pistol to my breast, and said if I did not tell all about it he would

sons said, he can verify the scrupulous exactness of their testimony by reference to two official acts on the subject; viz., a law of Theo-

blow my brains out; I again said I knew nothing about it; he then called for a rope, saying he would hang me if I did not tell; a rope was handed him by a soldier; he put it around my neck, and, followed by a guard, carried me out to the woods, threw the rope over a limb, and pulled me up, not quite off the ground, but enough to choke me; let me down, and told me to confess; pulled me up again, and went through the same process three times, after which he started back to camp with me; on the way I fainted; when I came to, he and the guard were standing around me cursing violently; Bergen then told the men to take me to camp, and said he would make me tell all about it; he took the rope off my neck, tied it around my wrists, tied me to a box near by, and left me there all night.

"It must be remembered that similar outrages as those detailed above were inflicted upon others, and that they were all, after an imprisonment of five weeks, released upon writs of habeas corpus by a Federal judge, without any charge whatever being preferred against them.

"Among the witnesses examined yesterday was the Hon. John Kerr, of Caswell County. Judge Kerr is decidedly one of the ablest men in this State, and one of the most eloquent orators in America. He has always been very prominent in the politics of this State. Was a member of the United States Congress twenty years ago; was the Whig candidate for Governor in 1852, and afterward wore the judicial ermine with honor to the judiciary. Yet this gentleman was one of Holden's many victims; was torn from his family, closely incarcerated by a drunken soldiery or rabble for five weeks, insulted day after day, threatened with death, and finally released with not a single charge preferred against him. The probate judge of Caswell County testified that Kirk took forcible possession of his office, scattered, lost, and destroyed bushels of his official papers and records, and a letter from Holden was read justifying Kirk's conduct. It has been also proven that Kirk told his prisoners that his orders were, 'if an attempt at rescue was made, to shoot down the prisoners, burn up the town, and put to death the women and children.'"

Now, these events occurred in the 19th century of the Christian era, only a few short months ago; and the purpose of this "gentle persuasion," was to continue Governor Holden in power, under the assumed name of Republicanism, that he and those acting with him might *collect taxes, ad libitum,* from the people of North Carolina. So the world, after all, has not changed much in nineteen centuries. See the testimony of the Rev. J. B. Smith, before the committee of investigation on Southern outrages, February 17, 1871. The Rev. Mr. Smith is a Northern man, who went to North Carolina, at the suggestion of General O. O. Howard, to establish a normal school for the education of negroes. He says:

"I asked a leading member of the House of Representatives of North Caro-

dosius the Great, dated at Milan, in March, 391,[1] and a novel of Valentinian the Second, dated at Rome, February, 451.[2]

Nevertheless, in spite of wrecks, in spite of the famine of barren years, in spite of the poverty or bad faith of the farmers, the Roman unions would perhaps have been industrious and rich enough to supply all the wants of the empire, without serious injury to their own interests, if a new cause, more powerful than all the others, had not fatally hurried on their ruin. That cause was the unbounded luxury of the emperors.

We moderns have no idea of the incredible extravagance of these masters of the world. They had the wealth of Europe, Asia and Africa in their hands, and certainly they made that fact well known. We have had in France some royal spendthrifts — for example, Francis I. and Louis XIV. It is doubtful whether Caligula would have found the first enough of a good liver to take part in his gayeties, and the whole fortune of the latter would not have sufficed to pay the board and wages of Nero's lackeys.

It is truly a "*History of a Thousand and One Nights*," that of the first Roman emperors — for example, Caligula, Claudius, and Nero. On a banter made to him, Caligula constructed a bridge over the sea from the port of Baia to the mole of Puteoli. This bridge was 3,600 paces long; it was paved, and had the width of the Appian Way.[3] He, with all his courtiers, made on it a triumphal procession for two successive days. The first day he rode a horse caparisoned

lina, knowing him to be a man of principle, 'How could you vote for the Shoffner bill, to empower the Governor of the State to declare at will a county to be in insurrection, if none existed?' — the word insurrection being a well-defined term. He said, 'Oh! we passed such a law, but it will never be executed.' Said I, 'Then why did you pass it?' 'Now, doctor,' said he, 'it is necessary to hold this State as Republican for three or four years longer, and the passage of that bill was necessary to enable us to hold it.'"

The Rev. Mr. Smith also testified that, in conversation with him, Governor Holden said that, "in his opinion, General Grant would hold the government of the United States, no matter what the election was in 1872; that he (Governor Holden) desired him to be emperor, and his son to succeed him as emperor." Governor Holden also told Mr. Smith, that he, Holden, had 80,000 negroes of the loyal leagues, whom he could and would arm to accomplish his wishes.

[1] Cod. Theod., lib. iii., tit. iii., lex unica.

[2] Cod. Theod., leg. novel. D. Valentin., tit. xi.

[3] Suet. Tranquil., C. Cæsar Caligula, cap. xxvi.

with magnificent housings, himself clothed in an imperial robe of cloth of gold, and armed *cap-à-pié*. His courtiers came after him, clothed in like apparel. The second day he appeared in the dress of a charioteer of the circus, in a chariot drawn by magnificent horses, followed by the equipages of his courtiers and all the prætorian guard. This bridge was constructed for these two promenades only, and the imperial caprice let it fall to ruins as rapidly as it had been constructed. Claudius, curious to see the bottom of Lake Fucinus, to draw the water off had a canal made across a mountain, 3,000 paces long.[1] This fancy cost him the board and wages of 30,000 workmen for eleven years. But Nero left far behind all these essays of power. Never did man show like profusion. When he played in the evening, after supper, his wager was never less than 400,000 sesterces.[2] If he wished to see a naval battle, he had a lake dug, large and deep enough for the manœuvres of two fleets.[3] Always clothed with silks and stuffs of the Orient, he never wore the same dress twice.[4] When he fished in his ponds, he had a line of purple and gold thread.[5] One year, during the feasts he gave to his good city of Rome, in his character of a great artist, the idea occurred to him to give a daily lottery to the people. As long as the feasts lasted, he distributed a thousand tickets daily. The prizes were warehouses filled with grain, complete wardrobes, collections of all rare birds, gold, silver, pearls, diamonds, pictures, slaves, horses, and domesticated wild beasts. On the last day, the prizes were ships, cities, and kingdoms.[6] Nero had a monkey, which he dearly loved. He assigned to it a palace in Rome, a castle and lands in the country, and regulated its housekeeping on an analogous footing.[7]

When he went to contend for the prize in the races of the Olympic games, Nero set out with his ordinary equipage; a train of a thousand chariots. The 2,000 mules, that drew him and his train, were shod with silver, and his three or four thousand coachmen and lackeys were clothed with the finest stuffs of Italy. A great multitude of Moorish couriers preceded him, clothed *à l'Africaine*, with

[1] Sueton. Tranquil., C. Cæsar Caligula, cap. xxvi.
[2] Sueton., Nero Claud. Cæsar., cap. xxiii.
[3] Ibid., cap. ix.
[4] Ibid., cap. xxii.
[5] Ibid., cap. xxii.
[6] Ibid., cap. ix.
[7] Ibid., cap. xxiii.

silk scarfs, collars, and bracelets. It was with this, his usual equipage, that he came to the Olympic games.[1] He carried off the prize, although he was thrown twice,[2] and afterward he returned to Rome in his racing chariot, drawn by ten white horses. On his return, he granted to the cities of Naples, Antium, and Alba the honor of a visit; he came clothed with a cloak of purple strewn with golden stars; and as conqueror in the Hieronic games, he entered Syracuse by a great breach in the walls.[3] Arrived at the gates of Rome, he caused to be thrown down an arcade of the grand circus, and made a magnificent road across the Velabrum and the Forum to the temple of Apollo on Mount Palatine. The road was covered with saffron powder; victims were immolated on both sides during his progress; and to the right and left, for his retinue and the people, there were endless tables covered with all sorts of birds and pastry, and crowned with bows of ribbons.[4]

Alas! it was the trades' unions, which in great part paid for these feasts, this profusion, these follies. They paid for the emperors' mistresses, eunuchs, minions, lackeys, their lions and panthers, their parrots, and their monkeys. And if we bear in mind that, between Augustus and Constantine, there were fifty-two emperors: that is, nearly fifty-two spendthrifts; and that among them one, Heliogabalus, dying at eighteen years, spent in one day, perhaps more than all the others, in paving the court of his palace with all the diamonds, all the emeralds, all the precious stones of Italy, it is easy to account for the exhaustion of the empire in the fourth century, and for the tyrannical laws against the trades' unions, which in the end had to provide for the people and the government at the same time. This explains how these tyrants, these fools, these ambitious men, who passed away so quickly, carried off, each, some portion of the wealth of the world; how the most frightful vexations were resorted to to raise money; how all the statues of the gods, which were of gold, and even the penates of Rome, were melted down by Nero;[5] how the ancient subsidies paid by the state to the priests and vestals were suppressed; how, in fine, to the great scandal of idolatrous devotees, the immense

[1] Sueton., Nero Claud. Cæsar, cap. xxiii.
[2] Ibid., cap. xvii.
[3] Ibid., cap. xix.
[4] Ibid., c. xix.
[5] Ibid., cap. xxvi.

property of the pagan clergy was confiscated and sold throughout the empire, for the benefit of the public treasury; which was the subject of the doleful epistles of the prefect Symmachus to the Emperor Valentinian the Second!

From the middle of the fifth century, the Roman trades' unions were completely disorganized. All their members sought to escape, by flight or voluntary exile, the ruinous burdens that weighed them down. We have cited the two laws of the years 412 and 445, which required the governors of provinces to seize and send back to Rome the fugitive members of the unions. But when institutions can only be maintained by such violence, they are truly dead. The trades' union, then, fell piece by piece, with the empire; or at least they detached themselves from Rome and Constantinople, which were successively their centre of administration. The feeble unions disappeared altogether; the rich ones continued to exist independently. Of these were the bakers' and sailors' unions. The fragments of the latter, in all the ports of the Mediterranean and of the ocean, became the nucleus of mercantile associations. Some of their counting-houses, established on great rivers, became the foundation of cities since become celebrated. The commune of Paris, called in the charters *la marchandise de l'eau*, originated from a Roman counting-house established in the city.[1]

[1] This clearly appears from the history of the primitive commerce of Paris, and from the following inscription found in the excavations made in 1711, under the choir of Notre Dame:

Tiberio Cæsare
Aug. Jovi optimo
Maximo Monumentum
NAUTÆ PARISIACI
Publice posuerunt.

See dissertation of M. le Roi on the origin of the Hotel de Ville, in Felibien's History of Paris.

# CHAPTER XV.

## BEGGARS AND HOSPITALS.

WE have already seen that slaves, once set free, divide into two classes. Some accept labor, and live at their own cost. Others reject labor, and live at the cost of others. The former constitute the trades' unions, whose history we have just given. The latter produce pauperism, of which we will present a picture.

Beggars were not a social element cotemporaneous with the first formation of peoples. Pauperism was only introduced as a consequence of the emancipation of slaves, and everything concurs to establish that this emancipation was very recent. We find the poor mentioned in the primitive poets, as Moses, Homer, and Hesiod; but in those early times they were very few in number. In fact, as long as slavery existed, whether among the ancients or the moderns, pauperism could not make much progress; because all being either masters or slaves, the masters had some fortune, and the slaves had masters, who naturally supplied all their wants during life. It was only in proportion to the emancipation of slaves that small proprietors, or working-men without capital, or laborers subject to all the chances of sickness, began to exist; and these small proprietors, working-men and laborers, at the first serious difficulty, at the first violent crisis, at the first grievous derangement of health, especially if they had a numerous family to support, found themselves in misery, and were reduced to pauperism.

Thus we see paupers increasing among the ancients in proportion to the multiplication of freedmen. As, however, the emancipations of slaves were not done systematically and in mass, but individually, according to the good will of the masters, and the good conduct of the slaves, there was at the commencement of the Christian era a very limited number of paupers; so few that there was no establishment of public charity. It was only in the cities that beggars were to be found; for the reason, that there the freedmen most did congregate. They were to be seen every morning collected around the temples, carrying in their hands small images of the gods, and asking alms from the good pagan souls. Among them were the priests of Cybele, who, in the pagan clergy, or, to speak more historically, in the *college of priests*, constituted a congregation of religious mendicants. Minutius Felix mentions them in his book entitled Octavius.[1] Tertullian, in his Apology, reproaches them for the effrontery, with which they prowled around the hostelries;[2] and Juvenal, who is very reliable in these matters, represents them as lazy, and lying under the tables of the lowest pot-houses, among ruffians, sailors, thieves, and fugitive slaves, butcher-boys, and coffin-makers for the funeral pomps of Rome.[3]

Things remained in this condition, that is to say, the poor, still few in numbers, had no hospital, in which to take refuge, in the first centuries of the Christian era.[4] The Christians indeed multiplied alms, and fed the needy; but they were not yet masters; they were still in the minority; they could not act publicly, collectively, legally; but only individually, and separately, each for himself. On their part, the pagan clergy — who had immense territorial wealth, derived, first, from the perpetual endowments paid by the public treasury, the legal institution of which goes back from the Roman empire to Numa, and, secondly, from numberless inheritances and legacies — never conceived the idea of organizing any system of public charity; and when, toward the end of the fourth century, Symmachus addressed to Valentinian II., Theodosius, and Arcadius his two celebrated letters on paganism, which was falling to ruins,[5] in which he complains so bitterly of the confiscation by the emperors of the property of the priests and vestals, St. Ambrose, in the first of his two replies to Symmachus, addressed to Valentinian II., contrasts the avarice of the pagan clergy, who kept their riches for themselves, with the self-denial of the Christian church, which, said St. Ambrose, possessed nothing of its own but its faith, and whose property was the property of the poor.[6]

Nevertheless it is true, that although the number of permanent

[1] Minuc. Felic. Octavius, chap. 24. See also Tertullian, Apologet., chap. 42.

[2] Tertul. Apologet., cap. xiii.

[3] Juvenal, Satir. viii., v. 173–175.

[4] There is no example in all antiquity of the establishment of a place of refuge for the poor. Thucydides mentions in his History of the Peloponnesian War a kind of hospital built near the temple of Juno, at Megara; but this hospital, although the beds were sacred to the goddess, was nothing more than a tavern. (Thucydides, lib. iii., cap. lxviii.)

[5] Symmach. Epistol., lib. x., epist. liv.

[6] S. Ambros. Epistol. ii., contra Symmachum.

poor, of professional beggars, was still very inconsiderable from the first to the third century of the Christian era, there came terrible times, when this number was frightfully increased. It was in the years of famine, when the crops failed in Sicily or in Africa, and when the two unions of the sailors and bakers, who had charge, the first of the transportation of the breadstuffs of the empire, the second of the general management of the flour and the distribution of bread, were brought to a standstill, that those horrible famines occurred, from which the administrative organization of modern times preserves the peoples of to-day. Then all the slaves of Italy, who were no longer fed by their masters, were seen hastening to Rome to ask for bread. But as this increase of population was not long in bringing famine on Rome herself, they expelled from the city, on a given day, all these parasitical inhabitants, who went to die where they could. This was the habitual mode of proceeding of the administrators of the republic in times of crises: and Symmachus, who was prefect of Rome, about the year 383, wrote as follows: "We fear a total want of food, even after having driven off all the foreign population, who have taken refuge in Rome, and whom the city feeds." [1] (*a*)

On their part, the Christians protested loudly against this cruelty of the burghers of Rome, who refused to share their food with the refugees. St. Ambrose, who mentions these expulsions in many places of his works, strongly denounced this want of feeling. He said: "Those, who drive strangers from Rome, cannot be justified. It is acting inhumanly to repel any one at the moment he most needs succor. Animals do not drive off animals—man drives away man." [2] Sometimes the pagans themselves have protested loudly against the expulsion of poor strangers, when famine menaced the cities.[3]

Finally, it results from many writings of the third and fourth century, that, as soon as the charity of the Christians became well known, the poor crowded round the churches. At Rome they gathered around the Church of the Apostles in the Vatican. There

[1] Symmach. Epistol., lib. ii., epist. 7.

(*a*) We find analogous instances in more modern history; for example, the treatment of the Irish by Cromwell, and the *banishment from their homes*, by General Sherman, of the *women* of Roswell Factory and Atlanta.

[2] D. Ambros. de offic. ministr., lib. ii., cap. xvii.

[3] Cicero de offic., lib. iii., cap. xi., § 47.

alms were distributed to them daily, as we see in Ammienus Marcellinus[1] among others, and from the poem of Prudentius against Symmachus.[2] It appears that all kinds of fraud were practised by these vagabonds to impose upon the compassion of the bishops. St. Ambrose, in the second book of his treatise on the duties of ministers,[3] thus expresses himself on this subject: "There must be some limit to liberality, that it may not be useless. Priests principally ought to use circumspection in this regard, that they may proportion the alms to the justice, and not to the urgency, of their supplications. Never was anything like the avidity of the beggars. Strong men, strolling about for the mere pleasure of vagabondizing, seek to absorb the aid due to the truly poor. Some feign to have debts. Let this be strictly examined into. Others pretend to have been robbed. Let exact information be had as to these persons, etc., etc." The scandal, caused by these false beggars and their frauds, went so far that the Emperor Valentinian II. made a law, dated at Padua, 1st July, 382, to expel from Rome all those, who were not truly paupers incapable of gaining a living.[4] (*a*)

This law of Valentinian is very curious, in that it contains certain and valuable data on the state of pauperism in Italy, toward the end of the fourth century. Thus, we see that the greater part of the beggars, who flocked to Rome, were either fugitive slaves, or serfs whom agriculture could not support.[5] They rushed to Rome, which was then the greatest city of the world, and in which they could more easily than anywhere else escape the pursuit of their masters. Valentinian exhorts the inhabitants of Rome to point out these beggars, and orders that it shall be carefully ascertained whether they were able-bodied. He adjudged the slaves to those, who informed upon them; and as to the serfs of the glebe, he gave them also, and by the same title, to those, who discovered them; saving to their

[1] Amm. Marcel., lib. xxvii., cap. iii., § 5.

[2] Prudent. contra Symmach., lib. i., v. 581–583.

[3] D. Ambros. de offic. ministr., lib. ii., cap. xvi.

[4] Cod. Theod., lib. xiv., tit. xviii., leg. 1.

(*a*) We have modern instances of this in all the Southern cities; and especially in Washington, where the control of all political power, given to fraudulent beggars, has produced a wonderful political phenomenon for the nineteenth century; viz., nothing less than a voluntary surrender by the citizens of Washington and Georgetown of their commune, or right of local self-government. See note (*a*) to chapter vii.

[5] Cod. Theod., lib. xiv., tit. xviii., leg. 1.

seignior recourse against those, who had counselled or facilitated their flight.[1] Justinian reproduced, in his eightieth novel, the law of Valentinian in very nearly the same terms, but with this difference, that he condemned all able-bodied beggars to the public works.[2]

All this great increase of beggars took place from the third to the fifth century. It seems that they took literally the character given to the Christians by St. Jerome, when he called them, in his twenty-sixth epistle to Pammachius, the *subordinates* and *candidates* of the poor.[3] The dominant historic and social fact, during the fourth century, is this vast increase of proletaries: and, after numerous fruitless experiments, the creation and organization of a great system of public charity, to provide for the wants of the poor, and take care of the old, the sick, and abandoned infants. This provident system, which has only been developed in the lapse of centuries, and which is still the only palliative put in use by modern societies, to cure, or rather to cover up, the sores of civilization, was created by Christianity.

Seeing that antiquity in four thousand years did not emancipate slaves enough to produce any considerable mass of proletaries, and that in four centuries Christianity had multiplied them so, that regular society was encumbered and disquieted by them, we might be tempted to believe that Christianity had declared a war of extermination against slavery, and that, contrary to what we have said above, it proceeded by great trials of systematic emancipation. This, however, would be an error. In general, Christianity did not touch the positive laws of the society, in which it was introduced. It left to Cæsar what belonged to Cæsar. St. Paul wrote to the slaves of Ephesus that the new religion in no manner changed their duties.[4]

[1] Cod. Theod., lib. xiv., tit. xviii., leg. 1.

[2] Authent. Collat. vi., tit. ix., novel. 80.

[3] D. Hieron, epist. ad Pammach. xxvi.

[4] It is generally said that Christianity abolished slavery, and that is true in the sense that it made liberty desirable for the slaves, and human dignity a respectable dogma for the masters; but it would be entirely wrong to believe that Christianity ever preached against the *legitimacy* of slavery, or excited the slaves to free themselves by violence. The following passages of St. Paul faithfully sum up the doctrine of Christianity on this subject:

"Servants, be obedient to them that are your masters according to the flesh, with fear and trembling, in singleness of your heart, as unto Christ;

"Not with eye-service, as men-pleasers; but as the servants of Christ, doing the will of God from the heart;

"With good-will doing service, as to the Lord, and not to men." (The Epistle of Paul to the Ephesians, vi. 5–7.)

Alongside of the ancient moral world, Christianity only produced a new moral world, into which it admitted all, who were willing to accept its conditions. It was by this attractive power that Christianity drew to itself successively all the members of pagan society; and the magnificent application, which it gave to its ideas of fraternity, charity, and love, was the principal cause, which, indirectly, led to so many emancipations, and created so many proletaries.

In pagan society, few slaves desired to become free, and for a very simple reason. As slaves, they had from their masters all the necessaries of life; they were sure of never suffering from cold, or hunger, or thirst; of being taken care of and well treated in old age as in infancy, in sickness as in health. Free, they had to provide, not only for their own wants, but also for those of their wives and children; not only in the vigor of manhood, but in old age and sickness: without taking into account that, poor and feeble as they would necessarily be on emerging from slavery, they would have to encounter all the risks of a perpetual struggle with society, a struggle, in which even the rich and the strong often succumb. But in Christian society, the slave felt very differently drawn to liberty. Firstly, the Christian freedman was not repelled by the pitiless prejudice of caste. Without refusing to recognize the nobility of race, Christianity had no exaggerated preference for it. The apostles and fathers extended the hand to the freedmen, and generally to all the common people, whom the gentiles, that is to say, the nobles of antiquity, had till then disdained. St. Paul wrote to the Romans that "there is no respect of persons with God;" and St. Gregory of Nazianza, and St. Ambrose, scattered broadcast through their works the philosophical railleries of Christianity on the domination of the flesh, which fell plumb on nobility, which is nothing else than the tradition of power by blood.[1] The freedmen, and the children of freedmen, were therefore welcome among the Chris-

[1] The war of Christianity against *gentility*, that is to say, against the nobility among the pagans, constitutes a very curious epoch in the polemics of the fathers. It will naturally find its place in the second volume of this work. We confine ourselves now to citing this passage of Saint Ambrose:

Quid te jactas de nobilitatis prosapia? Soletis et canum vestrorum origines, sicut divitum recensere; soletis et equorum vestrorum nobilitatem, sicut consulum predicare. Ille ex illo patre generatus est, et illa matre editus. Sed nihil istud currentem juvat. Non datur nobilitati palma, sed cursori. (D. Ambros., in lib. de Nabucha Izraelita, cap. iii.)

tians; all the degrees of clerical ordination were open to them; they could become deacons, priests, bishops; that is to say, they could leap over the interval, among the ancients immense and impassable, that separated extreme humility from extreme glory.[1]

Thus, Christian slaves becoming freedmen were sure of having no moral prejudice against them, and of having all religious prejudices for them; of not being repelled as plebeians, and of being aided as Christians. Therefore, they hastened to be free, and so imprudently, and in such numbers, that, having become suddenly their own masters, and responsible for their own welfare, the greater number were soon overtaken by improvidence and misery; misery unheard of before; a frightful misery, of which the reminiscences of the fourth century present a picture full of horror.

It was this mass of proletaries, created by Christianity, that gave birth to establishments of charity. The first document relative to their history is of the year 315.[2] It was a law of the Emperor Constantine relative to Italy. It provides that, to assist poor families, who gave away, hired, sold, exposed, or killed their children, for want of means to feed them, the necessary aid to provide for their support should be granted annually from the public treasury. A second law, of the year 321, facilitates and encourages legacies and gifts to churches, whose wealth was the property of the poor;[3] and a third law, of the year 322, renews for the province of Africa what that of 315 had already sanctioned for Italy.[4] A law of Valentinian and Valens, of the year 368, established a sort of *maximum* in the price of food and merchandise; to the end, says the law, that the poor may be able to purchase necessaries.[5] We see, by a law of Arcadius and Honorius, of the year 396, that this maximum was fixed in the provinces by an officer, called *discussor;*[6] and a law of Valentinian, Valens, and Gratian, of the year 369, makes known that the principal functions of the *discussor* consisted in visiting the provinces periodically, to collect the balances of taxes, or remit

[1] We have shown, in many places, what an ineffaceable stigma slavery among the ancients impressed on a man and all his race, and what scandal there was at Rome, when Ventidius Bassus, who had been a hostler, was made augur. In Christianity, however, the original stain disappeared completely, and nothing is more common than to find slaves become bishops.

[2] Cod. Theod., lib. xi., tit. xxvii., leg. 4.

[3] Cod. Justin., lib. i., tit. ii., leg. 1.

[4] Cod. Theod., lib. xi., tit. xxviii., leg. 2.

[5] Cod. Justin., lib. i., tit. iv., leg. 1.

[6] Cod. Justin., lib. i., tit. ix., leg. 9.

them; that is to say, to do very nearly what in the ancient financial system of France was done by the *controleurs et receveurs des restes*.[1]

At the commencement of the sixth century we first find hospitals and houses of refuge. A law of Justinian of the year 528 contains, very much at length, regulations for their management. There were houses for travellers, under the name of *xenones;* for the sick, under the name of *nosocomia;* for the poor, under the name of *ptocotrophia;* for orphans, under the name of *orphanotrophia;* for foundlings, under the name of *brephotrophia*.[2] Another law, of the year 530, mentions houses for the aged, under the name of *gerontocomia*, and for sick laborers, under the name of *paranomaria*.[3] A subsequent law provides for a *xeno*, that is, an hospital, in every city.[4] Another law of the same year, modifying that, which declared legacies to uncertain persons void, provided that legacies *for the poor* should be valid, and turned over to the hospital of the city where the testator died.[5] Two other laws of the Justinian code give the same direction to gifts or devises made in favor of Jesus Christ,[6] and all sorts of legacies given to the martyrs, prophets, and angels.[7] Finally, a law of the emperors Valentinian and Martian decreed that the public treasury should pay annually to the churches a sum for feeding and keeping the poor.[8] This law, which is the counterpart of the two ordinances of Constantine, of the years 318 and 322, and which, with those of Justinian, completes the regulations for hospitals, was of the year 454.

By this series of laws Christianity verified the language of St. Ambrose about the goods of the church; that they were the patrimony of the poor. It accepted the legacy of misery and ruin, which the ancient world left to it; it gave a real value to the enfranchisement of slaves, by admitting them even to the highest grades of the sacerdotal hierarchy; and for those, in whose hands liberty was barren, and who were dying of hunger, in spite of their rights as citizens, it created asylums always open to want, old age, and sickness; giving thus to some bread for the soul, to others bread for the body, according to their need.

1 Cod. Theod., lib. xi., tit. xxvi., leg. 1, 2.
2 Cod. Justin., lib. i., tit. iii., leg. 42, § 6.
3 Cod. Justin., lib. i., tit. iii., leg. 49, § 3.
4 Ibid., lib. i., tit. iii., leg. 49, § 6.
5 Ibid., lib. i., tit. ii., leg. 26, in proem.
6 Lib. i., tit. ii., leg. 26, § 1.
7 Lib. i., tit. ii., leg. 15.
8 Lib. i., tit. ii., leg. 12.

# CHAPTER XVI.

## LITERARY SLAVES.

IN following the slave races through the vicissitudes of their fortune, we have seen them leaving the bosom of the noble family, in which they were absorbed, to reach by emancipation the communal association. Once become burghers, the children of the old slaves were distributed among the industrial fraternities; for the commune only regulated their civil interests. The trades' unions regulated their labor.

When the slave races entered the commune and the trades' unions, they had just been freed. Landed property, therefore, was to them almost unknown; for besides that their means were very limited, the ownership of land presupposed certain seignorial qualifications, which they did not possess. Labor, manual labor, applied to the trades, to the arts, to small traffic, thus became the necessary condition of the infant burghers.

Now, labor does not suffice for all the world. Labor is like land; its returns are proportioned to what is given to it. He, who brings to his work the most activity and intelligence, is also the one, who derives most profit from it. The inequality of physical, intellectual, and moral faculties, therefore, produced inequality of condition among the freedmen, become burghers and members of trades' unions. Some prospered, others failed. Some had children, who found themselves rich; others had children, who found themselves beggars. We have seen that the numbers of beggars increased by the multiplicity of emancipations; for the greater the number to be fed by manual labor, the more there will be left without bread.

But, whether the freedmen found in labor the means of living, or want of work forced them to beggary, it may be said that the slave races produced two great classes of men resigned to their condition, viz., the laboring burghers, and the beggars. Both, confined to their position of freedmen, happy or unhappy, never dreamed of looking higher or farther. To work well, or to beg well, such was the principal effort of each day. And as to the superiorities of every kind of the noble races over them; superiority of intelligence, of grace, of command; they saw them without envy, because they were so far above them, or they accepted them without hatred, because they were so formidable.

Well! from the bosom of these same slave races, men arose, of noble souls and bold spirit, to whom nothing seemed too high or too great; who found their chains light enough to be carried with ease, or broken without effort; who felt or believed they had a nature above the nature of their fellows, and who would not be content with the rank, in which God had placed them; who, seeing the authority conferred by intelligence, grace, and strength, determined that they too would become intelligent, gracious, and strong; and who, forgetting their low origin, ennobled themselves by a profound faith in their destiny.

Thus there arose, among the ancients, from amidst the slaves, legions of poets, of courtesans, and of bandits; poets as illustrious as Terence, courtesans beautiful as Aspasia, bandits formidable as Spartacus; all produced by that moral courage, of which we have just spoken — triple protest of strong and proud souls, who seemed to say to God that he had made a mistake, and who, subject to the noble races by the accident of birth, subjugated them by mind, beauty, or terror.

Poetry, prostitution, and brigandage, among the slaves of the ancients, were then facts of the same historic nature, and of the same social signification.

The literature of the slaves is one of the most curious nooks of antiquity. It has special characteristics, which constitute it, give it a form of its own, and make it a domain apart. Thus, the slave is an artist, who does not work indifferently at all kinds of labor. He has not, and does not seek to have, any but a certain order of ideas, which he prefers, for which he is most apt, and in which he loves to shut himself up. For example, the slave never touches politics, law, or history; all ideas, which he leaves to his masters; but he excels in philosophy, in poetry, grammar, rhetoric; in all things that can be done in a corner, and which only require reflection, compilation, and meditation.

The literary studies of the slaves among the ancients were a natural result and logical consequence of their servitude. Their masters sought to make the most profit out of their capacities. They sent to the fields those, who had only muscular strength; they applied to domestic uses those, who manifested facility, elegance, and docility; and when they discovered in them intellectual aptitude, they had them educated with great care, either to derive some day an income from their talents, or a profit by their sale. Literary and artist slaves were of great value. Suetonius mentions Lutatius Daphnis, a slave grammarian, who was bought by Quintus Catulus for 200,000 Roman sesterces, and Lucius Appuleius, also a slave grammarian, whom the knight Calvinus hired from his master for 40,000 sesterces per annum.[1] Talented slaves were therefore a great fortune for their masters, and their education was pushed to the extreme of refinement. (*a*) The custom of the ancients to be served entirely by slaves, caused the latter to be divided into classes, ac-

[1] Suetonius de illust. gramm., cap. iii.

(*a*) These talented slaves, poets, grammarians, and rhetoricians, were not of the race of Ham — negroes — but descendants of Shem and Japhet, of the same blood as their masters. Quære: Does this account for the fact that, since the day when the pious and benevolent Christian priest, Las Casas, first suggested the substitution of African, or negro, for American Indian slave-laborers, down to the present hour, no owner of negro slaves has ever discovered sufficient intellectual aptitude in any one of them, to induce the experiment of education, with a view to profit, either by hire or sale?

In France, the two Dumas, father and son, *novelists*, would seem to confirm the views of our author.

With us, Fred Douglass, who has been prominent in POLITICS at the North, would seem to contradict his theory.

The philosophic historian should not overlook the fact that the two Dumas in France, and Fred Douglass in America, were all more white than black. All have manifested decided intellectual aptitude, very superior talents, in a certain order of ideas. The phenomenon of Fred Douglass's prominence in Northern politics is easily explained. He was forced into that prominence against his nature, and almost against his own will, by those who sought, by abolishing negro slavery, to *divorce* Southern capital from Northern labor, and thereby to reduce the wages of a working-man in the North below the cost of feeding and clothing a negro, and to enlist capital at the South, as well as at the North, in support of a system of legislation, that would make labor cheap and living dear.

But surely those are short-sighted politicians, utterly undeserving the name of statesmen, who permit themselves to believe that 35,000,000 of the Caucasian race will long permit them to use 4,000,000 of ignorant negro freedmen, as voters, to enforce such a system of legislation.

cording to their employment. There were in every grand seignior's house, independently of the slaves of low estate, slave overseers, slave huntsmen, slave singers, slave musicians, and buffoons, who played comedies during meals; finally, slave poets, grammarians, and rhetoricians, to educate the children.[1] Plutarch and Xenophon testify that throughout Greece and Italy education was entirely turned over to slaves. Cato the elder had many intrusted with the education of his children,[2] and Xenophon, in his treatise on the Republic of Sparta, regrets that in Greece, where they boasted of educating children best, they always gave them slaves for preceptors.[3]

It was in consequence of these educational functions that the slaves, among the ancients, monopolized all that may be called the meditative arts; that is to say, all that, like grammar, poetry, and philosophy, may be studied in private and in the silence of thought.

Grammar was considered by the ancients a great and beautiful art, comprising not only what we call philosophy, but also a multitude of facts and ideas properly belonging to history, philosophy, poetry, and the divine science of augury. We can judge what their books of grammar were by the treatises of Varro, the Saturnales of Macrobius, and the Floridæ of Apuleius, all works of great interest, but which never had among the ancients the reputation of some other treatises on grammar; as, for example, those of the grammarian Didymus, whom Plutarch frequently cites.

The study of grammar, as, indeed, the study of all the arts that have made the West illustrious, had its origin in Greece. The Greeks distinguished the *grammarians*[4] from the *grammatists*, as we distinguish *quacks* from *physicians*. Between the second and third Punic war, one Crates Mallotes, says Suetonius, was sent as ambassador to Rome by Attalus. One day, in passing through a street on Mount Palatine, he fell into a sewer and broke his thigh-bone. During his ministry, or rather during his convalescence, he had at his house literary reunions.[5] Ennius and Livius Andronicus, who were poets and rhetoricians, half Greek, and recently deceased, had also held these philological exercises. The example of Crates decided the public taste, and grammar was the fashion at Rome.

[1] Plutarch, Paulus Æmilius, cap. vi.
[2] Plutarch, Cato, cap. xx.
[3] Xenophon de repub. Lacedæm., cap. ii.
[4] Sueton. de illust. gramm., cap. iv.
[5] Ibid., cap. ii.

After that, grammarians abounded. There were sometimes more than twenty celebrated schools open at Rome at the same time.[1] The grammatic frenzy reached the provinces. Masters of renown established themselves there. Suetonius mentions, among others, Octavius Teucer, Siscennius Iacchus, and Appius Chares, who went into Cisalpine Gaul, and there taught to such an advanced age, that they became blind, and were carried to their schools in a litter.[2]

All these professors of grammar were slaves or freedmen; for their masters sometimes preferred to leave to their intelligent slaves the free control of their industry, and to emancipate them on condition of their paying a certain sum, and without prejudice to the patron's right to succeed to the estate of the client. Thus, in the war against Tigranes, the grammarian Tyrannion having been taken prisoner and made a slave, Murena asked him of Lucullus, obtained, and set him free.[3]

Suetonius has given a long list of these slave or emancipated grammarians. He mentions, as one of the first who acquired some celebrity, Suevius Nicanor, who was also a satiric poet.[4] Next, Antonius Gnipho, a Gaul, born free, but exposed in his infancy, and emancipated by the person who found and raised him. He had his first school in the palace of Julius Cæsar, and afterward opened one in his own house. This school was attended by the most illustrious youths.[5] Cicero attended it, even during his prætorship. Antonio Gnipho gave lessons in grammar every day, and declaimed on market days. These declamations were, in prose, what the improvisations of the Italians, French, and Germans, which we have witnessed of late years, were in verse; that is, an amplification in places of resort, more or less public, on a given subject.

In the time of Antonius Gnipho, and for some time after him, Atteius, the philologian, an Athenian and a freedman, lived at Rome in great reputation. He was intimate with Sallust and Asinius Pollion, and composed for the former an abridgment of Roman history.[6] It appears from the remarks of Pollion on the writings of Sallust, that Atteius scattered through the books of the latter that antique terminology, which has often been objected to.[7]

[1] Sueton. de illust. gramm. cap. iii. [2] Ibid., cap. iii. [3] Plutarch, Lucullus.
[4] Sueton. de illust. gramm., cap. v. [5] Sueton. de illust. gramm., cap. vii.
[6] Ibid., cap. x. [7] Ibid., cap. x.

Valerius Cato and Cornelius Epicadus were also very nearly cotemporaneous with Antonius Gnipho. The first was a grammarian and professor of poetry. Cornelius Epicadus was a freedman of Sylla,[1] who made him herald of the college of augurs. On the death of Sylla, he finished the memoirs, which the dictator had left imperfect. Staberius Eros, bought at the market-place, and shown naked on the selling-block, and afterward freed by his master, was the preceptor of Brutus and Cassius.[2] Lenæus, the freedman of Pompey,[3] and the companion of all his wars, had his school in the Carini, that noble suburb of Rome, where were the temples of Juno and of Terra, and where Pompey, Cicero, and a great number of rich and illustrious nobles had their hotels.

Quintus Cæcilius Epirota, with three names like a gentleman, freedman of the knight Atticus, the friend of Cicero, had something of the fate of Abelard.[4] Intrusted with the education of the daughter of Atticus, he fell in love with her, and the expression used by Suetonius on this matter does not forbid us to suppose that he was favorably listened to by his scholar.[5] The intrigue being discovered, the preceptor was discharged, and the young girl married to Marcus Agrippa. From the house of Atticus, his patron, Quintus Cæcilius Epirota passed into that of Cornelius Gallus. The grammarian lived with him in the strictest friendship, and in the struggle, which Cornelius Gallus had to sustain with Augustus — a fatal struggle, which brought his head to the scaffold — his intimacy with the freedman became the subject of the most serious charge. Deprived of this second patron, Quintus Cæcilius Epirota opened a school. He received very few pupils, and only very young ones, which caused the poet Domitius Marsus to give him the name of "nurse to sucking poets."[6] To the last, Quintus Cæcilius Epirota manifested the moral characteristics, which had begun the misfortunes of his life. He was the first, who gave lessons on Latin subjects. While the other grammarians recognized the Greek only as the language of learning and literature, he dared to scandalize his auditors by reading Virgil and other cotemporaneous poets.[7]

[1] Sueton. de illust. gramm., cap. xi.
[2] Ibid., cap. xi. See also Pliny, Hist. Natur., lib. xxxv., cap. lviii.
[3] Ibid., cap. xv. [4] Ibid., cap. xv. [5] Sueton., cap. xv.
[6] Ibid., cap. xv. [7] Ibid., cap. xv.

Alongside of grammarians like Cæcilius Epirota, Rome had others of less brilliant but more peaceable fortune, such as Verrius Flaccus, Scribonius Aphrodisius, Caius Julius Hyginus, and Caius Melissus.

Verrius Flaccus[1] established public debates, in which he gave the victor, as a prize, some rare book. Augustus chose him as preceptor of his nephews, and he had his school at first in the palace, afterward in Catiline's hotel, which was part of the palace. Scribonius Aphrodisius,[2] freedman of Scribonia, first wife of Augustus, and the cotemporary of Verrius, left a treatise on orthography. Caius Julius Hyginus,[3] a freedman of Augustus and friend of Ovid, was the emperor's librarian, which did not prevent his giving lessons. Caius Melissus,[4] exposed in infancy, saved and given to Mæcenas, and by Mæcenas to Augustus, was made by the emperor librarian of the portico of Octavia.

Finally, we have to speak of Quintus Remmius Palemon, who was a curious type of the slave artist, disdainfully revolting against his condition. Palemon commenced as the slave of a weaver.[4] Then he accompanied his master's son to the schools, and learned belles-lettres by stealth. Fortified by study and freed, he became, under Tiberius and Claudius, the most celebrated grammarian of Rome. Full of faults and vices, nevertheless he captivated the sternest minds by the inexpressible attraction of his speech and the surprising retentiveness of his memory. At need, too, he wrote good verses. Bold, conceited, and arrogant, he affected the greatest contempt for the learned Marcus Terentius Varro, and carried the elastic vulgarity of abusive latinity to its utmost stretch, by telling him that he was nothing but a hog.[5] He pretended that Virgil had clearly predicted him, in his third eclogue — by making Palemon the judge of the verses of Menalchus and Dametas — as the one, whose opinions on all matters of poetry posterity would accept;[6] and he related, with an exquisite fatuity, how the robbers, who had captured and wished to hold him for ransom, let him go with the greatest deference,[7] out of respect to the celebrity of his name.

Bold as a knight, Quintus Remmius Palemon was voluptuous as

[1] Sueton., cap. xvii. [2] Ibid., cap. xix. [3] Ibid., cap. xx.
[4] Ibid., cap. xxi. [5] Ibid., cap. xxiii. [6] Ibid., cap. xxiii.
[7] Ibid., cap. xxiii.

a Sybarite. He took an exorbitant number of baths each day, and his domestic luxury absorbed not only the income from his school, but his whole estate. His excessive fondness for gallantry ended by ruining him, and he spent in gayeties the income of his broker's warehouses, and even that of his vineyards, which he had himself planted, and which yielded him, according to Suetonius, 365 amphoræ of wine.[1]

*Rhetoric*, although near akin to *grammar*, was nevertheless so far separated from it, as to require men of different condition. Nearly all the grammarians were slaves. On the contrary, very few slaves became rhetoricians. For this essential difference, there were simple and natural reasons, which may here be given.

Grammar was an art for youth, rhetoric for manhood.[2] The former taught the principles of spoken and written language. The latter taught the practice of speech. Rhetoric, therefore, belonged directly to politics, by senatorial or tribunitial orations, and to jurisprudence, by the pleadings before the prætor.

Now, never, in any country of the world, have slaves applied themselves to the study of politics, or law, which belong exclusively to free men. Although shut up in a circle of generalities by the conditions of all public instruction, and, therefore, sustained by mere commonplaces, rhetoric requires a knowledge of law, and this, we say, it is that raises it above the sphere of slaves. Pompey, Cicero, Julius Cæsar, Brutus, and Cassius might well go to learn the rules of good speaking of Greece in the schools of grammarians like Marcus Antonius Gnipho or Staberius Eros; but what could slaves teach those great men on the law of the Twelve Tables, the science of augury, which was part of the law, or on the affairs of the republic? An orator, in his speeches, had always either the senate to convince or the judges to win over. Now, a miserable slave, deprived of all civil or domestic personality, was not qualified even to speak of matters so far above him as were judicial and political affairs.

There were, therefore, among the ancients, and especially in Italy, hardly any examples of orators among the slaves or freedmen.

It was, also, for the same reason that history with the ancients was never written by slaves. The ancients had no idea of what we

[1] Sueton. de illust. gramm., cap. xxiii. [2] Ibid., cap. iv.

call philosophical history; that is to say, no idea of a general recital and classification of human facts for the demonstration or justification of a principle. It seems that they were too near the starting-point to have been able to study the tendency, and learn the direction of events. They confined themselves, therefore, to writing memoirs on very narrow topics. We have only a very small part of the numberless historical works composed by the ancients; but those we have justify this opinion marvellously. The books of Thucydides and Xenophon, among the Greeks, of Sallust and Tacitus, among the Romans, are memoirs like those of Philippe de Comines or the Maréchal Blaise de Montluc; and as to general histories, like those of Herodotus, Polybius, and Titus Livius, they are general only in name; amounting only to meagre summaries, presenting the personal views of the author, or abridging former chronicles.

Among the ancients, historians generally were divided into two classes: those who wrote what they had seen, and those who compiled from the books of others. The former were much the most numerous. Thus, military men, who, like Thucydides, Xenophon, Arrian, Polybius, Pausanias, Cato, Sylla, Cæsar, Hirtius, Augustus, Tiberius, Claudius, King Juba, and Tacitus, had taken part in the wars, or travellers, who, like Herodotus and Strabo, had visited distant countries, ordinarily became historians. Now, slaves and freedmen, who were not free to travel, were not regularly admitted into the armies, and never could acquire the grade of officers, could not find a place among this class of historians.

There remain the compilers, like Diodorus of Sicily, Sallust, Cornelius Nepos, Titus Livius, Plutarch, Suetonius. But the nature of their work required numerous collections of memoirs, rare and costly. Besides, to write history, even after another, always involves the necessity of judging men, and, consequently, of sometimes condemning them. Now, it would have seemed intolerable to the generals and statesmen of antiquity to be judged by slaves; that is to say, by men totally ignorant of the military art and the science of statesmanship.

We say, then, that among the ancients, history was written exclusively by gentlemen. We scarcely find one or two exceptions. Suetonius mentions one Lucius Otacilius Pilitus, who was a slave porter, and, as such, fastened by a chain, as we do with dogs, to his master's door.[1] His natural talent impelling, he became a distinguished rhetorician, educated Pompey, and wrote a history, in many books, of the military expeditions of the Pompeys, father and son.[2] Suetonius mentions this fact, which he characterizes as very strange; adding, on the authority of Cornelius Nepos, that he was the first slave, who undertook to write history, which up to that time had been exclusively reserved to writers of noble birth.[3]

Poetry and philosophy were especially the literary labor suitable for slaves, because they required neither travel, nor the patient study of chronicles, nor high position in the state; and because for them a little quiet corner sufficed, where the slave could meditate, until his thoughts were elevated by degrees to the imaginations that make the poet, or to the reflections that make the philosopher.

We must make this general remark on the slaves, who cultivated poetry at Rome, at least before the Christian era: that they were nearly all Greek by birth or education, and nearly always used the Greek language in their compositions.[4] We have already seen, that from the time of Augustus, Q. C. Epirota introduced a great novelty in citing Virgil and other cotemporaneous poets as models. In the estimation of the literary men of Italy, there was but one language that was learned, complete, and worthy of being used for literary composition. That was the Greek. The grammarians lectured in Greek, and quoted Greek authors. The rhetoricians declaimed in Greek. The Latin was considered the national idiom, it was true; but more proper for the medical receipts of the elder Cato, or for the judicial proceedings of the prætor, than for the elegant creations of the poets.

From the period of which we speak, the Latin poets may be divided into two classes; the comedians, and the epic and lyric poets.

The comedians, as we understand them, were all those, who composed tragedies, comedies, and farces, and generally acted them; all, who composed songs and sang them in the streets; all, who wrote

[1] Sueton. de clar. rhetor., cap. iii. [2] Ibid., cap. iii.

[3] Ibid., cap. iii.

[4] The ancients generally remarked that the Syrians and Asiatic Greeks appeared destined by nature for slavery. "Hic Syri et Asiatici Græci sunt levissima genera hominum et servituti nata." (Tit. Liv. Hist., lib. xxxvi., cap. xvii.)

satires, and recited them on the boards in public. We may add to these different kinds of comedians, buffoons, jugglers, sword-swallowers, fortune-tellers, magicians; in fine, that eternal and universal Babel of men of talent, frothing always and everywhere on the surface of the people — mysterious river, flowing on a level with the earth, over the slime of every nation, having no known source, fattening on the condensed clouds of the occult sciences, and having two estuaries, the gallows and the hospital.

Perhaps there does not exist one piece of stage literature written in Latin, that was not a translation or imitation of the Greek, and on a Greek subject. Plautus and Terence have done little more than translate Menander, Aristophanes, Diphilus, Philemon, Demophilus, Epicharmus the Sicilian, Eubulus, Apollodorus, Posidippus, and the other dramatists of Greece.[1] The sale of slaves raised in Sicily, the Ionian Isles, or Asia Minor, or the vicinity of the Greek colonies established along the Adriatic Sea, were the two sources, whence unpolished Rome derived her poetry and fine language.

Plautus was the first Italian slave who wrote comedies. He translated or imitated the Greek classics, while turning a handmill in one of the establishments belonging to the bakers' trade's union of Rome. Three Greek philosophers, Menedemus, Asclepiades, and Cleanthis, turned a mill, as he did.[2] Plautus lived in the first half of the second century before the Christian era. Shortly after him came Terence, the slave and freedman of the noble house of Terentius Lucanus. Terence followed the example of Plautus, and translated the stage classics of the Greeks, as he boasts in the prologue to his Andrienna.[3] The stage literature of the Romans is, in fact, represented by Plautus and Terence; although we find other freedmen, who attempted it; among others, Caius Melissus, a slave grammarian, who was given, as a present, to Augustus by Mæcenas.

Alongside of the Greek stage literature, *comedia palliata*, there was also at Rome a national stage literature, *comedia togata*, taken from Italian subjects. Of this there were four kinds, one of which belonged exclusively to the young nobility, who composed the *Atellanes*, and acted them in society.[4] The other three were of the province of the slaves.

1 Philip. Parei, de Script. M. Acc. Plaut.
2 Ibid.
3 Terent. Andr., prolog., v. 17–20.
4 Tit. Liv. Hist., lib. vii., cap. ii.

There were in ancient Italy troups of strolling comedians, under the orders of a director, who bore the title of "*leader of theatrical performances*,"[1] or sometimes the title of "*emperor of the actors*."[2] The actors and actresses were always slaves or freedmen, and their education corresponded to the part they acted. Those who played in the classic comedies, or in tragedies, were generally highly cultivated grammarians; for Cicero relates that they were hissed pitilessly, if they happened to make a mistake in the prosody of a single syllable.[3]

We comprehend that there naturally were companies of every kind, according to the fortune of the director and the taste of the public. All directors did not possess comedians like Ofilius Hilarus,[4] Pylades, and Bathyllus, nor tragedians like Æsop and Roscius. Besides, only Rome could pay for such talents as theirs. Cities of the second order, and Rome herself, overflowed with buffoons and mimics, who played in the open air, without brodekins or mask, and only with some fantastic dress, as in the Atellan farces.

Troups of jugglers, mimics, and buffoons traversed Italy. The pieces, which they played, were sometimes written and learned by heart; but more often they were reduced to some burlesque parade. Suetonius mentions a freed grammarian, named Lucius Pansa, who wrote pieces for the buffoons.[5] Generally, the mimics and buffoons were the scum of the theatres. Their ordinary representations on the boards were a mixture of dances and epigrams, obscene pantomime, and moral sentences. There were cities where buffoons were not admitted; for example, Marseilles.[6]

Rome produced, under the emperors, mimics of great reputation. Vossius cites Publius Laberius, Publius the Syrian, Philistion of Nice, Cneius Mattius, Lentulus, Marcus Marullus, and some others.[7] The fondness of the emperors for the theatre had not a little increased the number of mimics. Caligula and Nero treated them with extraordinary favor. Caligula especially carried his fondness for them to frenzy. Sometimes in the intervals of the play he em-

1 Tacitus, Annal., lib. i., cap. xvi.
2 Plaut., Pænal., prolog., v. 4, 43, 44.
3 Cicero, Parad., iii., cap. ii.
4 Pliny, Hist. Natur., lib. vii., cap. 54.
5 Sueton. de illust. gramm., cap. xviii.
6 Valer. Maxim., lib. ii., cap. vi., § 7.
7 Vossius, institut. poetic., lib. ii., cap. xxxiii.

braced with transport the pantomimic Mnester.[1] One day, a knight having annoyed that dancer by some noise, Caligula wrote a note, and sent it at once to the knight by a centurion, with orders to leave immediately for Ostia, and thence for Mauritania, to carry the note to King Ptolemy. Now, the note contained literally these words: "Do neither good nor harm to the bearer." [2]

We know that Caligula was stabbed by Chæreas, behind the scenes of the theatre, while enraptured by gazing at some young Asiatic dancers of great celebrity, who were performing a dance of their country.[3]

Below the classic comedy, below the Atellan farce, below even the pantomime of the buffoons, there was another kind of dramatic poetry cultivated by slaves. This was satire sung in the streets, with the accompaniment of music and gesture. Perhaps it would be well to trace the connection of this dramatized satire, derived, like all the Latin literature, from Greece, from the *sillus*, cultivated by Timon Phliasius, the cotemporary of Ptolemy Philadelphus, and Xenophanes of Lesbos, down to the severe prohibition of it by the law of the Twelve Tables; for the license of the strolling singers was carried to such extremes that it became necessary to moderate their rapture by the rod.[4] The model of these poet-comedians of the streets was Livius Andronicus, a cotemporary of Ennius, and anterior to Plautus, and whom Suetonius calls a semi-Greek orator.[5] Valerius Maximus relates that when the artist, who had been set free by Livius Salinator, his master, had grown old, he hired a boy who sang the stanzas, and a flute-player, who accompanied him, and that he, broken down and blind, translated to the crowd by pantomime the poem, as the singer and musician progressed.[6]

Finally, and this is the lowest stage of the world of slave artists, there were bands of jugglers, sleight-of-hand players, fortune-tellers, and magicians, who lived as they could on the curiosity of passers-by. Sometimes the jugglers had sufficient reputation to be called by great lords, at the end of their feasts, to amuse the guests by their repartees and tricks. In the satiric poem of Petronius, Trimalchion had moun-

[1] Sueton. Caligula, cap. lv. [2] Ibid., cap. lv. [3] Ibid., cap. lviii.
[4] Cicero de Repub., lib. iv., fragm. 33. [5] Sueton. de illust. gramm., cap. i.
[6] Valerius Maximus, lib. ii., cap. iv., § 4.

tebanks, who danced on top of a ladder, and jumped through hoops during his famous dinner.[1] Generally, they danced and exhibited at public places, swallowing Lacedæmonian swords, to the great satisfaction of the idle.[2] The fortune-tellers had become so numerous at Rome, in the time of the first emperors, that they had a union;[3] and the day after Caligula was killed, magicians arrived from Egypt and Syria, who were to have given in the theatre a representation of hell.[4]

Epic and lyric poetry belongs less properly to slaves than dramatic poetry. Generally, the ancient Greek and Latin poets, who composed poems, odes, and hymns, were men of noble houses. The *gnomiques*, Theognis, Phocylides, Pythagoras, Solon, Simonides, all belonged to more or less powerful houses. Only Callimachus, librarian to Ptolemy Philadelphus, and Tyrteus, the Athenian general, commenced life as schoolmasters, which is a sign of very humble extraction. At Rome, Ennius was of a great family, and lived in intimate friendship with Cato the elder, and Scipio. Pacuvius, his nephew, was not less illustrious. Catullus and Lucretius, Tibullus and Propertius, Gallus and Ovid were born of distinguished parents. Juvenal and Perseus were gentlemen.[5]

There were scarcely any others then but Horace, Virgil, and Phædrus, who were poets of the slave race.

Horace, son of a freed salt-fish-monger,[6] also belonged to the slave poets by his Greek studies. Virgil, son of a poor village potter — that is to say, also born of the slave race — followed the bent of all his kind, learned grammar, rhetoric, medicine, mathematics, which then comprehended physics and astronomy, and even jurisprudence, which was an exception for men of his rank, and made him one of the most learned men of antiquity. Phædrus, a slave, full of the sententious (*gnomiques*) poets, of the study of Æsop, of the Milesianisms introduced into the Latin literature by Ennius and Plautus, lived at the latter end of the Greek revival, when the Latin language had ceased to copy Homer and Plato, to try, with Seneca,

[1] Petron. Arbit. Satir., cap. liii.

[2] Plutarch relates the taunt of an Athenian to King Agis, that the swords of the Lacedæmonians were so short that the mountebanks swallowed them without difficulty. (Lycurgus, cap. xix.)

[3] See note to page 213.

[4] Sueton. Caligula, cap. lvii.

[5] Suet. Horat. Vita.

[6] Donat. de Virgil. Vita.

Lucan, Juvenal, Perseus, the two Plinys, and a host of others, to revive the traditions of Roman taste, interrupted since the arrival of Greek rhetoricians and grammarians in Italy.[1]

After grammar, the theatre and poetry, philosophy was the study most liked by the slaves. There were slaves in all the notable ancient schools of philosophy. Phædon, to whom Plato dedicated his treatise on the soul, was a young boy of great beauty, exposed for sale at the house of a slave-merchant, who also kept a house of prostitution ; and he was bought by Cebes, the disciple of Socrates.[2] The beautiful books, which he composed on the doctrine of Socrates, still existed in the time of Aulus Gellius, who mentions them with honor. Menippus, a slave like Phædon, also became an illustrious philosopher. He devoted himself particularly to a kind of philosophical composition, under the form of satire, which he called *cynic*, and which Varro afterward imitated.[3] These *cynics* appear to have been satires of the same kind as the *Cyclops* of Euripides. Varro, in imitating them, wrote moral treatises, and gave them the name of *Menippian satires*. It is not known to what philosophic sect Menippus belonged. There was a slave peripatetic philosopher, named Pompylus, who belonged to the philosopher Theophrastus.[4] Perseus, slave of Zeno the stoic, shared the doctrine of his master, and Mys, the slave of Epicurus, had no other philosophy than his. Diogenes the cynic, although born free, was reduced to slavery, and bought in the market at Corinth by Xeniades, who made him the preceptor of his children.[5]

Epictetus, of the sect of the Stoics, was one of the most celebrated slaves, who cultivated philosophy. He was a Greek, like all the learned slaves, and belonged to Epaphroditus, the freedman of Nero. Two verses which he composed on himself, and which

1 It was this return of Latin literature to its primitive and national traditions, which gave birth to a style called "*the style of the decay*." The rhetoricians, pedants infatuated with Greek and habituated to the classic manner of Virgil, Cicero, and Horace, could not reconcile themselves to a turn of style, which did not recall their consecrated models, and they treated it as barbarous; while it only strengthened the language from the old and good sources of the time of the republic, from which great orators, like Appius Cæcus, the Gracchi, and Cato, had drawn. From the time of Seneca the return to the primitive traditions of the Latin language became general, and even extravagant. (Senecæ Epist., lib. ad Lucil., epist. cxiv.)

2 Aul. Gell., Noct. Attic., lib. ii., cap. xviii.

3 Ibid., lib. ii., cap. xviii. 4 Ibid. 5 Ibid.

Aulus Gellius has preserved, show that he was deformed.[1] Under Domitian, a senatus consultum having expelled the rhetoricians and philosophers from Italy, Epictetus, who was then a freedman, quitted Italy, and retired to Nicopolis.[2]

---

## CHAPTER XVII.

### THE COURTESANS.

THE ancient courtesans, whose history we are about to sketch, are not those, who were exposed in public houses. These latter offer no lesson for history. They were poor girls, bought in the market, naked, or nearly naked, on great tables called *catastæ;*[3] that purchasers, who were hard to please, could examine the offered merchandise closely.[4] These *catastæ* were sufficiently elevated, so that from the ground to the upper platform, on which were the slaves, large and high closets could be constructed. On top of the catastæ, slaves of ordinary value were exposed, naked, their feet rubbed with white chalk,[5] and a crown of holly-leaves on their heads.[6] In the catastæ were kept the slaves of great price, who were only shown to purchasers of some importance.[7] Generally, the trade of slave-dealer was connected with the profession of

[1] Aul. Gell., Noct. Attic., lib. ii., cap. xviii. [2] Ibid., lib. xv., cap. xi.

[3] It was commonly said of a slave that he had been "*bought on the catasta*" Staberius eros hero suo emptus de catasta. (Suet. de illus. gram., cap. xiii.)

[4] Statius says that the catasta turned on a pivot, so that the slaves could be examined by purchasers on all sides. (Stat. Sylv., lib. ii., carmen i., v. 72.)

[5] Tibullus, lib. ii., eleg. iii., v. 59, 60. Pliny also mentions three slaves, who afterward became celebrated, Staberius Eros the grammarian, Publius the mimic, and Manilius Antiochus the astrologer, who were sold with their feet rubbed with chalk.

[6] Aul. Gell., Noct. Attic., lib. vii., cap. iv. A passage of Justin on Philip, King of Macedon, shows that the usage was general. (Justin., lib. vii., cap. iii.)

[7] Martial gives the curious details, as follows :

In septis Mamurra diu multumque vagatus
. . . . . . . . .
Inspexit molles pueros, oculisque comedit:
Non hos quos primæ prostituere casæ:
Sed quos arcanæ servant tabulata catastæ,
Et quos non populus, nec mea turba videt.
(Martial., lib. ix., epigram lx.)

keeper of a house of debauch. Moreover, this business presupposed a consummate experience in the science of the toilet, of which we at this day have only a very incomplete idea. These merchants had the art of making women, otherwise least calculated to charm, appear young, elegant, and fresh.[1] As fairness of skin was a quality much prized by the ancients, the women exposed for sale were painted with a preparation of white moss,[2] which gave them a violet color much prized by connoisseurs. Pliny relates that they rubbed the bodies of those, who were too thin, with resin; a proceeding which was intended, he assures us, to give them the appearance of strength and size.[3] Pliny and Galien mention many other details, which the curious in antiquities of this kind will do well to consult; but to the recital of which the French language refuses absolutely to condescend. In a word, the slave-traders possessed thoroughly the art of the toilette, according to the ancient taste; an infinite mystery, in which the most skilful make mistakes, and of which we can appreciate the difficulties; we, who have proved them in the art of the toilette among the moderns; a toilette confined to dress, while the other undertook to manage the body itself.

But, we repeat, these are not the courtesans, whose lives we wish to recount. What could we say that is not summed up in a few words? To be exposed, as long as they were young, at the door of some house of ill fame, dressed from morning to night in that strange costume of prostitutes, which shocks by its splendid uniformity all the customs of honest life; and to wait, always wait, with feigned pleasure, between two lights, which burned day and night;[4] such their life, until, ruined and blasted, they were sold at low price for some less horrible work, which substituted fatigue of body for bitterness of sentiment and thoughts of ignominy.

[1] Slave-traders were called *mangones*. Many authors give the details of their business. Pliny mentions them in some places as men, who excelled in making perfumes and pomades. (Plin. Hist. Natur., lib. xii., cap. xliii.)

[2] Quintil. Inst. Orat., lib. ii., cap. xv., § 25.

Plautus says, in his comedy of the Ghosts, that old women rubbed their bodies with pomades, and painted themselves with white moss, to hide their wrinkles; but that, not being expert in the art of the toilette, they heaped, one upon the other, such a mixture of odors, that the result was a very questionable perfume. (Plaut. Mostellar., act i., sc. iii., v. 117–121.)

[3] Pliny, Hist. Natur., lib. xxiv., cap. xii.

[4] It is from Tertullian that we learn that the custom was to have two lighted candles before the doors of houses of debauch. (Tertul. Apologet., cap. xxxv.)

The courtesans, whose history is curious and instructive, were the freedwomen; women, whose beauty made them free, and who subjected the rich and powerful by their graces, as the slave grammarians or slave poets subjected them by talent.

We must first correct an error, very old and widespread, in relation to the different women spoken of by the ancient poets. The elegy-writers of the eighteenth century, as Dorat, Bertin, Parny, and some others, who more or less translated or imitated the ancient elegies, have borrowed from them the various gallant speeches, which they addressed to Greek and Latin women, and have applied them to French women. Now, they have not taken notice of the fact, that all the women addressed by the ancient poets were freedwomen courtesans.[1] Yes; all the women, to whom Horace addressed his verses, Pyrrha, Lydia, Leuconia, Tyndaris, Glycera, Chloe, Barina, Asteria, Lycea, Neobula, Chloris, Phidela, Galatea, Phyllis, Phryne, Neæra, Cinara;[2] all, of whom Catullus speaks, Lesbia, Hypsithylla, Acme, Quintia, Aufilena;[3] all whom Tibullus mentions, Delia, Næara,[4] were courtesans, freedwomen, freed by loss of virtue, and with more or less brilliant fortune, in proportion to their beauty and their talent. We will presently show what splendid and incredible fortunes some of these women made. Meantime we will speak of their domestic habits and daily life.

Nearly all these courtesan freedwomen were Greeks. The names of all we have mentioned indicate as much. Without our being able to say exactly what was their costume, it is certain that at Rome the sumptuary laws forbade their dressing like noble ladies. Tibullus urges Delia to be chaste, notwithstanding that the law would not permit her to wear bands on her hair or a long dress

[1] This is proved *morally* by the sense of all the verses addressed to these women, and *literally* by passages like the following:

Me *libertina*, neque uno
Contenta, Phryne macerat.
(Horat. Epod., lib., od. xiv., v. 15, 16.)
Grata detinuit compede Myrtale
*Libertina*, fretis acrior tradrice.
(Horat. Carm., lib. i., od. xxxiii.

Besides, there is in the Athenæum a passage, which admits of no reply; for it is in these words: "Not only the courtesans, but all the other slave women." (Athen. Deipn., lib. xiii, cap. vi.)

[2] See odes of Horace. [3] Catullus, passim. [4] Tibullus, passim.

with a train,[1] which was the privilege of women of noble condition. Catullus, in a comparison of Lesbia with the mistress of Formianus, says that Lesbia had smaller feet and longer fingers,[2] which indicates that she did not wear the dress of Roman dames; for that dress concealed the feet and hands.

These freedwomen were very devout, or, at least, they frequented the temples. Propertius complains of Cynthia that she did not go there exclusively to pray.[3] It was generally at midday that these dames received the fashionable world,[4] in a very light dress, and in summer under a large silk net,[5] to keep off the flies. The rich youngsters and poets joined their circle, on leaving the forum,[6]

[1] Sit modo casta doce; quamvis non vitta ligatos
Impediat crines, nec stola longa pedes.
(Tibul., lib. i., eleg. vi., v. 67, 68.)

[2] Salve, nec nimio puella naso,
Nec bello pede, nec nigris oculis,
Nec longis digitis . . .
(Catul., carm. xliii.)

[3] Fanaque peccatis plurima causa tuis.
(Propert., lib. ii., eleg. xv., v. 10.)

[4] This appears from a very coarse note from Catullus to Hypsithylla, of which we will only cite one verse:

Jube ad te veniam meridiatum.
(Catull., carm. xxxii.)

[5] The net, which seems to have been an importation from Greece to Rome, was only used by the courtesans, who were nearly all Greeks. It was called in Greek κωνωπειον, from κώνοψ, a gnat, and was Latinized into conopeum, which we find in many authors, and among others Horace:

Interque signa turpe militaria
Sol adspicit conopeum.
(Horat., Epod. lib., od. ix.)

The use of the net by courtesans made it an object of contempt among the Romans. Propertius gives us to understand that it was introduced into Rome by the Egyptians, and he is indignant that they had sullied with it the Tarpeian Rock.

Fœdaque Tarpeio conopea tendere saxo.
(Propert., lib. iii., eleg. ix., v. 45.)

Toward the end of the reign of Domitian, the net had grown into frequent use at Rome. The following lines of Juvenal show that it was used to cover the cradles of babies:

Ut testudineo tibi, Lentule, conopeo
Nobilis Euryalum mermillonem exprimet infans.
(Juvenal, sat. vi., v. 79, 80.)

[6] It is established by much testimony that the business of the forum ended at midday, and that thence the idle went to their pleasures. It is in the sense of this general fact that we must understand these two verses:

Varus me meus ad suos amores
Visum duxerat e foro otiosum.
(Catul. carm. x.)

when the business of the morning was over. The strictest decorum prevailed in these visits, which the most eminent statesmen made openly before all the world, to fashionable freedwomen, and there was no gentleman so distinguished as not to feel flattered, when one of them borrowed his carriage and livery. Catullus relates, that having gone with Varus to visit his mistress, and having said, in the conversation, that he had just had made new dresses for the Moors who carried his litter, she asked him bluntly to loan them to her, that she might go to the temple of Serapis.[1]

With the freedwomen the day was devoted to society, the evening to gallantry. At dusk the rich and idle youngsters started out. When the courtesans were considered easy of access, or had compromised themselves, their visitors observed no ceremony in making a noise at their doors, or rattling their window-shutters.[2] But when they had acquired some consideration by their talent or by their dignity, they came, humbly and respectfully, to sing romances under their windows. Horace has preserved a refrain of one of these romances, which was sung for Lydia in her youth, which is a very proper and touching compliment.[3] Sometimes, lovers did not confine themselves to simply singing romances, but brought with them bands of musicians, to regale the hard-hearted beauty with a serenade. Thus Horace recommends to Asteria not to show herself at the window in the evening, when the plaintive flutes begin

[1] Quæso, inquit, mihi, mi Catulle, paulum
Istos commoda; nam volo ad Serapim
Deferri. (Catul., Carm. x.)

[2] Parcius junctas quatiunt fenestras
Ictibus crebris juvenes protervi,
Nec tibi somnos adimunt . . .
(Horat., Carm., lib. i., od. xxv.)

[3] The two following verses appear to us to have been evidently the refrain of a romance sung to Lydia in her youth:

Me tuo longas pereunte noctes,
Lydia, dormis.
(Horat., Carm., lib. i., od. xxv.)

This fact seems to us clearly established; first, because Horace says to Lydia, grown old, that she no longer heard these words as formerly, *audis minus et minus jam;* — next, because he said, in a note to Asteria, that they called her *cruel* to the sound of music, which could only be in a song:

Et te sæpe vocanti
Duram difficilis mane.
(Horat., Carm., lib. iii., od. vii.)

to be heard in the streets.[1] Not unfrequently two or three serenades, intended for the same woman, came together at the same time under the same window, and the gallants bravely drew their swords, or ordered their people to make place for them with their daggers. Propertius, writing to Delia, who had gone to pass the summer at Tibur, congratulates her that she is no longer exposed to having her sleep broken by the nightly brawls of her followers under her windows.[2]

The domestic life of the courtesans depended on the position they had made for themselves, and the relations they had formed. The richer ones had sumptuous houses, numerous servants, and a costly retinue ; [3] the greater number owned slaves ; the less fortunate hired them. What every courtesan, rich or poor, wished to have was a mother. We have already said that they were freedwomen, consequently born in slavery, and without parents. What principally distinguished a courtesan from other women was having no family ; and this was precisely why they attached so much importance to making one for themselves, though incomplete, illusory, and pretended. They could not dream of having a father. A father was completely impossible in their position. So they fell back upon a mother.

The mother of a courtesan was not she, who gave birth to her ; but a woman, who gave her a rank. To have a mother, that was as much as to say, that they were not mere foundlings ; that they were entitled to some consideration. It brought them nearer to the women of society. Gentlemen displayed their titles ; courtesans displayed their mothers.

For ordinary courtesans the mother was an old woman, who had served her time as a courtesan, with an ambiguous look and familiar smile. For rich courtesans the mother was a kind of domestic

[1] The serenades given to women under their windows are very clearly referred to in these verses :

Prima nocte domum claude ; neque in vias
Sub cantu quærulæ despice tibiæ.
(Horat., Carm., lib. iii., od. vii.)

[2] Nulla neque ante tuas orietur rixa fenestras
Nec tibi clamatæ somnus amarus erit.
(Propert., lib. ii., eleg. xv., v. 5, 6.)

[3] For example, the house and retinue of Theodota were magnificent. See note on this subject to page 204.

fetich, pompously dressed, idle, a part of the stationary furniture of the room where visitors were received.[1] Zenophon relates that Socrates one day visiting Theodota, a young courtesan of Athens, then much the fashion, she insisted on presenting him to her mother,[2] who was splendidly dressed, and surrounded by a swarm of servants in attendance on her.

We readily conceive that the women of ancient days, like those of to-day, were fruitful in a thousand devices to enhance their beauty, or supply the want of it. In elegant houses,[3] the walls of the chambers were hung with tapestry, and the floors, laid in mosaic, were covered with Babylonian carpets.[4] As to the dress of the courtesans, it would be very difficult to reproduce it exactly; because, the fashion changing, both in Greece and Italy, we should be exposed, by insufficiency of data, to mix up the styles of different epochs. We can only indicate the general features.

[1] Tibullus draws a picture of Delia's mother, who was a model of the *genus*:

Non ego te propter parco tibi, sed tua mater
  Me movet, atque iras aurea vincit anus.
Hæc mihi te adducit tenebris, multoque timore
  Conjungit nostras clam taciturna manus.
Hac foribusque manet noctu me affixa, proculque
  Cognoscit strepitus, me veniente, pedum.
Vive diu mihi, dulcis anus. . . .

(Tibul., lib. i., eleg. vi., v. 57–63.)

[2] Xenophon. Memorab., lib. iii., cap. xi., § 4.

[3] The use of hangings for the walls was general in the houses of the rich of antiquity, and many examples can be cited. Thus, when the assassins sent by Lysander had set fire to the house of Alcibiades, they tried to put it out by smothering it with coverlets and the tapestry hangings. (Plut. Alcibiades.) The use of hangings came from the East. Tertullian thus speaks of the Medes and Parthians: "Sed et parietes Tyriis et Hyacinthinis, et illis regiis velis, quæ vos operos resoluta transfiguratis, pro pictura abutuntur." (Tertul. de cult. femin., cap. viii.)

[4] We find carpets used throughout the East from the earliest times. Homer mentions them often. To cite but one example, see Odys., lib. x., v. 12. These carpets were of fine wool, as is proved by this passage from Pliny: "Est et hirtæ (lanæ) pilo crasso in tapetis antiquissima gratia: jam certe priscos iis usos, Homerus auctor est." (Plin. Hist. Natur., lib. viii., cap. lxxiii.) Plautus, in his comedy of *Pseudolus*, mentions tapestry of Alexandria, on which animals were represented:

Neque Alexandrina belluata conchyliata tapetia.

(Plaut., Pseud., act i., sc. ii., v. 14.)

And in his comedy of Stychus, the tapestry of Babylon:

Tum Babylonica peristromata, consutaque tapetia.

(Plaut., Stych., act ii., sc. iii., v. 53.)

The height of magnificence was carpets of purple. Martial mentions them thus:

Stragula purpureis lucent villosa tapetis;
Quid prodest, si te congelat uxor anus?

(Mart., lib. xiv., epigr. cxlvii.)

First, we must not accept, as the costume of Greek and Roman women, the ridiculous dress put upon the stage in France since fifty years. This dress, designed after antique statues and cameos, is altogether imaginary, and was invented by the artists. Never would the most shameless woman have the impudence to appear in public, in Athens or at Rome, in that state of nudity, which does very well in statues, but of which a woman of the Lupercal would be ashamed. We repeat, the costume of ancient statues is conventional,[1] and the moderns have made a mistake in taking the rules of architecture and sculpture for the rules of domestic life. Nor were the statues of the pagan deities exposed naked in the temples. They were always dressed more or less magnificently,[2] and their hands and faces were painted flesh-color. At Rome, on the same day that the censors entered upon their offices, the usage was to repaint all the statues in the city.[3]

Ancient women, both Greek and Roman, had a passion for bright colors, pearls, precious stones, and tinsel. They stained their hair of a ruddy blond color, which made it look like gold.[4] Nearly all painted their faces.[5] They painted their eyebrows and lashes, prolonging them by encircling their eyes with two rings of purple.[6] Saint Cyprian reproached them for thus giving themselves the eyes of the serpent.[7] The headdress differed with the young and old. The young wore nothing on their heads, the old wore

[1] One very simple reflection will suffice to show that the ancient costumes preserved by medals, cameos, and statues were fanciful, and never had any real existence. For example, scarcely any cameo represents a Greek or Roman man with his hat, or a Greek or Roman woman with a covering for the head; and besides that it is not only logical to believe that the ancients did not go out in the rain with heads uncovered, it is positively established by numerous texts that the women had coverings for the head, and the men hats. Moreover, why should ancient sculptors have represented their models in their real costume, when modern sculptors take great care to leave off the cravat, and frequently the shirt, of those whom they portray. Scarcely any painter puts a hat on his portraits. Must it then be inferred, a thousand years hence, that hats are not worn?

[2] Instance the saying of the soldier, who carried off the cloak of cloth of gold from the statue of Jupiter at Ephesus, that it was too hot for summer, and too cold for winter.

[3] Plin., Hist. Natur., lib. xxxiv., cap. ix.

[4] D. Cyprian. de habit. virgin., p. 179.

[5] Tertul. de virgin. veland., cap. xii.

[6] D. Cyprian. de habit. virgin., p. 177. Another passage of St. Cyprian gives other details relative to eyebrows and lashes, showing that the women sometimes dyed them with a black powder. (D. Cyprian. de lapsis, p. 191.)

[7] D. Cyprian. de habit. virgin., p. 178.

always veils.[1] Young courtesans wore neither coif nor veil. Moreover, the courtesans were nearly all Greeks, and retained everywhere something of the fashion of their country. They wore the hair curled and frizzled, standing up on the head like a pyramid of many stories, very like the style of the end of the eighteenth century, *minus* the powder. (*a*) It is also probable that they wore wigs.[2] The necks of elegant women were covered with pearls and diamonds, according to their fortunes.[3]

Their robes would require so many details, because of numerous changes, that we must limit ourselves to a few general indications.[4]

[1] This clearly appears from many passages of Tertullian, and notably from that, in which he says that the pagans were accustomed to veil their women from the day of marriage, and when conducting them to their husbands. Tertullian approves the custom by saying that the girl thus becomes a wife in spirit before becoming so corporeally. (Tertul. de virgin. veland., cap. xi.)

(*a*) The author's account of the costume of the Greek and Roman women of easy virtue is so exact a description of the fashionable style of this day, that, if his book had not been published many years since, he might be suspected of making a war, disguised or open, upon the present fashions. But it is curious, and worthy of serious thought, to note the close analogies, political and civil, social and domestic, between the present condition of things in the United States, and the condition of things that marked the rapid decline and fall of the great Roman Empire. Nearly all the fifty-two tyrant and spendthrift emperors between Augustus and Constantine owed their power to play "such fantastic tricks" to the "Grand Army" of the Roman Empire. To-day we have a "Grand Army of the Republic," a great political machine, the real designs of which (to use M. Guizot's language) are centred in a few minds, while the greater part of those engaged in executing its work have no conception of them. General, now Senator Logan, of Illinois, is its Grand Commander; and as Constantine owes much of his fame to his having moved the seat of empire of the Old World from Rome to Constantinople, and thereby accelerated the decay of Roman greatness into precipitate ruin, so Grand-Commander Logan has conceived the idea of moving the seat of empire of the New World from the city of *Washington*, to establish elsewhere a great metropolis, to be called, probably, *Logansport*. At the same time, our great and fashionable ladies have gone back to the styles and fashions of dress of Greek and Roman freedwomen of easy virtue in the times of the decline and fall.

[2] The iron with which the courtesans frizzled their hair was called *calamistrum*. Varro describes it thus: "Calamistrum, quod his calefactis in cinere capillus ornatur." The slave, who used this iron for dressing his mistress's head, was called *cinerarius*, because he heated it in the ashes. (Varro, de ling. Lat., lib. v., cap. 129.)

[3] D. Cyprian. de lapsis, p. 191.

[4] We take, or rather we continue to take, from the Latin fathers of the second

At Rome, only noble women had the right to wear a long robe with a train, which was called *stola*.[1] This robe, fastened at the waist with a clasp of emeralds, was open in front, and showed a petticoat of a different color. The courtesans did not wear the stola. They wore short robes, descending only to the feet. When they were rich, this robe was of silk or wool, with figures of gold.[2] When they were limited in fortune, the robe was of cotton.[3] The most celebrated woollens were those of Miletus and Selga in Asia Minor, of Altino and Terentum in Italy, and of Grenada in Spain.[4] The black wools of Grenada were used without dyeing, and the scarlet wools of Grenada never faded.

All the elegant women of antiquity wore stockings, or rather drawers coming down close over the feet. At home they wore white satin shoes,[5] or rather slippers,[6] embroidered with pearls.[7] Abroad they wore galoshes or pattens, with wooden soles, the upper part of purple cloth, embroidered with gold.[8] It was in fact a rule, in Greek costume, never to wear purple without gold.[9] They also wore abroad boots of Venice[10] leather, which came so high up toward the knee, as to dispense with stockings, which was very elegant.

and third century, and principally from St. Cyprian and Tertullian, the details of the domestic life of the freedwomen. We should remark that the passages of their books, which we cite, are strictly applicable to our subject, because, in censuring the different details of this elaborate dress, they strove to turn Christian women from it, as being excessive, and only used by courtesans. This is what the fathers say repeatedly; but we limit ourselves to transcribing these words of St. Cyprian: "Fugiant castæ virgines et pudicæ incertarum cultus, habitus impudicarum, lupanarium insignia, ornamenta meretricum." (D. Cyprian. de habit. virgin., p. 177.)

[1] Tertul. de pall., cap. iv.

[2] D. Cyprian. de habit. virgin., p. 177.—De lapsis, p. 191.

[3] Tertullian speaks of trees, which the Indians spun, which clearly designates cotton. "Si ab initio rerum et Milesii oves tonderent, Seres arbores nerent." (Tertul. de cult. feminar., lib. i., cap. i.)

[4] Tertul. de pall., cap. iii.

[5] Pes malus in nivea semper coletur aluta.
(Ovid. de arte amandi, lib. iii.)
Aut mulleolum inducit calceum.
(Tertul. de pall., cap. iv.)

[6] The use of pearls for embroidering shoes came from the East. The Roman ladies, who saw them for the first time on the Parthians, were astonished at such magnificence, says Tertullian. (De cult. feminar., lib. i., cap. vii.)

[7] Tertullian says that the Roman ladies, to be more free, threw aside the pattens. "Crepidulam ejeravere." (Tertul. de pall., cap. iv.)

[8] Tertul. de idolatr., cap. viii. [9] Tertul., de pall., cap. iv. [10] Ibid., cap. v.

Such very nearly and generally, with earrings set with precious stones,[1] with many chains around the neck, and many rings on the fingers, was the costume of the elegant courtesans of Rome or Athens. We have already seen that they never lost a chance of appearing in a carriage, as this brought them nearer to the customs of noble women.[2]

As to the care of the person, it was extreme. The bath was for all, men and women, an every-day affair. What does not suit our ideas, not only the courtesans, but ladies of society, and even young girls, went to the public baths, and appeared in the water before all the world, which would be incredible, if we did not read it in St. Cyprian.[3] It is true that the bath was part of the hygienic rules of the ancients. They bathed as regularly as they ate, and the universality of the custom removed all malicious ideas. Independently of the baths of the city, they bathed in summer in the Tiber. It appears that respectable people used the river as a matter of preference. A good swimmer was at Rome a notable man with the women. Horace cites a lover of Lydia, whose passion made him forget his baths in the Tiber;[4] and he advises Asteria to turn a deaf ear to the proposals of a knight, although he was the best swimmer of the republic.[5] Suetonius, after recounting at great length the dexterity of Caligula in many exercises, stops short to make this singular reflection: "It was always a matter of surprise that this prince did not know how to swim."[6]

[1] Tertullian reproaches Alexander for having had his ears pierced like a woman. (Ibid., cap. iv.) As to chains and other jewelry the testimony is abundant. (D. Cyprian. de lapsis, p. 177.)

[2] We have mentioned above that Catullus was obliged to lend his litter to the mistress of Varus. Tertullian censures the noble ladies of his time for giving up theirs to appear in the streets on foot. (De pall., cap. iv.)

[3] D. Cyprian. de habit. virgin., p. 179. Spartian, in his Life of Adrian, says that that emperor ordained that the baths of the two sexes should be separate. Julius Capitolinus reports that M. Antoninus did the same. Ovid has pointed out the inconvenience of mixed baths in this verse:

Celant furtivos balnea mixta jocos.
(Ovid de arte amandi, lib. iii.)

[4] Cur timet flavum Tiberim tangere?
(Horat., Carm., lib. i., od. viii., v. 8.)

[5] Nec quisquam citus æque
Tusco denatat alveo.
(Horat., Carm., lib. iii., od. vii., v. 27, 28.)

[6] Atque hic tam docilis ad cætera, natare nesciit. (Sueton. Tranquil., C. Cæsar, Caligula, cap. liv.)

During the bath, the women, who prided themselves on their elegance, had themselves rubbed with perfumed soap. It appears that the consumption of soap by some of them was considerable; for Demetrius Poliorcetes, having gained a pitched battle against Menelas, brother of Ptolemy, during the long wars of the successors of Alexander, imposed upon the Athenians, who had surrendered at discretion, a fine of two hundred and fifty talents to buy soap [1] for the fair Lamia, his mistress, whom he had found among the baggage of the conquered. After the soap came precious ointments, with which the coquettes had their bodies rubbed to make the skin soft and fragrant,[2] and their custom was during the heat of the day to powder their bodies with an astringent powder, which possessed the double advantage of drying the skin, and giving to the flesh firmness without being hard, and elasticity without being soft.[3]

It is easy to believe that the living of a Greek or Roman courtesan of some celebrity cost very dear; and also that it was generally paid for by some one person. According to the expression of one of them, this was called having a friend, and being under obligation to him.[4] Moreover, the sons of wealthy families, who were bold enough to approach them, generally left in their hands the better part of their fortunes.[5] Catullus, in speaking of Lesbia, with whom he had a quarrel, uses an expression, the energy of which requires no comment. He says that she *peeled* the magnanimous posterity of Remus.[6]

This brings us to speak of the twenty-three odes, addressed to courtesans, which are found in the works of Horace. The poet,

[1] Plutarch, Demetrius, cap. xxvii.

[2] Tertul. de virgin. veland., cap. xii.

[3] Plutarch. Sympos., lib. i., quest. vi.

[4] This was the reply of Theodota to Socrates in their interview. See note to page 204.

[5] Horace speaks in these terms of the kind of terror, with which the beauty of Barina inspired the wealthy families:

Te suis matres metuunt juvencis
Te senes parci, miseræque nuper
Virgines nuptæ, tua ne retardet
Aura maritos.
(Horat., Carm., lib. ii., od. viii., v. 21–24.)

[6] Nunc in quadriviis et angiportis
Glubit magnanimos Remi nepotis.
(Catul., Carm. lviii.)

who was not very rich, used his verses, as far as he could, as money. Unfortunately, the fair freedwomen, whom he has immortalized, bore a slight resemblance to Chrysala, and didn't live on fine speeches; with one exception, however, who seems never to have asked Horace for anything but verses. See also with what gratitude he speaks of her! In an ode to Lycea, he blames her for having grown so old, while Cinara died in the flower of youth.[1] In an ode to Venus, he speaks with rapture of the reign of the *good* Cinara.[2] These eulogies are very touching, until we find an explanation of them in his epistle to his gardener, where he recalls with satisfaction his having in former times pleased the *rapacious* Cinara, without having had to pay for it.[3]

It remains for us to speak of the political part which these courtesans played in Greece and Italy.

There were two courtesans who enjoyed immense political power at Athens and Rome: Aspasia, mistress of Pericles, and Præcia, mistress of Cethegus. Some others, as Thargelia, Theodota, Timandra, Lais, and Flora, although of less elevated position, nevertheless deserve mention, for the relations they had with the most eminent men of their times.

Thargelia was an Ionian, mistress of King Xerxes, who gained him many partisans among the cities of Greece.[4] Theodota, of whom we have already spoken, was a beautiful woman, whom Socrates went to see, on the strength of her reputation, and who returned his visit.[5] The history of Timandra is connected with the exile and tragic end of Alcibiades. When he was for the last time banished by the Athenians, he retired to one of his castles in Phrygia. Timandra followed him. There Lysander, who feared his return, had him assassinated. Timandra, assisted by her slaves, took the body, washed the stains that covered it, wrapped and

[1] . . . Cinaræ breves
Annos fata dederunt,
Servatura diu parem
Cornicis vetulæ temporibus Lyceæ.
(Horat., Carm., lib. iv., od. xiii., v. 22–25.)

[2] Qualis eram bonæ
Sub regno Cinaræ. (Ibid., od. i., v. 2, 3.)

[3] Quem sis immunem Cinaræ placuisse *rapaci.*
(Horat. Epist., lib. i., epist. xiv., v. 33.)

[4] Plutarch, Pericles, cap. xxiv.

[5] Xenophon, Memorab., lib. iii., cap. xi.

buried it in the *finest cloths she had.*[1] Lais, the Corinthian, was her daughter.[2] Flora was the favorite of Pompey. Geminius, a noble Roman and friend of Pompey, having long followed her up, she replied to him one day, to get rid of him, that she belonged to Pompey, and must have his permission to listen to Geminius, believing that Pompey, who loved her, and whom she loved, would not consent. Pompey, solicited by Geminius, and relying on Flora's love, gave his consent, under the belief that it would amount to nothing. From levity or vexation, Flora listened to Geminius. Pompey, indignant, never saw or spoke to her again; and Flora, overwhelmed with regret and despair, attempted to kill herself.[3] Flora was of such majestic beauty, that Cæcilius Metellus, who ornamented the temple of Castor and Pollux with pictures, placed her portrait there.[4]

Aspasia was the most celebrated courtesan of antiquity. She was of Miletus.[5] Her wit and beauty gave her so high a position at Athens, that she managed all the affairs of Greece. She received at her house all the philosophers and poets of her time, and her visitors even took their wives to see her — a strange thing to believe, since we know that she kept a house of debauch.[6] Socrates went often to see her, and Plato writes, in his dialogue entitled *Menexenus*, that many Athenians of distinction went to learn good language from her.[7] Pericles excused himself for seeing her every day, because she guided him in managing the affairs of Greece. The general belief was that he loved her passionately.[8] The comedies of that day called her the new Omphale and the new Dejanira,[9] and all believed that it was Aspasia who persuaded Pericles to make war against the Samnians, in aid of the inhabitants of Miletus.

Præcia was at Rome in the time of Pompey, Lucullus, and Cethegus, what Aspasia was at Athens in the time of Pericles. She took care to have no relations except with eminent men, and to use her influence for the benefit of those whom she distinguished with her favor.[10] She was openly the mistress of Cethegus, who then managed the affairs of the republic, and all the young men of any

1 Plutarch, Alcibiades, cap. xxxix.
2 Ibid.
3 Plutarch, Pompey, cap. ii.
4 Ibid.
5 Plutarch, Pericles, cap. xxiv.
6 Ibid.
7 Plato, Menexen.
8 Plutarch, Pericles, cap. xxiv.
9 Ibid.
10 Plutarch, Lucullus, cap. vi.

ambition or aspirations made assiduous court to her, as one who could make or unmake them. Lucullus, who wanted the government of Sicily, and the command in the war against Mithridates, succeeded in winning her by his wit, and, above all, by the magnificence of his presents.[1] Præcia praised him to Cethegus; Cethegus praised him to the whole city, and Lucullus had the government he desired. (*a*)

[1] Plutarch, Lucullus, ch. iv.

(*a*) *Poeta nascitur, orator fit.* Horace was a born poet, and his "rhythmic money" passed as current coin even with the "rapacious Cinara." Many of our *Radical* high officials, legislative and executive, are not born poets, nor could any amount of study and preparation *fit* them for oratory. But native shrewdness, or the high culture of New England civilization, has (for some of them) supplied the lack of poesy and oratory, and made their official position and influence pass as current with the fair and frail portion of the Government machinery at Washington, as Horace's verses did with Cinara.

The system of employing female clerks in the Government offices at Washington, originating during the Civil War, doubtless sprang from the purest and loftiest sentiments. Certain it is, that in their distress, consequent upon the loss of their natural protectors, it has afforded relief to some of the best, purest, and noblest women of the land — women who would adorn any society, and of whom any country might be proud.

The use was noble; the abuse infamous.

But it was not long before *Radical* ingenuity discovered in that system a way of transferring Lesbia's *peeling* process from themselves to that gentleman with full pockets, who is known to the people of the United States as "*Uncle Sam.*"

As prominent in this business, the concurrent testimony of the scandal-mongers of the metropolis, and of the young bloods, who have encountered his rivalry, points to a New England legislator, whose boast is that his virility has not been impaired by age or strong drink.

The following verses would not entitle their author to rank among the poets with Horace. But they are not unworthy of notice in a history of the working and burgher classes. For, they secured for their author a lucrative and important office, involving the responsibility of the expenditure of a very large amount of the taxes paid into the treasury of "*Uncle Sam*" by the working and burgher classes. Moreover, they illustrate a phase of governmental administration under the Radical regime, as worthy of the notice of history as Præcia's influence in securing for Lucullus the government of Sicily and the command of the war against Mithridates.

It happened thus:

At a period of the late Civil War, when business was paralyzed, the writer found himself in debt, with mortgages hanging over his property, and likely soon to be foreclosed, unless, by some lucky chance, he could raise the money to meet his maturing obligations. He went to Washington, called on President Lincoln, and told him of his difficulties. In a moment of care and irritation, Mr. Lincoln gruffly said, "Do you expect me to take cognizance of every man's mortgages in the United States?" Soon, however, recovering his customary good-humor, he told his visitor to go and consult his member of Congress, decide upon what he wanted, and then he, Mr. Lincoln, would do what he could to aid him.

He called upon his member of Congress, who said: "What female influence can you bring to bear?" He replied: "What has that to do with this matter?" The answer was, "Everything. Now-a-days, offices, contracts, honors, all are controlled and disposed of by and through the women."

Despairing of success through any of the Præcias of the period, the poet went sadly back to his home in New England. There his good genius inspired the following verses, copies of which he sent back to Washington. By return mail he was notified that, if he would not publish them, he could have anything he wanted. He got what he wanted, and was enabled to pay off his mortgages.

"My friend, if you will just take a look
Between the leaves of the great and good Book,
You will find that a woman, Delilah by name,
Played off on old Samson a terrible game.
She bothered and teased, and then she did cry,
'Tell me now truly where your strength doth lie.'
At length the old fool, I vow and declare,
Told his Delilah that it lay in his hair.
Old Samson then, his Delilah to please,
Laid his head down upon her two knees.
He there fell asleep, among petties and frocks,
And in that condition she cut off his locks.
The old man awakes, and finds out at length
That by a pretty woman he was shorn of his strength.
The next thing in order took him by surprise;
For she called in the Philistines, who put out his eyes.
So honest old Abe took the President's chair,
With two good eyes, and a nice head of hair.
His Delilah played with him '*poor pussy*' and '*cat*,'
Till he was bald as an eagle, and blind as a bat.
To Congress, too, we have sent of the best,
From the North and the East, the South and the West:
They've played with their Delilahs the '*ass*' and the '*goose*,'
Till the hair on their heads is getting quite loose.
The cabinet officers, too, take a nap,
Each one with his head in his Delilah's lap;
With eyes upturned to her beauty so fair,
While she keeps a-clipping away at his hair."

The above is but a fragment of the mortgage-lifting verses; my informant who furnished me with them, himself a *Radical* and an office-holder, not being able to remember the other lines, or to obtain a copy. He also gave me some details of the private and official profligacy prevailing at Washington during the war; and *especially in the Interior Department under Secretaries Harlan and Usher.* If only a small part of what he narrated was true, the picture is appalling to the working and burgher classes, who pay the taxes, which now go to the support of the men (and their MISTRESSES) who seek to *unify* the United States of America into *one nation,* as the Roman Empire was *unified* under Caligula, Claudius, and Nero. (See Senator Wilson's article on *unification,* and Father Hecker's reply in the *Catholic World for April,* 1871.)

---

## CHAPTER XVIII.

### THE BANDITS.

THE pirates and bandits of antiquity were runaway slaves, in open war with their masters. It is well, before sketching their history, to correct some false ideas, which our morals might suggest as to the cause of these escapes.

It would be a great mistake to believe that the ancients had the notion of the equality of men, and that this notion was constantly impelling the slaves toward liberty. With the exception of the Essenes, who were a schismatic sect among the Jews, and whose basis of association was the dogma of equality, all antiquity remained completely strangers to the notion of human equality until the coming of Christianity; and when Jesus Christ announced it as a part of his doctrine, he uttered a sentiment, for his times, rash and factious; in opposition to all the adopted moral creeds, and which was calculated to offend, and did offend the pagans.

The two philosophers and the poet, who most powerfully influenced the ancient world, Homer, Plato, and Aristotle, were unanimous in considering men as naturally divided into two classes: those who were born to command, and those who were born to obey—the masters and the slaves. Homer says, in so many words, that God gave slaves only half a soul.[1] In his treatise on law, Plato cites and relies on this testimony of Homer. In the dialogue entitled Alcibiades, he makes Socrates ask this question: "Is it in

[1] See page 125.

the nobility, or in the common people, that we find the better nature?" to which he makes Alcibiades reply: "Beyond question, in the nobility."[1] Aristotle, for his part, presents the question of the inequality of the races with remarkable clearness and candor. "Among all created beings," he says, in his treatise on politics, "some are born to obey, and others to command."[2] Farther on he says, "Nature itself has marked with different characters the gentlemen and the slaves."[3]

Pagan antiquity had no other ideas on this subject. Cato the elder, whose slaves always boasted that he was a good master, sold them when they were old and broken down, which caused Plutarch to say, that he would never have the hard-heartedness to abandon an ox or a slave, who had labored and worked for him, to the end of their days.[4] It should be noted that Plutarch said this in an excitement of benevolence and indignation.

On their part, the slaves of antiquity never dreamed, in their revolts, of invoking any idea of human equality. They found slavery very just and reasonable in itself; they only tried sometimes to see whether they could not impose it on others, (*a*) in place of being subject to it themselves. The facts presently cited prove this com-

[1] Plato, Alcibiades, i.
[2] Aristot. politica, lib. i., cap. ii., § 8.
[3] Ibid., § 14.
[4] Plutarch, Cato Major, cap. v.

(*a*) Mr. Calhoun, in the speech from which we have quoted in our Preface, said prophetically: "We would soon find the present condition of the two races reversed. They (the negroes) and their Northern allies, would be the masters, and we the slaves."

Has not this prophecy been literally fulfilled? If deprivation of civil rights be slavery, then have the *loyal*, as well as the *disloyal*, whites of the South been enslaved. They, the loyal whites, who furnished, or had taken from them, quartermaster's and other supplies for the United States army, were denied, by the acts of Congress of the 4th July, 1864, and 21st February, 1867, their civil rights of property — rights guaranteed to them by that clause of the Constitution, which provides that private property shall not be taken for public use without just compensation. In the use made of the freedmen, to enslave and pauperize the whites, the spirit and purpose of radicalism were even more strikingly manifested, than in emancipating the slaves, to make "free labor more profitable than slave labor." In fact, this thing called radicalism is an *unholy alliance* of *imperialism* and *brigandage*, masquerading under the disguise and assumed name of Republicanism. Its politico-economical theory is that "free labor is cheaper and more profitable than slave labor." But, as practically illustrated in Georgia

pletely. We mention but one now, but it will suffice to prepare for an understanding of the others.

Twelve hundred Roman citizens, that is to say, twelve hundred men, more or less rich and educated, of fortune and family, were made prisoners in the second Punic war, carried to Greece by the merchants, sold as slaves in the Peloponnesus, and used by their masters in the work of the fields. If ever slaves ought to have had the sentiment of human equality, certainly these should, who were not born in slavery, and who, in regaining their liberty, would only have been regaining what had been violently taken from them. But see what they did.

They had long been slaves when the league of Achaian cities asked succor from the Romans against the usurpations of Philip, King of Macedon. T. Quintius Flaminius led some legions to their aid. Arrived in Greece, he vanquished the Macedonians. He was master of the country, when his troops one day encountered the twelve hundred Roman citizens, who were digging the earth. The soldiers and the slaves threw themselves into each other's arms, as compatriots, neighbors, friends, kinsmen, brothers. But the idea never occurred to one of them, either soldier or slave, that the slavery of twelve hundred Roman citizens was a monstrous thing. When they had embraced, they separated, the soldiers resuming their pikes and the slaves their hoes; and, as this meeting made a great noise in Greece, the grateful Achaian cities raised a common fund, purchased the twelve hundred slaves, and made a present of them to the general of the Roman army. He, to whom they belonged from that moment, and who might have employed them on his own estates, was pleased on his return to emancipate them; which, however, did not restore them to their primitive condition of Roman citizens, but placed them in the class of freedmen, and imposed on them the obligations and duties of clients.[1]

Thus, as we have said, never in pagan antiquity did our modern ideas of equality and the rights of man germinate in the mind of

under Governor Bullock, in South Carolina by Governor Scott, and in North Carolina by Governor Holden, that theory would be more correctly rendered thus: "It is more profitable to plunder the State Treasury and the tax-payers, like bandits, than to have slaves to feed and clothe, as masters."

[1] Plutarch, Flaminius, cap. xiii.

master or slave. The three most eminent men among the poets and philosophers, Homer, Plato, and Aristotle, believed ingenuously, profoundly, in the duality of human nature. No one in all the West, not even among the slaves, maintained or proposed a contrary doctrine; and it is, under the impression of this general oblivion of human dignity, that we must study the revolts of slaves among the ancients, and their organization into bands of pirates and bands of thieves.

If we confine ourselves to Roman history, we find ten revolts of slaves more or less serious. Titus Livius mentions six, without giving their details.[1] The sixth was that of Eunus the Syrian, reported at length by Diodorus of Sicily. The seventh was that of Athenion, which Florus also relates fully. The eighth, which was the most celebrated and formidable, was that of Spartacus. Plutarch, Florus, and Appian have related all the circumstances. The ninth, of small importance, broke out in Sicily, during the civil wars of Pompey and Cæsar. Appian, who mentions it, adds that it gave rise to the formation of a body of military, or guards, who afterward served to watch over the safety of Rome.[2] The tenth, which broke out in Italy under Tiberius, is related by Tacitus.[3]

There were principally three causes that impelled slaves to revolt: tampering with them by the chiefs of parties in the civil wars, excessive harshness of the masters, and the failure to execute the regulations relative to labor.

In the turbulent government of ancient Rome, there was always some conspiracy hatching or miscarrying, and poor Rome had always need for the spy and the executioner. The first idea of conspirators, we may well believe, was to incite an insurrection of the slaves. (*a*) The continual wars had thinned out the free population, and given the slave population a formidable preponderance. Seneca relates that in a discussion in the senate on the sumptuary

[1] The first in lib. iii., cap. xv.; the second in lib. iv., cap. lxv.; the third in lib. xxxii., cap. xxvi.; the fourth in lib. xxxiii., cap. xxii.; the fifth in lib. xxxix., cap. xxix.; the sixth in the summary of lib. lvii.

[2] Appian. de bell. civil., lib. v., cap. cxxxii.

[3] Tacit. Annal., lib. iv., cap. xxvii.

(*a*) So, after all, it appears that JOHN BROWN'S SOUL was not born, nor cradled on Plymouth Rock, but has been "*marching on*," like the Wandering Jew, ever since the days of Marius and Catiline.

laws, it having been proposed to require all the slaves to wear an uniform dress, the reply was that they must guard against giving to the slaves a means of counting their masters.[1] While the quæstor, Curtius Lupus, was putting down the tenth revolt of the slaves, which broke out in Italy in the 24th year of the Christian era, Rome trembled, says Tacitus, at the idea of the frightful multitude of slaves, and the small number of freemen that she contained.[2]

Party chiefs endeavored, as we have said, to attract the slaves to their ranks by offering them freedom. But we must add, in compliment to the good sense of the slaves, that they did not always listen to such propositions. During the civil wars, Marius having, by sound of trumpet, promised liberty to all the slaves, who would enroll under his banner, only three presented themselves.[3] (*a*)

[1] Seneca, de clementia, lib. i., cap. xxiv.
[2] Tacit. Annal., lib. iv., cap. xxvii. [3] Plutarch, C. Marius.

(*a*) The good conduct and fidelity of the Southern slaves, through the four long years of the Civil War, won for them, deservedly, the gratitude and good-will of the Southern whites, and astonished the Northern humanitarians. In thousands of cases, when their masters were in the army, they were left alone, without a white man on the place, with none but women and children to direct or control them. Nobly — yes, nobly is the proper word — did they respond to the confidence reposed in them by their masters. Their conduct was uniformly good; even better than when their masters were at home. They seemed to feel that the confidence reposed in them had put them "on good behavior," and we have never yet heard of the first instance in which that confidence was abused. Even since the war, outrages on their part have been the exception, not the rule; and the exceptional cases are directly traceable to the pernicious influence of the Freedmen's Bureau, the carpet-baggers, and the scalawags, who, for political purposes, have sought to excite a "race hatred" between them and the (so-called) rebels, by urging them to arson and other crimes. We do not class as *outrages* petty pilfering and stealing; for these are natural and unavoidable consequences of throwing a large mass of slaves, without prevision or preparation, on their own resources for a support. On a question so important — on which such strenuous efforts have been made, and so much public money spent, to create false impressions at the North, for party purposes — it is fortunate that we can add the unimpeachable testimony of the Rev. J. B. Smith, before the Senate Committee on Southern Outrages. (See Senate Document, 42d Cong., 1st Sess., Report No. 1, pages 214–224.)

Mr. Smith was the Secretary of the Board of Missions of the Protestant Episcopal Church, for that department of work among the colored people. He was requested to go from New Jersey, where he had resided up to 1867, to the South,

Appian lets us know that Catiline was contriving a slave revolt, when he attempted his celebrated conspiracy.[1] The first and third of the six revolts mentioned by Livy, were also incited by conspira-

to establish a normal school for the purpose of educating colored people, to make them competent to teach their own race. On consultation with General Howard, the latter requested him to go to North Carolina. He went there in December, 1867, and established at Raleigh a normal school for the education of colored teachers. His testimony will surely be taken at the North. He said:

"With regard to the people of North Carolina — and I have had a great deal of intimate, close conversation with gentlemen from various parts of the State — I regard them as an extremely kind people — I mean kind toward the colored people; they have a kindly feeling for them; I have evidence of it on all sides in expressions and in acts. I find that the relationship, which formerly existed between master and slave, has left a feeling of kindness on the part of the master toward the slave. I find masters continually recognizing the old relationship, and aiding and assisting their former slaves. I know of no feeling, upon the part of any one in North Carolina, that I have ever talked with and met, of antagonism toward the colored people.

"Question. Have you, since you have been in North Carolina, found any prejudice against you, or unkindness on account of your occupation?

"Answer. I have not found any unkindness toward me among the people of North Carolina; no one has treated me unkindly.

"Question. Have you, on the contrary, met with personal kindness from the people there?

"Answer. Yes, sir; the very best people of the State, all through the community, have treated me with the utmost kindness; visited my family and myself.

"Question. In your opinion, is it perfectly safe for any man, white or black, to keep a colored school anywhere in that State, if he confines himself to the legitimate duties of his profession?

"Answer. That is my opinion.

"Question. With perfect safety?

"Answer. I think so.

"Question. Would you hesitate to establish a colored school in any portion of the State, under the care of a judicious and sensible man?

"Answer. Not at all.

"Question. Would you think his life and personal property safe?

"Answer. Perfectly.

"Question. You said you voted for General Grant in the last election?

"Answer. Yes, sir.

"Question. Have you had any conversation with Governor Holden, relative to the late election?

"Answer. I have had several conversations with him.

[1] Appian. de bell. civil., lib. ii., cap. ii.

tors;[1] and the tenth, reported by Tacitus, was instigated by Titus Curtisius, an old soldier of the prætorian cohorts.[2]

"Question. How did he express himself in regard to the politics of those who were opposing his election?

"Answer. I had a conversation with him, I think, last April. Colonel Hayman was in charge of the camp. He was an Episcopalian, and I had called on him to pay my respects. I found Mr. Barringer, Mr. Kingsland, Colonel Hayman, and Governor Holden together. Mr. Kingsland was connected with the North Carolina Land Company. He was talking to Governor Holden about the great injury done to the State by his proclamation — that it kept persons from coming into the State to buy land. The proclamation was in regard to certain outrages. I do not know whether at that time he had declared the County of Alamance in insurrection. Mr. Kingsland was talking upon that subject when I went in. *Governor Holden was very much excited about the recall of the United States troops, and had received no assurance then that there would be any troops to supply their place.* Well, I spoke to Governor Holden, and said, 'Governor, what distresses me is, that you should put these colored men up for Congress, for responsible offices. I notice in my work among these people that there is a great moral injury done to them throughout the State; the effect is very bad; it unsettles them; they do not seem to be disposed to go to any regular labor, because they are looking to political preferment.' He then expressed himself in regard to the colored people, and said that Congress had seen fit to pass a law, by which they were admitted to seats in the State Legislature, and he wanted them to have some of the same themselves, and, therefore, he went for sending them to Congress. Then he said to me, or rather to us all, 'Now, if the Government does not send these troops, I shall arm the colored people. I can control by my word 80,000 men. I can go to the convention that is to meet here next week, (a Republican convention,) and control them by a word.' I remarked at the same time, 'That is dangerous power — very dangerous power to be in the hands of one man.' He then said to me, in the presence of these gentlemen, 'What is to hinder the Ku-Klux from taking you, Dr. Smith? Are you not afraid?' 'Not at all,' said I. Said he, 'There is nothing to hinder them from taking you or any other Radical.' Said I, 'Excuse me, but that is not my name. I am not a Radical.' Well, then he went on to say that, for his own part, in his opinion, General Grant would hold the government of the United States, no matter what the election was in 1872; that *he desired him to be emperor, and his son to succeed him as emperor.*

"Question. That is, that he, Governor Holden, wished it?

"Answer. That he, Governor Holden, wished it.

. . . "There is one thing I would like to state. I asked a leading member of the House of Representatives of North Carolina, knowing him to be a man of prin-

[1] Hist., lib. iii., cap. xv. Ibid., lib. xxxii., cap. xxvi.
[2] Tacitus, Annales, lib. xiv., cap. xxvi.

The severity of the masters was also a powerful cause of irritation and revolt; for, until the time of the Emperor Adrian, there

ciple, 'How could you vote for the Shoffner bill to empower the Governor of the State to declare, at will, a county to be in insurrection, if none existed?' — the word insurrection being a well-defined term. He said, 'Oh, we passed such a law, but it will never be executed.' Said I, 'Then, why did you pass it?' 'Now, doctor,' said he, '*it is necessary to hold the State as Republican for three or four years longer, and the passage of that bill was necessary to enable us to hold it.*'

"Question. Give his name.

"Answer. Augustus S. Seymour, of Cleveland County.

"Question. Where did he say that?

"Answer. In the legislature that passed the Shoffner act of last year."

Are our Northern readers surprised that we in the South, who have always claimed to be republicans, should not like that *kind* of republicanism, which requires United States troops, or such legislation as the Shoffner bill of North Carolina, with such militia as that of Kirk and Bergen, to hold the State as Republican? That they may realize what they are preparing for themselves by supporting the men who in Congress support such men as Holden of North Carolina, Scott of South Carolina, and Bullock of Georgia, and voted for the Shellabarger Ku-Klux Bill, we urge them to ponder well this testimony of a Northern man, whose integrity is unquestionable, and whose opportunities of knowing the truth are so abundant. He was asked:

"Does this (his connection with the normal school for the education of colored teachers) lead you to the examination generally of the condition of the black people of the State?

"Answer. Certainly; I am interested, and constantly inquiring and conversing with the colored people; and I may say that I organized, on going there, a land and building association, for the colored people, which brought me into intimate contact with them. I am the treasurer of it. The object is to secure to them homesteads.

"Question. Has the question of the treatment of the colored race and the outrages of the Ku-Klux assumed in any form a political aspect in that State?

"Answer. I have stated that numbers of the Union League assumed the badge of the Ku-Klux, and whipped colored people — *their own race;* so that I do not believe, from the information I have received, the organization (Ku-Klux) has any political character whatever."

Dr. Smith's testimony is fully confirmed by that of Daniel R. Goodloe, which will be found in the same document, pp. 224–236. Mr. Goodloe is well known at the North by his long connection (as a contributor and assistant editor, from 1847 to 1860) with the National Era, the Washington organ of the Abolitionists. He was one of the corresponding committee of the Republican Association of Washington City, to whom Mr. Frank P. Blair, in 1855, addressed his declara-

was no law that intervened, in any case, for the protection of the slaves. Under Adrian they were withdrawn from the domestic tribunal and transferred to the tribunal of the magistrates.[1] Now, a great number of facts testify that, during this long period of their history, while they remained subject to the discretion of their masters, the latter were often ungrateful, harsh, and even odiously barbarous. We do not wish to speak in detail of the mutilations, to which they subjected some of their slaves, to fit them for the purposes of the gynæceum, or preserve their freshness of color, and firmness of voice for the theatre. Generally, the slaves, who were subjected to this kind of mutilation, became of great value, and were the best treated; although Appian says that, for this, they had a mortal hatred of their masters.[2] But what irritated, exasperated, and sometimes, with good reason, provoked the slaves to rebellion, was the excessive and useless bad treatment, which they suffered

tion of adhesion to the Republican party, in which he denounced the Democratic party as a "combination" to extend slavery from ocean to ocean. Being asked as to the state of things existing in North Carolina, affecting the security of person and property, Mr. Goodloe answered:

"In that portion of the State, of which I can speak from personal knowledge, it is as good as it is anywhere in the world; there is no more steady-going and quiet people that I know of anywhere in the world. There is just as much security for life there as there is in Massachusetts; more than there has been in this city about election times, to my certain knowledge. . . . I have never been afraid to go anywhere in North Carolina; while I was marshal, I went all over the State, without any other weapon than a pocket-knife." . . .

"I have heard it stated from authorized sources, and it has been sworn to, that there has been no instance of violent resistance to civil process."

See also pages 232 and 233, where Mr. Goodloe proves that the State of North Carolina has been brought to the brink of hopeless insolvency by Governor Holden and "a set of swindlers, native and foreign, who ought to be in the penitentiary for the balance of their natural lives;" and that they had fraudulently squandered and dishonestly spent the State revenues and credit, until "State insolvency was looked upon as an already accomplished fact."

[1] Ulpian, in the eighth book of his treatise *De officio proconsulis*, under the title "*De Dominorum Sævitia*," cites the rescript of Antoninus, the Pious, which commences thus: "Dominorum quidem potestatem in servos suos inlibitam esse oportet, nec cuiquam hominum jus suum detrahi." (Mosayc. et Romanar., leg. collat., tit. iii.) Pithou also mentions the law of Adrian, as given by Spartian, in his notes, thus: "Spartianus in ejus vita (Hadriani) servos, inquit, a dominis occidi vetuit, eosque jussit damnari per judices, si digni essent."

[2] Appian. de bell. civil., lib. iii., cap. xcviii.

from avaricious, capricious, and ferocious masters. When old age, or disease, began to make them useless, there were masters, who forgot the former services of these poor helpless slaves, and let them die of hunger and misery. This is what made Plutarch so indignant, and made him say that his ox and his slave merited the same kind treatment. Sometimes, though rarely, masters treated their slaves with horrible ferocity. We know the history of that Vedius Pollion, of whom Seneca speaks, who fed the fishes in his ponds with the flesh of his slaves.[1]

The third cause of slave discontent and revolt was the inexecution of the regulations concerning them. Although the intervention of the magistrate in the relations of master and slaves was not complete until the time of Adrian, there were, nevertheless, even under the republic, general regulations as to slaves — some established by custom, others decreed by the senate. Diodorus testifies, in the most positive manner, that the revolt, of which the shepherd Athenion was the chief, broke out on account of the impossibility of a faithful execution by the prætor of Sicily of the established regulations as to slaves.[2] Plutarch clearly shows that the revolt of Spartacus had no other cause.

The three revolts, which were truly serious and terrible, broke out very nearly in the last sixty years of the republic. The two first took place in Sicily, the last at the gates of Rome. Eunus, the Syrian, and Athenion were the leaders of the former, Spartacus of the latter.

Eunus the Syrian, as his name indicates, was a slave originally from Syria. Generally, the slaves brought from that country were active, elegant, and industrious, and were employed in the houses of the great in the service of the table, which was the most difficult and nice. Syria also furnished excellent mimics, dancers, and magicians. Eunus presented himself at the prisons, where the slaves worked in chains, as a prophet, who was in communication with the gods. He called, to witness the sanctity of his mission, the tower-crowned headdress of the Syrian Venus; and concealing in his mouth a nutshell filled with lighted sulphur, he threw out, with his words of ecstasy, light flames, which astonished his hearers.[3]

[1] Seneca, de clement., lib. i., cap. xcviii.
[2] Diod. Sicul., fragm., lib. xxxiv. 2.
[3] Flor. Hist., lib. iii., cap. xix.

This prodigy immediately drew to him two thousand partisans. These broke the doors of the prisons, and Eunus soon counted an army of more than sixty thousand men.[1] The war was fierce and long. The slaves took the camps of four prætors. At last they shut themselves up in the city of Enna, there defended themselves with courage, and nearly all died of famine, pestilence, and the sword.[2]

Sicily had scarcely recovered from this frightful shock, which deprived her of more than sixty thousand workmen, when the second revolt broke out. It was caused, as we have said, by the inexecution of the regulations. A slave shepherd, originally from Cilicia, and named Athenion, assassinated his master, roused the slaves to revolt, and in a short time gathered together an army as numerous as that of Eunus the Syrian.[3] Athenion also stormed two prætorian camps; but his slaves, like those of Eunus, perished by famine.[4]

A very characteristic trait, common to Eunus and Athenion, was, that in revolting, neither had any idea of abolishing slavery or of establishing equality. Scarce had they drawn armies around them, before they hastened to forget that they had had the chain around their necks, and to enjoy with delight the prerogatives of lordship. First, as may easily be believed, castles, villages, and cities were pillaged.[5] Then the two chiefs, with puerile delight, decked themselves out with the insignia of royalty. Athenion, the shepherd, especially always appeared clothed in a rich robe of purple, with a cane of silver in his hand, and a diadem on his brow.[6]

The revolt of Spartacus was still more terrible, and Florus speaks of it with dolorous humility. For, this time, it was not a mere revolt of slaves. It was a revolt of gladiators.[7]

One Lentulus Batiatus, of Capua, was by profession a raiser of slaves, whom he trained to fencing and made gladiators.[8] He had nearly a hundred pairs of them, whom he kept confined, and destined to fight each other to the death, although they had committed no offence. These slaves, nearly all Gauls, Germans, or Francs, resolved to escape and flee. They elected three leaders, Spartacus, Crixus, and Œnomaus.[9] Their project having been discovered, only

[1] Flor. Hist., lib. iii., cap. xix. [2] Ibid. [3] Ibid. [4] Ibid.
[5] Ibid. [6] Ibid. [7] Ibid. [8] Plutarch, M. Crassus, cap. viii.
[9] Ann. Flor., lib. iii., cap. xx. § 1. The writers differ greatly as to the number

half of them succeeded in getting out, armed with knives, cleavers, and spits, which they took from the kitchens.[1] Scarce out of Capua, they met some carts belonging to their masters, carrying to the neighboring cities arms destined for a combat of gladiators, which they seized. Some troops of the garrison of Capua, having been sent to bring them back, were beaten and disarmed, and the fugitives profited by this victory to lay aside their gladiatorial weapons, which they considered as infamous, and take those of Roman soldiers, which were the arms of free men.[2] Thus, neither the gladiators of Capua nor the slaves of Sicily had any idea, in revolting, of proclaiming the equality of men. Both were ashamed of the condition, from which they were trying to escape, instead of boasting of it like the *Jacques* of the middle ages, or the *Gueux* of the Netherlands.

Plutarch, Florus, and Appian relate in detail the war of the gladiators. It lasted three years. From the first, Spartacus was recognized as the principal chief,[3] and for him it was a succession of victories. He successively defeated five prætorian or consular armies. At last the senate charged Crassus with the conduct of the war, and recalled, to aid him, Lucullus from Thrace, and Pompey from Spain. At one time it was thought that Spartacus was about to march against Rome,[4] and the terrified republic recalled the time of Hannibal.

Spartacus, who was a man with a heart above his condition, had but one idea. He wished to cross the Alps, reach Gaul, and, once there, let every man take the road to his own country.[5] The strategy of the consuls and the mutiny of his companions prevented the realization of his project. He therefore turned about for three years in Lower Italy, like a red deer in a cage, passing and repassing the Apennines, trying to reach Sicily, and even throwing two thousand men to aid some pirates, who deceived him;[6] then burning

of gladiators, who accompanied Spartacus. Florus is the one who puts it at the lowest figure. We have taken a mean number. See Cicero ad Attic., vi. 2; Epit., lib. xlv.; Vellei. Paterc., lib. ii. 30, 6; Eutrop. vi. 2; Oros., v. 25; Frontin. I, 5, 21, lxxiv. Pacatus (Paneg., Theod., cap. xxiii.) says that he had a battalion, *agmen*.

[1] Plutarch, M. Crassus, cap. viii. [2] Ibid., cap. ix.

[3] Ibid., cap. viii. — Appian. de bell. civ., lib. i., cap. cxvii.

[4] Appian. de bell. civ., lib. i., cap. cxvii.

[5] Plutarch, M. Crassus, cap. ix. [6] Ibid., cap. x.

and pillaging the country, emptying the wine-cellars of the friends of Epicurus, to the great disgust of the gourmands,[1] and sacking Nola, Nuceria, Thurium, and Metapontus.[2]

At last two of his lieutenants, Caius Cannicius and Castus, weakened his army, by separating from him.[3] In his last battle, as they brought to him his horse caparisoned, he killed him with a blow of his sword, and chose to fight on foot.[4] He fought with the skill of a gladiator and the courage of a hero. Wounded in the thigh in searching for Crassus, he fell, and received so many sword-cuts before dying that his body could not be recognized.[5] He had with him his wife, the daughter of a Thracian herdsman, somewhat versed in magic, who had loved him "in the bush," and who, having one day found him asleep with a snake coiled around his face, predicted that he would become a terrible and fortunate king.[6] Florus thus sums up his history. He was, he says, first a Thracian hireling, then a soldier, then a deserter, then a brigand, then a gladiator.[7] This war ended, there remained, of all the companions of Spartacus, six thousand prisoners. Six thousand crosses were erected on the two sides of the road leading from Capua to Rome, and there they were all crucified on the same day.[8]

The characteristic of all these revolts, however well they may have appeared to be put down, was always, as may easily be believed, to leave a great residuum of bandits and robbers, who established themselves near the Roman highways, and from the thickly wooded swamps or mountain gorges rushed out to carry off sheep and cattle, or put travellers to ransom. The disorders of the civil war, which preceded or followed the death of Cæsar, had produced such numbers of them, that Augustus was obliged to distribute troops through all Italy, to prevent their taking the field with armed bands, and carrying off slaves and free persons.[9] Under Tiberius, brigandage had grown so bold, that this emperor aug-

[1] Et cadum Marsi memorem duelli
Spartacum si qua potuit vagantem
Fallere testa. (Hor. Carm., lib. iii., od. xiv.)

[2] Flor., lib. iii., cap. xx.

[3] Plutarch, M. Crassus, cap. xi.

[4] Ibid., cap. xi.

[5] Appian. de bell. civ., lib. i., cap. cxx.

[6] Plutarch, M. Crassus, cap. viii.

[7] Florus, lib. iii., cap. xx.

[8] Appian. de bell. civ., lib. i., cap. cxx.

[9] Sueton. Tranquil., cap. xxxii.

mented the troops (*corps de garde*) and detailed the prætorian cohorts to guard the city.[1]

It should be understood that the system of the ancient was different from that of modern robbers. The ancient robbers hardly ever killed. They ransomed, and when the person captured had not the money, they sold him, as a slave, which was another mode of ransom. These robbers even acted on certain rules, on which one could depend. If taken by them, the prisoner had only to send to a relative or friend, and he was conducted immediately to the place designated and set at liberty, if the relative or friend acted with caution. Appian mentions Decimus Brutus, who killed Cæsar, and who was taken in Gaul, as he fled after the death of the dictator, and carried, at his request, to the Gallic lord, on whose territory he had been captured.[2]

Sometimes these brigands formed small armies, which they placed in the service of a general. During the wars of Fabius Maximus Æmilianus in Portugal, there were two companies of brigands, of ten thousand men, who gave much trouble to the Roman army.[3] The same thing has occurred often in modern history. During the wars which followed the death of Charles VI., in 1418, "*there reigned* (says Monstrelet) on the marches of Poutoise, Isle-Adam, and Gisors, a brigand chief, named Tabary."[4] This Tabary, who was small and lame, but brave, espoused the cause of the Burgundians, which did not prevent his cutting the throats of the Duke of Bedford's English. He had the honor of being killed in 1420, in an assault, at the head of his band, and in company with the Maréchal Villiers de l'Isle-Adam, Antoine de Croï, Robert de Saveuse, the Seigneur de Noyelle et de Lyonnel de Bournonville, on the fortress of Toussy, in Auxerrois, defended by the Seigneur de la Tremoïlle.[5]

We should add a few words relative to a specialty included in the general profession of robbers — that of a corsair. We have already said that, among the most ancient peoples on the coast of the Mediterranean Sea, the profession of a corsair was not dishon-

[1] Sueton. Tranquil., Tiber., cap. xxvii.
[2] Appian. de bell. civ., lib. iii., cap. xcviii.
[3] Appian. de bell. Hispan., cap. lxviii.
[4] Chroniq. d'Enguer. de Monstrelet, liv. i., cap. ccii.
[5] Chroniq. d'Enguer. de Monstrelet, liv. i., cap. ccxxxiii.

orable.[1] It was then followed by free men. In the Odyssey, the heroes, in a very amicable[2] spirit, ask this question: "My lord, are you a pirate?" Within a few centuries, fugitive slaves also took to piracy. Plato assures us that, in his time, all the pirates, who infested the coasts of Italy, were previously slaves.[3] What is worthy of notice is that, as soon as these fugitive slaves came together at any one point—took possession of some strong castle, and founded some durable establishment—they hastened to establish slavery among them. When Pompey had delivered the Roman republic from the crowd of pirates, whom Mithridates had let loose on the Mediterranean; when he had taken from them 378 ships, and killed 10,000 men, he opened the 120 cities, or castles, which they had seized,[4] and found there all that constituted a complete *state* at that epoch: captives in chains, who waited to be ransomed, arsenals full of timbers, iron, sails, hemp, and a great multitude of slaves, who worked in the prisons.[5]

The most illustrious pirate, whom antiquity has produced, was Agathocles, tyrant of Sicily, who succeeded to all the splendor of the elder Dionysius. Son of a poor potter, he passed his infancy in houses of ill-fame.[6] Grown to manhood, he became a pirate, and began his career by robbing his own fellow-citizens.[7] Exiled twice from Syracuse, he took refuge with the Murgantines, who elected him their general. Syracuse, which had banished him as a robber, recalled him as a general; and then commenced those brilliant wars against Carthage, which made him the most powerful monarch that Sicily ever had.[8]

[1] Thucyd., lib. i., cap. v.—Polyb. Hist., lib. ii., cap. viii.
[2] Odys., lib. iii., v. 71–73.
[3] Plato de legibus, lib. vi.
[4] Appian. de bell. Mithridat., cap. xcvi.
[5] Ibid.
[6] Ibid.
[7] Justin., lib. xxii., cap. i.
[8] Ibid.

# CHAPTER XIX.

## MODERN TRADES' UNIONS.[1]

WE have reached a point where those who have followed, step by step, the development of this book, will raise a grave objection to the historic theory, which it proposes. If it be true, as this book teaches, that the commune and the trades' union are, one the administrative, and the other the industrial association, which slaves form on attaining liberty, so that these two species of associations are reproduced simultaneously and necessarily in all slave countries, how does it happen that, after the fall of the Roman Empire, the trades' unions and the communes disappeared, although there were slaves still in Europe? and that we had in France to wait until the reign of Philip Augustus to again find burghers and trades' unions? Does it not seem, if the theory of this book is correct, that with the general tendency to emancipation, which Christianity introduced in the Old World: with the trouble and tumult caused by the invasion of the barbarians in the West: the multitude of freedmen ought to have been greater and greater, and that there ought to have been, on the contrary, more communes and more trades' unions than ever?

The objection is real and serious. It requires us to present a phase of the invasion of the peoples of the North, which no historian that we know of has as yet explained and pointed out.

There is in history a custom, to call the peoples of the North, who invaded the Roman Empire in the fifth century, *barbarians;* but no one has given us a clear idea of what constituted their *barbarism.* We will endeavor to settle this question, which, we hope, will illuminate and fix some points heretofore undecided and obscure.

As we have already said, if we consider the family in the primi-

[1] We have not thought it necessary to support the ideas contained in this chapter by justificative notes. For us, learning is not a luxury, but a necessity. Now, this chapter being based entirely on the testimony of well-known books, such as the *History of Paris* by Felibien, the *Treatise on Police*, and the *Register of Trades*, we have not thought necessary to enlarge this book by superabundant citations.

tive times of history, we find it entirely constituted in the father and absorbed by him. The wife was bought, and consequently a slave; the son could be sold, and was therefore a slave; the servant was completely a slave. At this epoch of the family, the wife, the son, and the servant were owned; they owned nothing—neither name, nor personality, nor property. They existed only by the father and in the father. Such, we have shown, was the primitive state of the family.

As ages rolled by, the constitution of the family was modified. The authority of the father diminished, and the personality of the wife, the son, and the servant was disengaged. Things finally reached the point where the wife had her portion in the joint property, and could demand a divorce; when the son, at twenty-one years of age, was independent of the father, and had his legal part in the succession; when the servant ceased to be a slave to become a hireling, and thenceforth discuss the conditions of his labor.

This revolution in the family is a human fact: that is to say, a fact produced in the Jewish family, in the Greek, the Roman, and the German; in the East and in the West; in humanity.

Well! *Barbarous* peoples are those who, as compared with others, have not passed through so many phases of the history of the family. As facts invincibly establish that the family does not remain stationary between the two extreme points of its constitution, which we have indicated, it necessarily follows that every people (who are but an aggregation of families) must pass through all the degrees successively. Hence, the most *barbarous* people are those, who have made the least of this inevitable journey; the most civilized are those, who have made the most.

The nations of the North, who invaded the Roman Empire in the fifth century, were, in fact, barbarians, as compared with the nations invaded—that is to say, the Goths, the Franks, the Burgundians, the Saxons, the Vandals, the Quadi, the Heruli had not reached the point in the history of the family, to which the peoples of Gaul, Spain, Italy, and Greece had arrived. With them, the authority of the father was more entire and more absolute. For example, the servant, who in the Roman Empire had almost generally reached the condition of a hireling, was, among them, still in the condition of slavery, and consequently they knew nothing of communes, or trades' unions, or of any of the associations, to which freedmen give birth.

Thus, the peoples of the North, who inundated the empire in the fifth century, were, properly speaking, more primitive than the vanquished. To find in the history of Italy an epoch when its institutions were analogous to those of the Goths or the Franks, we must go back at least to the time of Tarquin the Proud. Already, from the time of Marius, the feudal relations of the great families of Rome were weakened. We have seen that a judicial decision was necessary to force Marius to recognize the suzerainty of the house of Herennius. Among the Goths, the Saxons, and the Franks, on the contrary, the feudal hierarchy was still, in the fifth century, predominant.

When, after the invasion, the barbarian society of the North was infused in exaggerated proportions into the civilized society of the South, there resulted from the mixture a third society, much less advanced than that, which for some years previous covered the face of the Roman world. Greece, Italy, Spain, Gaul were obliged to recommence—recommence is the term rigorously correct—many successive steps of progress, which those countries had already passed through. For example, they recommenced the emancipation of slaves, to arrive, in the twelfth century, at the communes and the trades' unions, two things, which they already had long before the invasion of the barbarians.

This sudden and immense backset, impressed on the Roman world by the invasion, is a phenomenon so clear and striking that the greatest annalist history ever had, Vico, has based upon it his celebrated theory of the *Recorsi*—that is to say, of the *returns* of humanity upon itself at given periods of the life of peoples. Vico shows with admirable art how all the West recommenced, as we have said, in the fifth century, what it had already done and perfected seven or eight centuries before. This idea of Vico is mathematically true. But if Vico was right in affirming that the West repassed, under the peoples of the conquest, through the same laws, the same institutions, the same progress, which the Roman people had already given to it, he is wrong in concluding that this constitutes *a circular revolution of humanity upon itself*. For the Franks recommenced the Romans, it is true; but having recommenced, they continued them. This is what Vico did not observe, and what ruins his theory. (*a*)

(*a*) This theory of Vico has been very generally adopted, and, in another form, is expressed by the adage, "*History* repeats itself." Doubtless it is on this theory that Generals Grant, Sherman, and even Logan, rest their hopes of wearing some day the imperial purple — when, by the misrule of carpetbag-negro-scalawag barbarism, Radical policy shall have accomplished its object of *disgusting* the people with republicanism, and shall have prepared them for a *transition* to a monarchical or imperial form of government, as John Adams, a great man and a patriot, though a monarchist, anticipated and foretold. (See Translator's Preface, fol. xvi.)

General Logan bases his hopes on the Grand-Commandership of the Grand Army of the Republic, and on his great *projet* of removing the seat of government from *Washington* to a new metropolis, *Logansport.* But his aspirations are simply ridiculous; as *bogus* as the *paste* diamonds, with which, after having first tendered his services to the rebel States, he is said to have bought his major-general's commission, valuing them at $1,500, when they were not worth 1,500 cents.

The simple fact that his Grand-Commandership should cause a man of General Logan's mediocre mental calibre to "*dream dreams*" of becoming the EMPEROR CONSTANTINE of the New World, through the influence and by the instrumentality of the G. A. R., proves two other facts, viz.:

1. The general acceptation of the idea that in the circular revolution of humanity upon itself, the republican — that is to say, the municipal and State — rights of the working and burgher classes will inevitably be swallowed up by the *unification* and centralization of all political power, in America as in Europe, in the hands of an emperor or a king, and of the nobility, which that emperor or king may create.

2. The anti-republican, imperialistic tendencies of such an organization as the G. A. R., which is not a trades' union, nor a labor union, but is a *political, office-seeking union* of men, who have no sympathy, nor any point of contact with the working and burgher classes, except a desire to *put into their own pockets the taxes*, which the working and burgher classes pay for the support of the government.

General Grant bases his aspirations on his brilliant military services. But their lustre is now obscured behind a big black cloud — *auri sacra fames* — the "accursed greed for gold," which cannot say "*no*" to any who come "*dona ferentes,*" (bringing gifts,) but clutches with miser's grasp at houses and lands, U. S. bonds and Sto. Domingo shares, railroad land-grants and stocks, fast horses and fat cattle — anything and everything, on which there are no express charges to be paid. The aspirant for an imperial throne and sceptre must be more noted for *giving* than *accepting.*

The most dangerous man to republican liberty in this country is General W. Tecumseh Sherman. He has all the requisite qualifications of a successful mili-

Now, if we apply this idea to the history of the slave races of the middle ages, we account with precision, and clearly, for the kind of

---

tary usurper. He has the military genius; the ruthlessness of his savage namesake, Tecumseh; an unscrupulous disregard of all the obligations of honor, clemency, good faith, truth; the prestige of *giving* to his followers "*all that his quartermasters could n't take possession of, or did n't want.*"

He accepted the surrender of Columbia, S. C., having pledged his military honor for the protection of noncombatants and private property. He then applied the torch and burned Columbia to the ground, reckless alike of feeble womanhood and innocent childhood.

He is the very man to sweep remorselessly over all obstacles that might stand in his way to imperial and absolute power.

He afterward charged the "*enormous crime*" of the destruction of Columbia on General Wade Hampton. General Hampton replied by the following letter, which the Radical Senate refused to receive or act on, because they *knew* that an investigation would acquit General Hampton and convict General Sherman, both of the burning and the slander.

WILD WOODS, Miss., *April* 21, 1866.

To the Hon. REVERDY JOHNSON, U. S. Senate:

*Sir*—A few days ago I saw in the published proceedings of Congress that a petition of Benjamin Rawles, of Columbia, S. C., asking compensation for the destruction of his house by the Federal army, in February, 1865, had been presented to the Senate, accompanied by a letter from Major-General Sherman.

In this letter General Sherman uses the following language: "The citizens of Columbia set fire to thousands of bales of cotton rolled out into the streets, and which were burning before we entered Columbia. I myself was in the city as early as nine o'clock, and I saw these fires, and know that efforts were made to extinguish them; but a high and strong wind kept them alive.

"I gave no orders for the burning of your city, but, on the contrary, the conflagration resulted from the great imprudence of cutting the cotton bales, whereby the contents were spread to the wind, so that it became an impossibility to arrest the fire.

"I saw in your Columbia paper the printed order of General Wade Hampton that, on the approach of the Yankee army, all the cotton should thus be burned; and from what I saw myself, I have no hesitation in saying that he was the cause of the destruction of your city."

This same charge, made against me by General Sherman, having been brought before the Senate of the United States, I am naturally most solicitous to vindicate myself before the same tribunal. But my State has no representative in that body. Those who should be her constitutional representatives and exponents there are debarred the right of entrance into those halls. There are none who have the right to speak for the South; none to participate in the legislation which governs her; none to impose the taxes she is called upon to pay; and none to vindicate

interruption, which the barbarians brought with them in their march toward civil life. The people of the South had passed through

---

her sons from misrepresentation, injustice, and slander. Under these circumstances, I appeal to you, in the confident hope that you will use every effort to see that justice is done in this matter.

I deny emphatically that any cotton was fired in Columbia by my order.

I deny that the citizens "set fire to thousands of bales rolled out into the streets."

I deny that any cotton was on fire when the Federal troops entered the city.

I most respectfully ask of Congress to appoint a committee charged with the duty of ascertaining and reporting all the facts connected with the destruction of Columbia, and thus fix upon the proper author of that enormous crime the infamy he richly deserves.

I am willing to submit the case to any honest tribunal. Before any such, I pledge myself to prove that I gave a positive order, by direction of General Beauregard, that no cotton should be fired; that not one bale was on fire when General Sherman's troops took possession of the city; that he promised protection to the city; and that, in spite of his solemn promise, he burned the city to the ground, deliberately, systematically, and atrociously.

I therefore most earnestly request that Congress may take prompt and efficient measures to investigate this matter fully. Not only is this due to themselves and to the reputation of the United States army, but also to justice and truth.

Trusting that you will pardon me for troubling you, I am, very respectfully, your ob't serv't,

WADE HAMPTON.

Not long after the war, yet long enough for the passions of war to cool, we read and were shocked at a report of a speech made by General Sherman, in defence and justification of the outrages committed by his *bummers* on the helpless women and children of Georgia and South Carolina; the substance of which speech was that, because of the great crime of their male relatives, i. e. rebellion, these women and children had no rights, which his bummers were bound to respect. In a hasty examination of the files of the *Washington Chronicle* for that speech, we find in that paper of the 30th of August, 1865, the following extract from a speech made by General Sherman at a soldiers' picnic at Lancaster, Ohio:

"When the rebels ventured their all in their efforts to destroy our Government, "they pledged their lives, their fortunes, and their sacred honors to their cause. "The Government accepted their wager of battle. Hence, when we conquered, "*we by conquest gained all they had. Their property became ours by conquest.* "*Thus they lost their slaves, their mules, their horses, their cotton, their all; and* "*even their lives and personal liberty, thrown by them into the issue, were theirs* "*only by our forbearance and clemency.*

"*By this right of conquest we own this ground we stand on to-day, conquered* "*from the Indians — the Shawnees, I believe.*

nearly all the successive phases of the family. The people of the North had passed through but few. The Greeks, Italians, Span-

" *The State of Ohio is ours by conquest from the French and English.*

" So, soldiers, when we marched through and conquered the country of the " rebels, *we became owners of all they had; and I don't want you* TO BE TROU- " BLED IN YOUR CONSCIENCES *for taking, while on our great march, the property* " *of the rebels. They forfeited their right to it, and* I, BEING AGENT FOR THE " GOVERNMENT TO WHICH I BELONGED, GAVE YOU AUTHORITY TO KEEP ALL THE " QUARTERMASTERS COULD N'T TAKE POSSESSION OF, OR DID N'T WANT."

Now, it is difficult to believe that General Sherman, with all the advantages of a West-Point education, was so *ignorant* as not to know that his statements about having conquered the State of Ohio from the Shawnees, the French, and the English, were untrue. Almost every schoolboy knows, and, in view of his Connecticut origin, it is difficult to believe that General Sherman did not know, that the State of Ohio is a monument of the magnificent patriotism of the State of Virginia on the one hand, and of the directly opposite characteristics of the State of Connecticut on the other. Excepting only the "*Connecticut Reserve*," the State of Ohio is a part of that "*magnificent gift*" from the State of Virginia, which was conveyed to the United States by a deed executed and signed by Thomas Jefferson, Samuel Hardy, Arthur Lee, and James Monroe, on the 1st of May, 1784, and which so excited the admiration of the great Webster. It would seem, therefore, almost an act of madness for General Sherman thus to subject himself to the risk of being thought so *ignorant* on the one hand, or so prone to imaginative statements, destitute of truth, on the other. But there was a method in this madness. Unfortunately mankind are so constituted, as the history of all successful usurpations proves, that nothing is so well calculated to attract adherents as the idea that their leader is ready to *give to them all the property of his opponents* "*that his quartermasters can't take possession of, or don't want.*"

Connected with the destruction of Columbia is a question of some curious interest. It appears from a pamphlet published to vindicate General Hampton from the charge brought against him by General Sherman, that the soldiers, who did the burning, said that the duty of burning Columbia was assigned to them as a special honor or privilege. The theory of the writer of the pamphlet was, that the reason of this assignment was, that there were no Roman Catholics among them; and that all the Roman Catholics of Sherman's army were carefully and purposely kept out of the city, because they were opposed to the burning, *lest the Roman Catholic institution in that city should be involved in its destruction.* If this theory was correct, the Roman Catholics may well be proud of their exclusion from a participation in the *honor* (?) of burning down the (falsely so-called) "*hotbed and cradle of secession.*"

The city of Atlanta, Georgia, was also surrendered by the mayor to General Sherman, under a "*solemn promise*" of protection to noncombatants and private property. Even General Sherman will hardly dare to assert that the

iards, Gauls, had reached the regime of freedmen. The Franks, Burgundians, Saxons, and Visigoths were still under the regime of

---

"citizens of Atlanta set fire to thousands of bales of cotton rolled out into the streets," or that they "were burning before he entered the city." For he stayed in Atlanta many weeks. In spite of his "solemn promise," he gave the city up to sack and pillage. He gave his soldiers "authority to seize and keep all that his quartermasters could n't take possession of, or did n't want." When he was about to leave, he burned the city of Atlanta to the ground, "deliberately, systematically, and atrociously." An eyewitness assures us that, at the lowest calculation, 500 pianos, the private property of the ladies of Atlanta, were taken and sent North before the burning.

Attila, Alaric, Genghis Khan—the barbarous Hun, the brutal Goth, the savage Tartar—sacked and burned cities; but not *after* they had pledged a soldier's honor for the protection of private property. Had they been guilty of such "enormous crime," yet they would have scorned to "slander" so spotless a name as that of Wade Hampton.

POSTSCRIPT.—*Washington, May* 29, 1871.—To-day, a friend met me and said: "What do you think now of your friends, the communists? They have burned the greater part of Paris, and have murdered the archbishop and many priests." I replied: "The first part of the statement may be true. A great part of Paris may have been burned; but if so, I do not believe that it was deliberate, systematic, atrocious, like the burning of Atlanta and Columbia. Certain it is, that the fires of Paris did not occur after a surrender tendered and accepted, but in the heat of the fight; and they were most probably accidental. As to the latter part of the statement, I hope it is not true, and I do not believe it." He said: "Our minister, Mr. Washburne, telegraphs it officially." I replied: "Perhaps as a mere rumor, started by the imperialists and monarchists, to cast odium on the name and cause of the republican communists. Moreover, there is much reason to believe that Mr. Washburne is himself an imperialist, as anxious as Governor Holden to see General Grant an emperor, and his son succeed him as emperor. I take such telegrams from Mr. Washburne *cum grano salis*, and await more reliable information. Besides, in judging the communists, whom our imperialist journals delight in stigmatizing as 'the dangerous classes,' we must not forget that they have to carry the worse than dead weight of the three branches of the proletariat—the beggars, prostitutes, and thieves—for whose misdeeds the imperialists are more responsible than the working classes, though they are all charged to the latter."

A gentleman from Pennsylvania said to me a few days since: "It has always surprised me that no Southern man has ever taken the trouble to contradict a charge, which was made against the rebels during the war, and which excited more bitter feeling against them at the North than almost everything else that they were charged with. I myself know that there was not one word of truth in the charge." I asked: "What do you refer to?" He replied: "To the charge that the rebels

slavery. The former had produced around them a multitude of municipalities, in which the slave races entirely effaced, by the

set fire to the woods in the Wilderness for the purpose of burning up the Union wounded. I know that this charge was untrue, for I was in all those fights. The ground was covered with dry leaves, which took fire accidentally from the burning paper of the cartridges which fell among the leaves. The rebels had no more to do in starting the fire than we had; and as many of the rebel wounded perished by the fire as of our men. But this story was almost universally believed at the time. I have never seen any contradiction of it, and to this day thousands of our people believe that the rebels fired the woods purposely to burn up our wounded."

*June 1st*, 1871.—I have just received the following:

ATLANTA, GA., *May* 29, 1871.

Mr. B. E. GREEN:

*Dear Sir*—I received yours of the 23d inst., requesting me to send you a copy of the correspondence between General Sherman and myself in regard to the *surrender* of Atlanta, and the *protection* afforded by him.

I lost the manuscript copy of my letter and his original letter to me in reply, but you will find them in the book containing the history of his march through Georgia. I forget who wrote it, but presume you can find it in any of the bookstores at Washington. That copy is correct.

The correspondence did not relate to the *surrender* of Atlanta, as that took place about a week before. My letter was one of expostulation against his order exiling the citizens, and asking him to revoke or modify it; and his was a long argumentative letter in reply.

I send you a brief history of the circumstances attending the surrender, copied from the Atlanta City Directory, which is substantially correct. You will see I surrendered the city to Colonel Coburn, of General Ward's Division of Slocum's Corps; and you will see that Colonel Coburn promised protection to *private property*, and that the words used by me were reduced to writing the next day at his request; *but his were not.* I did not notify General Sherman of his promise,

privileges of burghership, the almost forgotten stain of their origin. The latter still lived in pure feudalism, without any mixture of com-

---

and acted on the presumption that he knew what his officers did in so important a matter; but in thinking about it since, I have concluded that it might be this promise of Colonel Coburn never came to his knowledge, *else he would not have allowed the houses and other property of poor widows and orphans to be burned up.* And I think so for this reason, also: General Sherman, for the most part, was very particular to observe all the promises he made to me. For instance, he told me to cause the citizens to put their *fine* furniture in one of the churches, and he would guard it, etc. They did put as much of it in one house as it would hold, and *he did guard it.* That house, I don't suppose, held the hundredth part.

When I was verbally complaining to him of the hardship of expulsion, and the loss of property it would occasion, etc., he told me they might take out every "*smithering*" of their personal property; but, notwithstanding I reminded him of the promise, he would not allow them to take out cotton, tobacco, spirits, and cattle.

One day I told him a poor widow wanted to take out her milch cow, and his officers would not allow her. He replied he "reckoned it would be difficult to drive a fat cow by the commissary's office." *He had probably forgotten his promise.* My cows were taken, and others. Some did take them out. The officers prevented buggies from being taken out. This was probably without the General's knowledge. I supposed they wanted them for their own use. If I was well, and had more time, I might throw more light on the subject. Yours, etc.,

JAMES M. CALHOUN.

(Extract from the Register of the City of Atlanta.)

On the morning and until the night of the 1st of September, 1864, Major-General Stewart's Corps, General Ferguson's brigade of cavalry, and the Georgia militia were in the city.

mune or trade's union—all masters, all seigniors, all barons, all kings.

---

and a corps under command of General S. D. Lee came within six miles of Atlanta, (to Killis Brown's, on South River.) In the afternoon, General Slocum's command were at the Chattahoochie River, eight miles distant. At night, the Confederate forces were withdrawn from the city, except Ferguson's brigade; and the following day, the Hon. James M. Calhoun, then Mayor of Atlanta, with a committee of some twelve citizens, after going more than two miles up the Marietta road, and first meeting with Captain Scott, obtained an interview with Colonel John Coburn, of Indianapolis, Indiana, the substance of which we give below.

After having been introduced by Captain Scott, Mayor Calhoun said: "Colonel Coburn, the fortunes of war have placed Atlanta in your hands. As mayor of the city, I come to ask protection for noncombatants and for private property." To this Colonel Coburn replied: "We did not come to make war on noncombatants, nor on private property. Both shall be *respected and protected by us.*" On this day, also, the command of General Slocum regularly invested the city, General W. T. Sherman himself coming in September the 7th. On the morning of the 3d, the above remarks on the part of Mayor Calhoun were, by request, reduced to writing, and addressed to General Ward instead of Colonel Coburn; *but the reply was not reduced to writing.*

The foregoing calls for a few brief comments.

1st. All honor to the brave men of the United States armies—and they were not a few—who did not go South to make war on noncombatants, (that is, women and children,) nor on private property. They were not Vandals.

2d. How should we characterize the general, who in the moment of victory could so brutally make a jest of the petition of a "*poor widow*"?

3d. Ex-Mayor Calhoun's handwriting bears the tremulous impress of age and sickness. See how, by their softening influence on the heart, charity, which covers a multitude of sins, seeks to find some palliation for the great spoiler! But his "*enormous crime*" *burns* through the mantle of that charity, which, hoping all

We may, then, compare the peoples of the South and the peoples of the North, toward the fifth century, to two liquids at differ-

---

things, believing all things, would even hope, if there was no room to believe, that "*it might be*" he did not know, or had forgotten, that through his officers he had promised protection to women and children and to private property. When the ex-mayor comes to speak of *how* General Sherman did keep a promise to him, his charity becomes sarcasm as bitter as that of the Yankee soldier, who said to his comrade Charley, "I believe Sherman has set the river on fire." Sherman, wanting to get together all the *fine furniture and articles of value which might otherwise be concealed*, told the mayor to cause the citizens to put them in one of the churches, and he would guard it. He did guard it, *from*, not *for*, the owners. It was a "*wooden-nutmeg*" trick — shrewd, but not consistent with the ideas of a soldier's honor, as understood by Robert E. Lee, Stonewall Jackson, Joseph E. Johnston, John B. Gordon, Hood, and others of that stamp — to get all the fine furniture and other valuable personal property together, so that his men could more conveniently "*keep all that his quartermasters could n't take possession of, or did n't want*," and that he might more surely burn and *smither* what his men did n't care to keep.

4th. Worcester gives this definition:

*Smithers, n. pl., fragments, atoms.* (*Local Eng.*) *Halliwell.*

General Sherman's promise to the mayor, that the women and children, whom he was driving from their homes, might take out every "*smithering*" of their personal property, was made to the ear, with the intent of breaking it to the hope. He intended first to *smither* it into fragments, and then they might take out the *atoms, if they could.* This corresponds with what he said at Memphis before the Vicksburg campaign: that he "did not intend to leave to any old woman in the South even her . . . . . ;" using the most vulgar term for that necessary domestic utensil, with which an old woman of antiquity is said to have slain as great a warrior as Sherman, by throwing it from a housetop. Perhaps General Sherman's resolve to *smither* the crockery of all the old women in the South may have been suggested by a prudent precaution against a similar tragic end for himself.

Colonels Bowman and Irwin, in their *Sherman and his Campaigns*, page 222, say:

"On the 11th of September, the town authorities addressed the following petition to General Sherman, praying the revocation of his orders:

"'*Sir*—The undersigned, mayor, and two members of council for the city of Atlanta, for the time being the only legal organ of the people of the said city to express their wants and wishes, ask leave, most earnestly, but respectfully, to petition you to reconsider the order requiring them to leave Atlanta.

ent degrees of saturation —one ready to crystallize; the other, more limpid, more corrosive, farther from the condensation of its ele-

---

"'At first view, it struck us that the measure would involve extraordinary hardship and loss; but since we have seen the practical execution of it, so far as it has progressed, and the individual condition of many of the people, and heard their statements as to the inconveniences, loss, and suffering attending it, we are satisfied that it will involve, in the aggregate, consequences appalling and heart-rending.

"'Many poor women are in an advanced state of pregnancy; others, now having young children, and whose husbands are either in the army, prisoners, or dead. Some say: I have such a one sick at home; who will wait on them when I am gone? Others say: What are we to do? We have no houses to go to, and no means to buy, build, or to rent any —no parents, friends, or relatives to go to. Another says: I will try to take this or that article of property, but such and such things I must leave behind, though I need them much. We reply to them: General Sherman will carry your property to Rough and Ready, and General Hood will take it from there on. And they will reply to that: But I want to leave the railway at such a point, and cannot get conveyance from there on.

"'We only refer to a few facts, to illustrate, in part, how this measure will operate in practice. As you advanced, the people north of us fell back, and before your arrival here, a large portion of the people had retired south; so that the country south of this is already crowded, and without houses to accommodate the people; and we are informed that many are now starving in churches and other out-buildings. This being so, how is it possible for the people still here (mostly women and children) to find any shelter? And how can they live through the winter in the woods —no shelter nor subsistence—in the midst of strangers who know them not, and without the power to assist them, if they were willing to do so?

ments—and when their mixture took place, that one of the two which was nearest to crystallization was suddenly thrown back, and,

---

"'This is but a feeble picture of the consequences of this measure. You know the woe, the horror, and the suffering cannot be described by words. Imagination can only conceive of it; and we ask you to take these things into consideration.

"'We know your mind and time are constantly occupied with the duties of your command, which almost deters us from asking your attention to this matter; but we thought it might be that you had not considered the subject in all its awful consequences, and that on more reflection you, we hope, would not make this people an exception to all mankind; for we know of no such instance ever having occurred—surely none such in the United States. And what has this helpless people done, that they should be driven from their homes, to wander as strangers, outcasts, and exiles, and to subsist on charity?

"'We do not know, as yet, the number of people still here. Of those who are here, we are satisfied a respectable number, if allowed to remain at home, could subsist for several months without assistance, and a respectable number for a much longer time, and who might not need assistance at all.

"'In conclusion, we most earnestly and solemnly petition you to reconsider this order, or modify it, and suffer this unfortunate people to remain at home and enjoy what little means they have. Respectfully submitted.

"'JAMES M. CALHOUN, *Mayor.*
"'E. E. RAWSON, *Councilman.*
"'L. C. WELLS, *Councilman.*'"

Page 226.—"As soon as his arrangements were completed, General Sherman wrote to General Hood by a flag of truce, notifying him of his orders, and proposing a cessation of hostilities for ten days from the 12th of September, in the country included within a radius of two miles around Rough and Ready station, to enable him to complete the removal of those families electing to go south.

in an instant, all the embryos of sediments which were already deposited on the sides of the vase dissolved and vanished.

---

Hood immediately replied, on the 9th, acceding to the proposed truce, but protesting against Sherman's order. He concluded:

"'Permit me to say, the unprecedented measure you propose transcends in studied and iniquitous cruelty all acts ever before brought to my attention in this dark history of the war. In the name of God and humanity, I protest, believing you are expelling from homes and firesides wives and children of a brave people.'"

Porus, after a brave and stubborn resistance, was defeated and brought captive before Alexander. The latter asked: "What have you to say?" Porus answered: "That you shall treat me as a king." Alexander said: "Make of me some special request." Porus replied: "Everything is included in what I have said." Alexander restored him to his throne, added to his dominions, and made him a friend.

Mark the contrast!

After a brave and stubborn resistance of the Confederate armies, the captive *women and children* kneel at the feet of the victor, Sherman; some far advanced in pregnancy, some "in the perils of childbirth," some with babes just born. Mark this, ye working and burgher classes of the North, who were deceived into believing that the war was made to put down the rebellion of a slaveholding aristocracy. General Sherman's own aide-de-camp tells us that these suppliant women and children were "*almost entirely of the lower class.*" They were the wives and children of the white working and burgher classes of the South. They came beseeching General Sherman to treat them as *women and children.*

How did he reply to their supplications? Practically, his answer was:

"I, at the head of my army, and my brother John in the Senate, have an understanding with the imperialists and with the capital that *hires* labor. I want to be an emperor; my brother, the senator, wants to get rich. The capital that *hires* labor wants to reduce wages, increase the cost of living, make labor pay the taxes, spend those taxes for the profit of capital, and establish a moneyed aristocracy, freed from the restraints of all usury laws.

"Now, your fathers and husbands and brothers and sons and sweethearts are opposing us — have committed the great crime of fighting us, who came to *divorce* capital from labor in the South. For *their* great crime I intend to punish *you.* I will not leave to any old woman among you, out of her crockery, so much as a . . . . . . I will drive you from your homes to starvation or worse. I will *smither* into fragments your little property, and you can take the fragments with you into exile, if you can. For my purpose is to *burn!* BURN! BURN!"

But let the horrible story be told in the words of the great modern Vandal's own aide-de-camp, Brevet-Major George Ward Nichols. He says:

Page 23.—"A long train of wagons and ambulances from Atlanta, provided by General Sherman, had driven into the space between the outposts, and deposited their freight of women and children with (the *smitherings* of) their house-

Thus, the arrival of the peoples of the North truly arrested the peoples of the South in their progress; it suspended emancipations,

---

hold furniture. *These people seemed to be almost entirely of the lower class. The wealthier citizens removed from Atlanta when the firing began, those only remaining who were willing to take the risk of shot and shell, and the possibility of Federal occupation.*

"The dust from our wagons had hardly subsided, when the sharp crack of the whip and the loud cries of the train-masters and mule-drivers announced the arrival of the rebel convoy to remove the people (that is, the women and children) whom General Sherman had refused to permit Hood to throw upon him as a burden."

Page 26. — "Meanwhile, under Sherman's orders, the removal of the citizens of Atlanta outside our lines was continued. . . . The rebels howled forth threats and objurgations at what they termed a fiendish act of cruelty; but General Sherman little heeded their ravings. *He had taken this step only after due premeditation. Atlanta was a captured city.* . . . It would have been an absurd incongruity daily to fill the mouths of the wives and children of men in arms against the Government."

Page 37. — "Nov. 13th. Behind us we leave a track of smoke and flame. Half of Marietta was burned up — not by orders, however; for the command is that proper details shall be made to destroy all property which can ever be of use to the rebel armies. Stragglers will get into these places, and dwelling-houses are levelled to the ground. In nearly all cases these are the deserted habitations formerly owned by rebels who are now refugees. Yesterday, as some of our men were marching toward the Chattahoochie River, they saw in the distance pillars of smoke rising along its banks — the bridges were in flames. Said one, hitching his musket on his shoulder in a free and easy way: "I say, Charley, I believe Sherman has set the river on fire."

(The aide heard the words of the soldier, but was so blinded by the smoke that he could not see the point of this bitter sarcasm on the General.)

Page 38.—"Atlanta is entirely deserted by human beings, excepting a few soldiers here and there. The houses are vacant; there is no trade or traffic of any kind; the streets are empty. Beautiful roses bloom in the gardens of fine houses; but a terrible stillness and solitude covers all, depressing the hearts even of those who are *glad to destroy it.* In the peaceful homes of the North there can be no conception how these people have suffered for their crimes."

"*Atlanta, night of the 15th November.* A grand and awful spectacle is presented to the beholder in this beautiful city, now in flames. *By order,* the chief engineer has destroyed by powder and fire all the store-houses, depot-buildings, and machine-shops. The heaven is one expanse of lurid fire; the air is filled with flying burning cinders; buildings covering two hundred acres are in ruins or in flames. Every instant there is the sharp detonation or the smothered booming sound of exploding shells and powder, concealed in the buildings; and then rendered impossible the communes and trades' unions which were ready to be formed, and dried up the source of the communes and

---

the sparks and flame shoot away up into the black and red roof, scattering cinders far and wide."

Page 41.—"A brigade of Massachusetts soldiers are the only troops now left in the town; they will be the last to leave it. To-night I heard the really fine band of the Thirty-third Massachusetts playing 'John Brown's soul goes marching on,' by the light of the burning buildings. I have never heard that noble anthem when it was so grand, so solemn, so inspiring."

Nero was a great artist, (see page 232.) His enjoyment of the sight of burning Rome was enhanced by the music of his own fiddle. General Sherman also is a great artist in "studied and iniquitous cruelty," in punishing women and children for the crimes of their male relatives, and in Vandal incendiarism. It was altogether a fitting and artistic climax, this band of a Massachusetts regiment playing "John Brown's soul goes marching on," by the light of the burning buildings of Atlanta, on that night of the 15th November.

The great Webster once represented Massachusetts in the Senate of the United States. Speaking there for her, in reference to the gift by Virginia of those lands in Ohio, which Sherman claims to have conquered from the Shawnees, French, and English, he said:

"And a most magnificent act it was. I never reflect upon it without a disposition to do honor and justice—and justice would be the highest honor—to Virginia, for the cession of her Northwestern territory. I will say, sir, it is one of her fairest claims to the respect and gratitude of the United States, and that, perhaps, it is only second to that other claim that attaches to her: that from her counsels, and from the intelligence and patriotism of her leading statesmen, proceeded the first idea put into practice of the formation of a general Constitution for the United States."

The great Webster passed away. Men of very different stamp spoke for Massachusetts in the U. S. Senate. New ideas sprang up with new men. Almost before the grand tones of Webster's majestic eloquence had died away, Massachusetts sent John Brown, a border-ruffian, horse-thief, murderer, and *incendiary*, into Virginia, to apply the torch by night to her peaceful homes, and excite a servile insurrection, with all its attendant horrors.

How artistically appropriate it was, then, that on that night of the 15th November, a brigade of Massachusetts soldiers should be the last to lose the *gladdening* sight of the effects of fire on the homes of Atlanta—on "the beautiful roses blooming in the gardens of fine houses," which (Major Nichols says) they were "*glad to destroy*"—and that a Massachusetts band should play "John Brown's soul goes marching on" by the light of the burning buildings! The *mise en scène* was perfect, and placed General Sherman alongside of Nero as a *grand artist* in INCENDIARISM WITH APPROPRIATE MUSIC.

For his artistic war of starvation on the women and children of the white

trades' unions already existing, viz., emancipations. Then, as we have said above, everything recommenced. Emancipations began anew, and few at a time, as in the primitive ages of ancient history. The asylums so long closed were reopened; and after seven centuries of this new preparatory labor, the conquering races in their turn attained to the same degree of civilization in which they found the

---

"*lower classes*" of the South; for his systematic, deliberate, artistic burning of Atlanta, Rome, Marietta, Columbia, the University of Alabama at Tuscaloosa, etc., etc., the advocates of imperialism, low wages, and high taxes glorify him; while they cry out with well-affected horror at the barbarism of the republican leaders of France, because, in all the hurry and tumults and excitements of a siege, they could not prevent a few fires, or control the demoniac fury of stragglers. See what the aide-de-camp says of the burning of Marietta:

"*Stragglers will get into these places, and dwelling-houses are levelled with the ground.*"

How inconsistent! how absurd! how unjust! how hypocritical! to praise Sherman for burning systematically and artistically, and denounce the French republican advocates of local self-government, because it was not in their power to afford protection against fire to every part of beleaguered Paris!

Disgusting as is this *hypocrisy*, of those who wilfully misrepresent the French republicans, it is yet more sad to witness the *ignorance* of others, who, without knowing what they do, unite in vilifying and traducing the communists, as the rebels were vilified and traduced by the false charge that they purposely set fire to the woods in "the Wilderness," to burn up the Union wounded.

We read, this morning, in a Washington City paper, opposed to centralism and imperialism, the following:

"The communists pretended to regulate the price of labor, and to exalt it, by defiance of all law, human and divine. Who can contemplate the sad spectacle of poverty and degradation which is the work of these infidel destructives, without a feeling of deep and stern resentment?"

Now, all this deep and stern resentment, as our readers will see from our author's very clear and precise explanation of what a commune is, (see, *ante*, page 138,) grows out of a total ignorance and misapprehension of the subject.

It is not true that "the communists pretended to regulate the price of labor." This was a matter of the trades' unions. All that the communists contended for was the right of local self-government—the right to levy and collect and spend their own local taxes for local purposes, through officers chosen by themselves from among themselves—instead of being tyrannized over in their local affairs, and plundered, by the appointees and favorites of a central despotism, emperor, king, or president. (See, *ante*, p. 138; see, also, note, pp. 148–150.)

The following is taken from the *New York Herald* of June 2, 1871:

races whom they conquered. Then they, also, had communes and trades' unions.

Seven hundred years of time and efforts—from the fifth to the

---

## DELESCLUZE'S DEFENCE.

### WHAT THE BROTHER OF THE DEAD COMMUNIST LEADER HAS TO SAY ABOUT THE COMMUNE.

To the Editor of the Herald:

In spite of the profound sorrow I feel at the assassination of my brother Charles, there is one sentiment that encourages me to speak as I do in this letter. It is, that his dear memory should be placed beyond those perfidious calumnies to which the press of New York has given currency with regard to the Commune of Paris. Whether it be from ignorance or bad faith, the journals of this city have been the echo of the misrepresentations of the royalists at Versailles. It has been said that the Commune of Paris aimed at the destruction of private property; that it wanted to divide the domains of the State; that its programme forbade the existence of religion or of family ties in society, etc. All these ridiculous allegations are nothing but lies. The Commune of Paris has nothing to do with these doctrines, which were originated by a few misguided individuals, ignorant of the wants of our society. The commune has never had any other programme than that of building up a republic in France, based upon justice and morality. It has claimed, with an energy and courage which one day will be admired, complete municipal franchise for its city, and, consequently, for other cities. It was resolved to destroy the centralization of the Empire, and to substitute in its place the decentralization of administration—that is to say, the right to every commune to govern its own affairs. But it meant, above all, to maintain the political centralization vested in a national assembly, to be elected by all the departments, and sitting in any one city in France. Some time hence, I shall, perhaps, take occasion to give exact details as to the principles and the future of the commune. To-day my heart is too much oppressed for that task. To return, therefore, to my brother. Never has he had other ideas than those above stated; never did I meet with a man who had more respect for the rational laws of his country. For him the ties of family were an object to be cherished.

Hear what he said in a book he published in Paris after his return from Cayenne, and you will know his thoughts on the subject:

"If there is any one thing in this life which should be above the combinations of interest and the selfish exaggeration of passions, which has nothing to fear from the reverses of fortune, it is undeniably the love of family—this mysterious chain which descends from father and mother to the children, and makes all of them, as it were, partakers of the same life.

"How is it that this sentiment only appears in all its purity and force in the midst of trials and sufferings? In the course of an existence which has never been clouded by tempests, habit and security seem to render dormant an affection

twelfth century, from Clovis to Philip Augustus — were required for France to remount to the level from which the invasion precipitated her.

---

unmenaced by danger. Such beings love as they breathe, without being aware of it. It is only in evil days that one knows the value of these ties, if they are based on esteem and self-denial."

Let those who accuse the radicals of desiring the obliteration of family life think on these words, and they will acknowledge, if they are sincere, that this sacred institution, being, as it is, the only foundation of an advanced society, has nowhere had better supporters than our poor vanquished friends in Paris. And how about this war between the two selfish and criminal monarchs — I mean those of France and Prussia? Was it not vehemently opposed before its outbreak by the radicals? The unanimous cry of all their journals was, "No war." Among them was distinguished the *Reveil*, the editor in chief of which was my brother.

(Extract from the *Reveil*, September 3, 1868.)

"France does not want war, and she proclaims it aloud. She protests against an adventurous policy, carried on in the name of peace and liberty."

Here is another of July 26, 1870:

"And what have the people of the Rhine Provinces done to us? True, they have been French, but their interests and habits are German. Do they ask us to incorporate them with our country? No, not at all. It is only intended to revive the spirit of imperial conquest, to blind our people, and to profit by it by securing the tottering dynasty of Louis Bonaparte. Will France follow this man, who is only absorbed by his personal interests. We hope not."

These quotations will suffice. They will free the radical party in this respect from all responsibility. From personal information I have learned that the inhabitants of Paris would have eagerly accepted a conciliation, if based on the condition above mentioned. In all the sittings of the commune, my brother did ever invoke the best sentiments of the human heart. Certainly he believed in the necessity of a revolution, but he desired to carry it on without denying respect to law and public opinion.

When he was appointed deputy, he saw that in the presence of a resistance of the Parisians against the monarchical plots of Thiers, it was his duty to return to his electors, to remain with them to the last, and to await there the triumph of the right, whatever may be the means necessary to attain it. He has fulfilled his duty. The work which he and others have undertaken will be completed by the future generation. But his profound conviction did not efface the melancholy presentiment which weighed upon his mind. Thus, during his stay in the Ministry of War, he, in private conversation, often let out that he had given up all hope of conciliation, and that he was doubtful of success for the present. In his proclamations he told the National Guard that it might happen that they who

It was, in fact, under Philip Augustus, as we have seen, that the greatest municipal movements of the middle ages took place. Then feudalism finished its gestation of the slave races.

It was also under Philip Augustus that the trades' unions, those twin-sisters of the communes, were formed. To better understand their history, we will clear away some facts, which encumber their approach.

We have said, that, when the invasion presented itself on the banks of the Rhine, all Gaul had reached the regime of the commune. The territory was divided into one hundred and fifteen cities, which had for their capitals one hundred and fifteen municipal towns, governed by one hundred and fifteen *hotels de ville.* The fury of the barbarians fell entirely upon the towns. In fact, the institutions, the life were there. All the towns were taken; many were ruined.

The Abbé Dubos, Montesquieu, M. de Savigny, and some others have written works, more or less curious, to show how far the barbarians destroyed the Roman government in Gaul. In our opinion, all these historians have made mistakes, because they put the question on a false basis. In fact, by the government of Gaul under the Romans, these historians have understood something which was only a part, and a very feeble part, of that government. They have understood the action which the prætorian prefect of the diocese of Gaul exercised in the name of the emperors, through his vicar, his seventeen governors, his one hundred and fifteen counts, and his four treasurers-general of the finances of the province. Now, we repeat, the action of all these officers constituted but a part, an accessory part, of the government. They established a connection between Gaul and Rome or Constantinople — that was all — but they did not govern it.

What governed Gaul was the municipal councils, the *curiæ.* In fact, the four treasurers-general received the taxes; but who levied,

combated would reap no advantages from the social revolutions, the fruits of which will, however, certainly be enjoyed by their children. And he was right, sir. On this man, who was so devoted, so sincere, so much attached to the right — who had throughout his life fought for the right — have the journals of this city cast a slur with regard to his tragic death, making him alone responsible for the massacres of Paris, caused by the obstinacy, disloyalty, and the royalist intrigues of Thiers, MacMahon, and the like. HENRY DELESCLUZE.

who were responsible for them? The municipal councillors, or *curiales*. The seventeen governors commanded the troops; but who raised and who paid them? The *curiales*. The counts presided over the tribunals; but who composed them, who studied and who decided the causes? The *curiales*. The real government of Gaul, then, resided entirely in the municipalities. The counts, the governors, the treasurers-general, the prætorian prefect did nothing but report the results of this government to the emperors, and in some sort stamp his coat of arms upon the province.

Then the question whether the barbarians destroyed the Roman government in Gaul is reduced to this: did the barbarians destroy the municipalities?

Put in these terms, the question is at an end. Yes; the barbarians did destroy the Roman government in Gaul, because they destroyed the column which sustained the edifice, the soul which animated the body. What matters it, after that, that the emperors affected not to know that Gaul was no longer under Roman dominion, and that Anastasius conferred on Clovis the powers of prætorian prefect, and sent him the patrician robe? Does that prove that this dignity had any real value in a province where the true supports of government had perished; where the municipalities—that is to say, the power which was responsible for the taxes, which furnished the troops, which administered justice—were dispersed? What would the Emperor Anastasius himself have done with Gaul, without taxes, without soldiers, without tribunals? (*a*)

(*a*) This suggests several questions relative to the conquest, by the people of the North, of the people of the South, in the late civil war in the United States. First. Did the people of the North destroy the "true supports" of republican government in the South?

Answer. Yes; they did. They tore down the column that supported the edifice; they sought to destroy the soul that animated the body. They sought to disfranchise the intelligence, the virtue, and the worth of the South, and to place the political, the governing, power in the hands of ignorant negroes just emancipated, *suddenly*, and with far less knowledge of the science of government than the barbarians, whose predominance threw Europe back seven centuries in her march of progress and civilization.

Second. Who did this?

Answer. Not the people of the North or of the South — not the working and burgher classes — but the *monarchists* and *imperialists*; a few corrupt and design-

Yes; the barbarians of the invasion destroyed the Roman government in Gaul, because they destroyed there the municipalities. Now,

ing men, "in whose minds," to use the language of M. Guizot, "the plans of the great machine were centred," and who, like Governor Holden of North Carolina, "wished to see General Grant (or some other despot) an emperor, and his son succeed him as emperor."

Third. Why did they do this?

Answer. For several reasons.

1st. Because the tendency of the Southern institution of *negro* slavery, unlike the *white* slavery of Europe, was to strengthen the principles of social and political equality among *all whites*, a tendency odious to the aristocrats, monarchists, and imperialists of the North.

2d. Because the tendency of negro slavery, which *married* Southern capital to labor, was to a system of high wages, cheap living, moderate taxation, honest and economical government expenditures; while the interests of Northern capital, *divorced from and hostile to* labor, called for a system of low wages, dear living, oppressive, unequal, and unjust taxation of labor; wasteful, corrupt, and extravagant government expenditures, *for the profit* of capital.

3d. Because certain Northern leaders hoped that a very short experience of government by negro slaves — just emancipated, without prevision or preparation, totally ignorant of the alphabet, the A B C of political science, led, and, by the aid of Ku-Klux bills, controlled by white men more depraved than the negro slaves — would disgust the people with republicanism, and prepare them for a "*transition*" to an imperial and aristocratic form of government.

Fourth. What will be the results of such governments in the South, sustained by Ku-Klux bills, and upheld by fabricated reports of Congressional committees, a majority of whom repudiate all legal rules of evidence to accomplish their wicked partisan purposes?

Answer. A sudden and immense backset to civilization, and to all development, social, political, commercial, and industrial. For a few — ex. gr. for General Howard and his brothers in the Freedmen's Bureau, for Holden and the swindler Littlefield in North Carolina, for Governor Scott and his "pals" in South Carolina, for the bandits Bullock and Blodgett in Georgia — sudden and immense fortunes. For labor, Asiatic wages and diet. For the people, individual and State bankruptcy. For industry and commerce, paralysis.

Finally. If Gaul under the barbarians of the North of Europe was worthless to Anastasius, will not the South, under the deeper barbarism of carpetbag-negro-scalawag misrule, soon be worse than worthless to the people of the North?

We leave the answer to this question to the "sober second thought" of the working and burgher classes of the North, trusting that their own self-interest will open their eyes to the fact that they are not benefited but directly injured by permitting the South to be plundered and impoverished; that the South can only be valuable to them as customers in a legitimate trade; and that that trade will

from this, for the modern trades' unions, two consequences result, which we proceed to deduce, and which will open to us their history.

First, in destroying the municipalities, the barbarians destroyed the trades' unions; for the trades' union and the municipality, in ancient as in modern history, are two facts which are never separated. In ruining Spires, Worms, Strasbourg, Rheims, Amiens, Arras, Tournay, the city of Morins, and all the towns of the two Aquitaines, of Guienne, Lyonnaise, and Narbonnais, what could the trades' unions, which had their seat in those cities, do but disperse and perish? Moreover, these nomad people, living as it were in tents, composed exclusively of two species of men, the nobles and the slaves, without freedmen, who precisely formed the trades' unions of the Roman world — what had they to do with these industrial and sedentary associations?

Secondly, in destroying the trades' unions with the municipalities, the barbarians destroyed them in the same manner — that is to say, imperfectly and gradually. The Franks, Burgundians, Saxons, and Visigoths had not, and had no idea of having, any logic in their destruction. They threw themselves brutally, as soldiers, athwart the Gallic-Roman civilization, and what could save itself was saved. Thus, some towns, and principally those which were at the same time capitals of provinces and capitals of a diocese, succeeded, by the influence of the bishop and the respect obtained by the Church, in preserving some fragments of their municipal government. We have already seen in the course of this book, that when the edict of Moulins took from the municipalities of the kingdom the jurisdiction of civil matters, the hotels de ville of Rheims, Toulouse, Boulogne, and Angoulême resisted, alleging and proving that they had that jurisdiction since the time of the Romans. For this reason, M. Raynouard and M. de Savigny have produced a great number of documents establishing that the municipalities in Gaul did not absolutely perish in consequence of the invasion.

Well! For the same reason, we find in the middle ages, long before the known establishment of modern trades' unions, traces of mysterious associations which the historian knows not where to place. These are some lost children of the vast system of the Roman unions

be more and more profitable to them as the South becomes more and more prosperous, and happy and contented because prosperous.

which the barbarians of the invasion overlooked in their seclusion, and which there lived a poor and sickly life, deprived of air and sunshine — that is to say, deprived of their support, viz. emancipations — like those mutilated and invalid municipalities for which we must seek long and minutely in the charters of the first and second races, and whose history, fall, and misfortunes must be known to recognize in them what Aulus Gellius calls "little Romes, made after the image of the great Rome."

We have, then, in the history of the middle ages, two kinds of trades' unions, as there were two species of communes. These were, first, the Roman unions, which perished, and of which we find here and there the ruins; next, the French unions, which came into existence, or rather were developed, under Philip Augustus, and were organized after the time of St. Louis.

For example, traces of the Roman unions are recognizable, among other documents, in a capitular of Dagobert II., of the year 630, concerning the organization of the bakers; in another capitular of Charlemagne, of the year 800, directing that the corporation of bakers should have their complement in the provinces; in a passage of the edict of Pistes, of the year 864, concerning the goldsmiths' union; finally, in what Ducange relates of the *rex arcariorum*, the *rex arbalestariorum*, the *rex merceriorum*, the *rex alatariorum*, the *rex juglatorum*, and the *rex ministellorum*. Moreover, the modern bakers' union of Paris seems to have been grafted on the ancient Roman corporation; for it was subject to a tax (*droit de hauban*) of a hogshead of wine paid to the king annually, and this tax is mentioned in a capitular of Dagobert II., of the year 630, and in another of Charlemagne, of the year 803.

We have already said that the trades' or labor unions always develop themselves parallel with the communes, and we have shown how they were two associations of the same origin, the same nature, almost for the same end. It is in the towns, then, that we must seek for the trades' unions; there where the freed races concentrate in the commune. Now, although the greater number of communes differ in some peculiarity of their interior organization, and the trades' unions of each town, formed from the point of view of the persons and things of that town, always present something peculiar and individual, nevertheless, both of these two species of associations are cast in the same mould almost, and it may be said that it is enough to know one commune and one trades' union to know all the communes and all the trades' unions. We therefore confine ourselves to an exposition in detail of the organization of the trades' unions formed in the commune of Paris, which will be in the main an exposition of all modern trades' or labor unions.

The first written and official document on the trades' unions of Paris dates from the year 1258, under the reign of St. Louis. It is the ordonnance of Stephen Boileau, prévôt-guard, known under the name of "*Register of trades and merchandise.*" To better comprehend the situation of these unions in relation to the government, we must say something of the different powers which governed the city of Paris in the middle ages.

We have already said that Paris had a commune — that is to say, the right of self-government. The seat of this government was the hotel de ville, which primitively bore the name of "*Parloir aux bourgeois.*" The inhabitants of Paris were divided, like those of every communal city, into burghers and dwellers. The burghers were those who were inscribed on the municipal rolls, and who enjoyed the right of commune. The dwellers were those who had their domicile in the city, without participating in its privileges.

The government of the city resided in the municipal council, and the supreme chief was a magistrate, who did not bear the name of mayor, as in most of the communes, but that of prévôt of merchants, (*Prévôt des marchands.*) See the historic reason for this special nomenclature.

There was at Paris, from the time of Tiberius, a Roman counting-house belonging to the general union of the boatmen of the empire. These boatmen carried on the commerce of the river, and their statutes served as the basis of the *customary* charter of Paris; for this charter was not written until 1411. Moreover, in 1170, Louis the Young, in speaking of the *custom* of Paris, called it ancient. The commune of Paris had, therefore, this peculiarity from its origin: that it was an association, a commune of merchants; which caused the name of prévôt of merchants to be given to its first magistrate, instead of the name of mayor, which was more usual.

However, the city did not include the seigniory of the commune only. It also included the seigniory of the king. The seigniory of the king was in virtue of his title of viscount, and it was under the charge of a lieutenant of the king, who bore the name of Prévôt of Paris.

We therefore must not confound the prévôt of merchants with the Prévôt of Paris. The former was a municipal magistrate; the latter an officer of the king; and, consequently, their jurisdictions were perfectly distinct and separate.

Stephen Boileau, who reduced to writing in 1258 the statutes of the trades' unions, was Prévôt of Paris; that is to say, the trades' unions received their institution from the royal power, like the Roman trades' unions after the reign of Trajan.

When Stephen Boileau reduced to writing the statutes of the trades' unions, they had already long been in existence. Philip Augustus is cited in many places of the register, and notably in the first title, as having regulated the trades. The prévôtal ordonnance of the year 1258 did not, therefore, create the trades' unions. It only brought them into relations with the royal power; and the work of Stephen Boileau consisted chiefly in bringing together into one body the peculiar customs of each trade, most of which had probably never been written.

The register of trades contained the statutes of one hundred industrial professions. We give them in the order of the register, and in their bare announcement we have a sort of summary of French industry in the thirteenth century.

They were the talmeliers, (bakers,) the millers, the corn merchants, the grain measurers, the auctioneers, the gaugers, the tavern keepers, the beer brewers, the hucksters of bread, salt, and sea fish; the hucksters of fruits and vegetables, the goldsmiths, the tinners, the ropemakers, the workmen in small lead and tin wares, the smiths, (workers in iron,) the farriers, the edge-tool makers, the cutlers, the locksmiths, the box and case makers, the brass-wire beaters, the copper and brass buckler makers, the iron-wire drawers, the brass-wire drawers, the nail makers, the hauberk makers, the bone-bead makers, the coral-bead makers, the amber and jet bead makers, the glass cutters, the gold and silver thread beaters, the tin beaters, the gold and silver leaf beaters, the thread and silk net makers, the spinners of silk with big spindles, the spinners of silk with little spindles, the thread and silk fringe makers, the workers in silk tissues, the branliers en fil, (breeches makers,) the silk and velvet drapers, the founders, the book-clasp makers, the shoe-buckle makers, the silk weavers, the lamp makers, the barrel makers, the carpenters, the masons, the stone cutters and plasterers, the dish and cup makers, the cloth weavers, the *sarrazinois* (quære, Saracen?) tapestry makers, the common tapestry and coverlet makers, the fullers, the dyers, the hosiers, the garment cutters, the linen merchants, the hemp and thread merchants, the hemp-cloth merchants, the pin makers, the sculptors of images of the saints, the painters of images of the saints, the oil makers, the tallow-candle makers, the scabbard makers, the scabbard trimmers, the comb and lantern makers, (*a*) the writing-desk makers, the cooks, the poulterers, the playing-dice makers, the button makers, the bath keepers, the clay potters, the mercers, the brokers, the bursars, the house painters and the saddlers, the saddle-tree makers, the blazon painters on saddles, the harness makers, the horse-bit makers, the leather dressers, the cordwainers, the sheepskin-shoe makers, the cobblers, the curriers, the glove makers, the hay merchants, the flower-headdress makers, the felt hatters, the cotton hatters, the peacock's-feather hatters, the furriers, the bonnet makers, the furbishers, the archers, the fishermen in the king's waters, the fresh-water fishermen, and the fishermen of the sea.

If, before going farther, we wish to find what points of resemblance the French trades' unions may have had to the Roman trades' unions, we must consider them in their relation to the chief of the State, in their relation to the persons composing them, and in their relation to each other.

Considered in their relation to the chief of the State, the French unions were divided, in the third century, into two categories. The first comprises those which required an authorization; the second, those which were only required to conform to the regulations of the trade. The Roman unions were never in an analogous condition; for we have seen that they were all free by conforming to the laws up to the time of Trajan, and that after that prince's time they were subject to a previous authorization. Besides, this division of the unions seems to have been very arbitrary, or at least it seems now

(*a*) Query, what natural connection was there in the thirteenth century between combs and lanterns? The compositor suggests that lantern frames as well as combs were made of horn.

impossible to find the theoretical reasons for it, if any there were. Thus, sometimes there were professions of great importance which were free, as that of goldsmith; and others, of small importance, which required an authorization, as that of farrier. Sometimes, on the contrary, professions of great importance, as that of baker, required the royal authorization; and others of less consequence, as that of ropemaker, were only subject to the customs of the trade. We have only observed one species of trades' unions which were always subject to a previous authorization, viz., those which involved public functions as it were, such as auctioneer, grain measurer, and gauger.

The situation of the free trades or professions was very simple. Any one could enter them on three conditions: first, of knowing the trade; second, of having the necessary capital, (*s'il a de quoi*, says the register;) third, of complying with the customs which governed the union. Subject to these three conditions, there was no limit to the number of their members.

The authorized professions were of two sorts: those which obtained their authorization from the Prévôt of Paris, and those which obtained their authorization from the prévôt of merchants; that is to say, which depended on the municipal authority. These were limited to three, viz. grain measurers, auctioneers, and gaugers.

Naturally, the necessity, for certain professions, of a previous authorization, limited, or at least restricted the number, which raised them to the condition of offices hereditary and salable for money, provided always that the heir or purchaser fulfilled the conditions of the trade. This is expressly stated in many titles of the register, and especially in title L, relative to cloth weavers.

To obtain permission to enter a profession, it was necessary, according to the nature of that profession, to present a petition either to the prévôt of merchants, at the hotel de ville, or to the Prévôt of Paris, at the castle. Then the applicant paid a fee in silver, was examined by the guards of the trade, and, if admitted, was installed, having taken the oath.

Considered in reference to the persons composing them, the French unions had still less resemblance to the Roman unions. We have seen that from the time of Constantine the latter formed a kind of necessary corps, impressing an indelible character, and that none who once entered could ever leave them — neither they nor theirs;

neither their persons nor their property. No such principle is observable in the French unions. Their members could always withdraw; and, although each profession possessed a common fund and a general treasury, the patrimony of the associates remained completely free and invariably distinct. This characteristic, peculiar to the trades' and labor unions of the middle ages, of leaving to their members perfect liberty of withdrawal, did not prevent their being connected, like the Roman unions, with the administrative system of the kingdom. For St. Louis and his successors employed the unions to collect the taxes. It was the peculiarity of different ancient institutions, tainted with the spirit of fatality or of absolute solidarity, to divest themselves of that on entering upon modern times. The trades' and labor unions and the curiæ may be cited as memorable examples.

There is, however, one exception to what we have said of the liberty of withdrawal possessed by members of the unions. Undeniable facts establish that the butchers could not quit their unions. In 1260, the great butchery of Paris belonged to twelve families, which, at the end of four hundred years, in 1660, were reduced to three. We easily comprehend how the extinctions enriched the survivors. Now, toward the middle of the fifteenth century, the butchers wished to retire from the union, or at least to rent their stalls to others. Then a decree of parliament, of the 2d April, 1465, intervened, requiring them to occupy their stalls in person. A century later, on a new occasion, this decision was confirmed by another decree of parliament, of the 4th of March, 1557.

We must not, however, exaggerate the importance of this fact, true as it is, in the general history of the trades' and labor unions. It is certain that it constituted an exception. Moreover, we should add that this exception is only relative to the epoch in which it manifested itself; for, under the first, and even under the second race, there still existed some Roman unions which were governed by the principles of Roman law. We have cited a capitular of Charlemagne, of the year 800, directing that the provincial judges should see to it that the bakers kept up their complement. The principle of absolute obligation, (*solidarité*,) which in the fifteenth century still oppressed the butchers, is then, as we have said, strange only for its time; and it only proves that the Roman traditions have penetrated much farther than is generally believed into some specialties of our history.

We find in the modern unions an element which was totally wanting in the ancient, and which requires a separate notice, viz. apprentices.

The ancient unions had no apprentices, for the very simple reason that the workmen they employed were slaves. Hence the complete absence in the Roman laws of regulations on apprenticeship, masterpiece, and admission to mastership.

The modern unions, at least from the time of the prévôtal ordonnance of 1258, which is their first charter of organization, have never employed any but free workmen. Besides, slaves commenced to become rare at that epoch.

Apprentices were divided into two classes, the sons of the masters, and strangers. Between these two kinds of apprentices there was this profound difference, that the number of the first was unlimited, that of the latter restricted. We add that the sons of the masters who were not legitimate, or born in lawful marriage, (*nés de loyal mariage*, as the register of trades says,) were in all respects assimilated to strangers.

A very important part of the internal laws of the unions was that which regulated the conditions of the work of the apprentices; and that is readily conceived when it is said that apprenticeship was the school of the masters, and that no one reached the first rank without having regularly passed through all the degrees of the hierarchy. It appears, without being able to find the reason for the fact, that the masterships were divided, in reference to apprentices, into two categories; some admitting an indefinite number, and others a very limited number. For example, the professions of silk draper and fringe maker, of gold and silver leaf beaters, of amber and coral bead makers, admitted only a restricted number of apprentices; those of gold and silver thread beaters, tin beaters, hauberk makers, admitted them at will. In the professions in which the number of apprentices was limited, the masters could ordinarily have but one, often two — sometimes, but rarely, three. The spinners in silk on big spindles had three, the goldsmiths but one, the cutlers two.

Generally, all apprentices were subject to two conditions: they engaged to serve their masters for a fixed time, and paid him a certain sum of money.

A goldsmith's apprentice was required to serve six years, a ropemaker's four, a cutler's six, a box maker's seven, and a buckle maker's eight. The amount paid for apprenticeship also varied. The box maker's apprentice paid twenty Parisian sous, the bead maker's thirty, the silk draper's six Parisian livres. Almost always the apprentice could substitute for the payment of money an increased length of service. Thus, a silk draper's apprentice paid nothing if he was willing to serve eight instead of six years; the box maker's, by serving eight years instead of seven.

The contract of apprenticeship was so strict and rigorous for the apprentice, that he not only could not quit before the expiration of his time, but the master could *sell* him to another for the remainder of his term of service. Nevertheless, this right of selling an apprentice was fixed and limited to certain extreme cases, such as a lingering sickness of the master, his quitting the business, excessive poverty, or departure for beyond seas. The apprentice, on his part, could buy his time; but if he did so before the expiration of his legal term of service, he could not receive the mastership. If the master workman died, his widow retained his right and kept the apprentice. If the master had no heirs, the apprentice could apply to the guards of the trade to which he belonged for a new master. The guards referred him to the Prévôt of Paris, who immediately granted his request.

When the time of their legal service was ended, the apprentices who wished to become masters made a *masterpiece* before the guards of the trade, presented a petition to the Prévôt of Paris or to the prévôt of merchants to obtain the mastership, and, on payment of the fees, were established. It often happened that the apprentices did not aspire to mastership, which always involved an establishment, and required a certain capital. Then, their service ended, they became what was called in the thirteenth century *vallez* or *sergans*. These were free workmen, going from shop to shop, from city to city, and working with masters for wages. Title II. of the register of trades, relative to goldsmiths, speaks of these workmen, who "knew how to gain a hundred sous a year, and their food and drink." Generally, masters could take as many *sergans* or *vallez* as they pleased.

Finally, we must consider the French unions in themselves; that is, in reference to their administrative organization.

We have already said that the number of their members was not fixed. This depended on the public necessities, and increased or diminished according to the bent of manners and the tendency of industry. At the commencement of the sixteenth century, the money-brokers' union, reduced to five or six heads of families, was so poor that it declared that it could not pay the expense of the silk robes they were required to wear on the entry of Mary of England, second wife of Louis XII.; while, sixty years later, the mercers' included twenty-five hundred families, and, in 1557, Henry II., on a general review of the infantry of Paris, found under arms a body of three thousand mercers, perfectly equipped.

However large or restricted it might be, every union, considered in itself, had two points of view, viz. administrative and religious.

The invocation of such and such holy personages, by every union of the middle ages, was no novelty. Among the pagans, the merchants specially invoked Mercury; the sailors, Neptune; laborers, Ceres and Triptolemus. In the middle ages, the drapers invoked Our Lady, (*Notre Dame*;) the grocers, St. Nicholas; the mercers, St. Louis; the furriers, St. Sacrament; the hosiers, St. Fiacre; the goldsmiths, St. Eloi.

Every union, then, as we have said, had two aspects, one religious, the other administrative; and two centres, a church and a bureau. In the church, the ceremonies and prayers of the union were held; in the bureau, the common interests and general affairs were discussed. To take the six corps of Paris in their order: The drapers had their brotherhood (*confrèrie*) at the principal altar of St. Pierre des Arces, and their community (*communanté*) in the *rue des Dechargeurs*, (street of porters,) in a house called the *carneaux*, (vent-hole,) which belonged in 1527 to Jean-le-Bossu, Archdeacon of Josas. The grocers had their brotherhood at Grands-Augustins, the mercers at St. Sepulchre, the furriers at Carmes des Billettes, the hosiers at the Church of St. Jaques-de-la-Boucherie, the goldsmiths in a chapel in the rue des Deux Portes; and as to their bureaux, the grocers had theirs in the cloister of St. Opportune, the mercers in the rue Quincampoix, the hosiers in the cloister of St. Jaques, and the goldsmiths in the rue des Deux Portes.

The French, like the Roman unions, had a general administration. To understand its mechanism, it is necessary to make first a short digression.

Between the thirteenth and sixteenth century, a kind of centralizing movement occurred in the unions, which consisted in grouping a certain number of them, under the name of *métiers*, (trades,) around a master-union, under the name of *corps*. In the time of St. Louis there were only the *métiers;* in the time of Louis XII. there were the *corps* and the *métiers*.

The primitive administration of the *métiers* was much less fixed and less regular than that of the *corps* was subsequently. There is no doubt that each of the *métiers* had a treasury, which in the register bore the name of "*boîte de la conflairie.*" It results, also, from a donation of twenty-four houses by Philip Augustus, in the commencement of his reign, to the drapers, and another of eighteen houses to the furriers, that these two unions, and probably all the others, had certain material interests in common. The administrators of the general interests of each union differed in their number, in the mode of election, and in the length of their terms of office.

These administrators bore the name of *prud'hommes* or *gardes*. Most of the trades had two; for example, the beer brewers, the tin potters, the rope makers, the iron cutlers, the locksmiths, the bone-bead makers, and the silk spinners. Others had three, as the goldsmiths and the knife cutlers; some four, as the fullers; some six, as the farriers; a small number eight, as the thread and silk fringe makers; finally, we find some which had twelve, as the talmeliers (bakers) and fruit hucksters.

It is certain that, primitively — that is to say, when the Roman traditions had not yet entirely disappeared, and at the epoch when royalty was not completely mixed up with the unions, the prud'hommes were elected by the corps. There were even in the register some trades that elected their guards, as the goldsmiths; but in most of the trades the prud'hommes were, at the beginning of the thirteenth century, nominated by the Prévôt of Paris; that is to say, by the king. For all the unions whose prud'hommes were nominated by the Prévôt of Paris, the duration of their functions was unlimited; for the prévôt maintained or changed them at will. But the fullers were an exception to this. Their prud'hommes, by special law, were changed every six months. In the unions in which the prud'hommes were elective, the usual term of their functions was for a year. The goldsmiths' union had this peculiarity, that the guards were not re-eligible until after the expiration of three years.

There remains one point to exhaust all that is necessary to be said about the *métiers* — that is, their jurisdiction. We know that in the middle ages, an epoch full of small associations, forming so many small and almost independent states, the jurisdictions were numerous. Thus, the scholar appealed to the university; the priest to the bishop; the burgher to the hotel de ville; the gentleman to the king. The trades, also, had a jurisdiction. This jurisdiction was not complete; that is to say, the trades had no tribunal before which every member of the union had the right of demanding a trial for any offence, as every scholar had the right of claiming the jurisdiction of the university. That could not be, because every member of an union of Paris was at the same time a burgher, and hence this latter character subjected him to the jurisdiction of the hotel de ville. The jurisdiction of the trades was partial, and only embraced offences committed against the statutes of each union.

Well! this jurisdiction of the trades was exercised either by the prévôt of Paris or by the grand officers of the crown. We know that the Roman unions all depended on the officers of the palace. It was the same with the unions of the middle ages, which royalty had subjected to its grand officers. Thus, the grand pantler had under him the bakers; the grand cook, the fishermen; the grand chamberlain, the mercers, drapers, furriers, and frippers; the grand butler, the wine merchants. The jurisdiction exercised by these grand officers carried with it an annual tax on the part of the trades, besides fines and confiscations. For this reason, the supreme mastership of the trades was, in fact, an endowment worthy of being conferred by feudal title.

Such was the situation of the trades toward the middle of the thirteenth century. We can follow the different variations which they subsequently underwent, first, in the forty or forty-five ordonnances relative to the unions, issued by the Prévôts of Paris down to the commencement of the fourteenth century, and, next, in the royal ordonnances down to the sixteenth, the epoch when they acquired a fixed organization.

Since the end of the fifteenth century, as we have said, the *corps* were already formed. Under Louis XII., on the entrance of Mary of England, there were six, called the *six corps of Paris*, and they ranked in this order: the drapers, the grocers, the mercers, the leather dealers, the hosiers, and the goldsmiths. Henry III. erected the wine merchants into a seventh corps, and their letters-patent were confirmed by Henry IV., Louis XIII., and Louis XIV. Nevertheless, the other corps were unwilling to receive them into their assemblies. Moreover, it was only after an infinite succession of troubles, disputes, wranglings, revolts, and suits that the rank of the corps was definitely settled as we have stated.

The six corps formed, as it were, the aristocracy of the trades, in this sense, that they expressed their interests and were their head. Their emblem was a Hercules, seated, trying to break a fasces of six rods, with this device: *Vincit concordia fratrum.* The six corps represented industry in great ceremonies, and in truth summed up all its political value.

At the commencement of the seventeenth century, the six corps petitioned the city for special arms. Master Christopher Sanguin, prévôt of merchants, granted their request, and accorded to them arms, as follows:

The drapers bore: azure, a ship of silver, with the banner of France, an open eye *en chef*, with this legend: *Ut cætera dirigat.* In fact, the drapers were the first corps. Others blazoned their escutcheon thus: silver, a vessel of gold, sails and flag azure, sailing on a sea of sinople. These were, as we see, the arms of inquiry. We have found no author who gives a reason for it.

The grocers bore: azure and gold couped. On the azure a silver hand holding golden scales. On the gold two ships floating gules, (red,) with the banner of France; two red stars en chef; with this device: *Lances et pondera servant.* In fact, the grocers had charge of the standard of weights at Paris.

The arms of the mercers were: sinople, three silver ships, with the banner of France, placed two and one, en chef a golden sun with eight rays, between two ships. Their device was, *Toto orbe sequimur.*

The leather dealers, who claimed to have received their arms from a Duke of Bourbon, Count of Clermont, grand chamberlain of France in 1368, bore: azure, a silver paschal lamb, holding a red banner; on it a golden cross. The shield was supported by two ermines, and had a ducal crown for its crest.

The hosiers, who only became a corps under Louis XII., by the withdrawal of the money-changers, bore: azure, five silver ships with the banner of France; en chef, a golden star.

The goldsmiths, confirmed in their privileges and statutes by Philip IV., received from him in 1330 their arms. They were: gules, (red,) a golden cross dentelled, cantoned on the first and fourth quarters with a golden cup; on the second and third, a golden crown; en chef, France. Their device was: *In sacra inque coronas.*

It is to be remarked that four of the six corps, viz. the drapers, grocers, mercers, and hosiers, had their arms by municipal grant, which explains why the ship (*nef*) of the coat of arms of the hotel de ville of Paris appears so abundantly on their escutcheons.

Such, with perhaps some other details of small importance, was the organization of the trades' unions of the middle ages. If the reader has observed with some care the general spirit of their statutes, he will have seen that they were at once a guaranty for society, for industry, and for the public.

The unions were a guaranty for society, first, because they regulated the condition of the working classes, maintained order and emulation among them, and were, in a measure, the guards of the most restless and turbulent parts of the population; next, because corporations of every kind are always conservative in their nature, and the countries where they exist can always venture more in liberal enterprises, as they are strongly restrained by the chains of traditions.

The unions were also a guaranty for industry, because they created a hierarchy among the laborers, establishing among them degrees, which were reached by time, labor, and intelligence; and because they inexorably closed the door of the professions to all those who did not bring in their hands the golden branch of talent and good conduct.

The unions were, finally, a guaranty for the public; for the strictness of those who guarded their statutes admitted to mastership only those who were long practised in a profession, and could prove, by the perfection of their *masterpieces*, that they accepted all its obligations, and were proficients in its exercise.

But how did it happen that, with all these incontestable advantages, the unions ended by becoming the objects of general animadversion, and the constituent assembly abolished them with as much enthusiasm as they did titles and feudal rights? How happened it that the masterships, that knighthood of the people, found no mercy at the hands of the democratic destructives of the end of the last century? And if burgher institutions fell pell-mell under their hands, along with royal institutions, was it blindness, contempt, or stupidity?

No! It must be admitted that it was not solely the fault of the constituent assembly that the unions fell. It was also the fault of the unions themselves.

From the middle of the fourteenth century, in 1358, Charles of Valois, Duke of Normandy, Dauphin of France, and regent of the kingdom during the captivity of King John, expressed in these terms, in an ordonnance relative to tailors, the coming condemnation of the unions. Speaking of the regulations concerning the unions, he said: "Generally they are made more in favor and for the profit of individuals of each trade than for the common good." Behold the true germ, which, in its development, has killed the unions — egotism.

In fact — and this was, however, less a crime of intention than a misfortune of the times — when the unions were established, it was without any general plan, and without any social preoccupation. Each of them only thought of itself, and thought only of aggrandizing itself, no matter at whose or what cost. Instead, then, of being co-ordinates, they were rather in a state of strife. This is why they perished.

Toward the end of the eighteenth century, the clashing of the opposite interests of the several unions rendered almost all progress in industry impossible, because each union was absolute master in the kind of work which the statutes guaranteed to them respectively. For example, if four or five trades had to co-operate in any product, each one of them could stop all improvement by refusing, through ignorance or interest, to do otherwise than their forefathers had done. It is, then, certain that the unions which founded professional industry in France, ended by becoming obstacles to its development; but as the evil came from want of unity and general agreement in their statutes, the remedy was to be found in their revision, and not in their destruction. The destructives of the constituent assembly therefore overstepped the mark; for, instead of removing the disease, they killed the patient.

---

# CHAPTER XX.

## SUMMARY.

HERE ends the task we have imposed on ourselves in this book; and that its general course may remain clearly traced on the mind of the reader, we sum up its principal ideas.

We commenced by stating the fact, subsequently proved in the course of the work, that the laboring and burgher classes, in all countries where they exist, came from a previous emancipation of slaves.

This fact once established, we were led to prove that primitively slavery existed among all the peoples of the world, without exception. Then we have inquired whence came this slavery universally existing in the first ages of every nation; and we have concluded, from the study and comparison of a great mass of facts, that slavery was born in the primitive family and, consequently, it was not originally established by the hand of man.

These ideas stated and discussed, we have followed the slave races to their emerging from slavery by emancipation, and have seen them divide into two great columns—one formed of the industrial freedmen, who gathered together in the cities; the other formed of the agricultural freedmen, who were scattered through the country. The first form the commune and the burghers; the second, feudalism and the peasants.

Arrived at this point, we have treated separately the history of these two great divisions of the freed races.

The commune appeared to us to be the administrative association of the freedmen; the trades' union their industrial association. As there are freedmen among all the peoples of the world, we have concluded that there were also communes and trades' unions among all the nations of the universe.

Feudalism seems to us to be the government which regulates the relations of the agricultural freedmen to their masters; and, as there have been agricultural freedmen in all countries, we have concluded that feudalism was an element of ancient as of modern history.

Below the burghers and the peasants, outside of the commune and feudalism, we have found those who *could not* support themselves, who form the class of beggars, and constitute pauperism.

Alongside of the burghers and the peasants, we have found those who were *unwilling* to live their life, and who, in the three great categories of literary slaves, courtesans, and bandits, gained by intellect, beauty, or force, what birth had refused to them.

Such, excepting some transpositions of chapters required by the logic of our ideas, is the book which we present to the public. It is a faithful picture of the historic fortune of the slave races, in which we see what they were before becoming, and to become, what they are.

We are stopped on the threshold of the present: there, where the historian meets the publicist; the affirmation theory; facts the idea.

# POSTSCRIPT.

WE have already alluded briefly (see p. xlviii.) to the repugnance of the non-slaveholding whites of the South to the proposition for negro enlistments in the Confederate armies; a repugnance which even the great name and magic influence of Robert E. Lee could not overcome. This proposition was advocated by General Lee at a late period of the civil war—perhaps too late to have changed the results. Reluctant as we are to detain our readers, we would feel that our part of this work was incomplete if we failed to notice the fact, that long before General Lee came to that conclusion, there was one man whose forecast anticipated that some such measure would be indispensable to the success of the Confederate cause. That man was Colonel John T. Pickett, who was selected, on account of his previous Mexican experience, as the first diplomatic agent of the Confederate States in Mexico. Early in the war—under date of Vera Cruz, February 22, 1862—he submitted, for the consideration of the Confederate Government, the following

"MEMORANDUM.

"Is there no mode by which we may be able to neutralize the hostility existing throughout the world against our institution of domestic servitude? It is in vain to attempt to correct the gross misapprehensions prevailing with regard to it. The word 'slavery' is sufficient to condemn it among the peoples. Can we not invent a better and more appropriate name for it? It is not 'slavery' as understood among men; but we bear the odium as though it were. The enactment of laws which would prohibit the separation of mothers and children, (though what white family is not so separated?) the granting to the negroes certain civil rights, (so to speak,)

— such as protection from cruel and arbitrary punishment, right to change their masters if maltreated, privilege to purchase their freedom, etc., etc.,— might go far toward the end so much to be desired. Practically, these things do exist to a certain extent. The force of public opinion is protection to the negro, not to speak of the interest and even affection of the master. But the world at large knows not these things, and cannot or will not be convinced; whereas, an expression of the supreme legislative will would appeal to the governments and to the enlightenment of the age. I resided for years in the British West Indies, made many visits to Hayti and to the Dominican Republic, have seen only too much of the fruits of indiscriminate equality among the mongrels and hybrids of Spanish America, and therefore no one can entertain sounder views on the great domestic question than I do. In short, emancipation *without* deportation would be national suicide; *with* it, a chimera."

These suggestions were not acted on for two reasons: first, because the question was a *local* one, belonging exclusively to the States, and the Confederate authorities had no constitutional power to touch it in any way; secondly, because their whole time, attention, thoughts, and energies were absorbed in the question of *defence* — of repelling the armed invasion of their territory.

Colonel Pickett's idea was, that the inauguration of a scheme of gradual emancipation would emasculate the Abolition party of the North, satisfy Europe, and secure intervention, peace, and independence; and that although the Constitution of the Confederate States gave to the Confederate Government no right to interfere with the local institutions of the States, yet the Confederate Congress might, by joint resolution, recommend some such action to the State Legislatures, and justify their recommendation by the plea of "*military necessity*," which in time of war covers, like charity at all times, a multitude of sins.

Colonel Pickett soon found that he could accomplish nothing by remaining in Mexico, and, without waiting for instructions from his Government, returned to take part in the active service of the field, as chief of staff to General Breckinridge. As Mr. Colwell, under the excitements of the war, came to the conclusion that negro slavery should be sacrificed to save the Union, so Colonel Pickett, from his standpoint, under the influence of his associations with the diplomatic representatives of the monarchies and empires of Europe, came to the conclusion that *the institution* should be sacrificed to secure European intervention, peace, and independence.

Subsequently, he ran as a candidate for the Confederate Congress, against General Humphrey Marshall, that he might officially and more effectually ventilate his views in favor of negro enlistments and gradual emancipation. He was defeated, not, as he supposes, by any intrigues of General Marshall, but because it got bruited about among the non-slaveholding whites that he was in favor of negro enlistments and gradual emancipation.

Still later, he learned that the Confederate Government contemplated sending another minister to Mexico, and, for the benefit of his successor in that mission, submitted the suggestions of his experience, as follows:

"The cause of Mexican hate toward us, as individuals and as a nation, is patent. . . . It may be said to arise, firstly, from the great aversion of the Mexicans to negro slavery; and, secondly, from jealousy of race, the natural dread a weaker people have for a stronger neighbor, and from the artfully contrived teachings of the United States Government as to past and future aggressions upon Mexican territory.

"As to the first proposition. It is impossible to unteach the Mexican mind on the subject of slavery. We daily feel what an abolition propaganda has done among a more enlightened people. But it ought to be in our power to persuade Mexican statesmen (for it will be with Mexicans that our diplomatist will have to deal, even under the government of Maximilian) that, although slavery has both its moral and political blessings, and as practised in the Confederate States, it is but a mode of hiring servants for life, while in other countries they are employed by the day, month, or year, yet we have never designed to force the institution upon our neighbor. It can be shown, too, that free colored people are regarded with more consideration and entitled to more substantial privileges among us, though not admitted to social and political equality, than in the United States. Our history will furnish instances. General Jackson treated the free colored inhabitants of New Orleans as 'citizens,' in a certain sense. We know that a large class in Mobile, of the present day, termed 'creoles,' are colored people, (whence the popular error as to the true signification of that word,) of French and Spanish admixture. It is also a fact that many adopted citizens of Texas have African blood in their veins. Neither did our Southerners in California object to the eminent Don Pio Pico because of his negro blood. But California, an Abolition State, refuses citizenship to the Chinese, (to which refusal the writer does not object, individually,) while, to my knowledge, some of the best families in Mexico have Chinese blood in their veins — the natural consequence of the annual galleon between Acapulco and Manilla. I was on very friendly terms with the head of one of these families, Don Luis Jauregui. But the most striking contrast of this whole picture would be the treatment which the negroes received from a New York mob not many months ago.

"It would be an ungracious office, but we might remind the Mexicans that they enslave their own race. Indeed, white *peons* are very numerous, and *peonage* is the most atrocious system ever conceived of. It is slavery for debt, without provision for infancy, sickness, or old age. It is transmitted from father to son, while with us the child takes the condition of the mother only. But hear Commodore Perry on the subject of Mexican peonage. 'God pity these poor creatures!' says the commodore in his journal, in reference to the laboring classes of the Lew Chew Islands. 'I have seen much of the world, have observed savage life in many of its conditions, but *never*, unless I may except the miserable *peons* of Mexico, have I looked upon such an amount of apparent wretchedness as these squalid slaves would seem to suffer.'

"It is a system which would have disgraced the laws of Draco, which are said to have been written in blood. If we were as hypocritical and meddlesome as our Northern brethren, and were in a condition to do so, we might *cajole* the world by a *crusade* against this enslavement of white men. We might create a great sensation, too, by broaching a scheme for the amalgamation of the white and red races of the continent. Why should it not be as great an honor to claim the blood of Montezuma as that of Powhatan? At least, let us impress Mexicans with the fact that we have no prejudice against their native race — that Indians are citizens with us, and sit in our national legislature. It would be well, also, to explain to them that it is in the abolition programme to colonize Mexico with North American negroes of the Protestant (i. e. 'heretic') faith, and speaking the English language.

"As a proof that Mexico is thoroughly abolitionized, I will mention that, during my long residence as United States Consul at Vera Cruz, I never succeeded in reclaiming, by intervention of local authority, a single negro deserter from the vessels of my nation; while, on the other hand, I scarcely ever failed to have the white sailors returned promptly. I think the accomplished gentleman* mentioned in connection with the secretaryship of the new mission has some official knowledge of this fact. I will dismiss this part of my theme by suggesting that the envoy procure some of our standard Southern works on the slavery question. They may be useful to him, and cannot, probably, be procured in Mexico. He can easily obtain the published Northern view of the subject in that capital, and should do so. *Fas est ab hoste doceri.*"

Colonel Pickett is an accomplished scholar, a sound thinker, a quick and acute observer. Yet the standpoint from which his observations were taken did not command a view of the whole field. He looked at the subject only as a diplomatist, intent on one object, viz. peace and independence through the instrumentality of an European intervention. Consequently, like M. Guizot, (see *ante*, p. 134,) with many clear and correct views, he stopped halfway on his road to a great discovery. He saw that the world is governed by *sensations;* but he did not prosecute his inquiries far enough to discover *who created* these *sensations*, and for what purposes. If he had done so, he would have seen that *self-interest* was at the bottom; that "man advances in the execution of a plan which he has not conceived, of which he is not even aware, and which he comprehends very imperfectly," while "its designs are centred in a single or in few minds."

He saw that the diplomatic representatives of European despotisms were bitterly and unchangeably opposed to the *peculiar institution of negro* slavery in the Southern States, while they had no word

* Walker Fearn, Esq., Secretary of Legation to Mexico with the Hon. John Forsyth, Minister Plenipotentiary.

of sympathy for the far more wretched condition of the *peons* of Mexico, nor for the slaves of the Lew Chew Islands and of the British East Indies.

He did not stop, or rather he did not go on, to inquire why this was so. If he had, he would have discovered that negro servitude, as it existed in the Southern States, being a *peculiar* institution, produced *peculiar* political and politico-economical results.

1st. Its tendency was to strengthen the democratic principle of political and social equality among the rich and poor whites.

2d. It elevated the whites, however poor they might be, above the degradation of selling their votes.

3d. It *married* capital to labor, by making it the interest of capital to keep up wages, which went into its pocket, and to keep down the cost of living, which came out of its pocket.

4th. The result of these *peculiar* influences was to give *stability* to *free* institutions, causing the Southern States to be "*constantly inclined most strongly to the side of liberty; the first to see and the first to resist the encroachments of power;* and, by the *marriage* of capital to labor, it enlisted capital on the side of labor against that legislative policy which seeks to cheapen labor, to increase taxes, and to squander the taxes paid by labor for the profit of capital." (See Calhoun's speech, *ante*, p. xxxii.)

If Colonel Pickett had pushed his observations beyond the diplomatic into the politico-economical field of inquiry, he would have discovered that, on the part of the advocates of centralism and of capital, emancipation was the chief object of the war; because,

1st. Emancipation would *divorce* Southern capital from labor;

2d. It would destroy the chief support of the democratic principle of equality among the whites, and place the Government on *the inclined plane* to monarchy;

3d. It would substitute for the *incorruptible* votes of the poor whites of the South the *cheaply purchasable* votes of negro freedmen, to neutralize the votes of the working and burgher classes of the North and West.

When Colonel Pickett said that "emancipation without deportation would be national suicide; with it, a chimera," he spoke of *immediate emancipation in mass.* His observations and experience in Mexico and the West Indies doubtless satisfied him, as ours did us, that *deportation* was surrounded with practical difficulties which made the scheme chimerical. Those difficulties were, first, the enormous expense of moving 4,000,000 of people, and of taking care of them *in transitu*, and until located in new homes; second, their inability to take care of themselves after they were located, as shown by the fate of the American negro colony on the island of Santo Domingo; third, the inhumanity of the "frightful misery" which must inevitably result from turning them off to take care of themselves; and, finally, because their labor was indispensable where they were, and could not be supplied except by a slow and gradual system, running through a long course of years.

This idea of gradual emancipation *with* deportation originated with Mr. Jefferson, fifty years ago—long before the very *peculiar* politico-economical results of the *peculiar institution* were analyzed by the master mind of Calhoun. Up to the close of the war, deportation of the negroes was a favorite idea with most of the prominent leaders of the *monarchical cheap-labor* party.

On the 8th of December, 1859, Senator Trumbull said:

"When we say that all men are created equal, we do not mean that every man in organized society has the same rights. We do not tolerate that in Illinois. I know that there is a distinction between these two races, because the Almighty himself has marked it upon their very faces; and, in my judgment, man *cannot, by legislation or otherwise*, produce a perfect equality between these races, so that they will live happily together. . . . I trust that an idea foreshadowed by Mr. Jefferson will hereafter become, although it is not now, part of the creed of the Republican party. I mean the idea of the deportation of the free negro population from this country. . . . It seems impracticable to transport this great population to Africa. Let us obtain a country nearer home; and I know I may say for the people whom I represent, we will contribute liberally of our means to relieve the country of the free negro population. I hope it may become the policy of the Republican party . . . to deliver the country from the only element which ever seriously threatened its peace, and furnish the means of relieving it from the evils of a large free negro population. By such a course we may lay the foundation for continued and permanent prosperity."

On the 13th of April, 1860, Senator John Sherman, in a speech at the Cooper Institute, New York, favored the idea of the "gradual colonization of the negro population of the United States in the Central American States," where they might be "free from the domination of the white race."

On the 7th of March, 1860, Senator Wade, of Ohio, said, in the Senate of the United States:

"This great Government owes it to various pressing considerations to provide a means whereby the free negroes may emigrate to some congenial clime, where they may be maintained to the mutual benefit of all. This would insure a *separation of the races.* Let them go into the tropics. There are vast tracts of most fertile and inviting lands, in a climate perfectly congenial to that class of men, where the negro will be predominant, where his nature seems to be improved, and all his faculties, both mental and physical, are fully developed, and where the white man degenerates in the same proportion as the black man prospers. Let them go there; *let them be separated;* it is easy to do it. They will be so far removed from us that they cannot form a disturbing element in our *political economy.* . . . I hope, after that is done, to hear no more about negro equality, or anything of the kind. We shall be as glad to rid ourselves of these people as anybody else can."

On the 21st of August, 1858, at Ottawa, Ill., Mr. Lincoln said:

"I have no purpose to introduce political and social equality between the white and black races. There is a physical difference between the two, which, in my judgment, will probably *forever* forbid their living together upon the footing of perfect equality; and, inasmuch as it becomes a necessity that there must be a difference, I am in favor of the race to which I belong having the superior position."

In the course of his canvass with Mr. Douglas, in Illinois, in 1858, Mr. Lincoln repeatedly declared that he was opposed to "a social and political equality between the white and black races;" that he "was not in favor of negro citizenship;" and that he would "to the very last stand by the law of Illinois which forbade the marriage of white people with negroes." He also declared that, in his "opinion, it would be best for all concerned to have the colored population in a State by themselves."

Finally, in his messages to Congress and otherwise, Mr. Lincoln urgently advocated *gradual emancipation with deportation.*

In his annual message, December 3, 1861, he said:

"To carry out the plan of colonization may involve the acquiring of territory, and also the appropriation of money beyond that to be expended in the territorial acquisition. . . . If it be said that the only legitimate object of acquiring territory is to furnish homes for *white* men, this measure effects that object; for the *emigration of colored* men leaves *additional room for white* men remaining or coming here. Mr. Jefferson, however, placed the importance of procuring Louisiana more on *political* and commercial grounds than on providing room for population.

"On this whole proposition, including the appropriation of money with the acquisition of territory, does not the expediency amount to absolute necessity—that *without which the Government itself cannot be perpetuated?*"

This amounts to an assertion by Mr. Lincoln that emancipation without deportation would be national suicide.

But why tear from their homes, and from the "kind, protecting care" they then enjoyed, 4,000,000 of negroes, to banish them to the "frightful misery" of taking care of themselves in the Central American States? Did any idea of good will for the negroes enter into this scheme for their banishment? Surely not; for when Mr. R. M. T. Hunter, at the Hampton Roads conference, alluded to the sufferings which would result to the old and infirm, and to the women and children, who were unable to support themselves, the only answer was the following story, told by Mr. Lincoln:

"An Illinois farmer was congratulating himself with a neighbor upon a great discovery he had made, by which he could economize time and labor in gathering and taking care of the food crop for his hogs, as well as trouble in looking after and feeding them during the winter.

"'What is it?' said the neighbor.

"'Why, it is,' said the farmer, 'to plant plenty of potatoes, and when they mature, without either digging or housing them, turn the hogs in the field, and let them get their own food as they want it.'

"'But,' said the neighbor, 'how will that do when the winter comes, and the ground is hard frozen?'

"'Well,' said the farmer, '*let 'em root!*'"

(See the War between the States, by A. H. Stephens, vol. ii., p. 615. Barrett's Life of Lincoln, p. 827.)

From the inhumanity of saying to the old and infirm negroes, and to the women and children who were unable to support themselves, "*Root, hog, or die,*" the Southern people shrank with greater indignation than Plutarch felt for Cato. (See p. 275.) There was no trace of benevolence or pity for the negroes in that sentiment.

Did an overcrowded territory require that the negroes should be driven out, like the Indians, to make *additional room* for white men? It is true that Mr. Lincoln's message of December 3, 1861, gives prominence to this argument, and his message of December 1, 1862, elaborates the idea that the time is fast approaching when our population will have so increased, that, "*instead of receiving the foreign-born, as now, we shall be compelled to send part of the native-born* (*the negroes*) *away.*" To show when that time would probably arrive, Mr. Lincoln, or rather Mr. Seward, (for his handiwork is clearly perceptible in both messages,) said: "Several of our States are already above the average of Europe — 73⅓ to a square mile. Massachusetts has 157, Rhode Island 133, Connecticut 99, etc., etc."

Then he gives a tabular statement of decennial increase, showing that in 1930 our population *may* reach the overcrowded number of 251,680,914; and concludes thus:

"These figures show that our country *may* be as populous as Europe now is, at some point between 1920 and 1930 — say about 1925 — our territory, at 73⅓ persons to the square mile, being the capacity to contain 217,186,000."

Now, this argument of Mr. Seward, and his ingenious sophistries about capital and labor in the same messages, were as false and as deceptive as his dogma of the irrepressible conflict between free labor and slave labor. They were adroitly and ably prepared for the express purpose of misleading and enticing the working and burgher classes of the North into an indiscretion, a false step, against their natural ally and *politically-wedded spouse;* the consequence of which would be, and since has been, a declaration of the Attorney-General that labor is now a divorced grass-widow!

The so-miscalled Republican party were not acting in good faith with white labor when they endeavored, in 1861 and 1862, to make it appear that their purpose was to drive out the negroes to make additional room for the rapidly increasing white population. This is apparent from the fact that, since their object has been accomplished, by *divorcing* capital from labor by emancipation, we hear nothing more said about deporting the negroes. So far from being the special friends of the negroes, they were actuated by a malevolence to the negro almost as atrocious as Sherman's treatment of the women and children of the white working classes of Atlanta. This is apparent from the proposition to drive away the negroes from their comfortable homes, and say to their old and infirm and women and children, "*Root for yourselves, like hogs, or die!*"

Moreover, in the same message, in speaking of our vast territory of 2,963,000 square miles, Mr. Seward admits that they furnish abundant room, a broad national homestead, an ample resource against an overcrowded condition for at least fifty years to come — perhaps much longer. Then, why drive the poor negro away now, into the Central American States, to Santo Domingo, or elsewhere?

Mr. Seward, the Oily Gammon of politics, throws out a cautious intimation that, like Mr. Jefferson's acquisition of Louisiana, there was a *political* object to be gained. Bluff Ben Wade, in his bluff way, blurts out the true answer, and says, "*The negroes form a disturbing element in our* POLITICAL ECONOMY."

Why disturbing? We have already given the true answer, but it cannot be repeated too often. If Mr. Wade was candidly and confidentially explaining this *disturbance* to one of his party friends or followers, his language, substituting *dashes* for the oaths with which he sandwiches his discourse, would be about as follows:

"This — — peculiar institution, under which these — — negroes exist in this country, has — — peculiar results. — — —, it marries capital to labor. It makes the — — owners of negroes vote with the — — working-men in the North and West. — — they want to keep up wages, because wages go into their — — pockets. They legislate with a view to keep down the cost of living, because they have to feed and clothe and nurse and take care of the — — negroes, and that comes out of their pockets. And — —, they go in for what they call an honest and economical administration of the Government, and — — they oppose our little occasional appropriations of a few millions or so, with which to enrich our party friends; and — —, they whine about these paltry millions coming partly out of their own pockets and partly out of the pockets of the — — working and burgher classes of the North and West. But — — —, these — — owners of negroes treat — — poor white men as equals. Now, all these — — disturbances of our political economy grow out of this — — *marriage* of capital to labor in the South. We must *divorce* them. We must separate the white from the — — negro race. We must send the — — negroes off into the tropics. Then Southern capital will vote with Northern and Western capital, and we can, by subtle and artful fiscal contrivances of legislation, impose as many burdens on the — — working-men, and grant as many privileges to capital, and make as many and as large appropriations for the benefit of our party friends as we — — please. And if we can get *rid* of these — — negroes by sending them away into the tropics, we can get rid of the — — democratic notion of the — — slave power about the equality of white men, which this — — peculiar institution fosters."

As we have said, there can be no doubt that Mr. Seward prepared those portions of Mr. Lincoln's annual messages of 1861 and 1862 relative to the deportation of the colored population. It is not to be supposed, however, that Mr. Lincoln would have sent those messages to Congress without the concurrence and approval of the other members of his cabinet. These were S. P. Chase, Simon Cameron, Gideon Welles, Caleb B. Smith, Edward Bates, and Edwin M. Stanton. Now, if Mr. Lincoln and these his cabinet officers, and Senators Trumbull, Wade, and Sherman are to be accepted as the authorized exponents of the principles and policy of the so-miscalled Republican party, we have, in these messages and in the speeches of those senators, an official declaration of a purpose to drive the colored population out of the country, to make more room for white population, accompanied with the suggestion that it was a *necessity, without which the Government itself could not be perpetuated!*

Let the colored population bear this always in mind!!

Let the white population of the North and West bear in mind that since then the so-miscalled Republican party have taken a new departure!!!

Now, instead of "sending the negro population into the Central American States, where they may be free from the domination of the white race," they have subjected the white race in the South to the domination of the negro. Why this new departure? Because they wish to use the cheaply purchasable votes of the negro freedmen to neutralize the votes of the white working and burgher classes of the North and West, and hope so to use 4,000,000 of negro freedmen as to secure to themselves the power to govern and tax 40,000,000 of whites.

What Attorney-General Akerman says is true: "*Emancipation has* DIVORCED *the interests of* CAPITAL *from the interests of* LABOR." By this divorce the working and burgher classes have lost their "*natural ally.*" Now, they must, single-handed and alone, resist the encroachments of power, and the "subtle and artful fiscal contrivances by which capital seeks to divide the wealth of all civilized communities so unequally, and to allot so small a share to those by whose labor it was produced, and so large a share to the non-producing classes."

This divorce was intended to be, and is, complete and perpetual. It is a divorce *a mensa et thoro* and *a vinculo.* There is no appeal. The decree is irreversible, and *it forbids the parties from marrying again.* No one at the North or West, not one in ten thousand at the South, indulges in the delusive dream of a restoration of negro slavery.

What remains? Much of hope and encouragement in the future of the working and burgher classes. With their eyes opened to the *tricks* by which centralism and capital *cajoled* them into a crusade against their natural allies, and by brute force "divorced capital from labor by emancipation," they may find in the experience of the past a light to guide them in the future. If they would successfully resist the encroachments of power, and the artful contrivances of capital, they must go back to the political principles of Washington,

Jefferson, and Calhoun; principles which Washington, Jefferson, and Calhoun termed *republican*, while the monarchists and capitalists of New England, in derision and by way of reproach, called them *democratic*.

A few more words to the National Labor party. On the 25th of January, 1871, their committee, under a resolution of the National Labor Congress held at Cincinnati, in August, 1870, called a convention to meet *at Columbus, Ohio, at* 10 *o'clock, A. M., on the third Wednesday of October*, 1871, for the purpose of nominating candidates for the offices of President and Vice-President of the United States, and the transaction of such other business as may properly come before them.

On the 29th of May, 1871, H. M. Turner, (negro,) as President of the Georgia State Convention, issued a proclamation addressed "to the *colored citizens* of the States of Alabama, Arkansas, Delaware, Florida, Georgia, Kentucky, Louisiana, Tennessee, Maryland, Mississippi, Missouri, North Carolina, South Carolina, Texas, Virginia, West Virginia, and the Territory of Columbia."

This proclamation calls a convention of the *colored citizens* of the States above named to meet at *Columbia, S. C., on the* 18*th day of October*, 1871, *at* 12 *o'clock, M.*

Now let the working and burgher classes of the North and West take special notice of these dates! Why this call, in May, 1871, for a negro convention at Columbia on the *same day in October* selected by the committee of the National Labor party as early as January, 1871?

It is another *trick* of imperialism and capital to organize the negro vote of all the Southern States in the interest of imperialism and capital, and to neutralize *by that negro vote of the Southern States* any action that may be taken at Columbus, Ohio, by the working and burgher classes of the North and West, against the interests of imperialism and capital.

Look into and think about the purposes and objects of this *little trick!*

BEN. E. GREEN.

WASHINGTON, *June* 12*th*, 1871.

# ADDENDA TO TRANSLATOR'S PREFACE.

SUPPLEMENT TO THE FOURTH ANNUAL REPORT OF THE SPECIAL COMMISSIONERS OF THE REVENUE. COST OF LABOR AND SUBSISTENCE IN THE UNITED STATES. TABLES SHOWING THE COMPARATIVE AND AVERAGE WEEKLY WAGES PAID, ETC., ETC. PREPARED BY EDWARD YOUNG, IN CHARGE OF THE BUREAU OF STATISTICS. WASHINGTON: GOVERNMENT PRINTING-OFFICE. 1870.

THE foregoing is the title of an official document sent to us by a Member of Congress,* to convince us, by the statistics it professes to give, that we are wrong in our historic theory that one of the main purposes and results of the late civil war was to reduce wages and increase the cost of living.

On careful examination, we find this document remarkable alike for the absurdity of its multitudinous errors, and for the very manifest purpose of deception, with which it has been carefully and elaborately prepared, as a campaign document, to mislead and *again* betray the working and burgher classes into the support of the (so-*mis*called) Republican party.

In seventy-five octavo pages the Bureau of Statistics gives sixty-seven tables of figures, doubtless supposing that no one would ever take the trouble to wade through them.

The first fifty-eight tables are intended to produce the impression that, under the policy of the (so-*mis*called) Republican Administration, there has been an increase in wages, amounting to an average of forty-eight per cent., as summed up in Table 57, on page 57, as follows:

* Hon. John Coburn, of Indiana.

TABLE SHOWING THE PERCENTAGE OF INCREASE IN MONTHLY WAGES, WITH BOARD, PAID FOR FARM AND OTHER LABOR, IN THE UNITED STATES, IN 1869 OVER 1860.

| STATES. | Experienced hands (summer.) | Experienced hands (winter.) | Ordinary hands (summer.) | Ordinary hands (winter.) | Common laborers other than farm. | Female servants. | Average increase per cent. |
|---|---|---|---|---|---|---|---|
| Maine | 55 | 48 | 45 | 45 | 36 | 44 | 46 |
| New Hampshire | 46 | 46 | 45 | 33 | 55 | 64 | 48 |
| Vermont | 65 | 59 | 62 | 59 | 53 | 75 | 62 |
| Massachusetts | 60 | 58 | 62 | 76 | 58 | 59 | 62 |
| Rhode Island | 57 | 80 | 50 | 100 | 67 | 100 | 75 |
| Connecticut | 88 | 50 | 67 | 50 | 87 | 75 | 69 |
| New York | 66 | 57 | 55 | 50 | 55 | 93 | 62 |
| New Jersey | 81 | 76 | 81 | 81 | 96 | 89 | 84 |
| Pennsylvania | 64 | 70 | 59 | 64 | 51 | 65 | 62 |
| Delaware | 43 | 20 | 50 | 29 | ... | 100 | 40 |
| Maryland | 67 | 75 | 60 | 50 | 60 | 100 | 69 |
| West Virginia | 38 | 38 | 40 | 42 | 25 | 40 | 37 |
| Ohio | 48 | 48 | 46 | 45 | 44 | 59 | 48 |
| Indiana | 36 | 60 | 41 | 33 | 42 | 47 | 43 |
| Illinois | 46 | 42 | 42 | 40 | 50 | 69 | 48 |
| Michigan | 62 | 64 | 53 | 60 | 62 | 53 | 59 |
| Wisconsin | 42 | 42 | 42 | 31 | 36 | 44 | 39 |
| Minnesota | 60 | 59 | 66 | 58 | 69 | 59 | 62 |
| Iowa | 50 | 48 | 56 | 51 | 54 | 61 | 53 |
| Kansas | 35 | 69 | 58 | 32 | 48 | 48 | 48 |
| Nebraska | 83 | 83 | 67 | 50 | 50 | 46 | 63 |
| Missouri | 65 | 37 | 65 | 75 | 63 | 102 | 68 |
| Kentucky | 28 | 37 | 32 | 20 | 27 | 29 | 29 |
| Virginia | 22 | 15 | 21 | 18 | 15 | 25 | 19 |
| North Carolina | 40 | 26 | 25 | 15 | 25 | 38 | 28 |
| South Carolina | 36 | 25 | 33 | 38 | 19 | 50 | 33 |
| Georgia * | 11 | 20 | 1 | 9 | 10 | 17 | 11* |
| Alabama | 30 | 26 | 25 | 27 | 15 | 16 | 23 |
| Mississippi | 46 | 54 | 46 | 66 | 50 | 20 | 47 |
| Louisiana | 88 | 85 | 60 | 31 | 34 | 33 | 66 |
| Texas | 54 | 71 | 24 | 40 | 38 | 15 | 40 |
| Arkansas | 35 | 48 | 37 | 66 | 50 | 20 | 43 |
| Tennessee | 23 | 26 | 27 | 24 | 38 | 40 | 29 |
| Average in United States, exclusive of Pacific States and the Territories | 51 | 51 | 47 | 46 | 46 | 51 | 48 |

* The percentages of increase here given, although accurately computed, do not indicate the true advance in the wages paid. This arises from the fact that while there were nineteen returns from Georgia giving the wages in 1869, but six of them gave those of 1860. The true increase in the monthly wages paid in 1869 over 1860 was about 23 per cent. instead of 11.

Under the heading, "EXPENSES OF LIVING," Tables 59 to 66, both included, (pages 58 to 73,) are intended to produce the impression that the cost of living has been reduced, while wages have gone up 48 per cent. on an average. In order to make this appear, the Bureau of Statistics selects the years 1867 and 1869 for comparison, and gives prominence to wheat flour, which, for New England, it puts at $12.35 in 1867, and $9.15 in 1869; for the Middle States, at $12.50 in 1867, and $7.85 in 1869; for a portion of the Western

States, at $12.71 in 1867, and $6.41 in 1869; for other Western States and Territories, at $8.67 in 1867, and $5.35 in 1869; and for the Southern States, at $10.72 in 1867, and $9.50 in 1869.

The poet says:

> "Oh! what a tangled web we weave
> When first we practise to deceive."

The Bureau of Statistics, absorbed in its figures, had never read these lines, or did not appreciate the exhortation to honest dealing which they contain; or else it relied on its formidable array of figures to deter any one from attempting to unravel its tangled web of deceit. It is obvious that the Bureau was "*practising to deceive*" when it selected the years 1867 and 1869, and gave this prominence to the varying price of wheat flour, in order to produce the impression on the working and burgher classes that the effect of Radical policy had been to reduce the cost of living. For, this difference in the price of flour was caused, not by any beneficial influence of Radical policy, but partly by the difference in the seasons, and partly by that subtle and artful fiscal contrivance, by which the wheat-growers of the West are placed in the power of the great moneyed aristocracy for the means, with which to move their crops to market; thereby enabling Eastern capital to depress the price of Western wheat at pleasure.

But even admitting that the Bureau's figures are correct and reliable, (which they are not,) they disprove the very idea, which this elaborate document was concocted to sustain. For on pages 74 and 75 we have a table of the "comparative cost of building-materials, and of dwelling-houses," in 1861 and 1869, which shows that "the *true average increase in the cost of materials and labor required in building a dwelling-house suitable for workmen was* 88 *per cent.*"

Now, this is a much more reliable criterion of the increase or decrease of the cost of living than the difference between the cost of wheat flour in 1867 and 1869; and even if it were true that wages had advanced 48 per cent. from 1860 to 1869, how are the working and burgher classes benefited, when that increase of wages is accompanied by an increase of 88 per cent. in the cost of living?

As to Table 57, page 57, (above quoted,) which pretends to show the percentage of increase in monthly wages, with board, etc., we *know* that in Georgia, where we have lived since 1855, and we *believe* that in the other Southern States, instead of an increase of 23, or even 11 per cent., there has been an actual decrease of from 25 to 50 per cent. on a general average, and not taking into account the exceptional cases of high wages paid for hands in some of the swindling railroad operations, based on State bonds, which, if not repudiated, will bankrupt the States for the profit of a few individual carpet-baggers and scalawags.

Neither can we believe that this table is reliable as to the Eastern, Middle, and Western States.

First, because we *know* that it is wrong as to Georgia, and *believe* it to be wrong as to other Southern States.

Secondly, because it is obviously got up with great care in the interest of the Radical party, and with a premeditated design to "practise to deceive."

Thirdly, because, as the Bureau of Statistics admits, in an introductory note, it is "*the result, mainly, of inquiries made through the assistant assessors of internal revenue in the various collection districts of the United States*"—a very unreliable authority.

Finally, because a mere reading of Table 65, on page 72, which professes to give a summary of the results of all these inquiries and figures, will show to any man of common sense that it is utterly unreliable, not to use the much stronger language which the absurdities of that table would suggest.

It is as follows:

TABLE SHOWING THE AVERAGE WEEKLY EXPENDITURES OF WORKMEN'S FAMILIES IN SOME OF THE MANUFACTURING TOWNS OF THE UNITED STATES IN 1869.

| ARTICLES. | Two adults. | Parents and one child. | Parents and two children. | Parents and three children. | Parents and four children. | Parents and five children. | Parents and six children. | Parents and seven children. | Parents and eight children. | General average. | General average in 1867. |
|---|---|---|---|---|---|---|---|---|---|---|---|
| Bread and flour | $0.75 | $0.78 | $0.85 | $0.95 | $1.29 | $1.37 | $1.73 | $2.50 | $2.37 | $1.39 | $1.99 |
| Meat of all kinds | 1.25 | 1.60 | 1.75 | 1.92 | 2.21 | 3.09 | 2.92 | 3.00 | 4.68 | 2.48 | 2.46 |
| Lard | 24 | 33 | 33 | 44 | 40 | 35 | 63 | 33 | 61 | 39 | 33 |
| Butter | 1.00 | 71 | 82 | 1.10 | 1.26 | 98 | 1.35 | 1.32 | 2.88 | 1.27 | 1.12 |
| Cheese | 20 | 12 | 14 | 16 | 20 | 11 | 26 | 22 | 18 | 16 | 26 |
| Sugar and molasses | 69 | 74 | 92 | 92 | 1.18 | 85 | 1.18 | 76 | 1.80 | 1.00 | 1.01 |
| Milk | 59 | 41 | 44 | 37 | 50 | 58 | 26 | 56 | 1.26 | 55 | 46 |
| Coffee | 30 | 20 | 23 | 32 | 32 | 34 | 34 | ....... | 65 | 30 | 25 |
| Tea | 63 | 23 | 39 | 38 | 46 | 57 | 75 | 50 | 35 | 47 | 46 |
| Fish, fresh and salt | 10 | 13 | 25 | 20 | 22 | 24 | 23 | 20 | 16 | 19 | † |
| Soap and starch | 25 | 17 | 22 | 17 | 23 | 25 | 18 | 16 | 54 | 24 | 29 |
| Salt, pepper, and vinegar | 12 | 09 | 08 | 12 | 12 | 11 | 18 | 10 | 20 | 12 | 16 |
| Eggs | 30 | 25 | 21 | 24 | 29 | 15 | 06 | 20 | 58 | 25 | 31 |
| Potatoes and other vegetables | 30 | 44 | 61 | 47 | 73 | 80 | 60 | 40 | 88 | 58 | 83 |
| Fruits, fresh and dried | 30 | 26 | 33 | 21 | 42 | 46 | 27 | 50 | 62 | 39 | 36 |
| Fuel | 1.00 | 96 | 74 | 1.09 | 1.20 | 1.13 | 88 | 1.21 | 1.50 | 1.08 | 91 |
| Oil or other light | 30 | 22 | 25 | 23 | 21 | 23 | 19 | 16 | 22 | 22 | 22 |
| Other articles | 1.11 | 22 | 54 | 21 | 21 | 20 | 35 | ....... | 38 | 35 | 73 |
| Spirits, beer, and tobacco | ....... | 23 | 02 | 13 | 35 | 47 | 27 | 05 | 12 | 16 | † |
| House rent | *4.50 | 2.17 | 2.23 | 2.29 | 2.17 | *3.34 | 2.25 | 2.25 | 2.56 | 2.64 | 2.14 |
| Taxes | ....... | 37 | 03 | 12 | 05 | 24 | 18 | ....... | 30 | 13 | † |
| For benevolent objects | 39 | 34 | 58 | 40 | 34 | 25 | 30 | 2.00 | 60 | 57 | † |
| Total per week (clothing excepted) | 14.32 | 10.97 | 11.96 | 12.44 | 13.36 | 16.11 | 15.36 | 16.42 | 23.44 | 14.93 | 14.29 |

* The increased cost of house rent, and the use of more expensive provisions, render the expenses of these families higher than some of larger size.

† Not furnished in 1867. Deducting these, the average weekly expenses of families in 1869, as compared with 1867, will be reduced to $13.88.

This table presents results that would make Malthus, dead as he is, open his eyes with astonishment. We earnestly recommend to all, who are contemplating obedience to the Scriptural injunction, "*increase and multiply*," to study it carefully. It would be too tedious to point out all its peculiarities. A few will suffice to direct attention to the others.

1st. According to this table, the average expense per week of a workman and wife with seven children for bread and flour is $2.50; with eight children, only $2.37.

2d. With six children, their average weekly expense for lard will be 63 cents; with seven children, only 33 cents.

3d. Their average weekly expense for butter will be, without children, $1.00; with one child, only 71 cents; with two children, 82 cents; with three children, $1.10; with four children, $1.26; with five children, only 98 cents, etc., etc.

4th. Their average weekly expense for cheese will be, without children, 20 cents; with one child, 12 cents; with two children, 14 cents; with three children, 16 cents; with four children, 20 cents; with five children, 11 cents; and with eight children, 18 cents.

5th. Their average weekly expense, without children, for sugar and molasses, will be 69 cents; with four children, $1.18; with seven children, only 76 cents.

6th. Their average weekly expense for milk will be, without children, 59 cents; with one child, 41 cents; with two children, 44 cents; with three children, 37 cents; with four children, 50 cents; with five children, 58 cents; with six children, 26 cents; with seven children, 56 cents; and with eight children, $1.26.

Finally, and funniest of all — even funnier than the allowance, on a general average, of 59 cents for milk to a workman and wife without children, and only 26 cents for a workman and wife with six children — is the Bureau's estimate for soap and starch:

| | | | | | |
|---|---|---|---|---|---|
| It allows to a man and wife | without children, | per week | 25 | cents. |
| " " " | with 1 child, | " | 17 | " |
| " " " | " 2 children, | " | 22 | " |
| " " " | " 3 " | " | 17 | " |
| " " " | " 4 " | " | 23 | " |
| " " " | " 5 " | " | 25 | " |
| " " " | " 6 " | " | 18 | " |
| " " " | " 7 " | " | 16 | " |
| " " " | " 8 " | " | 54 | " |

Without wasting more time, the reader will find similar absurdities running through the whole of this and other tables of this precious production of the Radical Bureau of Statistics. It might excite merriment and laughter, if indignation at such palpable partisan patchwork would admit of pleasantry. But the question is too serious for mirth. These tables have been laboriously prepared in the interest of the monarchical, aristocratic, *cheap-labor* party, and on the supposition that the great mass of the people of the United States — lawyers, doctors, ministers of the gospel, merchants, civil engineers, etc., etc., as well as the working-men — were too busy with their own private affairs, or too ignorant, to discover and expose the deceit attempted to be practised upon them by this array of figures.

When we examined the figures, we thought, *surely*, these must be typographical errors. We therefore called upon Mr. Edward Young, at the Bureau of Statistics, in the Treasury Department, and asked him whether there were any typographical errors in his tables. He said, "No." We then asked him to explain by what process of computation he arrived at such wonderful results, according to which a husband and wife, without children, required 25 cents' worth of soap and starch per week; with one child, only 17 cents; with six children, 18 cents; and with seven childen, only 16 cents.

The reply, not very courteously given, was: "That table has been criticized before, and where there is a determination to criticize, anything may be criticized." Pursuing information under difficulties, we persisted, and at last drew out this explanation, viz. that the first nine columns of figures do not represent *averages*, as the heading would indicate, but only the expenditures of single selected families, the *averages* being given in the tenth and eleventh columns, so as to show a reduction in the cost of living from 1867 to 1869.

Our interview with the Bureau of Statistics convinced us that its tables were manufactured solely for partisan purposes, and are utterly unreliable, except in so far as they show, on page 75, that the true average increase in the cost of materials and labor required in building a dwelling-house suitable for workmen has been 88 per cent. in the ten years that the so-miscalled Republican party have been in power.

# INDEX

TO

## TRANSLATOR'S PREFACE AND NOTES.

---

FINIS.

www.ingramcontent.com/pod-product-compliance
Lightning Source LLC
LaVergne TN
LVHW010147110826
845151LV00002B/444